SEX ROLES

SEX ROLES

Sex Inequality and Sex Role Development

Jean Stockard
Miriam M. Johnson
University of Oregon

PRENTICE-HALL, INC., Englewood Cliffs, New Jersey 07632

Library of Congress Cataloging in Publication Data

STOCKARD, JEAN.
Sex roles.

(Prentice-Hall sociology series)
Bibliography: p.
Includes index.
1. Sex role. 2. Social role. 3. Socialization.
4. Sex differences (Psychology) 5. Sexism.
I. Johnson, Miriam M., joint author. II. Title.
HQ1075.S75 301.41 79–23286
ISBN 0–13–807560–3

PRENTICE-HALL SOCIOLOGY SERIES

Printed in the United States of America

10 9 8 7 6 5 4 3

Editorial production/supervision and interior design by Lynda Heideman
Cover design by Bill Agee
Manufacturing buyer: Ray Keating

PRENTICE-HALL INTERNATIONAL, INC., *London*
PRENTICE-HALL OF AUSTRALIA PTY. LIMITED, *Sydney*
PRENTICE-HALL OF CANADA, LTD., *Toronto*
PRENTICE-HALL OF INDIA PRIVATE LIMITED, *New Delhi*
PRENTICE-HALL OF JAPAN, INC., *Tokyo*
PRENTICE-HALL OF SOUTHEAST ASIA PTE. LTD., *Singapore*
WHITEHALL BOOKS LIMITED, *Wellington, New Zealand*

To our parents

Clement Nat Stockard
Anita Stockard McMilan

and

Herbert Neal Massey
Leola Paullin Massey

Contents

5: A Cross-cultural and Evolutionary View of Sex Stratification, 92

PART TWO
SEX ROLE DEVELOPMENT

6: Biological Influences on Sex Differences and Sex Roles, 115

7: **Psychological Sex Differences,** 145

8: **Becoming Sex Typed: Theories from Psychology,** 178

9: Psychoanalytic Explanations of Sex Role Development and Male Dominance, 201

10: Parents, Peers, and Male Dominance, 224

11: Sex Roles throughout the Life Cycle, 254

12: The Future, 276

References, 287

Index, 319

Preface

We would like to thank a number of people for making this book possible:

The Department of Sociology at the University of Oregon and its Center for the Sociological Study of Women have provided strong support for women faculty and students. It was good to be able to work in a nonsexist atmosphere where theory and research concerning sex roles are considered important and legitimate. Although probably none of our colleagues totally agrees with all we have said, they have helped us say it. Joan Acker and Marion Goldman collaborated with us on an earlier paper that served as a basis for some of the ideas in the book and have continued to encourage us in the writing of this book. We also thank Walter Martin for his help in gathering the statistical information given in chapters 2 and 6; Jeanne McGee for her help with chapter 11; our colleagues in the Department of Psychology, Mary Rothbart and Beverly Fagot, for their help with chapters 7 and 8; and Leslie Conton in the Department of Anthropology for her help with chapter 5. Among the graduate students in our department, we especially thank Adrienne Anderson, Johanna Esseveld, Mike Finigan, Sandy Gill, Linda Heuser, Jack Sattel, Gail Schroeger, and Alphons van de Kragt for their help with parts of the manuscript and their encouragement. We thank Sarah Hendrickson and Leslie Hendrickson for their editorial comments. For first suggesting that we write this book, we thank Robert Noll, and for his help in working through the maze of the publishing world we thank Terry Brennan. Finally, we thank the many students in our classes who used parts of the unfinished manuscript as a text and helped us enormously with their reactions and suggestions.

A number of people outside our campus have read various drafts of the manuscript. We would like to extend special thanks to Arlene Daniels and Francesca Cancian for criticizing the first overly long early drafts and for their encouragement in completing the project. We would also like to thank the following reviewers who took over this critical task at a later stage and led us to an even more drastic cutting and reorganization: Professor Janet G. Hunt, Department of Sociology, University of Maryland; Professor Elliott Kushell, Department of Sociology, California State University, Fullerton; Professor Judith Long Laws, Department of Sociology, Syracuse University; Professor John Scanzoni, Family Research Center, University of North Carolina at Greensboro; Professor Barrie Thorne, Department of Sociology, Michigan State University. However, any errors that may remain in the book are the responsibility of the authors.

A most essential part of completing any book is the typing and clerical work. We would like to thank the office staff of the Department of Sociology at the University of Oregon—Lynn Shy, Pearl Morgan, Barbara Kosydar, Jennifer Raines, Connie Ingram, and Evelyn Marczuk—who worked on the manuscript at various stages for their diligent efforts and their support. We would also like to thank Doris Boylan for fast and accurate typing under time pressure at crucial points.

Most especially we want to thank our husbands, Walter Wood and Benton Johnson, for helping in so many different ways. They are good enough feminists not to be insulted if we say that on many occasions, they gave us the kind of support that wives, not husbands, traditionally give. They took responsibility in the home; they were sounding boards for ideas; they did clerical work in a pinch and generally kept us going. We spent too much time on the book but they made us feel our efforts were worthwhile.

The order of authorship of this book reflects the fact that a somewhat larger share of the writing was done by Stockard, although the difference was not great. In looking through the completed manuscript, we find that it would be difficult to say precisely who wrote what. While initially, we took separate responsibility for chapters, by the time we had finished reworking and rearranging material, each chapter had become a genuine collaboration. Our strengths and weaknesses differ, and in the collaboration we believe that we produced a better product than either of us would have produced working alone.

We hope that this book may be used as the text or one of the texts in courses dealing with sex roles, sex differences, and sex inequality in a variety of disciplines including sociology, psychology, anthropology, political science, and women's studies. The book may also be used as a supplement in other courses focusing on social problems, social issues, the family, and social psychology. We also hope that the book will be useful to the general public and especially to those involved professionally and/or personally in issues of sex inequality. It can be a guide to understanding the wealth of material that has been written on sex roles and in developing a perspective on how change might come about.

Introduction

The most recent feminist movement is now well into its second decade and has prompted much scientific and scholarly work on sex roles and sex inequality in various disciplines including economics, anthropology, biology, psychology, psychoanalysis, sociology, and social history. To review this rapidly growing mass of material presented a formidable problem, not only of coverage, but also of organization and interpretation. Rather than producing an encyclopedia of information on sex roles, we wanted to produce a work based on broad scholarship that did justice to different disciplinary perspectives and the different insights and visions of individual theorists and researchers, but that also synthesized and transcended this work to some extent. We especially wanted to achieve an integration between work which focused on the development of sex differences in personalities and work which focused on sex inequalities in social roles and institutional structures.

In our view, sex roles and sex differences cannot be studied without reference to sex inequality. It is no longer possible to ignore or to deny the fact that the sexes are unequally valued and unequally rewarded. Throughout the book we refer on occasion to a male paradigm or male bias. Until very recently, not only was the world itself defined from a masculine perspective, but much scientific theory and research that examined sex differences and sex roles took place in terms of this male view of the world. Some of this work was little more than a justification and reinforcement for the unequal and male-defined status quo. Following the tradition of researchers such as Eleanor Maccoby and Carol Jacklin (1974), we have tried to review the research literature without the lens of a male paradigm, while maintaining strong scientific standards of accuracy.

However, we are not just concerned with sex inequality or, more accurately, male dominance, as a source of bias, but also as a social phenomenon to be examined in itself. We have now advanced beyond the stage of simply documenting sexism and are increasingly in a position to explore systematically the social mechanisms which tend to reproduce and sustain it. If the sexes are ever to attain equality, we need to understand the social and psychological bases for the current inequality. This book attempts to contribute to such an understanding.

Initially, we had planned to call this book something like *Sex Role Development and Sex Inequality.* We began by examining various theories concerning sex role development and then examined sex stratification in the adult world. We realized, however, that this organization could create the erroneous impression that we were trying to explain institutionalized sexism by socialization alone. Nothing could be further from our intent, especially since we had long been dissatisfied with the usual treatments of sex role socialization. These treatments assumed that most sex differences were learned. The problem, then, for some researchers became one of discovering what was wrong in women's socialization that brought about women's "inadequacy" and men's "accomplishment." Social learning theory was often invoked to argue that girls were reinforced in passivity and dependence early in life and that this handicapped them in the race for rewards in the adult world. More often than not, the responsibility for the presumed debilitating effects of women's socialization was laid at the feet of mothers, female teachers, and the mass media.

This view, which has been criticized by Jessie Bernard (1975b) among others, implies that institutional sex inequality can be blamed on some deficiency in women's personality make-up that was caused by socialization. In fact, these kinds of explanations generally are not justified by the evidence (see especially our discussion in chapters 7 and 8). Our own treatment of sex role development differs from the above in that we do not ask what it is about women that causes them to be secondary, but rather what it is about male socialization that motivates males to denigrate and dominate women. We believe that these male motives to dominate women are generated within a particular kind of institutional structure, which sharply divides sex roles within the family and assigns mothering to women.

We now begin the book you will read with a discussion of how inequality is built into our social institutions and into the whole system of cultural symbols through which we interpret experience. We not only show how sex inequality pervades our cultural symbol systems but we also try to give a picture of how most women are constrained in their everyday lives not to challenge this system. On the institutional level, we explore the wealth of evidence on how sex stratification operates in the polity and economy of our society. We critically examine the theories of economists as to why women workers face discrimination, as well as sociological theories concerning the impact of women's family roles on their status in the labor force. We also examine how the family became split off from the world of work and how the family and educational institutions help reinforce sex inequalities in the economy. We then broaden our scope and examine women's status in social institutions in other countries and, finally, across human history. We use theories of anthropologists to explain some of the variations and similarities in women's status and roles in societies with various kinds of kinship structures and at different stages of technological development. While arguing that in all societies the activities carrying the highest prestige are reserved for men, we explore factors related to both kinship systems and the organization of work that might mitigate this tendency.

Having established the foregoing institutional framework, we turn in the second part of the book to a consideration of sex role development. We prefer this term to sex role socialization because the latter has come to be associated for many people with the narrow reinforcement model described earlier. The term *sex role development* can suggest a much broader perspective, one that does not assume female deficiency, that does not leave out the possibility of biological influences on personality and roles, and that considers several other models of the acquisition of sex typing, including development throughout the entire life cycle.

In our canvas of theories and findings concerning sex role development, we describe biological differences between the sexes but argue that they cannot directly account for social role differences and certainly cannot account for socially defined sex inequality. After discussing on their own terms theories from academic psychology and psychoanalysis about the acquisition of sex typing and their implications for understanding sex differences and male dominance, we turn to a more role-oriented analysis. Among other things, we suggest that institutionalized patterns that make females primarily responsible for early child care affect both male and female motivation and personality structure and help reproduce male bonding and male dominance. Sex differentiated personalities and male motives to dominate are ultimately reproduced by institutional and cultural arrangements which give males access to greater power resources than females. This linkage of sex role development and institutional sex inequality provides clues as to how the system of male dominance may be altered, a topic we pursue in the last chapter of the book.

SEX ROLES

PART ONE:
SEX INEQUALITY

1: Sex Inequality in Cultural Symbolism and Interpersonal Relations

"Is it a boy or a girl?" This is the first question we ask when a baby is born, and the answer will profoundly affect the child's future. From birth on, we feel the need to know a person's sex in order to interact comfortably with her or him. Similarly a person needs to feel that she or he is indeed one sex or the other. While the decision to classify a child as a girl or a boy is obviously based on the child's physical characteristics, the major impact of this decision on the child's life results from the social distinctions we make between the sexes.

Societies vary in the degree to which they train children differently according to their sex. Some societies segregate the sexes quite early and begin training for differentiated adult roles right away. In others, as diverse as some nomadic hunting and gathering societies and the modern United States, girls and boys receive fairly similar early training. On the other hand, all human languages make a definite distinction between the sexes, and all societies use sex as a basis for assigning people to different adult roles. In the United States, men and women tend to enter different occupations and have different activities and opportunities in the economic world. Here too, as everywhere, women are more involved with nurturant and domestic activities than are men.

Furthermore, the social roles assigned to women and men are not simply different, they are also differentially evaluated and differentially rewarded. For instance, in the United States, not only is the labor force sex-segregated, but also among full-time employees, women earn on the average only about 60 percent as much as men. As more women enter the labor force, women's work continues to be defined as both different from and less important than men's. As we shall see in subsequent chapters, it is not women's inferior performance that causes an occupation held predominantly by women to be less rewarded, but rather the fact that it is a woman's occupation. This hierarchical ranking of the sex groups that involves their differential access to both resources and rewards is called *sex stratification.** Obviously there are other group inequities in societies besides sex based ones, most notably in the United States those based on class and race. Yet, because families include both sexes, inequities based on sex occur within both class and racial groups.

Sex stratification reflects the actual organization of societies and is reinforced by the shared symbol systems of a culture. These shared symbol systems provide the common understandings that people use in interaction. *Male dominance* refers to the beliefs, values, and cultural meanings that give higher value and prestige to masculinity than to femininity, which value males over females, men over women. Many anthropologists consider all known societies to be male dominant to some degree.

Male dominance does not mean that individual males in a society consciously conspire to keep women subordinate. Neither does it mean that women are helpless victims who have no way to prevail against men. Indeed, male dominance is hard to see unless one has become sensitized to it. The difficulty arises because male dominance is imbedded in our language and ways of thought. These built-in presuppositions limit the potential of all people and have personal costs for both males and females. In this chapter, we show how male dominance operates at the level of culture and in our everyday interactions.

CULTURAL SYMBOLISM AND MALE DOMINANCE

A cultural level of analysis or way of viewing human action focuses on the shared meanings individuals use in their interactions. Male dominance is passed from one generation to another partly through these shared symbol systems, including language and religions, as well as the mass media. These symbol systems picture and define our world for us and constrain us to interpret the world in masculine terms.

*Social scientists have used several other terms besides sex stratification, such as sex discrimination, sex/gender systems, and sexism, to describe sex inequalities. The term *sex discrimination* tends to focus attention on individuals and their unequal access to opportunities. We prefer the term *sex stratification* because it focuses attention on the systemic or built-in nature of sex inequality. We do, at times, however, use the term *sex discrimination* to refer to individual actions that promote and maintain the system of sex stratification. While the term *sex/gender systems* uses the word *gender* to remind us that the roles assigned to the sexes are social roles and not biological necessities, it does not imply any inequality in the system. The term *sexism* is derived as a parallel to *racism* and points to a parallel between sexual inequality and racial inequality. While there is some truth to this analogy, it should not be carried too far because the sources of sexism and racism are probably far from identical. Moreover, while the sexes are joined in families, an important aspect of racism is the prohibition of intermarriage.

It is important to remember that ultimately culture is a human product: we humans construct our social world. However, no one individual ever constructs an entire culture singlehandedly. Most of our culture was originally made by other people, and some of it is quite old. This is the reason why we often see cultural meanings as if they were facts of nature, like the weather, objective necessities that exert an irresistible control over us, rather than the products of human activity. Thus, humans are both creators and victims of culture. But because culture is a human product, created and re-created in human interaction, it can be changed and controlled by human will.

Language

Language, the means of our thought and of our communication with others, embodies male dominance. What is male in a language is generally basic; what is female is usually subsidiary and/or deprecated. Some languages such as Japanese, are used differently by male and female speakers. Although the basic form and syntax of the language do not change, males and females use different prefixes and suffixes, and at times the two "languages" sound quite different. When this happens, however, the language that the males use is always seen as the language of the society; the female version is called "women's language." Other languages such as those in the Romance and Germanic families use gender-differentiated pronouns for both the singular and plural forms, but again the male form is basic. In French, while *elles* refers to a group of females and *ils* to men, only *ils* may be used to describe a group of mixed sex. In English, this same practice appears in the use of the generic *he.* To refer in a general sense to a single person, one must use the masculine singular pronouns *he, him,* or *his.* The result can be absurd; "No person may require another person to perform, participate in, or undergo an abortion against his will" (Key, 1975:89). In other instances, the term *man* is used to refer to all human beings. We have many phrases with this meaning, including "good will to men," "man in the street," and even "all men are created equal."

English often describes females in terms of males. Thus, we may speak of an usherette, a poetess, an actress, even a tigress and a lioness. With occupations, we usually attach appendages, such as lady doctor or woman lawyer, to signify that the occupant is not a male. Only with family-related terms such as widower or with traditionally female occupations, such as male nurse or male prostitute, do we signify that the occupant is a male (Adams and Ware, 1979:491). Even the terms of address Mrs. and Miss indicate a woman's marital status. There are no comparable terms in the language to indicate whether a man is married. Even the recent attempt in English to use the undifferentiated Ms. for women may be in danger of being subverted. Although the originators of the term hoped it would be used to refer to all adult women, it now appears that Ms. is informally coming to refer only to single women or even to women who have been divorced! Thus, out of an undifferentiated category, yet a third differentiation has been made—a formerly married woman.

Finally, language usage deprecates and devalues women. In some instances, this may take the form of trivializing what women are and do, as in phrases such as "wine, women, and song" or using the term *girl* for women of all ages. One of our mature students described how she developed new sensitivity when a college choir director regularly called for women's voices with the phrase, "Now, girls," while eliciting male vocalization with, "Now, men." To call a full-grown adult male "boy" is an insult, but until recently it was no insult at all to call a full-grown adult female "girl." Actually, the words *woman* and *female* themselves have several deprecatory meanings. For example, the 1956 edition of Webster's dictionary gives, in addition to neutral meanings, the following meanings for *woman:* "One who is effeminate, cowardly, emotional, or weak, used of a man, as, he seemed to me a very woman." Another meaning given was "to cause to act like a woman, to subdue to weakness like a woman." In 1967, the Random House dictionary eschews the foregoing list but notes that the word *female,* which used to be used interchangeably with *woman,* has now developed a contemptuous implication, as in "a strong-minded female." The 1916 collegiate edition of Webster's dictionary was even more straightforward. It defined male as "denoting an intensity or superiority of the characteristic qualities of anything:—contrasted with female"!

Perhaps the ultimate form of this deprecation involves sexual overtones to words connected with women. One study found close to 1,000 English words and phrases that describe women in sexually derogatory ways, and many fewer such phrases describing men. While there are over 500 synonyms for prostitute, there are only about 65 for the masculine term of whoremonger (Schulz, 1975). Even terms that were once sexually neutral (such as hussy, which comes from an old English term for housewife; broad, which meant a young woman; and spinster, which once meant someone who ran a spinning wheel) have over the years developed negative meanings with sexual overtones (Schulz, 1975).

These language patterns reflect our male-dominated culture. They may also, however, reinforce and reproduce this culture because language reflects the ways in which we see the world.

Religion

Religions generally do recognize and include both masculine and feminine principles. For instance, Taoism includes both the principles of yin, symbolizing the feminine elements, and yang, symbolizing maleness. Hinduism and other indigenous belief systems throughout Oceania, Asia, Africa, and the Americas contain a theme of two basic masculine and feminine principles. Recently discovered writings of early Christian sects also show a strong feminine element in their conception of God (Pagels, 1976). All of these stress that the masculine and feminine principles are interdependent, both needed for the completion of the deity and the universe (Weitz, 1977).

Even so, the two principles have different functions. The female image is usually linked with fertility, the earth, and nurturance. Christianity in the Middle Ages referred to God and Christ as a mother who gave birth to, cared for, and nurtured the faithful. Also, priests and prelates were supposed to act as mothers to their flocks. The dualistic principle of the Christian God as containing some feminine traits declined after the Reformation.

Sister Marie Augusta Neal (1979) has suggested that in the West, God has usually been symbolized as the father of a family. Men, at times, have been depicted as the servants of God while women in many societies and across classes in the same society have been seen as the servants of men. While the concept of the Virgin Mary does allow women a spiritual existence that was not allowed in earlier times, her image represents less of the nurturing mother than that of the pure and chaste asexual "lady." (For a discussion of recent scholarship on religious imagery, see Neal, 1979.)

The major functionaries of religious systems are also male. For instance, although there have been a few strong women prophets, the major prophets and figures of Western religions, including Moses, Jesus, and Mohammed, were male. Females are included in Biblical stories, but their role is generally minor. They may be maternal and devoted helpmates as Mary Magdalene and Ruth were, or they may be evil or stupid, as were Lot's wife, Jezebel, and most especially, Eve.

Religions have different official roles for males and females, and males always have the closest ceremonial ties to the deities. In the Catholic church, men are priests and women are nuns. While nuns teach, nurse, and may hold very responsible administrative positions in hospitals and schools, they cannot celebrate Mass. Only priests may perform the ceremony that links the faithful directly with God. In some Protestant groups, only elders and deacons—who are men—may make the congregational decisions. Among conservative and orthodox Jews, only men may be rabbis. Jewish women serve important functions in the home, but in the orthodox and conservative synagogues they are seated apart from the men and are not involved in the official prayers and ceremonies.

Finally, religious rituals reflect and reinforce systems of male dominance. This occurs partly because the major religious functionaries are male. Thus, in Christianity, men ordain other men; in most denominations only men serve communion; and men generally perform wedding ceremonies. Sometimes the ceremonies themselves embody the principles of male dominance. For instance, the traditional Jewish male regularly repeats a prayer in which he thanks God that he was not born a woman. The initiation rites of males through which young men learn the sacred rules of a society may serve to bond men together and to separate them from and elevate them over women. Even female initiation rites serve to promote male dominance by legitimizing and helping women rationalize men's control over their lives (Weitz, 1977:185–87).

Because religion defines the ultimate meaning of the universe for a people, the impact may be deep and often emotional rather than intellectual. When male dominance is embodied within religion, it enters the arena that a society considers sacred. This may make it even less open to question and more resistant to change than other social areas.

The Mass Media

The media have an important impact on people's everyday lives. Americans spend an enormous amount of time with the mass media, especially television. Over 95 percent of the homes in this country have at least one television set. By the time an average child is fifteen years old, she or he has spent more time watching television than going to school. In adulthood, people do not break the habit. An average adult spends five hours a day with the mass media, four of these with electronic media such as radio and television and typically another hour with newspapers, magazines, and books (Tuchman, 1978). The way men and women are depicted in the media—in television shows, magazines, popular songs, and even school textbooks—reflects the assumptions of a male-dominant society.

Women tend to be both underrepresented and misrepresented in television programming, from children's shows and cartoons to prime-time comedies and dramas, game shows, crime shows, and commercials. With the exception of soap operas, where men are only about 50 percent of the characters, men are vastly overrepresented as characters. A study in 1975 found that 69 percent of the characters in all prime-time shows (74 percent of the characters in dramas and 60 percent in comedies) are men (McNeil, 1975). On children's programs, there are over twice as many males as females (Sternglanz and Serbin, 1974, cited by Schuetz and Sprafkin, 1978:72). A study of spot messages during children's shows, including commercials and public service announcements, revealed that over 60 percent of the characters, both human and cartoon, were male (Schuetz and Sprafkin, 1978:73). The situation on public television is even more dismal. An analysis of programs other than music and dramas found that only 15 percent of the participants were women (Cantor, 1978). This situation had not changed appreciably by the 1977–78 season (U.S. Commission on Civil Rights, 1979).

The roles men and women play also differ. Studies of commercials find that males are much more likely to do the selling, either in a factual or an "aggressive sales-pitchy" manner. Females tend to be seductive or soft-spoken in commercials (Chafetz, 1978). Analyses of role interactions of characters in prime-time shows also reveal sex differences that reflect male dominance. One study analyzed activities intended to influence or control the behavior of others in prime-time situation comedies and crime dramas in 1975. Both social class (measured by occupational status) and race influence dominance attempts, with higher-status people and whites more likely to dominate others. However, ignoring the impact of occupational status, men dominated women in 23 percent of the interactions involving both men and women in situation comedies and 47 percent of these interactions in crime shows. The reverse situation, with women dominating men, occurred in 13 percent of the interactions in comedies and in only 6 percent of the crime show interactions. Even though having a female star helped decrease the number of times men were dominant, the incidence of men dominating women on these shows was still much higher than the reverse (Lemon, 1978).

The roles women play on television have changed some over the last quarter century to reflect actual changes in women's activities. For instance, while Lucy Ricardo, of "I Love Lucy," was a housewife in the 1950s, Mary Richards, of the "Mary Tyler Moore Show," had a career and Maude was actively involved in community affairs in the 1970s. Nevertheless, Mary was always Mr. Grant's assistant, and, even though Maude has replaced Lucy Ricardo, her husband Walter, like Lucy's Ricky, still ruled the roost (Tuchman et al., 1978:45).

While commercial television is often accused of appealing to the lowest common denominator of popular taste, magazines do differentiate their audience and appeal. Thus, while researchers have found that fiction in contemporary women's magazines emphasizes the ideal of the traditional housewife role, the nature of these images do differ by class. Some evidence of change is apparent, especially in magazines aimed toward middle-class women. New magazines especially for working women have appeared, articles now commonly provide "tips for working wives," and twenty-eight women's magazines, *Redbook* and *McCall's* among them, have published articles in support of the Equal Rights Amendment.

An analysis of the top ten popular songs in each year from 1955 through 1974, songs that were so popular that they were played many times each day on radios and phonographs (especially by teenagers), found that while they made many references to women's beauty and sex appeal in the songs, they rarely mentioned males' physical attractiveness. The author concludes that the songs convey the message to boys that they "*should* dominate every relationship and that a girl's refusal to participate as the subordinate partner is evidence of the boy's personal failure." Girls would get the message that beauty, sex appeal, passivity, submissiveness, and dependence are appealing to boys and that by manipulating a boy's sexual impulses, a girl may control him (Talkington, 1976:149).

Finally, a number of studies have examined children's reading, mathematics, science, and social studies textbooks and found similar results there. Females are less often included as characters and, when they are included, are much less likely to be the main character. The behaviors that characterize the children and adults of each sex group in the stories also differ. Men are often portrayed outdoors, in business, and at school; women are much more often portrayed in the home (Saario et al., 1973).

In short, these images of males and females in the mass media as well as in school curricular materials attest to the male-dominant culture. That females are less often portrayed than males has been called a "symbolic annihilation," the removal of women from our cultural imagery (Tuchman, 1978). Women are more limited in the roles they hold and may be shown in devalued characterizations and in interactions controlled by men. While these portrayals reflect the male-dominated culture, by their very existence they—like religion and language—may also reinforce and support the existence of male dominance on the cultural level.

INTERPERSONAL RELATIONS AND MALE DOMINANCE

Not only does male dominance pervade our language, religion, and media; it also influences the everyday interactions of males and females. Sex segregation and the devaluation of women appear in everyday life. This involves *social roles,* individuals' actions in social groups based on the expectations of others in that group. When people are expected to play certain roles simply because they are males or females, these roles are called *sex roles* or *gender roles.* * These sex roles are both different and differentially evaluated.

*There has been a good deal of uncertainty and controversy over the use of the term *sex role(s).* When the term is used in the singular, many people prefer gender role to sex role and use it to imply all the expectations that are socially assigned to an individual on the basis of sex. Thus, they see gender role as preferable to sex role because it implies to them a social rather than a biological basis of role assignment. On the other hand, males and females are assigned different roles on the basis of physical differences related to biological sex. In addition, professional journals and societies commonly use the term *sex roles.* Our solution to this problem is to use the terms somewhat interchangeably. We generally follow the rule that when speaking of certain roles assigned to people on the basis of sex, we use the term *sex roles,* and when speaking of all the expectations for behavior that we have for an individual on the basis of being male or female, we use the term *gender role.*

Sex Role Differentiation in Everyday Life

Extensive role segregation appears in day-to-day interactions at home, at work, and in organizations. For instance, in the United States, men more often change the oil in the car and mow the lawn, and women more often dust and clean closets. At work, women much more often use a typewriter or copy machine; men more often use a dictaphone. While both upper-class men and women belong to exclusive clubs, the men may belong to the city clubs or the university clubs, and the women belong to the Junior League or have auxiliary membership in their husbands' groups. Middle- and working-class organizations are also sex-segregated. Only men may usually belong to the Elks Club, the Moose, the Eagles, the American Legion, and the Junior Chamber of Commerce. While women may belong to auxiliary groups such as the American Legion Auxiliary or the Jaycee-ettes and participate in social and service functions, they are generally barred from participating in the ceremonial activities of the groups. (These groups have also been segregated by race and religion. Nonwhites and non-Protestants have sometimes formed their own lodges, which are also sex-segregated.)

The intensity of people's feelings about this role segregation is most apparent in organizations threatened by change. For a number of years the Episcopal church had a strong controversy over the ordination of women into the priesthood. Before women were officially ordained, dissident priests who allowed women to give communion were threatened with excommunication. After women joined the priesthood, dissent continued. Some clergy and some parishes even left the established church for other church bodies or their own fellowship. Similarly, the United States Jaycees once expelled several chapters when they admitted women. Supporters of integrating the group took the case to court, and the Jaycees have spent much time and money fighting the possibility of integration.

The Devaluation of Women in Everyday Life

Not only women's activities, but also their very being are devalued in everyday interactions. This is well illustrated by the way men avoid anything feminine. For instance, if nursery school boys display behavior usually associated with girls, they tend to redefine the activity as masculine. Heuser (1977) tells about a boy who one day wore white tights and a woman's wig. He vehemently rejected other children's derision of his "girlish" behavior by explaining that his tights were "boy's tights" and his wig covered his balding head! Heuser did not find the parallel behavior of girls avoiding masculine activities. It is far worse for a boy to be called a sissy than for a girl to be called a tomboy. Grown men continue this pattern. The unisex fashion pattern primarily involves women adopting masculine clothes such as pants and T-shirts. Men may wear brighter clothes and jumpsuits and even carry purses, but they never wear skirts or dresses, and the purses they carry are always, as the fashion coordinators say, distinctively masculine.

Even the attribution of womanly traits may be considered an insult. In an informal basketball game we observed, when a boy would miss a basket the other boys would call him "woman!" On another occasion, we heard a younger boy turn to an older boy in the midst of an argument and say, "Shaddup, boy!" in the most deprecating tone he could muster. The older boy, however, immediately gained the upper hand by saying to his younger brother, "You shaddup, girl!" There is no comparable phenomenon among women, for young girls do not insult each other by calling each other "man."

By adulthood most men temper the open comments they make about women as they become more intimately involved with them. Yet signs of men's devaluation still appear, especially in all-male settings. In his classic study, *The American Soldier,* Samuel Stouffer describes how training for combat becomes entwined with the soldiers' definitions of themselves as men (Stouffer et al., 1976:180).

> The fear of failure in the role [of combat soldier], as by showing cowardice in battle, could bring not only fear of social censure, but also more central and strongly established fears related to sex-typing. To fail to measure up as a soldier in courage and endurance was to risk the charge of not being a man. ("Whatsa matter, bud—got lace on your drawers?"

Even in modern times men are urged on to war by threats to their masculinity. Wayne Eisenhart (1975) describes an "endless litany" from the drill sergeant in the Vietnam War along the lines of "Can't hack it, little girls?"

Men's sexual jokes may also reveal antagonistic attitudes toward women. Jokes about dumb blondes or traveling salesmen and the farmer's daughter are typical ways to convey devaluation of females. The woman in these jokes "is represented as naive or simply stupid, easily outmaneuvered by the male, who gets what he wants without cost" (Fry, 1972:139).

While women may not often witness military training or even hear men's jokes, they do come into contact with men at work. Michael Korda's description of office life illustrates how both expectations of sex segregation and the devaluation of women may be expressed (Korda, 1973:20–21):

> Leaning against the water cooler, two men—both minor executives—are nursing their cardboard cartons of coffee, discussing last Sunday's Giant game,

postponing for as long as possible the moment when work must finally be faced.

A vice-president walks by and hears them talking about sports. Does he stop and send them back to their desks? Does he frown? Probably not. Being a man, he is far more likely to pause on his way and join in the conversation, anxious to prove that he too is "one of the boys," feigning an interest in football that he may very well not share at all. These men—*all* the men in the office—are his troops, his comrades-in-arms.

Now, let's assume that two women are standing by the water cooler discussing whatever you please: women's liberation, clothes, work, any subject except football, of course. The vice-president walks by, sees them, and moves off in a fury down the hall, cursing and wondering whether it is worth the trouble to complain—but to whom?—about all those goddamned bitches standing around gabbing when they should be working. "Don't they know," he will ask, in the words of a million other men, "this is an office?"*

The Reproduction of Male Dominance in Everyday Interactions

In the final analysis cultural patterns of sex segregation and devaluation continue to exist because individuals perpetuate them. Sex segregation is usually much more strongly supported by men than by women, and it is men who express jokes and comments that devalue women. Men communicate their expectations of role segregation and devaluation to each other and thus reinforce these views. Obviously some men do not care as deeply as others about maintaining sex segregation. However, because they must actively work against long-established traditions and the often deeply held views of others, their attempts to end sex segregation and devaluation usually meet a good deal of opposition. Women also may reinforce sex segregation, the devaluation of women, and male dominance through their responses to these expectations.

Male power in everyday life In male-dominant societies, men have, as a group, greater power than women. Their verbal communications of women show that they know that this power differential exists. Males and females in our society tend to speak in different ways. Women tend to be more polite and less assertive than men are. Women also soften their requests more often with phrases like "Would you mind?" while men tend to be more direct and demanding (Lakoff, 1975). Men tend to interrupt women when they are speaking more than women interrupt men (Zimmerman and West, 1975). Contrary to the stereotype of talkative women, when men and women are in the same group, the men actually dominate the conversation and talk more than the women do (Henley, 1977).

*Michael Korda, *Male Chauvinism! How It Works.* Copyright 1973 by Random House, Inc., Reprinted by permission.

Men's greater power also shows in nonverbal interactions. Men take up more space than women do, even when the size of their bodies is taken into account. When both men and women are seated, for instance, men take up more space relative to their bodies than women do. Men also touch women without permission more than women touch men (Henley, 1977). In all of these interactions, women's actions are those found to characterize lower-status persons generally. This suggests that women recognize that men have greater power than they do and demonstrate this recognition in their interpersonal relations.

Women's responses to expectations of role differentiation Expectations of sex role differentiation often follow the lines of the *instrumental-expressive* distinction. Expressive actions are oriented toward relations within a group. Instrumental actions are oriented toward goals outside a group. Women are usually expected to be able to deal with the emotions and feelings of others, to be supportive and warm teachers, mothers, or nurses. Men are usually expected to be rational and analytical and to gain recognition in occupational and other nonfamilial arenas of achievement and creativity. Actually, however, both men and women must be both instrumental and expressive. It is virtually impossible for any adult to avoid both instrumental and expressive tasks. But, how, given expectations of role segregation as well as the overriding situation of male power and women's recognition of this, do women respond to men's expectations of role differentiation?

First, women may confine their instrumental tasks to typically female spheres. Here, even though they are instrumentally competent, they do not encroach on males' areas of endeavors and thus cannot threaten men's self-definitions. Housewives and mothers typically engage in many instrumental tasks, yet their work is seen as "women's work" and not at all in men's sphere. Many middle-class women routinely engage in volunteer work in their communities. The sociologist Arlene Daniels has studied the volunteer efforts of upper-class women in San Francisco.* She reports that many of these women engaged in high-level executive decisions, managed large charity budgets, and coordinated complex organizations and activities. Yet, perhaps because its ultimate aim was charity, their work was seen as feminine. Most of the women who work outside the home, work in predominantly female fields and do not challenge expectations of role segregation, for the job itself—no matter what it is—becomes defined as appropriate for women.

Yet, some women do participate directly in fields that include a substantial number of men. What may these women, who are directly challenging expectations of sex segregation, do? One possible response is for

*Arlene Daniels, 1974: personal communication.

the women to degrade their achievements, especially when compared to male colleagues; another is to redefine their work as actually being more in line with "feminine" roles.

Attempting to degrade one's own achievements seems most common when women directly compete with men in school or in sports, as grades or a game score give concrete evidence of the achievement of both the man and the woman. Mirra Komarovsky noted a tendency for women students to play down their academic achievements when talking with men friends. One young woman said, "When a girl asks me what marks I got last semester, I answer, 'Not so good—only one A.' When a boy asks the same question, I say very brightly with a note of surprise, 'Imagine, I got an A!' " (Komarovsky, 1953:78). Similarly, when a woman beats a man in tennis or in any sport at which the man typically excels, a woman may say (if she wants to play with the man again), "Oh, I just got lucky." Komarovsky finds the tendency for women to downgrade their intellectual accomplishments less prominent in the 1970s (1974:525), and this tendency for women to disparage their achievements may be generally declining.

The world of work lacks game scores or exam grades to compare. The reaction women may give then to males' expectations of role segregation is to redefine their activities as appropriately "feminine." The reasons women give for wanting to enter male professions often fit with an expressive orientation more than the ones men give. In our own research, we have found that, regardless of the kind of occupation, young women say much more often than young men that they want to enter a job because they want to work with people or help people. The reasons women give correspond to the expectations of what women should do. Because they have "feminine" reasons for wanting to be a lawyer or a doctor, the young women may defuse male objections to their actions.

Studies of women in male-dominated arenas suggest that women who emphasize some aspect of a feminine role meet with the fewest interpersonal problems on the job. For example, John Y. Brown, a millionaire from his investments in Kentucky Fried Chicken, once bought the Kentucky Colonels basketball team. His wife, Ellie, became chair of the board and placed her friends from the Junior League on the other seats on the board. Basketball team administrators up to that time had always been men. Yet, these women eliminated criticism of their entrance into the field by emphasizing their femininity in their statements, their dress, and their manners. As one member of the board put it, "We're all wives and mothers first" (Rich, 1974:56). Similarly, interviews with women professionals suggest that women who "act professional, but not especially formal or aggressive, who try to be gracious as women and not be one of the boys, face the fewest problems in male dominated work situations" (Epstein, 1970:979). Being feminine may take the form of playing the mother who is sympathetic and helpful to others, the sex object or seductress who plays on her sexuality, or the "pet" or kid sister who encourages the men in their work or acts as a mascot (Kanter, 1975; Tavris and Offir, 1977:211).

If women enter male areas but do not redefine their activities as feminine in nature, they may be seen as the "hard-boiled executive" or an "iron maiden" (Kanter, 1975). This response directly challenges male expectations of sex role behavior by asserting that the woman is indeed competent and is doing what the men are doing. There are two reasons why this response is relatively rare. First, it directly challenges male expectations, and men may react negatively. Second, professional women who marry and have families, if they are not well to do, still usually carry a heavy load of typically female household chores. Thus, even if they wanted to, only a small minority of married women would be able to limit their role behavior totally to the male sphere of activities.

Women's responses to devaluation Just as none of women's reactions to role segregation directly challenges it, the ways that women deal with males' devaluation of them do not directly contradict these sentiments. Instead, women often use coping mechanisms that maintain their self-esteem without directly challenging the system of male dominance and the associated female devaluation. All people, men and women, have a need to be loved, to feel good about themselves, to see themselves as worthy. Thus, women are motivated to find other ways to interpret men's devaluation than to see it for what it is. Even if women perceive the devaluation, they also know that men have greater power than they do, and they cannot challenge the devaluation directly without jeopardizing their own security.

One possible response to devaluation is for women to see it as correct on a general level but to insist that "it doesn't apply to me because I'm not like other women." Thus, women who have made it in a man's world often attribute their success to their being better than and fundamentally different from other women. Isolated professional women may feel, "I made it. Why can't the rest of you?"

Women may also deny that men's devaluation of women is true and may even put men down themselves. We suspect that this devaluation of men occurs almost exclusively in all-female groups. This would, of course, be expected given the views and the power of men. Many of the putdowns occur as small elements in conversations, as simple asides. Women, at least in this culture, apparently do not have the repertoire of jokes or insults that men use to indicate their devaluation of women. Much less do they base their solidarity on their power over men. Yet the bits of conversation are telling. Women often agree with the grandmother who said, "We really are smarter than men, we just can't let them know it!"

Perhaps implicitly believing this statement women have typically countered male dominance in day-to-day life by manipulation. Studies of interpersonal power document that this indirect manipulation is the most common means women use to assert control over men (P. Johnson, 1976). Women use their interpersonal skills to manage and control men whom they may think of as "fools" or "babies" that can be skillfully managed. This is reflected in the folk adage: "The best way to get a man to do something is to let him think it is his own idea." A television commercial once showed a mother and daughter preparing sandwiches for the family's lunch. Even though the father and son insisted that they didn't want mustard, the mother and daughter wanted to use a new brand and put it on the sandwiches anyway. Father and son liked it, and the women and their new brand of mustard triumphed.

Finally, women may deny that men devalue them by accepting the role of angel on the pedestal. For these women, having men open doors for them, hold chairs for them, and extend them courtesies indicates the high regard men have for women. These women may encourage men to give them special treatment by being especially appealing. Unfortunately, these special courtesies have more often than not been associated with a view of women as dependent, weak, and incompetent.

The popular Total Woman movement is an interesting amalgam of the angel-on-the-pedestal and the manipulation responses. Marabel Morgan, the leader of the movement, suggests that if a woman accepts her husband just as he is, admires him every day, adapts to his way of life, and appreciates all he does, he will "absolutely adore her in just a few weeks time. . . . It is really up to her. She has the power" (Morgan, 1975:106–7, back cover).

In order to be "adored," the woman gives up all thought of exercising power directly but uses the fact that she is "beloved" to get what she wants indirectly. Morgan denies advocating manipulation since one must sincerely appreciate one's husband in order to attain the pedestal. On the other hand, once the pedestal is attained, a woman gets her way by playing up his strength and her weakness. If a woman's efforts fail, she presumably must blame herself for not appreciating her man sufficiently. Becoming one man's special woman may occasionally work, but it weakens the power of women as a group and weakens women's solidarity with each other.

Just as all the responses to role segregation except the relatively rare "iron maiden" response do not directly challenge sex role differentiation, none of the responses just described challenges the devaluation of women as a group. These responses do allow individual women to maintain a favorable self-image in a male dominated culture, but they do not challenge the system itself. Indeed, individual women may get farther by not challenging the system, and they may have much to lose by challenging it. In short, as long as a culture *is* male dominant, women are constrained to play the game to survive and many have done so almost automatically.

In so doing, however, the basic rules of the game tend to remain unquestioned and unchanged.

THE FEMINIST RESPONSE TO MALE DOMINANCE

The current feminist movement has made people more aware of how our cultural symbolism and day-to-day interactions reinforce male dominance. The latest upsurge of feminism began largely among middle-class women in the latter part of the 1960s. The movement at first consisted of two somewhat different groups of women; the so-called radical feminists who challenged male dominance from the ground up, and the liberal feminists, who sought to bring about sexual equality essentially within our current institutional arrangements.

The radical feminists were young middle-class women. In working with men in New Left political projects, they became acutely conscious that their male coworkers were concerned about equality and justice for the poor and for blacks but *assumed* the inequality of women. These women, who were as educated and concerned as their male counterparts, were treated by males in the movement as flunkies and sex objects. In protest, they organized consciousness-raising groups in which women came to feel that what they had once considered their personal problems were in reality problems shared by all women, problems stemming from male domination. By contrast, the liberal-feminist National Organization for Women (NOW) was established before these consciousness-raising groups developed, and it consisted mainly of somewhat older professional women who were concerned with pressing for the implementation of laws that forbid employment discrimination on the basis of sex (see Hymowitz and Weissman, 1978).

Since these beginnings, many more and different types of women have become involved in feminist activities, and the movement has become very diversified. Although feminists do not always agree with each other on either analysis or strategy, they do tend to share a common desire for greater sex equality and less rigid sex-role differentiation. Male dominance has its rewards for males, but it also has psychological costs. Because male dominance is costly, moving toward more equality between the sexes would not just be a move toward women's liberation, but toward "human" liberation and a relative lack of differentiation between the sexes in attitudes, behaviors, traits, roles and status. Thus, men as well as women are now involved in the feminist movement.

While nineteenth century feminists were concerned with legal and voting rights for women, the current feminist movement has widened its area of concerns considerably. Feminists have called for changes in our language, in media representations of women, and even in religious practices. These attempts have met with considerable success. For instance, publishers now often require that at least their textbook authors phrase their writings in ways that do not use masculine referents for all people. Before 1975, women were rarely seen as newscasters on national or local television. Although men are still the majority, women reporters are now much more common. Women in a wide range of religious groups have also called for changes. The Episcopal church ordained some women in response to the urging of feminists within the church. Clerical roles for women in other denominations are becoming somewhat more common although their duties are usually teaching and counseling rather than pastoral.

Feminists have also encouraged people to challenge male dominance in their day-to-day interactions. For instance, contemporary feminists have questioned the existence of male-only organizations and have brought costly lawsuits against many of them, forcing them to allow at least some women to join. They have also encouraged women to try to replace manipulation with assertiveness in order to gain directly what they want in their daily lives. It is clearly true that less direct maneuvers tend to support male dominance.

While relatively few individuals call themselves feminists, feminists' activities have affected all of us in one way or another. One powerful influence has been among social scientists concerned with studying human behavior and social institutions. Sex stratification goes beyond cultural symbols and day-to-day interactions and is built into the organization of societies and the personalities of individuals. Sex stratification is a problem that must concern social scientists both as scientists and as individuals who profess to believe in human equality.

In the chapters to follow, we first consider in detail how social institutions embody and perpetuate sex stratification and then explore how these institutional arrangements generate individual motives and attitudes that may underlie sex stratification.

SUMMARY

Male dominance pervades both cultural symbols and day-to-day interactions. Males are depicted in different roles than women and are given more value and authority than women in languages, in religions, and in the mass media. In day-to-day interactions, men show their devaluation of women and the roles of the sexes are often sharply differentiated. While the actions of women often reinforce differentiation and devaluation, contemporary feminists have challenged these patterns of male dominance.

Suggested Readings

CATER, LIBBY, A., AND ANNE FIROR SCOTT, *Women and Men: Changing Roles, Relationships and Perceptions.* New York: Aspen Institute for Humanistic Studies, 1977. Contains essays and a report on the Aspen Workshop on Women and Men.

DALY, MARY, *Beyond God the Father.* Boston, Mass.: Beacon Press, 1973. Best known current challenge to male dominated theology.

HENLEY, NANCY M., *Body Politics: Power, Sex, and Non-Verbal Communication.* Englewood Cliffs, N.J.: Prentice-Hall, 1977. A readable description of how male dominance and male power appear in everyday settings in verbal and nonverbal communications.

HYMOWITZ, CAROL, AND MICHAELE WEISSMAN, *A History of Women in America.* New York: Bantam, 1978. History of the development of the current feminist movement.

THORNE, BARRIE, AND NANCY HENLEY, eds., *Language and Sex: Difference and Dominance.* Rowley, Mass.: Newbury House, 1975. Collection of articles on various facets of how language reflects sex stratification.

TUCHMAN, GAYE, ARLENE KAPLAN DANIELS, AND JAMES BENET, eds., *Hearth and Home: Images of Women in the Mass Media.* New York: Oxford University Press, 1978. Collection of articles describing the representation of males and females in the mass media, including television, newspapers, and magazines.

2: Sex Inequality in the United States: The Polity and the Economy

Compared to men, women play a minor role in the polity (political organizations and institutions) and the economy of our society. Much of the power men wield results, in fact, from their control of these institutional areas. Although we now have laws that guarantee women's rights, the inequities these laws are designed to counteract remain and are especially striking in the economy. In this chapter, we explore sex differences in political attitudes and participation and describe the important laws that affect sex stratification. We examine past and current trends in sex segregation in the labor force and sex differentials in wages. Finally, we consider the economic theories advanced to account for women's lower wages.

THE POLITY

While women definitely have views on political issues, participate in political parties, and are represented in political posts on the local level, they rarely hold national office. A number of laws have restricted women's activities in the past, yet the legal principles of the United States Constitution and some federal and state laws are designed to end sex stratification and promote equality in our institutions. Much of this legislation has come about through the efforts of feminists.

Sex Differences in Political Attitudes

Attitude polls and voting behavior over the past thirty years show some consistent sex differences in political views, but increasing similarity in political preferences in voting for candidates. Polls throughout the 1960s and 1970s show that women were much less likely than men to support

United States involvement in the Vietnam War. In 1975, only half as many women as men supported the sending of United States troops to countries attacked by Communist forces (Gallup, 1975, in Frieze et al., 1978:342). Similarly, polls from 1937 to the present day show that women are less likely than men to support capital punishment even though women are more aware than men of increases in crime and more fearful of personal attacks. Women are also more supportive than men of what has been called "prosocial aggression," including the jailing of child abusers and drunken drivers (Frieze et al., 1978:343). Even though women tend to oppose military aid to other countries more than men do, they are more supportive of nonmilitary aid. In fact, after World War II, women were much more willing than men to return to rationing so that food could be sent to other countries (Frieze et al., 1978:344).

Although in the past women tended to give responses in polls that indicated somewhat less tolerance of dissenters than men, these differences appear to have declined in recent years (Frieze et al., 1978:344). Similarly, differences in the party identification and voting patterns of men and women seem to have lessened so that only insignificant differences are generally now noted in polls of presidential preference.

Political Participation

Even though women rarely appear in the national political scene, both men and women are involved in politics. Sex stratification influences the nature of this involvement. Women's right to vote was first supported at a women's rights convention in 1848, yet suffrage was not won until seventy-two years later, when the Nineteenth Amendment to the United States Constitution was finally ratified in 1920. Although fewer women than men actually voted at first, in recent years the proportions have been almost the same. Because there are more adult women than men in this country, this means that more women than men actually turn out at the polls. In 1976, 53 percent of the voters were women (Frieze et al., 1978:339).

Men and women are quite similarly involved in party activities at the lower levels. For instance, from the 1968 through 1976 presidential election campaigns, there have been few differences in the proportions of men and women who wear buttons or display bumper stickers in support of candidates, who attend political meetings, or who actively work for the election of a candidate. Men, however, have been more likely to contribute money to a party, probably simply because they have more money and perhaps also because they are more often employed and thus are solicited for contributions (Lynn, 1979:410–11).

Beginning in the 1920s, both national parties included a man and a woman from each state on their national committees. On the local level, both precinct committee women and men are elected for each party. Over the years, more women have gone to the national conventions so that in recent years about one-third of the delegates are female. Women, then, are active in party activities, but this activity still reflects sex stratification and male dominance. Women are much more likely to stuff envelopes and answer phones, while men make decisions and plan campaign strategy.

Women are also political candidates and hold political offices, but they are much more likely to do so at the local than at the national level. Their chances of being elected may also be greater in urban than in rural areas. For instance, in the early 1970s, women were 12 percent of the members of school boards in the United States (Bers, 1978, citing National School Boards Association, 1974), but figures from only a few years earlier indicate that 23 percent of school board members in large cities were women (Frieze et al., 1978:342). Similarly, it was estimated in 1979 that 4 percent of all the mayors of municipalities in the United States were women. Yet, 6 percent of the mayors in cities with populations greater than 50,000 were women and five of the nation's twenty largest cities (Chicago; San Antonio, Texas; Phoenix, Arizona; San Francisco, and San Jose, California) had women mayors (Warren, 1979).

More women are being elected to state legislatures; by the beginning of 1978 they represented 9.3 percent of all state representatives and senators (Lynn, 1979:418). However, probably because the lower houses in each state are larger, they are much more commonly found there, rather than in the state senates. Women legislators tend to be more common in the New England states and, to some extent, in the West than in other areas. While their representation is associated with low pay (New Hampshire with 20 percent of all the women state legislators pays its representatives only $200 a biennium), an even more important correlate of women's participation appears to be a lack of competition for legislative seats. The New England states generally have very large lower bodies, perhaps as an extension of the town meeting practice. Because there are many legislative seats relative to the total population of the state, the competition for the seats is relatively low. In states with such large legislatures in relation to the population, women tend to predominate (Diamond, 1977).

Until 1974 only three women had been elected as a state governor. "Ma" Ferguson of Texas was elected in 1924 and 1932 after her husband was impeached as governor. Nellie Taylor Ross was elected in Wyoming in 1925 after the death of her husband, and Lurleen Wallace was elected in 1966 in Alabama when the state constitution prohibited her husband, George, from serving another term. Only in 1974 were two women elected on their own credentials: Ella Grasso of Connecticut and Dixie Lee Ray of Washington.

Until 1979 there had never been more than nineteen women in the United States House of Representatives and two women in the Senate. Few of these women have served long enough to have sufficient seniority to be on major committees or to hold powerful decision-making posts. Moreover, informal norms of cronyism may lock women out of many informal, behind-the-scenes decision-making meetings.

While from 1917 through 1976 only 3 percent of deceased senators and 9 percent of all deceased representatives had been succeeded in office by their wives, many of the women elected to the United States Congress have been widows, and a large number of them have filled their deceased husbands' positions. As Diane Kincaid (1978:96) put it, "Statistically at least, for women aspiring to serve in Congress, the best husband has been a dead husband, most preferably one serving in Congress at the time of his demise." While in general the widows who succeed their husbands have been less likely than those first elected in regular November elections to pursue a second term of office or to have political or professional experience similar to men in Congress (Bullock and Harris, 1972), the widows have not been mere figureheads. Many of them faced stiff opposition in run-off elections to fill their husbands' vacancies and many have been reelected many times (Kincaid, 1978). In fact, there is no difference in the total numbers of years served in Congress by the widows and those women first elected in November (Bullock and Harris, 1972).

Women are notably absent in high-level appointive posts. For instance, through the 1970s, no woman has served on the Supreme Court, and as of 1978 only nine women were federal judges. Only five women have been cabinet members, two of these during the Carter administration. When senators and representatives hire women, they pay them from 18 to 129 percent less than their male employees in similar jobs (Foreman, 1977).

Laws and Sex Stratification

Much of the legislation that is now viewed as restricting economic equality of women was originally designed to protect them from dangers in occupations such as mining, bartending, and policing (Gates, 1976:62). This protective legislation limits the hours women may work, the tasks they may perform, and the situations in which they may work. While the original intent of some of this legislation may have been to bar women from certain jobs, many of the laws were originally developed through the efforts of feminists, labor unions, and social reformers to eliminate the tragic sweat-shop conditions under which many women labored. Yet, a byproduct of these efforts has been to exclude women from certain jobs.

While this protective legislation is now being ruled unlawful, women are still sometimes excluded by entrance requirements that systematically discriminate against them as a class and often against groups of men. For instance, many police departments have minimum height standards. These serve not only to eliminate women from the pool of applicants, but also to screen out Asian and Hispanic men who, as a group, are shorter than Anglo men. Veteran's preference given in state and federal appointments also benefits men (Gates, 1976:63).

Other laws have affected access to education. For instance, it was once legal to bar pregnant girls from continuing their schooling and to restrict boys from taking home economics classes and girls from taking shop classes in high schools. Employers could legally fire married women workers (as they did with flight attendants) or restrict the employment of pregnant workers. Provisions of the Social Security laws restricted payments in ways that also promoted the ideal of the husband as the main breadwinner. For instance, unlike wives of working husbands, husbands of women who provided most of the family income were not allowed to earn survivor's benefits when their spouse died.

In recent years these and other such laws have been challenged. The basis for these challenges comes from the United States Constitution and the constitutions of the various states, laws passed by Congress, and various administrative regulations. The Fourteenth Amendment to the United States Constitution requires that no state shall "deny to any person within its jurisdiction the equal protection of the laws." This provision has been used in several lawsuits as the reason for requiring equal protection or equal treatment for men and women. Such court cases often prove lengthy, costly, and time-consuming, and Congress and state legislatures have passed other laws that deal more directly with elements of sex stratification in social institutions. An example is the Equal Pay Act of 1963, which requires that men and women be paid equal wages for the same work.

The most important prohibition against occupational segregation is Title VII of the 1964 Civil Rights Act. This landmark legislation prohibits discrimination on the basis of race, color, national origin, religion, and sex in any term or condition of employment. While the original intent of the act was to deal with racial discrimination, the inclusion of the criterion of sex (as an afterthought, apparently a tactic by southern legislators to defeat the total bill) has led to important legal support for women seeking to end occupational discrimination (Robinson, 1979). The act specifically forbids an employer "to limit, segregate, or classify his employees in any way which would deprive or tend to deprive any individual of employment opportunities . . . because of such individual's sex."

Another important legal tool for employment equality is Affirmative Action, an executive order that requires employers with federal contracts to take "affirmative" steps to make up for past inequities that minorities and women have faced. While it is probably still too early to assess the impact of this policy, for it has been in effect only a few years, preliminary evidence is not encouraging. Women listed in news articles as top officials in corporations and government are often merely "tokens" placed in ineffectual, inflated, and powerless positions (Geng, 1976). When women in these positions attempt to assert independent power, they are likely to be dismissed. For example, even though she was only the chair of an advisory committee that had no extensive power, Bella Abzug was fired by President Carter in 1979 when she criticized his policies to the press.

On the other hand, some evidence indicates that sex typing in certain skilled trades may have begun to lessen as a response to the civil rights legislation passed in the 1960s. In 1960, about 3 percent of all skilled craftsworkers were women; by 1970, 5 percent of these workers were women. Although this is still a very small proportion of the field (and only just matches the level attained in World War II), it is a higher rate of change in the sex ratio than in any other job category (Hedges and Bennis, 1974). (Of course, these broad census categories may mask the type of job segregation found in executive jobs, where the women are only in ineffectual positions with changed titles.)

The most important legislation for education is Title IX of the Educational Amendments of 1972. The provision prohibits discrimination in education on the basis of sex. The regulations developed by the Department of Health, Education, and Welfare for its enforcement prohibit sex segregation and discrimination in almost all areas of academic and extracurricular activities at the elementary, secondary, and college levels. One of the most far-reaching impacts of these regulations has been the requirement of equal expenditures in athletics for males and females.

While legislators and the courts sometimes are reluctant to intrude on the family because it is seen as a sacred and private area, the Supreme Court decision that legalized abortions provided women greater control over their own bodies. The laws promoting women's equality in the workforce may also help increase their status in the home. Laws pertaining to marriage and family relationships vary considerably from state to state because states have jurisdiction over domestic matters. Courts have been almost totally ineffective against wife battering because they, as well as the public, have tended to define marital violence as a private affair (Gelles, 1976). There is some effort now to devise a national family policy that would assess how legislation in various fields affects the family.

Much of the legal protection given to women derives from court decisions and legislation regarding the rights of minorities. Yet, unlike provisions regarding race, the United States Constitution does not specifically guarantee women equal rights. Thus, it is sometimes harder for women to win court decisions that charge sex discrimination than it would be for minorities to win a similar suit that charged race discrimination. Supporters of the Equal Rights Amendment to the Constitution hope that the inclusion of this constitutional guarantee of equal treatment will give the broad legal authority needed to guarantee this equality.

THE ECONOMY

The laws that provide the basis for ending sex stratification have been enacted for well over a decade, yet patterns of sex stratification remain. They are especially apparent in the economy, for here real dollars can be used to measure the extent of sex stratification. In recent years, more women have entered the labor force. Yet women tend to work in different jobs and are paid less than men, despite their educational level or job classification. Minority women face a double burden of race and sex and suffer more disadvantages than white women.

Participation in the Labor Force

Since 1900, the participation of women in this country's labor force has risen sharply, mainly because of the increased participation of married women. From 1900 to 1940, the percentage of married women in the labor force more than doubled, and from 1940 to 1970, it almost tripled. During that same time period, the labor force participation of single women and men fell. This increase in the labor force participation of married women has occurred with women of all ages (Kreps and Clark, 1975).

Married nonwhite women have participated more in the labor force than have married white women, mainly because the husbands of nonwhite women make substantially less money than the husbands of white women. Married women of Mexican, Puerto Rican, or American Indian origin do not have higher labor force participation rates than white women. Even though their families are poorer than white families, cultural prohibitions against women working as well as a possible lack of jobs and definitely lower educational levels probably influence their absence from the workplace (see Almquist and Wehrle-Einhorn, 1978:66–67).

While married women have continually increased their labor force participation, the rates for men have declined. Ninety-three percent of the married men sixteen and over who were living with their wives worked in 1947; in 1974, this figure dropped to 84 percent. Much of this decline can be attributed to lower participation rates of men over fifty-four years of age, who more often retire early—both voluntarily as higher pensions become available and involuntarily as it is more difficult for older workers to compete in the labor market—and of men between 16 and 20, who more often attend postsecondary schools. The difference in labor force participation rates for white and nonwhite married men is much lower than the difference with women. From about 2.4 to 2.9 percent more nonwhite men than white men worked from 1950 to 1970, in contrast to the gap of about 10 percent for nonwhite and white women (Kreps and Clark, 1975:14–16).

Women with small children are less likely to be in the labor force than are other women. In 1977, 39 percent of married women living with their husbands and with children under six years of age were in the labor force, 56 percent of those with children between the ages of six and 17 were working, and 45 percent of those with no children under 18 were in the labor force, (Statistical Abstracts, 1978:405). The largest increase in labor force participation in the last few years has been among women with small children, and Kreps and Clark (1975) predict that a continuation of these trends will eventually lead to no difference in the labor force participation rates of women with small children and of all married women (1975:18–19). While the smaller number of children young mothers have today and a greater availability of part-time work have contributed slightly to this increase, the most important influence seems to be a greater tendency for all young women to work. This cannot be explained by their higher educational level or by greater monetary needs of their families. It probably involves a different attitude by all young women, whether or not they are mothers, toward work outside the home (Darien, 1976). Since almost all married men between the ages of 20 and 55 are employed, the presence of small children has little effect on men's labor force participation rate. The age at first marriage has risen over the past few years, and the number of divorces has also grown. While widows (many of whom are over 65) have a lower labor force participation rate than married women do, single and divorced or separated women have a higher employment rate.

Sex Segregation of Occupations

While more and more women have entered the labor force, they do not work at the same jobs as men. A number of studies show that the occupational structure in the United States is intensely segregated by sex and that this pattern of sex segregation has persisted since at least 1900. In every decade, over two times more women than we would expect by chance are in occupations that are disproportionately female, given the number of women participating in the labor force as a whole. This sex segregation is so extreme that if men and women were to be represented in occupations the same way that they are represented in the labor force as a whole, fully two-thirds of all men and women would have to change jobs (Gross, 1968:202).

Valerie Oppenheimer (1970) concludes that the vast increase in the number of women in the labor force in this century has come not from women entering men's fields, but from the rapid expansion of the occupations in which women work. Over these years, female occupations have become more open to including men, while male occupations have been less open to including women (Gross, 1968).

The nature of women's jobs has remained remarkably consistent throughout this century. Of the seventeen occupations that had 70 percent or more women workers in 1900, fourteen of these were still largely female in 1960 (Oppenheimer, 1968). Women still predominate in areas such as librarianship, nursing, teaching, secretarial work, telephone operators, operatives in textile factories, housekeeping, and private service work. One-fourth of all employed women in 1969 were in just five occupations: secretary-stenographer, household worker, bookkeeper, elementary school teacher, and waitress (Blau, 1975:221). Except for teachers, these occupations fall in the clerical and service sectors. Occupational projections made for the period to 1985 suggest that these sectors will continue to grow rapidly and that there is no apparent reason to expect a decline in women's labor force participation (Carey, 1976). In general, women workers are much more concentrated in just a few occupations than are men. While half of all working women are employed in 21 of the 250 occupations listed by the census, half of all working men are employed in 65 occupations.

While the census categories are an invaluable source of data, they can often underestimate the amount of sex segregation and sex discrimination in the labor force. Within a given occupation listed in the census such as teaching or sales, the more prestigious and usually higher paid posts are held by men, the less prestigious and less well rewarded posts by women. For instance, in retail sales, men generally sell cars and large appliances, and women sell clothing and small kitchen goods. Also, salesmen tend to serve male customers, and saleswomen serve female customers.

Sex segregation may even be found within one department of a store. In the men's clothing department of a national chain of department stores, women sell the underwear, ties, and less expensive shirts and are paid an hourly wage. Men, however, sell the suits and more expensive clothing, are paid by commission, and earn much more than the women do. Similarly, while the census figures show that women predominate overall in the profession of teaching, most men teach in high schools and most women teach in elementary schools. Within the high schools, men usually teach the physical sciences and some of the social sciences while women teach languages and literature. In sex-segregated classes, men generally instruct boys and women teach girls.

Women also experience additional discrimination because of their color. Table 2–1 gives the distribution of black and white males and females in the major occupational categories used by the census. This table shows discrimination by both race and sex. White women are overrepre-

TABLE 2-1 OCCUPATIONAL DISTRIBUTIONS BY PERCENTAGE OF THE FOUR RACE-SEX GROUPS, DECEMBER 1978

OCCUPATION	WHITE MALES	BLACK MALES	WHITE FEMALES	BLACK FEMALES
Professional, technical	15.6	10.0	16.3	14.3
Managers and administrators	15.0	6.7	6.4	3.0
Sales workers	6.5	2.4	7.9	3.6
Clerical	5.9	7.7	35.6	27.9
Craftsmen, foremen	22.0	15.6	1.9	1.3
Operatives, except transport	11.2	15.5	10.3	14.8
Transport equipment operatives	5.6	8.5	0.8	0.8
Laborers, except farm	6.6	13.2	1.2	1.5
Farmers and farm managers	2.5	0.8	0.3	0.2
Farm laborers and foremen	1.2	3.1	0.7	0.3
Service workers, except private household workers	7.7	16.4	16.3	24.3
Private household workers	[a]	0.1	2.2	7.5
Totals[b]	99.8	100.0	99.9	100.1
Total N (in thousands)	(49,976)	(5,692)	(35,158)	(5,081)

[a] Less than 0.05 percent.

[b] Totals may not equal 100.0 because of error introduced through rounding.

Source: "Household Data," *Employment and Earnings*, 26 (January 1979), 38.

sented in clerical fields. Nonwhite women are overrepresented in low-paying service and private household work. White males are overrepresented in the professional, technical, administrative, craftsman and foreman job categories. Black males are overrepresented in the operative, laborer, and service categories. Although the aggregate figures show more black female than black male professionals, this statistic results from the large number of black female nurses and teachers. Using the 1970 figures, when nurses, dietitians, therapists, and teachers are eliminated from the category, 4 percent of black female workers remain in the professional category, compared to 4.4 percent of black male workers (Almquist, 1975:138).

Sex Differences in Wages

Men and women earn vastly different salaries, even when they both work full-time. In 1960, year-round, full-time male workers over the age of fourteen had median annual earnings of $5,435. For full-time, year-round women workers, the comparable figure was $3,296, which is 61 percent of the male rate (U.S. Department of Commerce, 1976:47). In 1977, the median earnings of full-time male workers was $14,626, comparable women's median earnings were $8,618—59 percent of the men's wages.

Over this decade and a half, women's wages relative to men's declined, whether the absolute or the percentage differences between the sexes are considered (Statistical Abstract of the United States, 1978:464).* While single women tend to earn more than married women, the gap between single and married women's incomes is so small that it is not at all comparable to the income gap between women and men.

People who have less education and are nonwhite generally earn less than people who have more education and are white. Yet, in each of the education and racial categories, women earn much less on the average than men do (see table 2–2).

Part of the wage gap between men and women comes because women tend to work in lower-status and hence less well paid positions. Yet, even when men and women work in the same occupational category, women tend to be paid less. Table 2–3 compares the median earnings of male and female full-time, year-round workers in each of the broad census categories of major occupational groups in 1974. In each of these categories (with the exception of nonfarm laborers), women earn less than two-thirds of what

*The gap between men's and women's wages becomes even more dramatic if the means, or averages, instead of the medians are compared. (While the median denotes the point that divides a distribution in half, the mean is the average, or "balancing point," of the distribution and is thus affected by extreme values in the distribution. Men are much more likely than women to have extremely high incomes; thus, their mean incomes are much larger than their median incomes.) In 1974, the mean income of full-time women workers was 45 percent that of comparable men, a much larger gap than that shown by the usually reported comparison of median figures (Fogg, 1977).

TABLE 2–2 MEDIAN ANNUAL INCOME OF YEAR-ROUND, FULL-TIME WORKERS OVER AGE 18 BY SEX, RACE, AND EDUCATION, 1976

	EDUCATIONAL LEVEL OF MALES						
	Elementary School	High School 1–3 Years	High School 4 Years	College 1–3 Years	College 4 Years	College 5+ Years	Total
Whites	$10,342	$12,114	$13,587	$15,014	$17,932	$20,676	$14,289
Blacks	8,258	9,165	10,278	12,305	12,778	17,827	10,222
Total	10,031	11,617	13,317	14,730	17,631	20,497	13,873
	EDUCATIONAL LEVEL OF FEMALES						
	Elementary School	High School 1–3 Years	High School 4 Years	College 1–3 Years	College 4 Years	College 5+ Years	Total
Whites	$ 6,114	$ 6,850	$ 7,931	$ 8,834	$10,612	$13,522	$ 8,381
Blacks	5,404	6,087	7,781	8,775	10,757	12,992	7,836
Total	5,923	6,712	7,910	8,845	10,611	13,426	8,317

Source: "Current Population Reports," Bureau of the Census, United States Department of Commerce, Series P-60, no. 114 (July 1978), 192–201.

TABLE 2-3 MEDIAN EARNINGS OF YEAR-ROUND, FULL-TIME CIVILIAN WORKERS 14 YEARS OLD AND OVER WITH EARNINGS BY OCCUPATION OF LONGEST JOB AND SEX: 1973 AND 1974

OCCUPATION OF LONGEST JOB	1974			1973		
	Women	Men	Women/Men (Ratio)	Women	Men	Women/Men (Ratio)
Total with earnings	$6,772	$11,835	0.57	$6,335	$11,186	0.57
Professional, technical, and kindred workers	9,570	14,873	0.64	9,093	14,306	0.64
Managers and administrators, except farm	8,603	15,425	0.56	7,667	14,519	0.53
Sales workers	5,168	12,523	0.41	4,650	12,296	0.38
Craft and kindred workers	6,492	12,028	0.54	6,144	11,245	0.55
Operatives, including transport	5,766	10,176	0.57	5,358	9,503	0.56
Laborers, except farm	5,891	8,145	0.72	4,956	8,158	0.61
Farmers and farm managers	a	5,459	b	a	6,697	b
Farm laborers and farm supervisors	a	5,097	b	a	4,727	b
Service workers, except private household	5,046	8,638	0.58	4,588	7,937	0.58
Private household workers	2,676	a	b	2,069	a	b

[a] Median earnings not shown when base is less than 75,000 persons.

[b] Not applicable.

Source: U.S. Department of Commerce, 1976.

men do, even though both the men and women included are working full-time.

No matter how one looks at the picture, women workers earn less than men. This wage gap appears in both traditionally male fields such as science and engineering and in predominantly female areas such as service jobs. Many of the areas where women work require extensive education and training. Yet, within specific fields where this is true, such as librarianship, nursing, teaching, and clerical work, women workers earn much less than males. Their lower pay does not represent lower qualifications than men have or employment in areas that require less education. Within occupational categories where men and women have quite similar educational levels, the women consistently earn less than the men. Even though men in predominantly female occupations do earn more than the women in those fields, they generally do not earn as much as other men in the labor force, presumably because they are employed in "female" jobs.

While women college graduates earn less than their male counterparts, even in traditionally masculine fields, there is some indication that by the mid-1970s this situation was changing slightly for the few women who had recently received degrees in traditionally masculine areas and were just entering the job market. "In 1975–76, the average national monthly salary offer for women bachelor's degree candidates was $1,198.43, almost $19.50 a month more than the average offer to the male candidates. Women candidates in accounting ($1,021), computer science ($1,045), and chemistry ($1,052) also received average offers of more than their male rivals by $4, $10, and $41 a month, respectively" (National Science Foundation, 1977).

Women and Poverty

At least since 1948, women's unemployment rates in the United States have tended to exceed men's. For instance, in 1978 the seasonally adjusted unemployment rate for men twenty years of age and older was 4.2 percent; for women, it was 6.0 percent (Current Labor Statistics, 1979:78). Although part of this difference may come from women's overrepresentation or crowding into just a few jobs (where they face more competition than men do in typically male jobs), within typically female occupations women's unemployment is also higher than men's. For instance, the unemployment rate of women in clerical jobs is one and one-half times that of men; in sales jobs, women's unemployment rate is twice that of men. Women are more likely than men to withdraw from the group of people who are actively seeking work and thus may not be counted in official unemployment statistics. The actual male-female difference in rate of unemployment, then, may be even greater than what is usually reported (Kreps and Clark, 1975:61).

We live in a highly stratified society where the highest paid one-fifth of all white workers earns 600 percent more than the lowest paid one-fifth (Jencks et al., 1972:14). The United States has no official policy of minimizing wage differences between occupational categories, and both working-class women and men face economic disadvantages relative to others in the society. Working women, however, are disproportionately at the bottom of the income distribution because, if they are married, their husbands often earn less than other men and their own salaries are usually too small to raise the family's income much. If they have no husband and must support families by themselves, their low wages make it even harder to survive.

One of every seven children in the United States lives in a family without a father present, and from 1966 to 1976 the number of female-headed families with children grew almost ten times as fast as two-parent families (Sawhill, 1976:201). Increases in the divorce and separation rates are the main reason for this rise. Families headed by a woman are much more likely than two-parent families or families headed by a single man to have incomes below the poverty level. Almost half of all female-headed families are officially categorized as poor (Sawhill, 1976:204).

All of these patterns affect minority families more adversely than white families. Table 2–4 compares the unemployment rates of nonwhite and white men and women. From this table, it is apparent that nonwhite women receive more than a "double dose" of discrimination. The sex differential in unemployment rates for nonwhites is higher than for whites, and the race differential is higher for women than for men.

Although black women are more likely than white women to be employed, the median wage of year-round, full-time, black women workers was 93 percent of the median wage of year-round, full-time, white women workers, 67 percent of the black male median, and only 55 percent of the median wage of the white male worker in 1976 (see table 2–2). In 1978, 32 percent of all employed black women were private household workers or working in the service sector outside the home, while only 18 percent of all employed white women were in these categories (see table 2–1). Since virtually no minimum wage legislation applies to these areas, such a pattern exacerbates the poverty of black women.

Minority women are also more likely than white women to be married to men with low incomes, for both minority men and minority women face discrimination. Full-time employed men in all minority groups in this country earn less than white men. So, while many minority women must

TABLE 2–4 UNEMPLOYMENT RATES BY RACE AND SEX OF WORKERS OVER 20 YEARS OF AGE, FEBRUARY 1979

	SEX		
	Male	Female	Sex Differentials
Race			
White	3.4%	5.0%	−1.6%
Non-white	8.6%	10.6%	−2.0%
Race differentials	−5.2%	−5.6%	

Source: "Current Labor Statistics: Household Data," *Monthly Labor Review*, 102 (April 1979), 78.

work for the family to make enough to live on, their earnings still rarely approach the average family income of white families.

Black, Hispanic, and American Indian families are more likely to be headed by a woman than are white families. (Asian families more often have both parents present than white families.) Black, Puerto Rican, Mexican-origin, and American Indian female-headed families are almost twice as likely as white female-headed families to have children under six. All minority families tend to be larger than white families (Almquist and Wehrle-Einhorn, 1978). Together, these variables show the extreme economic problems that minority women face. They earn less, their husbands earn less, they are more likely to be unemployed, their families are larger, and they are generally more likely to have to support a family by themselves than are white women.

Explanations of Sex Stratification in the Economy

Social scientists have long been interested in why men and women earn unequal rewards in the economy, and their explanations have tended to focus on the economic institutions themselves. Blau and Jusenius (1976) distinguish three theoretical approaches to this question in economics, and explanations common in the sociological literature can be subsumed under these categories. Most of these models were originally proposed to explain race discrimination and were later expanded to account also for sex inequalities. While they may all ultimately be used to explain institutional patterns of sex stratification, these models eventually use the more individual concept of discrimination—the idea that employers favor one group (males) over another (females)—as an explanatory variable.

Employees and employers Some economic models, often termed neoclassical, examine how the actions of employees and employers in the labor market relate to larger economic patterns. Some of the theorists using these models assume that we have a competitive economy and that discrimination is essentially the employers' preference or taste for one group over another. Because this discrimination is inherently inefficient and does not help the employer maximize profits, these theorists suggest that it will disappear as a more efficient system develops. Both the overcrowding hypothesis and the human capital model discussed below use this assumption. Other economists do not assume that the labor market is perfectly competitive and suggest instead that employers and favored employees benefit from discrimination. The monopsonistic model falls into this category.

The *overcrowding hypothesis* involves the notion that women tend to be "overcrowded" in certain areas of the labor force and that this overcrowding contributes to their lower wages. The idea first arose in writings of English economists in the early part of this century (Fawcett, 1918; Edgeworth, 1922) and appears again in the writings of contemporary economists (Bergmann, 1971, 1973; Stevenson, 1973, 1975). This theory rests on the traditional economic notions of supply and demand and the relation of wages to these variables. Demand refers to the need of employers or consumers for a given group of workers. Supply refers to how much of that group is available. If the supply of workers is higher than the demand for them, then a buyer's market exists and employers can afford to discriminate. The overcrowding hypothesis says that because women's occupations are overcrowded, the supply of workers exceeds the demand and the workers will receive lower wages.

Why does this overcrowding happen? If employers wanted to maximize their profits, it would seem that they would hire women, to whom they could pay lower wages than to men. Yet they do not. The proponents of the overcrowding model suggest that this overcrowding occurs because of discrimination, the desire to keep women in their "place"—only in certain jobs—and the acceptance of cultural stereotypes of women as inefficient and incapable of performing male jobs. This benefits not only employers, but also male workers, who do not have to compete with women in their predominantly male occupations.

Empirical studies give some support to the overcrowding hypothesis. Even when jobs are grouped by the training and skills they require, women in each group consistently earn less than men. Men and women with the same skills and experience are placed in different jobs, and these different jobs have different levels of pay.

The overcrowding hypothesis can also help account for women's higher job turnover and the growing wage discrepancy between men and women. About half of the difference between men and women in their turnover rates in jobs can be accounted for by the type of job that they hold. "Women are heavily employed in the kinds of occupations in which women *and* men tend to quit more often, whereas men are heavily employed in the kinds of jobs in which stability of employment is rewarded" (Bergmann, 1973:14, emphasis in original). Moreover, the wage discrepancy between men and women is growing because the jobs into which women are crowded are also the ones that are growing the most. More and more women are entering these lowest-paying jobs, and thus the average wages of men and women are getting even further apart (Bergmann and Adelman, 1973; also Ferber and Lowry, 1976). It must be remembered, however, that overcrowding cannot account for all of the gap in men's and women's unemployment rates and wages. Even in the typically female jobs, males appear to be preferred as employees and have a lower unemployment rate and higher wages than women.

Human capital theories offer another neoclassical explanation of women's job situation. Human capital refers to the resources men and women can sell to the labor market. Theorists who use this approach generally assume that in a perfect competitive system people with equal resources will earn equal rewards. The reason that men and women do not earn equally is that they do not have equal resources to offer. Because women generally have less experience in the labor force and may have higher turnover rates than men do, they are worth less to the employer and are therefore paid less (Blau and Jusenius, 1976:185–86).

Empirical tests of this model provide little support for it. Even when various human capital variables are taken into account—when the impact of women's disadvantage in work experience, training, occupational status, and so forth is statistically removed—a large wage gap between men and women remains. Moreover, women appear to benefit less than men from advanced education, working in male-dominated areas, and having continuous work histories (Treiman and Terrell, 1975; Suter and Miller, 1973). This situation does not appear to have improved over time. Between 1962 and 1973, education became a more important determinant of men's incomes, but its ability to predict women's incomes did not increase. Moreover, human capital variables explained about as little of the earnings gap between husbands and wives in 1973 as they did in 1962 (Featherman and Hauser, 1976).

The final neoclassical explanation is a *monopsonistic* model. Monopsony, in this case, refers to a system in which employers (the buyers of labor) are in a position to set the wages they have to pay to get the workers they need. Anyone who has such monopsonistic control over wages pays the lowest wage that still attracts workers. Janice Madden (1973, 1975) applies this model to sex discrimination. She assumes that males hold the power within the society and that it is to their advantage to discriminate against women. This discrimination may not be a "prejudice" or "taste." Rather, it is an economically rational way for employers to maximize profit, a "manifestation of male power" (Madden, 1975:155).

Madden argues that the wage differential between men and women and the extent of monopsony is a function of the wage elasticity of the supply of labor to a firm. She argues that because women's labor supply is less elastic (in other words, because women are less able to change jobs than men), a firm has greater monopsony power over them. Because women have fewer choices within the labor market and cannot respond as men do to wage changes, a firm can get women to work for less. Because the supply of female workers—women who want to work—is less affected by labor market conditions than is the supply of men workers (in other words, it is possible to find more women to work), women can be paid less than men. The model assumes that it is not inefficient to discriminate against women because men have power (a monopsony) over the female market anyway. In essence, then, this model is similar to the overcrowding hypothesis, except that it does not assume that all workers are paid for their actual contributions.

Madden suggests that the elasticity of the supply of women workers within specific firms is influenced by a number of variables, including the family and home responsibilities, as well as the fact that women are married to men, who have some control over their labor market decisions. (See Blau and Jusenius, 1976, and Madden, 1976, for a further discussion of this point.) Protective legislation has also been used to enforce male power in the labor force. Unions have often excluded women from membership or ignored their specific needs. Because males are more likely to unionize than females, they develop their own form of monopsony power. In the wage demands they can place on employers, they have advantages over nonunionized workers, many of whom are women. Male wages can also be determined relative to other work while female wages may be compared to work at home, which has been given no explicit monetary value.

Perhaps the most important aspect of the monopsonistic model, in contrast to both the overcrowding hypothesis and human capital models, is that it begins from the assumption that male dominance exists and affects women's labor force experiences. The model, then, can be used to further examine conditions that enhance men's power over women and women's disadvantage relative to men.

Work organizations Instead of focusing on the characteristics and motives of workers and employers, some analyses focus on the nature of jobs, occupations, and employing firms. These include the economic analyses of dual and internal labor markets as well as analyses of organizations, often a separate field in sociology.

Dual labor market analyses have often been used to explain the marginal position of minorities in the economy. This view posits that the labor market is divided into a primary and a secondary market. The primary market is well developed. There are only a few entry jobs and long promotion ladders. Worker stability tends to be high because there are high wages, opportunities for advancement, good working conditions, and provisions for job security. The secondary market, however, has many entry positions and short or nonexistent promotion ladders. Worker stability is low, probably because there are low wages and few opportunities for advancement, poor working conditions, and little job security (Blau and Jusenius, 1976:196). Minorities and, to some extent, women are more commonly found in the secondary market, and one can use the dual labor market analysis to explain why they have lower wages and advance less than white men.

Yet a great deal of sex segregation also exists within specific occupations. The *internal labor market* analysis deals with this situation. In this analysis, the jobs within a given organization are divided into two categories: those filled from sources outside the firm by recruiting new workers, and those filled by promoting or upgrading current workers. The various neoclassical approaches may be used to analyze the filling of the entry-level positions from outside the firm. The filling of the second category of jobs, though, is determined by administrative apparatus within the firm, the "internal labor market," and competition among those already hired or employed by the enterprise. An individual's advancement opportunities within this internal labor market are usually determined by the worker's original entry-level job (Blau and Jusenius, 1976:192). Thus, because men and women enter an occupational area or a firm at different points, these entry-level positions are linked with different career lines, and it is entirely possible that they would continue to be in different jobs and receive different wages. For example, male college graduates may be hired as junior executives. Female college graduates may be hired as secretaries, even executive secretaries. Yet, a man has a greater chance to move into administrative ranks than a woman does because his entry-level position is bureaucratically linked with those higher positions.

Civil service regulations in the state of California require that for an employee to be promoted, there must be less than a 10 percent difference in wages between the present classification and the one into which the employee wishes to transfer. Clerical salaries are so low that they are generally more than 10 percent lower than those of almost all other positions that would provide upward mobility. Because most clerical positions are held by women, women are effectively blocked from moving into other posts. Recognizing this, the state of California has moved in recent years to alter this pattern by adding bridging classes, new job classifications that pay enough to meet the requirements for movement into the new job and that also provide experience helpful in entering a new position (Lang, 1977). This policy is specifically designed to alter the internal labor market mechanisms that discriminate against women.

An internal labor market analysis can be used to explore the sex discrimination professionals face. A number of studies show how men and women in medicine, law, and academia have different experiences. For instance, women tend to be overrepresented in the specialties of pediatrics, anesthesiology, psychiatry, physical medicine, and public health and underrepresented in surgical specialties (except obstetrics), cardiovascular medicine, gastroenterology, and general practice (Quadragno, 1976). Women lawyers tend not to be in general practice and are concentrated in low-prestige specialties such as domestic relations, where many clients are women, or trusts and estates (Patterson and Engelberg, 1978:281). Academic areas also tend to be segregated by sex, with women greatly underrepresented in economics in the social sciences, in all of the physical sciences but astronomy and chemistry, and especially in plant pathology, biophysics, entomology, and genetics. They are somewhat overrepresented as anthropologists, sociologists, and social workers in the social sciences, in astronomy and chemistry in the physical sciences, and in general biology and cytology. Moreover, within specific fields, women are largely segregated in specialty areas. Women psychologists are overrepresented in developmental and school psychology and underrepresented in industrial, consumer, and psychopharmacology areas. Women anthropologists are somewhat more likely to be cultural anthropologists or linguists and much less likely to be physical anthropologists or archaeologists than would be expected by chance (Patterson, 1973).

As with the overcrowding and human capital models, this sex segregation is often explained by discrimination. Interviews with women physicians indicate that they avoid the masculine specialties because other physicians discourage their involvement and they wish to avoid conflict that might arise if they entered those areas (Quadragno, 1976). Similarly, researchers who have looked at the field of law suggest that women are put in "back rooms" where firms can make "sure they do not have contact with big clients who, the firms claim, would find it unacceptable to deal with women" (Patterson and Engelberg, 1978:281). Finally, a large number of studies in many academic disciplines show that in comparison to their male colleagues, women are more likely to receive initial appointments at lower ranks or in nonrank positions; that they are promoted more slowly and receive tenure at a later age, if at all; that they are less involved in administration or in decision making in either the department or the national professional association; and that they receive lower salaries (Patterson, 1973:299). While some of these differences are influenced by male-female differences in human capital variables such as degrees earned and publication records, these variables cannot account for all the sex differences in rank and salary (Patterson, 1973; also Astin and Boyer, 1973).

While many professional fields such as medicine, law, and higher education are dominated by men, women do predominate in other professional areas, including nursing, social work, teaching and librarianship. In the past few years, more men have entered these areas. In fact, it is possible that in the United States, these female fields have been more open to the entry of men than the male fields have been to the entry of women (Gross, 1968; Wilensky, 1968). Yet when men enter these professions, they often do not hold the same positions women do. Men more often teach in higher grades; male social workers are more often community organizers than group or case workers. These different starting points generally presage different incomes and opportunities for advancement (Grimm, 1978). In these traditionally female fields, the proportion of men has gradually increased over a period of years. Yet men are represented in the higher-status and administrative components more than would be expected by chance, and this tendency has not declined as more men have entered the fields. This is especially true when the administrative component of a profession expands. A "demand" for administrators apparently enhances the tendency of males to dominate the field.

Although the majority of working women in the United States are in nonprofessional jobs, relatively little research has been devoted to their problems. However, they experience both sex segregation and wage discrimination. Some of the occupational sex segregation for blue-collar workers involves segregation by firm. As the dual labor market analysis would predict, women tend to predominate in fields with low profits, relatively unstable employment opportunities, and, thus, low wages. These fields include such jobs as apparel manufacturing workers, beauticians, waitresses, laundry and dry-cleaning workers, and dressmakers (Baker, 1978:349–50). Yet, as an internal labor market perspective would predict, extensive sex segregation also exists within organizations, and because men and women start at different points in the firm, their advancement opportunities and career patterns differ greatly. Discrimination may occur in promotion patterns, wage advances, or entry points, but the end result is that women always tend to have lower wages and employment levels than men (Cassell et al., 1975).

While much of this discrimination results from decisions of employers, some of it arises from union practices. Union organizers have not penetrated some typically female areas. They believe that clerical workers and workers in some service areas such as waitressing are hard to organize. In fact, these workers have not formed unions as often as other workers have, even though women workers who are organized into unions do earn better wages than nonorganized women workers. Moreover, the gap between male and female wages in the service sector is greater for nonunionized than for unionized workers (Oleson and Katsuranis, 1978:319; Baker, 1978:351).

Yet, unions themselves, which are headed mainly by men, also discriminate against women. In contrast to the situation with service workers, the wage gap between male and female blue-collar workers is greater among unionized than among nonunionized workers, clearly showing a lack of concern by blue-collar unions for women workers (Baker, 1978:351). From their beginning many unions have had exclusionary policies or, when women were allowed to join they did not give women's needs high priority. Women have especially been excluded from apprenticeship programs in the skilled trades. Union leadership has been dominated by men, even in unions that serve mainly women, including the International

Ladies Garment Workers and the Amalgamated Clothing Workers (Falk, 1975).

To understand how this discrimination occurs in labor markets, sociologists have examined *women's experiences in work organizations.* Careful studies of several organizations show that women and men tend to have very different experiences, even when they are in the same structural positions and have the same work qualifications. In fact, women in high-status positions who have greater expertise and authority may face the most difficulty. They may lose friends and respect from others and actually have less influence and access to information than they did before. These women will experience more strains at work than they did before, and the situation will not improve, and may even worsen, over time (Miller et al., 1975).

Again, these organizational dynamics are explained by discrimination, but discrimination on the interpersonal level. An experimental study illustrates how this discrimination occurs. In the study, both men and women observed a man or a woman who performed either very well or less well on an assigned task. In some cases, the subjects competed with the man or woman; in some, they simply observed her or him; and in some, they were to cooperate with her or him. The male subjects tended to dislike the competent woman only when they directly interacted with her. In both the competitive and cooperative situations, men liked working with an incompetent woman as much as with a competent woman. They, however, always preferred to work with a competent man. Men also tended to report liking a competent woman only when observing her, not in cases where they interacted with her (Hagen and Kahn, 1975). Thus, the greater isolation and lack of power experienced by high-status women in organizations may be understood as coming from the reluctance of men to acknowledge the worth of competent women and to associate with them.

Capitalism Some contemporary economists informed by Marxism use an analysis that focuses on the segmentation of the labor force to show how the segregation of minorities and women into certain occupations and their lower pay benefits capitalists, private owners of businesses, and capitalism as a system. These theorists accept the dual labor market analysts' primary and secondary sectors. They further divide the primary sector into what they call "subordinate" and "independent" primary jobs. They suggest that while the independent jobs require and encourage creativity and problem solving, subordinate jobs are routinized and require dependability, discipline, and responsiveness to authority (Reich et al., 1975:71). Beyond these divisions, they recognize that the labor market is segmented by race, with minorities more often in the secondary sector and the subordinate part of the primary sector, and by sex, as we discussed earlier.

These theorists, then, suggest that this labor force segmentation benefits the system of capitalism. First, segmentation of the labor force increases capitalists' profits and forestalls challenges to the system as a whole by dividing workers among themselves and undermining unions that promote workers' interests. Because labor force segmentation usually follows ethnic, race and sex lines, when one group of workers goes on strike, another group of a different race, ethnicity, or sex may be enticed by the employers to be strikebreakers. For instance, when workers in paper mills on the West Coast, who are mainly men, went on strike in the late 1970s, the salaried and nonunionized clerical workers, who are mainly women, were required to work in the mills if they wanted to keep their jobs. Labor segmentation theorists also suggest that labor market segmentation limits women workers' aspirations for mobility and legitimizes inequalities between individuals. Most important, segmentation of the labor force is profitable. For instance, even though the women who worked in the West Coast paper mills during the strike were paid more than they earned as clerical workers, their wages were still less than those the men workers had before they went on strike. Thus, not only were the mill owners able to continue operations during the strike, they even made greater profits.

It would seem that rational employers would always prefer to hire women, to whom they could pay such low wages, rather than men. Yet many employers continue to hire men and still make profits. The reason may be partly that men workers tend to predominate in monopoly sectors with high profit rates and women workers predominate in less profitable industries such as the service areas and garment industry, which are also more competitive. The capitalists in the latter areas profit from hiring women workers, because they help keep their prices low and competitive. The employers in the monopoly sectors, because they can essentially set the prices they pass on to consumers, also make a profit and can still afford to refuse to hire women (Deckard and Sherman, 1974).

Comment In the sections above, we have reviewed several explanations of sex discrimination in the economy. With a neoclassical model, the overcrowding hypothesis suggests that because women are crowded into fewer occupations than men are, they can be paid less than their skills and abilities would warrant. The human capital theorists try to account for women's lower wages through their lower accumulation of education, job experience, and other such variables. Inequities that remain after the impact of these variables have been accounted for are attributed to discrimination. The monopsony approach recognizes that discrimination exists and that men have greater power than women in the economy. Because women are crowded into fewer occupations and hence, become a less elastic labor supply than men, firms can discriminate more against them. In other words, women have to take what they can get.

Other analyses focus on the discrimination women face within work organizations. They suggest that because women generally start at different points within the labor market, they have different opportunities and experiences than men do and that within work organizations, even when given responsible positions, women face discrimination. Finally, labor market segmentation theories accept many of the findings of the other approaches, but add the idea that sex segregation of the labor market benefits capitalism itself.

In explaining sex inequalities in the economy, each of these theories falls back eventually on the idea that employers discriminate by confining women to certain jobs and by not rewarding women for their actual contributions. While these theories explore how this discrimination occurs, they do not deal with the questions of why occupational sex segregation exists or why males and females are not rewarded equally for their work. In other words, they do not answer the *primary* question of why sex inequalities exist in the first place.

Sex segregation of occupations and discrimination in pay are specific examples of the tendency for males to differentiate their activities from those of women and to devalue women's roles. Men and women tend to have different job titles, even when the nature of their work is quite similar. Women and men workers with similar skills, experience, and responsibility are paid different amounts.

These patterns of discrimination are institutionalized in an economic system. While to some extent we can understand the perpetuation of occupational sex segregation and sex discrimination in incomes as stemming from the continuance of these traditional patterns, it is important to realize that these patterns are continually reproduced and reinforced by individuals who make decisions about the nature of the work place. These "gatekeepers" to the economic world make decisions on job classifications, hiring, firing, and income levels. They may be employers, personnel managers, and even union officials, but they are generally men, or women whose superiors are men.

Undoubtedly, the labor market segmentation theorists are correct when they see sex segregation of the occupational force as benefiting capitalism. Yet, not just employers, but male workers as well, benefit from sex discrimination against women in the economy. Moreover, countries that have explicitly tried to eliminate profits of capitalists and to minimize the overall discrepancies in income still have occupational sex segregation and sex discrimination in wages (see chapter 4). Thus, sex inequalities in the economy appear to be rooted in the system of male dominance. To end them, we must deal with the system of male dominance itself and its perpetuation from one generation to another.

SUMMARY

While women and men have similar voting behavior and political participation at the local level, men are much more frequently in the upper echelons of decision making. Women's labor force participation has risen throughout this century in the United States. Yet men and women generally work in very different occupations, and women, even with the same training and skills, earn much less than men. Women, especially those who are the sole providers for their families, are poorer than men in similar circumstances. Indeed, women represent a much higher proportion of those classified as poor than men. Explanations of this sex stratification in the economy may focus on the characteristics and situation of the employees and employers, on the nature of the job and work organization, and on how patterns of sex discrimination serve capitalism.

In recent years, laws have been passed that guarantee more equality to men and women; yet the wage gap and sex segregation of the labor force remain high. An underlying assumption behind discrimination in the economy and the polity is that women's primary social roles are in the family and that men's primary social roles are in the economy and occupational world. It is assumed that women should devote their major attention to their roles as wives and mothers and that the major focus of men's attention should be to the world of work outside the home. Thus, women's family roles are often used directly and indirectly as reasons for denying them equal access to public roles.

Suggested Readings

BLAXALL, MARTHA, and BARBARA B. REAGAN, "Women and the Workplace: The Implications of Occupational Segregation," *Signs* (Spring 1976 Supplement), 1, no. 3, part 2. Collection of papers from a conference on occupational segregation that includes many good articles from economists and sociologists; all deal with theoretical and empirical issues related to sex segregation of the work force.

DIAMOND, IRENE, *Sex Roles in the State House.* New Haven, Conn.: Yale University Press, 1977. An analysis of the representation of men and women in state legislatures and the reasons for women's underrepresentation.

KIRKPATRICK, JEANE J., *Political Women.* New York: Basic Books, 1974. A report of in-depth interviews with fifty women state senators and representatives in 1972; includes extensive comments on their background, personalities, and future plans.

LLOYD, CYNTHIA B., ed., *Sex Discrimination and the Division of Labor.* New York: Columbia University Press, 1975. Collection of papers by economists, some of which are fairly technical, that examines reasons underlying sex inequality in the economy.

Monthly Labor Review and *Employment and Earnings.* Two monthly government publications that are excellent sources of the most current data on sex differences in wages, unemployment, and occupational sectors of employment. s2

STROMBERG, ANN H., and SHIRLEY HARKESS, eds., *Women Working: Theories and Facts in Perspective.* Palo Alto, Calif.: Mayfield. Collection of works, mainly by sociologists, that deal with sex segregation and sex discrimination in the economy.

3: Sex Stratification in the United States: The Family and Education

Industrialization in this country has involved the separation of the world of the family from the world of paid work. The family has come to be seen as the seat of personal and private life, and work has become a means to sustain it. Although, as we saw in the previous chapter, women have increasingly entered occupations outside the family, men continue to be defined in terms of their outside work in a way that women are not. In the United States a man's primary role is his job or occupation, while a woman's primary role is her home and family. The separation of the family from economic production has important consequences for sex inequality since the family serves the economy far more than the economy serves the family.

With industrialization, education designed to prepare people for work and family roles has become a system of formal training removed from both the home and the workplace. In general, people in this society see education as a potential way to equalize opportunity for people from various socioeconomic class levels and for the two sexes. There is less sex inequality in education than in the occupational world. In addition, our educational system is an area where many strenuous efforts are being made to overcome sexual inequality in other institutional areas. We need to assess to what extent equal access to educational facilities for men and women can bring about their equality.

THE FAMILY

In this section we trace the emergence of the family as we know it today and ask how changing views about what families are supposed to do and be have affected the status of women. Certainly not all of the changes involved in industrialization have been detrimental to women. In fact, these changes have provided a new basis for women's equality. We shall also examine the situation of women today from the perspective of the interconnections between family and housework roles and paid work roles. We look at inequality within the family itself and directions of change with special reference to the areas of sexuality and child care.

The Emergence of the Modern Family

In the predominantly rural, preindustrial society of the colonial period, family life and work life were one and the same. Privately owned family farms were the basic enterprises, and other businesses were also usually family owned and operated. In the early period of capitalism, the family unit was the basic affectional unit and also the basic work unit. This early family also was likely to contain nonfamily members, such as servants (usually the children of other householders) and apprentices. The preindustrial family was not only the workplace; it was also "church, reformatory, school and asylum" (Hareven, 1976b:198). With increasing industrialization and urbanization, these functions were given over to other agencies and the family became a very "specialized" structure whose main functions were the early socializing of children and managing tensions, or stabilizing adult personalities. Talcott Parsons calls this process of assigning functions to increasingly specific structures "structural differentiation" (1966). While the husband/father provided for the family by his outside work, the wife/mother assumed major responsibility for housework, child care, and making a happy home. Thus, the male role became anchored in the occupational sphere outside the family and the female role was anchored in the family. Parsons describes this whole process as highly functional for industrial society. The privatization of the family, its separateness from nonfamily members, made it easy for a family to pick up and move with the worker/husband wherever occupational opportunity led him. Parsons gives the impression that this arrangement is ideal and will continue indefinitely.

Eli Zaretsky, a contemporary Marxist, analyzes the relationship of the family to the economy in a manner that does not contradict Parsons's analysis, but puts the emphasis in a different place. For Zaretsky, the changes Parsons calls structural differentiation have had the effect of removing work "from the center of life to become the *means* by which life outside work was maintained" (1976:50–51). He sees this "radical disjuncture" between personal life and work as a distinctive feature of developed capitalist societies. For Zaretsky, as the world of paid work becomes increasingly impersonal and alienating, the subjective world of the family becomes increasingly important to the individual. Both Parsons and Zaretsky see the family as very much needed by individuals in contemporary society precisely because it is the place we have come to expect to find personal fulfillment.

While this more specialized family may be functional for industrial society according to Parsons and for large-scale capitalism according to Zaretsky, its beginnings can be traced back to ideological, structural, and demographic changes that preceded both industrialization and large-scale capitalism. The Protestant idea that children were not just miniature adults or workers, but individuals whose souls (we would now say "personalities") needed parental care and guidance, had been emerging for a long time (Ariès, 1962). It is also true that certain demographic changes preceded industrialization by at least several decades. Both mortality and fertility declined before industrialization, suggesting (since the fertility decline occurred among married couples) that the attitude toward children had already changed (Hareven, 1976a:99).

Whatever the ultimate and proximate causes of the change, historians tell us that from about 1825, ideas and ideals about family life that are familiar to us today were disseminated from the pulpit and in middle-class periodicals (Jeffrey, 1972). The type of family, then, that Parsons and Zaretsky describe—the family that is the cradle of personal life, the specialized family that is removed from the world of work—emerged as both ideal and partial reality a little over 150 years ago. This family ideal posits love as opposed to financial considerations as the only legitimate basis for marriage, stresses the importance of mother love for children, and sees the home as a domestic unit, a psychological haven apart from the rest of society.

In the Colonial period before industrialization women too were producers. In addition to housekeeping, women made bread, churned butter, spun yarn, wove cloth, and made soap, candles, and medicines. (Ehrenreich and English, 1976:11). Women also had important roles in the community that were later to become the jobs of male professionals. For example, the functions performed by midwives have been taken over by obstetricians, almost all of whom are male (Lerner, 1969).

Some have argued that because women did play these productive roles, their status was higher in the Colonial period than in the nineteenth century, when work and family became more separate. Even though women's competence as workers was recognized and valued in the early days of this country's history, it must not be forgotten that married women did not have anything like equal status with their husbands. They were next in command, but they were certainly not the boss of these small enterprises unless the male head died or became seriously incapacitated. In addition, married women's legal and property rights were more limited than men's

(Hareven, 1976a). Women were not given higher education until well into the nineteenth century; and women were not allowed to vote until the twentieth century.

The new image of the family that began to emerge in the 1800s defined women in a very different way than as a worker. The home began to be discussed in highly sentimental terms as a retreat, and already it was clear that meaning and satisfaction in life were to be found at home and not in the workplace.

This ideal of the home as a retreat from the harsh and evil world had the effect of connecting women to domesticity and sentiment in a way unknown in the Colonial period. It further sharpened the perceived differences between the sexes, and it associated feeling and sensibility with women and intellect and assertion with men (Zaretsky, 1976:52). On the other hand, the sentiment and feeling associated with women was also associated with morality, and there were advantages for women in this new image. Even though nineteenth century middle-class men were clearly the heads of their households, they were, nevertheless, exhorted by popular moralists to model themselves on the virtues of their wives, who were "purer" beings. The purity and morality assigned to nineteenth-century women became a vital opening wedge for increasing women's political and educational rights. After all, since the home was seen as the moral bedrock of society, society would be helped by helping the home, which was represented by women. Thus, women's benevolent and temperance activities became, in part, a seedbed for feminist activities.

The first concern of nineteenth-century feminists was to reform the property laws and upgrade women's power inside the family. This goal was met with the Married Woman's Property Acts of the second quarter of the nineteenth century, which established a wife's right to act in economic and family matters with the same powers as a husband. Next, feminists sought to gain the vote in local elections by arguing that family morality and interests should be represented in the community. This approach was also used in 1920 when women secured the right to vote in national elections and thereby, at least formally, became the political equals of men. The rhetoric women used to get the national vote was that women's concerns with home and morality would clean up dirty politics. At about the same time that women got the vote, education for women in general began to be justified on the basis of their family role. Thus, women's loss of their productive roles by the separation of family and economy in the nineteenth century may have actually helped them attain greater legal equality.

The view of the family as a haven of sentiment and morality was far more characteristic of middle-class families in the nineteenth century than of working-class families. These families, for whom economic survival was relatively precarious, could ill afford the luxury of sentiment. In the first half of the century, families often retained their rural base while supplementing their incomes with the earnings of daughters who went to work in the textile industry. In other cases, whole families operated as a work unit in the manufacture of some item. Even when different family members worked in different places at different jobs, work continued to be a family enterprise in that each member's work was considered to be for the family and was regulated by an overall family survival strategy (Hareven, 1976a:101–3). On the other hand, most of the working-class women who worked outside of the home were not married. In the nineteenth century, 95 percent of women who were married did not work outside of the home (Hareven, 1976a:106).

In the middle class, the nineteenth-century idea of the housewife creating perfect bliss within the home on the basis of intuition later became transformed into a more "scientific" attitude toward home management. The Domestic Science Movement was formally begun by middle-class women at the turn of the century with the Lake Placid Conference on Home Economics. This movement, in essence, sought to professionalize the role of the housewife. As a result of this effort, scientific principles of health, sanitation, and nutrition along with efficient, economical management practices were taught in colleges, universities, and public schools. Even though the larger effect of the home economics movement was to keep women fully occupied within the home, the movement was supported by many feminists who used it as a way of justifying higher education for women. The domestic science movement itself gradually became less and less essential as the practices it espoused came to be taken for granted by more and more families. The movement encouraged families to live in single-family dwellings as an essential condition for successful homemaking, and the number of families owning their own homes burgeoned. Increasingly, the mass media and advertising have taken over the housewife's "education" in domestic science.

By the 1930s, sex and sexuality became increasingly acceptable for married women. For example, while people at the turn of the century thought that a woman who wore make-up was promiscuous and beyond the pale of respectable society, ordinary housewives adopted it after make-up was used by the semirespectable flappers of the 1920s. In general, as the Victorian dichotomy between good (asexual) and bad (sexual) women blurred, sexuality and sex appeal became something the middle-class woman could strive for. Women were (and still are) encouraged by advertising not only to have the cleanest floor in town, but also to look glamorous (for their man). Thus, being beautiful and buying products to make them beautiful became a part of women's job and one that women were encouraged to work at in order to maintain their husband's interest. Also, a good-looking wife became a new way for men to symbolize their own status; a glamorous wife was as much a status symbol as a shiny car. From a feminist standpoint, however, the glamour pattern increased sex role differentiation even further since men were not encouraged to be attractive, only occupationally successful. Moreover, it defined women largely in terms of their specifically sexual qualities as opposed to their more general humanistic qualities (Parsons, 1954a).

An alternative pattern at this time was for the middle-class housewife to play the role of good companion to her husband by emphasizing this common humanistic element in their relationship (Parsons, 1954). Actually, the humanistic element was usually not shared, since middle-class men tended to be totally immersed in their occupations. Essentially, this role is an updated version of the cultural interests, moral activity, and charity work that were seen as part of a good wife's duties in the nineteenth century. But as services became increasingly professionalized, the work of volunteers, no matter how useful, tended to be downgraded. The "club woman" was the butt of many cruel jokes in the 1940s.

During World War II, as many men went off to war and as the economy boomed with the opening of shipyards, aircraft plants, and munitions factories, many women, even those with small children, entered the labor force. Although sex segregation persisted in the jobs in these plants, women took over many jobs that were previously held by men or were newly created. They were paid better wages than women had ever received, and employers needed their services so much that many were willing to provide child-care facilities. In this crisis, women served as a reserve labor force that could be brought in when needed by the economy.

After the war, however, the men returned and took over the high-paying jobs. Although the proportion of married women working outside the home continued to climb, images in popular periodicals showed an almost compulsive return to images of domesticity after the war. Many couples had children that they could not have had during the war, and large families became fashionable for the middle class. While the idea of sex appeal and motherhood were at opposite poles during the flapper era of the 1920s, by the 1950s more and more people were getting married and at younger and younger ages. In the 1950s couples were buying single-family dwellings and having more children. The divorce rate was rising, but so was the rate of remarriage.

Betty Friedan, in her now classic *Feminine Mystique* (1963), criticized the situation of middle-class married women in the 1950s from a feminist standpoint. The book came at a time when feminism (as opposed to the feminine mystique) had never been less popular. As Friedan says, words like career and emancipation were embarrassing in the 1950s. Nevertheless, she found that the women she interviewed and talked with informally all shared "a problem that had no name." They spoke of feeling "incomplete . . . as if I don't exist," of meaninglessness. Many went to psychiatrists to see what was wrong and were told that what they needed was to enjoy being feminine. Advice columns told women who complained of accomplishing nothing that their successful husbands and children were their accomplishment. It seemed that all the weight of the culture argued that women should rejoice in their femininity. Essentially, being feminine in the 1950s implied getting all one's life satisfaction from being a wife and mother, of not wanting to do the things males did, of not wanting to be strong, independent, or personally accomplished, of being grateful for the luxury of not having to work outside the home.

The feminine mystique had influenced the entire class spectrum. More and more working class and immigrant families began to believe that the husband/father's duty was primarily to provide for his family and the wife/mother's duty was to make a home for him and their children. The definition of masculinity itself was closely tied to the provider role. While it was taken for granted in western Europe that working-class wives would work in the factories, in the United States working-class married women were expected to remain at home up until the 1930s. As immigrants became Americanized, they adopted the ideology that a woman's working compromised her husband's status and was not good for the children (Hareven, 1976a:106). While middle-class men's work was overly demanding, working-class men's work was likely to be deadening. In both cases, however, men saw home as offering the psychological solution to the problems generated in the work world. By the 1970s, working-class wives whose families had followed the middle-class move to the suburbs also began to be faced with the problem that had no name (Rubin, 1976:115):

> I don't know what's the matter with me that I don't appreciate what I've got. I feel guilty all the time, and I worry about it a lot. Other women, they seem to be happy with being married and having a house and kids. What's the matter with me?

The main exception to the ideology that married women should not work outside the home was black wives in the South, who worked in the homes of whites as domestic servants. Perhaps out of necessity black wives have tended to see outside work as part of their family role. Black families were often too poor for mothers not to work, and earning money for the children became part of the mother role.

One of the reasons that Friedan's book could strike a responsive chord in middle-class women was that it articulated the contradiction between their level of education and the actual life the feminine mystique required them to lead. Even though middle-class girls were very oriented to getting married, they were also being trained to do other things. Women were told to look on their education as a contingency plan to be put to use if something went wrong; nevertheless they were being educated. In college, they learned to value personal achievement; yet they were only allowed vicarious achievement through their husbands and children. For many women, vicarious achievement proved not to be enough.

Women and Men in the Contemporary Family

By the early 1970s, inspired largely by the new wave of feminism that had emerged in the 1960s, social scientists were asking different kinds of questions about the family and taking a more critical view of it. Most especially, they began to examine the family from the standpoint of its effect on women.

Although family ideology declares that marriage is supposed to be every woman's dream, considerable evidence indicates that marriage actually benefits men more than women. Some of the most clear-cut evidence for this contention comes from studies that compare the rates of mental disorder among married men and women. No matter how mental illness is defined or what stage of treatment is investigated, married women have higher rates of mental disorder than married men. By contrast, most studies of people who have never married find that single men have higher rates of mental troubles than single women. Men who are divorced, widowed, or never married have higher rates of mental illness than their female counterparts. While married people of both sexes have less mental illness than single people, the difference between the mental health of single and married people is much greater for men than it is for women (Gove, 1976). It appears that marriage does considerably more for men's mental health than it does for women's.

The findings concerning mental health differences between married men and women also apply to differences in physical health. In a more recent study, Gove and Hughes (1979) showed that married women's "nurturant" role was associated with their greater susceptibility to minor physical illnesses. The researchers found that because women take care of others, they are often not able to take care of themselves.

Some of the reasons for married women's poorer mental and physical health may be found in the characteristics of the modern family. First, because the family is geared to the world of work rather than the world of work being geared to the family, the wife must make the major adjustments. Her job is defined as giving her husband physical, psychological, and sometimes, in the middle class, social support in the pursuit of his occupation. Even when the wife works, she usually earns considerably less than her husband. Thus, his job is seen as more important and the husband tends to get the support.

Second, the modern family is relatively isolated from other families both physically and socially. People in the United States put great stress on each family having a home of its own and each wife keeping up that home—alone. Furthermore, our family norms decree that a wife's primary loyalty should be to her husband and children, and not to her relatives or to her friends. So, even though most women do not see their husbands at all during the day, they do not see other women or men either. Feelings of loneliness and isolation and the associated psychiatric symptoms appear to be most extreme among unemployed women with children under four years of age (Gove and Geerken, 1977).

There is another side of the coin, however: Work outside the family is not necessarily healthful for men. Men in our society are continuously under stress in the workplace from the pressure of decisions or from boring routine work. Thus, men use the family somewhat as they did in the nineteenth century, to recover from work. But women do not have "wives" to help relieve them of the strains of either housework or outside work. It is not clear from current research whether working wives are all that much happier with marriage than are nonworking wives (Wright, 1978.) As we shall see later, a wife's working does not necessarily bring the husband to her emotional aid.

The housewife role Whether women work outside the family or not, most married women consider themselves housewives. A study in London found that while neither middle-class nor working-class housewives particularly enjoy housework, working-class women identify psychologically with the housewife role more often than middle-class women do. For working-class women, being a housewife, even if they don't like housework, is tied to their sense of feminine identity (Oakley, 1975). They see being a housewife as both the privilege and the duty of being a woman. One reason working-class women are less resistant to the housewife role may be that the prestige of housewife is higher than that of the majority of the paid labor-force roles available to working-class women (Bose, 1976).

Some Marxist feminists have focused attention on the housework that women do precisely as work—socially necessary work that is not paid for by capitalists but by their wage-earning husbands as a hidden cost. A number of different analyses deal with how women's housework contributes to a capitalist economy and to women's secondary status. Some authors suggest that regardless of whether women work outside the home their household labor, including child care, constitutes a huge amount of socially necessary production that is not usually considered real work under capitalism. The reason is that housework does not involve producing goods or services to sell, and therefore it has only use value rather than exchange value (Benston, 1977). Others suggest that housewives do indeed produce commodities for exchange, but not in the usual sense of the term. In rearing children and in caring for their husbands, women under capitalism reproduce workers who sell their labor in the market. This is essential for capitalism, yet women are paid nothing for this work (Dalla Costa, 1973). Others note that one consequence of women's unpaid work in the home is that it makes them financially dependent on men and hence powerless and isolated in work that is not socially recognized (Secombe, 1974).

Other Marxist authors see housewives as engaged not so much in the work of production as in work related to consumption. The housewife serves as the connection between the private household and the highly rationalized, bureaucratized system of production. She not only buys food, clothes, and all the supplies for her family, but she also deals with (and adjusts her schedule to) the purveyors of services for the family such as the doctor, the dentist, the installer, and the repairer (Weinbaum and Bridges, 1976).

In spite of the technical differences in their analyses, all the foregoing writers would agree that capitalists profit from women being housewives and that the housewife role lies at the heart of women's secondary status. Most analysts do not advocate paying women for housework because this would only serve to lock them further into a role that has many other more basic disadvantages. They would agree that whether or not women work outside the home, their housewife role must be changed if their status is to improve significantly. They do not foresee this possibility under capitalism and not even under socialism unless specific attention is given to restructuring housework.

Non-Marxist feminists stress that the centrality of women's housewife role affects their access to more valued work roles. They argue that one important reason women are discriminated against in the occupational world is that employers assume that women cannot work as efficiently as men because their central commitment is to the home (Epstein, 1974; Acker, 1978). It is assumed, and in fact expected, that women neglect their job for the home—yet, with men it is assumed that they neglect their home for the job. Thus, regardless of the actual content of the work they do in their jobs, women's jobs are defined as replaceable (Coser and Rokoff, 1974). This rationalization, in turn, is used to justify giving them less prestige and pay. In sum, then, the family commitments that are normatively expected of women are used to justify downgrading women's jobs in the labor force and to justify not hiring women at all in some jobs and in not advancing them in others.

Although most feminist theorists would agree that women cannot obtain equality so long as the domestic sphere remains exclusively female, most of the actual changes in women's roles in the United States have not been related to the domestic sphere but to working outside the home.

Women's work outside the home and family roles The increase in women working has been especially great since 1940. In that year, 30 percent of American women aged eighteen to sixty-four were in the labor force; by the 1970s, the figure had passed the 50 percent mark. There has been a steady growth in the labor force participation of women in the thirty-five to forty-four year age group, and more and more young women are working, especially those who are single, divorced, widowed, or separated. While married mothers with preschool-age children are still the group least likely to be in the labor force, the fastest growing category of women workers is married women with children under five. Yet even though many women work now, the belief that women's primary role is in the home appears to remain strong. Some authors suggest that women's employment outside the home can alter sex stratification in the family by affecting women's decision-making authority as well as the division of labor in the home.

Power is a complex concept that is difficult to define and to measure. Most often, marital power has been studied in terms of decision-making. A trail-breaking study of marital power in the 1950s asked wives "who usually" made the final decision concerning eight family matters ranging from what job the husband should take to what doctor to call when someone was sick. In general, the researchers found that the husbands' scores were somewhat, but not markedly, higher (Blood and Wolfe, 1960). A similar study obtained almost identical results even when husbands were respondents instead of wives (Centers et al., 1971). Most important, the decisions that husbands tend to make, such as what job to take and what car to buy, have more long-range importance than the decisions women make, such as what doctor to call and the weekly food budget (Gillespie, 1972). Husbands with higher occupational prestige and incomes generally have greater voice in marital decisions.

Women who work appear to have more power in their families than nonworking wives, and nonworking wives with young children have the least power (Bahr, 1974a). Employed wives have greater power than nonemployed wives and are especially likely to make more decisions concerning financial matters and large expenditures than unemployed wives. The wife's employment also slightly increases her degree of control over decisions about whether to have children (Bahr, 1974b; Weller, 1968; Safilios-Rothschild, 1967, 1969). Those few studies that have found unemployed wives making more decisions in the family generally focus on relatively minor matters (e. g., Middleton and Putney, 1960).

Working-class wives may gain more power through employment than middle-class wives (Bahr, 1974a). In fact, employment may actually decrease the power of wives whose husbands have high white-collar jobs, while the power of wives with blue-collar husbands appears to increase in all areas when they become employed. Perhaps the power of wives of high white-collar workers does not increase because the income they add to the family budget is relatively unimportant. Also, the added income may not make up for the loss of the psychological and social support they can give to their husbands' careers when they are not working. Wives with no preschool children or with small families also appear to gain more power through employment than wives with large families, probably because if few or no young children are involved, the wives' work is seen as providing more resources without withdrawing needed child-care services.

When women work outside the home, it could be expected that the work previously assigned to them within the home would be reassigned to other family members, especially to the husband. Yet generally household tasks are still sex segregated. Time-use data on the actual number of hours spent in various tasks indicate that while employed wives spend less time working in the home, there is no compensating increase in the amount of time husbands spend working in the home. In fact, a number of these studies find that the husbands of employed wives spend about the same amount of time at family tasks as do the husbands of unemployed wives! (Pleck, 1977:420). Time-use studies, however, are based on cross-sectional rather than longitudinal data and cannot reflect any changes in husbands' participation at different stages of the life cycle (Pleck, 1977:420). The husbands of working wives may participate more when there are young children and less when the children are older than do the husbands of unemployed wives. Family size may also affect this participation, and husbands of working wives with large families may also help more in household tasks—including child care—than the husbands of nonworking women with large families (Hoffman, 1978).

There are many problems yet to be resolved in estimating how the wife's employment affects the division of labor within the family. It is clear that employed wives continue to take the main responsibility for housework and child care and that employment considerably increases the total hours the woman works. Even though the husband of a working wife may participate more in family work under some circumstances, his increase falls short of the wife's own increased participation in the world of work. Fully employed men do only a small part of the family work that fully employed women do (Pleck, 1977:420).

Female-headed families The major reason for the existence of female-headed families is divorce. Ross and Sawhill suggest that the increase in divorce is related both to a disparity in ideology about the proper roles for men and women and to women's increased social and economic power. They take the view that the rising divorce rate indicates that women now have more social and economic alternatives to marriage and therefore are less constrained to preserve their marriages at all costs. These alternatives relate not only to the fact that women's working directly increases their ability to survive alone, but also to the fact that women's working and divorce itself are more socially acceptable now. Ross and Sawhill predict that divorce rates may rise quite rapidly as women's economic opportunities expand, but they "expect some eventual restabilization accompanied by a redefinition of rights and responsibilities within marriage" (1975:63).

Ross and Sawhill's interpretation of the great increase in female-headed families may be overly optimistic. While it is undoubtedly true that the rising divorce rate is related to an increase in women's economic power, the fact that female-headed families have less than half the income of male-headed households (U.S. Department of Commerce, 1976:52) suggests that this power is not great. As long as women are paid less than men and continue to bear the major responsibility for children, women will be constrained to seek and maintain marriages, even though, as we have seen, marriage is not particularly "good for women."

The Symmetrical Family

Some writers predict that men will gradually decrease their commitment to work and increase their participation in the home. This will result in a "symmetrical" family (Young and Willmott, 1975). In this type of family, both husband and wife work outside the home and both share responsibility for work within the home more or less equally. Young and Willmott (1973:278) predict:

> By the next century—with the pioneers of 1970 already at the front of the column—society will have moved from (a) one demanding job for the wife and one for the husband, through (b) two demanding jobs for the wife and one for the husband, to (c) two demanding jobs for the wife and two for the husband. The symmetry will be complete. Instead of two jobs, there will be four.

Currently, we are very much at the stage where there are two demanding jobs for the wife and one for the husband. Also, as things stand now, expanding the male's family role without changing the male work role would produce strains for men similar to the strains now faced by working women (Pleck, 1977:424). Certainly, upper-middle-class men who see their jobs as careers are likely to claim that any greater commitment to the home would jeopardize their occupational advancement. In fact, they see part of their wife's job as helping them in their career advancement.

Clearly, without some major changes in our competitive economy to allow for flexible schedules, longer leaves, no penalties for part-time work, and adequate family income with less than two full-time jobs, it is difficult to see how men can participate more in the home.

Even if men had jobs that would allow them to take greater responsibility in the home, it is unlikely that men would do so spontaneously because of the norms of male dominance. If women's place is culturally seen as in the home and the role of housewife is seen as feminine, then men may consider it degrading to enter the feminine sphere. Men's work role is really not the primary determinant of the limited family role men play (Pleck, 1977:421). Instead, it is the traditional division of family labor by sex in which housework and child care are seen as women's work. Because of this, family symmetry is probably not just around the corner.

It is important also to understand that symmetry is not equivalent to equality. Young and Willmott themselves are explicit in saying that they do not mean "egalitarian" by "symmetrical." They say that to call the family egalitarian "would not square with the marked differences that still remain in the human rights, in the work opportunities and generally in the way of life of the two sexes" (1975:31). In spite of this demurrer most people talking about symmetrical families imply that they would eliminate sex inequality. One important deterrent to achieving husband-wife equality lies in the pay differentials between men's jobs and women's jobs, since full-time working women generally earn less than two-thirds what full-time men workers earn (see chapter 2).

Finally, two British sociologists, Colin Bell and Howard Newby (1976), argue that even as we move toward increasing symmetry with the wife and husband both working outside the home, wives will continue to symbolically express deference to their husbands. They refer to a process called swinging the norms, which means that even when traditional tasks are reversed, for example when the husband cooks, he receives deference for it that the wife does not. Many women have found themselves praising their husbands when they prepared a meal, did the dishes, or made a bed even though the women had equally demanding occupational roles. This deference to the husband reflects the norms of male dominance that may prevail even when roles are reversed.

Sexuality

Over the years, ideas about sexuality, especially women's sexuality, have changed considerably. Researchers have found that women's sexuality is far more like men's, at least in terms of physiological response, than was previously thought. The Kinsey report on women, based on interviews with almost 6,000 white nonprison women from a wide range of classes, was published in 1953. Kinsey and his associates noted the importance of the clitoris to women's orgasm (1953:158), and clearly stated that a vaginal orgasm was a "biologic impossibility" (p. 584). The Kinsey group also reported that some 14 percent of their female subjects had multiple orgasms (p. 375) and that women could climax quickly when they masturbated.

The work of Masters and Johnson, which involved the direct observation and physiological measurement of women's sexual responses in masturbation and intercourse, was published in 1966. Their findings regarding women's sexual capacities confirmed those of Kinsey and were given wide publicity. They indicate that women who achieve orgasm in intercourse do not do so through passivity and compliance, but by feeling free to seek their own pleasure. Feminists have used these findings concerning women's capacity for multiple orgasms and the greater effectiveness of masturbation over intercourse in producing orgasm to point out the extent to which male-dominated intercourse has worked against women's gratification (e.g., Koedt, 1973).

While Masters and Johnson's findings are potentially liberating, more often than not they have been interpreted in ways that do not seriously challenge male dominance. Even though women are being encouraged to take greater sexual initiative, popular books of sexual advice still consider men to be the controller in sexual activities. Most books give men the idea that they might feel power as they "play upon" the woman and cause her to respond. This is illustrated by the comment made by a male respondent to a survey, concerning his experience with an exceptionally responsive female (Hunt, 1974:162, italics ours):

> It was her enjoyment that got to me. Wow! Tremendous! It did more for me than my own pleasure ever did. I began to enjoy the playing with her even more than the intercourse, because I could see *what I had the power to make happen.* I could see that I was becoming a good lover.

Similarly, a study of advice concerning sexual dysfunction in sex and marriage manuals finds that women are often seen as being both the cause and the cure for their own and the males' most common sexual problems. A woman's sexual dysfunctions are seen as caused by her own parental background and her own religious or moral inhibitions, while men's dysfunctions are more frequently blamed on the partner's failure to be supportive (Peterson and Peterson, 1973).

Some have argued that sexual liberation, by increasing women's expectations, has put men under undue pressures to perform. In Victorian times a man need only avoid offending his wife's delicate sensibilities, but now that women have been declared deserving of pleasure, the male may see himself burdened with greater responsibilities. Popular magazines, in fact, have discussed the "new male impotence" and blamed it partly on the women's movement. Some men have argued that they want women to take the sexual initiative and to themselves be sexual, but women have not been wholly convinced of this and feel that in the last analysis, men choose more conventional ("unliberated") women for long-term relationships (Bengis, 1973). Lillian Rubin (1977) notes in her discussion of sexual relations in working-class marriages that the husbands are encouraging their wives to be more sexual. Yet the wives are still slightly afraid that in spite of their husbands' assurances to the contrary, if they show themselves to be too sexual, their husbands would actually disapprove.

Two widely publicized practices, open marriage and swinging, also illustrate that male dominance has not been overcome as a result of the sexual revolution. Although these "alternatives" claim to help liberate women sexually, neither has met this aim, essentially because they have been implemented within the context of a male-dominated society. In *open marriage,* espoused by Gena and George O'Neill (1972), both spouses agree that each may form relationships (which may or may not be sexual) outside the marriage. Yet, actually, men are in a much better position to establish relationships outside marriage than are most women, especially if the couple has children or the wife does not work. Furthermore, a woman who seeks outside relationships is likely to be defined as aggressive or as unhappily married, whereas a man who seeks such relationships is seen as merely normal.

Swinging is a form of deliberate mate-swapping in which the exchange is explicitly and exclusively for the purpose of sexual variety and in which a close personal relationship with the outside partner is strictly prohibited. Interviews with swingers reveal that the husband usually first suggests participating, and wives often feel compelled to go along with the idea to preserve the marriage. Interestingly enough, the husband may call a halt to swinging if his wife becomes too enthusiastic and appears to be enjoying other men too much. In general, however, more wives than husbands call a halt to swinging, not out of jealousy but out of distaste for the impersonality of the sexual contacts (Denfield, 1974).

Another alternative to sexual exclusivity has been the idea of expanding the boundaries of marriage itself into *communal forms.* While group marriage is very rare, a number of commune dwellers, especially in urban settings, have defined sexual exclusivity as oppressive. Joel Whitebook (1974), in a description of an urban commune, notes, however, that males tend to be the leaders in this talk, and he suggests that sexual liberation becomes yet another arena for macho competition. Whitebook describes how the men in the commune, while professing to be smashing monogamy because it was oppressive to women, managed to oppress women even more by their compulsive hustling.

Much of the advice to women that comes out of the sexual revolution, then, has encouraged women to be sexual, but in a context in which male dominance is essentially unchallenged. Yet there is considerable evidence that sexuality and dominance feelings go together in women as well as men. Kinsey's findings (1953) of greater frequency of orgasm among highly educated women support Maslow's (1942) earlier argument that self-esteem, dominance feelings, and sexuality positively correlate in women.

In saying that dominant women with high self-esteem tend to be sexual, we do not mean to imply that women wish to dominate in the sexual situation. Rather, what women probably want is truly egalitarian sex—mutual pleasuring that would emancipate men from the demands of dominance and women from the demands of compliance (Morgan, 1977). Now, however, ideas about sexuality imply that the male should be in control and the female should help give him the feeling that he is.

Communal Experiments

Those who have been interested in combatting the isolation of the family and the alienating aspects of outside work have sometimes thought in terms of communal living. They focus on personal growth through expanding the quantity and quality of personal relationships with both sexes. While both rural and urban communes share in these goals, rural communes made some attempt to combine work life and home life through farming activities. Most urban commune dwellers continue to have jobs outside "the family."

In rural communes, roles are likely to be divided along traditional lines with women doing the cooking and child care and men doing the heavy work. Children are considered to belong to their mothers, and norms requiring paternal solicitude for children are largely absent. As Bennett Berger and his associates, who have studied a number of rural communes, state, "What this means is that fathers are 'free'—at the very least free to split whenever they are so moved" (Berger et al., 1974:457). This does not mean the woman is entirely bereft, for she often has welfare payments and the support of other communards. But it does mean that child care is optional for the father and required for the mother. Berger and his associates report that women with children tend to hang together and help each other out. While it is true that unmarried women with children are not penalized and, indeed, have a certain status in communes, in part because of the welfare checks they bring in, the sex-segregated division of labor and traditional sex-typed behaviors have usually remained unchallenged.

While most urban communes maintain a separation between work life and home life, they have often been explicitly concerned with achieving sexual equality in domestic arrangements. One study of twenty-one urban communes found that men and women in these households share cooking, dishes, housecleaning, grocery shopping, and other tasks generally unrelated to child care. This was most effectively accomplished by breaking tasks down into small units and rotating them. While this task sharing fosters role crossovers in both sexes, the general behavioral norms stressed for both sexes in the households were feminine, since the primary activities of the communal household tend to be nurturant and expressive. Furthermore, power in these communes tends to be based on personal qualities and not, as in nuclear families, on the size of the financial resources brought in. All these factors tend to make the sexes equal at least in this context, but the issue of child care has not been specifically addressed (Kanter and Halter, 1976).

Urban communes are currently few in number and are subject to high turnover and dissolution (Kanter and Halter, 1976:215). While their numbers may increase, they hardly appear to be the wave of the future. More likely, they will continue to meet the needs of some people, particularly at certain stages of the life cycle such as transition—before marriage, after divorce, or for the widowed (Giele, 1975). As Kanter and Halter suggest, even if communes do not become "permanent institutions for a large part of the life cycle," they may still be important training grounds for breaking up old ideas about the proper sexual division of labor.

Men, Women, and Child Care

Much of the literature on both the symmetrical family and on the communal family has focused on male-female relations rather than on parent-child relations. This focus may reflect the fact that we have been assessing changes in the family and creating changes in the family in terms of a masculine paradigm. Alice Rossi (1977) contends that we have been designing women's lives, including their motherhood, to meet the needs of men and the economy, which men dominate, rather than to meet the needs of mothers and children. This occurs partly because the family is geared to the economy rather than vice versa.

Rossi contends that efforts to produce male-female equality will not succeed in the long run unless we consider that men and women view children differently. She argues that while children are of central importance to women, men tend to view them as consequences of or appendages to mating and tend to "turn their fathering on and off to suit themselves or their appointments for business or sexual pleasure" (1977:16). Rossi believes that the masculine way of viewing motherhood has led to practices that add stress to the lives of young mothers and impoverish the quality of their relationship with their children (1977:21). She criticizes traditional obstetrical practices, which give control to the physician rather than the mother, and endanger bonding between mother and child. She also suggests that our practice of spacing children close together may be unnatural and puts undue strain on mothers and siblings. Rossi sees us as moving ideally toward a greater emphasis on the relations between parents and children, which she feels have been neglected by women in their push for equality.

The United States is far behind most modern industrialized countries in providing child care facilities outside of the home. Much of the opposition to public support of day care has centered around the notion that such practices would destroy the family and remove children emotionally and even physically from their parents (see Keyserling, 1976). These charges seem ironic in view of the desperate need of many families for adequate care. Such care would seem only to strengthen the health and security of children as well as relieving worries of parents. The parents, then, could give their children better attention, and the children as recipients of quality and consistent care would be better parents when they have their own families.

Even when a mother does not work outside the home, child care benefits both the mental health of the mother and the health and education of the child. To be a loving and caring mother, one must also be a fulfilled adult. A mother cannot devote all of her waking hours to the care of a small child, especially when she herself is isolated from other adults, and hope to maintain a separate adult identity. Thus, some time in which others take over the child's care is essential for both the well-being of the mother and the assurance of good care for the child. Middle-class mothers have long recognized this necessity and have been able to afford the luxury of baby sitters and private nursery schools. Public nursery schools, however, except for the very poor, are almost unknown in this country.

Care outside the home is important for children. Specialists in early childhood development stress that group experiences are very desirable for children at the age of three and over. This applies not just to only children or to those with special problems or a working mother, but appears to be a developmental need of all children to expand their realm of significant others beyond the immediate family at that age. Experiments with quality group care for infants also show that with a good staff/child ratio, this experience can also be beneficial to children (Caldwell, 1973).

Summary

During the nineteenth century, the family as we know it today began to emerge. Households became smaller as nonfamily members were gradually excluded, and the family itself came to be viewed as the seat of personal life, "a haven in a heartless world" (Lasch, 1978) sharply different from the world of paid work outside. Women were defined as the moral core of the family, and on this basis feminists fought first for property rights and later for legal and educational rights. In the nineteenth century, very few married women worked outside the home, but the number of married women working has increased steadily in the twentieth century, especially since midcentury.

Although women's outside employment, at least in the working class, has somewhat increased their power in the family, women have not really achieved equality with their husbands. Married women are still defined primarily as housewives even when they work outside the home, and they are likely to be receiving less pay than their husbands even when they are doing more prestigious work. Furthermore, husbands generally do not share housework, perhaps because it is seen as women's work, and husbands continue to see themselves as dominant because of their higher incomes. Even in households where tasks are shared or reversed, males often continue to dominate on the basis of the symbolic advantages that accrue to masculinity itself. So far, then, instead of the symmetrical family, we find that women who work combine two demanding jobs while men have not increased their household work to any great extent. Also, while the patterning of men's and women's sexuality has changed considerably in recent times, women's greater sexual participation continues to be defined in such a way as not to threaten male dominance.

Communal alternatives to living in isolated nuclear families, so far at least, have not equalized the sexes, and problems have been particularly acute with regard to child care. As things stand now, with more and more women entering the workforce, the problem of child care looms large. So far, attempts to increase women's equality have largely taken the form of increasing women's workforce participation without compensating provisions for child care by fathers or day care centers. In other words, there has been more assimilation of women's roles to men's in the economy than assimilation of men's roles to women's roles in the family. If sex stratification is to end, family roles must also change.

THE EDUCATIONAL SYSTEM Women and men have generally been treated more equally in education than in other areas of the society. In general, individuals' educational attainment and achievement are more influenced by class status than by sex. Men and women usually have equal scores on intelligence and standardized achievement tests; indeed, women have higher grades than men at all levels from grade school through college. For many years, women have been more likely than men to finish high school. Yet when families must make decisions concerning who receives post-high school education, men are favored. Women attain less education than would be expected given their qualifications and may face discrimination in secondary and higher education.

Influences on Educational Attainment

Women graduate from high school more often than men largely because working-class men can get jobs without a high school certificate and women often need such certification for clerical work. In recent years, the importance of formal education has been increasingly stressed and educational requirements for employment have risen. As a result, more people graduate from high school and the proportions of men and women finishing high school have become more nearly the same.

A much larger percentage of both males and females in the total population are also going to college now, as job requirements change and community colleges burgeon. Universities have continually grown in size as shown by the number of faculty members, number of students enrolled, and the number of degrees awarded. Yet the proportion of women teaching, enrolled, or receiving degrees has fluctuated over the years, rising gradually to a peak in the 1920s and 1930s, dropping during the Depression and especially the post–World War II years, and rising again to the levels of fifty years ago in the late 1960s and 1970s.

These trends reflect cultural and class-specific definitions of the importance of a college education as well as specific economic conditions and educational policies. For instance, they show how the sexes are generally given the same education, unless specific economic or political circumstances require that some people be denied access to schools. The economic problems of the Depression caused a sharp decline in the rate of growth of total college enrollment. Although the number of both men and women enrolled in college continued to rise during the Depression, the number of women enrolled rose much more slowly than the number of men. This trend probably resulted from the decisions of families to invest more heavily in the college education of their sons than of their daughters. The even greater difference between the percentage increase of enrollment of males and females at the end of World War II probably reflects specific national educational policies as colleges set quotas limiting the admission of women in order to absorb men returning to school on the G. I. bill (Campbell, 1973). As a result of these quotas, the proportion of students enrolled in 1949–50 who were women was 30 percent, lower than the rate of enrollment in 1879–80! The vast enrollment growth after World War II altered the social class distribution of college students, as men of lower-middle-class and working-class backgrounds were able to attain education beyond high school. The rising representation of women in higher education in those years parallels the changes in the late 1800s and early 1900s as it became accepted by not just the upper-middle-class but also by a greater proportion of the population that both men and women should have a college education. While men were first sent to college, when families could afford to do so, daughters were also sent.

Table 3–1 gives the expected educational attainment of young people who were seventeen years old in the fall of 1973. It is clear from the table that almost as many women as men are expected to get bachelor's and master's degrees today. Sex stratification is most apparent with doctoral and other professional degrees. About 19 percent of the Ph.D.'s awarded in 1973–74 were to women, only slightly above the 1929–30 level. This percentage rose to 24 percent in 1975–76. Enrollment in degree programs at the graduate level is also segregated by sex. For instance, in 1975–76, women received 36 percent of the Ph.D.'s in the humanities, 33 percent of the Ph.D.'s in education, and 22 percent of the Ph.D.'s in social sciences. But only 11 percent of the mathematics Ph.D.'s, 9 percent of those in the physical sciences, and 2 percent of the Ph.D's in engineering were awarded to women. An increasing number of women are receiving graduate professional degrees, but they are far from achieving parity. For instance, while less than 1 percent of all dentistry degrees were awarded to women in 1950, 4 percent of the degrees were awarded to women in 1975–76. Ten percent of the medical degrees were awarded to women in 1950. This fell to 6 percent in 1960, but rose to 16 percent by 1975–76. Similarly, the percentage of law graduates who are women rose sharply from 5 percent in 1970 to 19 percent in 1975–76 (Grant and Lind, 1978).

To some extent, the pattern of sex differences in educational attainment varies among racial groups in this country. On the average, differences in educational attainment for white men and women balance out. The median years of education that both white women and men eventually attain in this country is 12.1 years. Among blacks, however, women

TABLE 3–1 LEVEL OF EDUCATION EXPECTED FOR BOYS AND GIRLS 17 YEARS OF AGE IN THE FALL OF 1973 BY PERCENTAGE OF TOTAL MALE AND TOTAL FEMALE POPULATIONS

	BOYS	GIRLS
Completing high school in 1974	73	77
Enrolled as first-time college students in fall 1974	47	44
Expected to receive bachelor's degree in 1978	25	24
Expected to receive master's degree in 1979	8	7
Expected to receive Ph.D. in 1982	2	0.5

Source: W. V. Grant and C. G. Lind, *1976 Digest of Education Statistics*, National Center for Education Statistics, United States Department of Health, Education, and Welfare, 1977.

have a median level of 10.0 years while men reach a median of only 9.4 years. This probably occurs because of race discrimination in the economy where black women are better rewarded—in terms of eventual income—for attaining more education than are black men (Suter and Miller, 1973). Thus, decisions of black men to go to work rather than further their education may be economically rational (Michelson, 1972). With Hispanic people, men have an average attainment of 9.9 years, women 9.4 years (Grant and Lind, 1977:15), perhaps reflecting the more traditional sex role patterns in Spanish-speaking ethnic groups. This pattern continues in institutions of higher education. In the total population, as well as in the subgroups of native American, Asian-American, and Spanish-surnamed peoples, more men than women are enrolled in all levels of college work including undergraduate, professional and graduate schools. Among blacks, however, more women than men are enrolled at all levels except the first year of undergraduate school and in professional schools and Ph.D. (not master's) programs (Grant and Lind, 1977:95, data from fall 1974). This reflects the sex-segregated employment patterns among black professionals (see discussion in chapter 2) with black men dominating the traditionally male professions of law and medicine and women entering social work and teaching, fields that require master's but not doctoral degrees.

A number of social scientists have examined influences on eventual educational attainment. While most of these studies have involved only men, in recent years a few have also looked at the educational attainment of women (see Sewell and Shah, 1967; Alexander and Eckland, 1974; and Treiman and Terrell, 1975). They find that women's educational attainment is highly influenced by family background status while for males academic ability is a stronger influence. Moreover, after controlling for variables generally found to relate to educational attainment, including academic ability, status background, performance, educational goal orientations, academic self-concept, curriculum enrollment, and the influences of significant others such as parents, teachers, and peers, females have lower expected educational attainment than males do.

Sex Discrimination in Access to Education

Sex segregation occurs in both academic and vocational curriculum areas. Males and females train in vocational education programs for very different jobs. Women are usually in the clerical or home economics areas, while men are more evenly distributed throughout the various possible fields and are most highly concentrated in trades and industry. Very few of the students in agriculture and technical education are women. Notably enough, the areas with more men have much higher wages than the areas for which women are trained. Moreover, women overwhelmingly teach the courses in home economics, health, and office skills, while men tend to teach the trades and industry, technical education, and agriculture courses (Roby, 1976).

In the academic areas, girls are much less likely than boys to choose to take math and science courses. Without this high school preparation they cannot enroll in college programs that lead to the lucrative male-dominated professions associated with science, including various research and medical fields. Even though 41 percent of all recipients of bachelor's degrees in mathematics in 1975–76 were women, they enroll much less often in other college majors requiring expertise in mathematics and science than young men do. For instance, men received 54 percent of the bachelor's degrees awarded in the United States in 1975–76; yet 81 percent of the architecture majors, 80 percent of the business and management majors, and 98 percent of the engineering majors were men. Seventy-three percent of the education majors, 80 percent of the foreign language majors, and 96 percent of the home economics majors were women (adapted from Grant and Lind, 1978:108–13).

Although well-qualified women are almost as likely as well-qualified men to be admitted to undergraduate schools, data from only a few years ago show that among less well qualified students, boys are much more likely to be admitted to college than girls are (Roby, 1973). Even in graduate school, men with low undergraduate grades were more often admitted than women with low grades, and, on the whole, women were overrepresented in the group with the highest undergraduate grades (Roby, 1973). Before laws banned most sex discrimination in admission, information about these discrepancies was regularly published to inform students of their chances for admission. Now it is hard to find such comparisons of the admission scores of male and female students. However, we do know that the traditionally male Ivy League schools are still legally allowed to limit the number of women admitted, thus assuring that the women are much more academically qualified than the men.

On the whole, of those women and men who begin college, women are somewhat more likely than men to attain their bachelor's degree within four years of beginning college. Yet, a nationwide study of students beginning school at over 200 institutions in 1966 found that when matched on measures of ability (high school grades and aptitude tests), fewer women than men of equal ability received their degrees by four years after entering school (Patterson and Sells, 1973). Women are also more likely than men to drop out of graduate school programs (see Patterson and Sells, 1973).

Men and women tend to differ in how they finance their college education. Supporting the finding noted above, that social status is a more important determinant of women's than men's educational attainment, women depend more than men on help from their parents to complete school. Also, because they have greater earning power, men may rely more than women on their own earnings in financing their education (Roby, 1973; also Grant and Lind, 1978:88). While it is more difficult to determine the extent of discrimination in the granting of financial aid by institutions, some scholarships specify the sex of the recipients. Married women as well as part-time students (who may more often be women) are sometimes excluded from competition. Moreover, some graduate departments subtly discriminate against women in their proportion in the department. If, because of earlier discrimination in admissions, the women are more qualified on the whole than the men, well-deserving women may not be given financial help.

While today the restrictive campus rules on closing hours and check-in policies as well as clothing regulations have virtually disappeared from most liberal arts campuses, women still may receive career counseling towards more traditional areas as well as subtle discouragement in less traditional female fields of endeavor. A comparison of male and female graduate students at the University of Chicago found that even though the women were slightly more committed to their career plans than the men, they consistently reported receiving less support from faculty members, parents, and friends for their graduate or professional school work as well as their career plans than the men reported (Freeman, 1975).

While this lack of encouragement for women can be seen in individual interactions, it can also be reflected in organizational policies. On many campuses only minimal child-care facilities are available. A study of women who were not attending graduate school but planned to do so indicated that they considered the availability of child-care facilities the most important condition for their graduate study (Roby, 1973). In spite of this need, universities have consistently resisted providing support for such facilities. Jo Freeman (1975:204) contrasts the concern universities showed for young men during the Vietnam War by providing letters and jobs to help them retain their draft-exempt status with the lack of concern shown pregnant women who must often leave school, lose a fellowship, and get medical care outside the university facilities.

It is important to note that the lack of child-care facilities and provisions for maternity leave becomes most important for women when they are in graduate and professional schools. It is widely accepted that middle-class women will attend and graduate from college, and because they usually major in different areas, they rarely compete directly with men during those years. When, however, they enter graduate and professional schools, they encroach more on traditional masculine territory, and it is here that they receive even less personal and institutional support, even though they are at an age where it is probable that they will want or already have children and be in need of such services.

Institutional Linkages

Institutional explanations of sex stratification in education generally focus on the relationships between education, the economy, and the family. A great deal of work has examined how students' social class and racial background influence their experiences in education. This work shows that the limited opportunities working-class and nonwhite people face in education reflect the limited resources and opportunities for them in the occupational world. This correspondence can also help account for sex stratification in education. While upper-middle-class boys become doctors and lawyers, their sisters most often become teachers or social workers as well as wives and mothers. Thus, they have different majors in college and graduate school, and males more often go to graduate and professional schools in male-dominated areas. While working-class men may enter skilled trades, their sisters probably enter much lower paying clerical and service occupations. The exclusion of women from the male-dominated areas in vocational training reflects their absence from those areas in the occupational world.

Because students generally choose their college majors and their vocational course work themselves, these patterns may appear to persist because of voluntary decisions by the students. Yet students do see the sex segregation in the occupational world and are aware of what is considered women's work and men's work. Although the laws and regulations that once enforced this segregation are now banned, more subtle and covert means discourage women from entering the highly rewarded male fields. Unofficial norms among both teachers and students support the maintenance of sex-segregated classes. These are reflected in expectations individuals hold and communicate to students and in organizational patterns including even the physical structures of school buildings. For instance, women's bathrooms are much less commonly found in shop, vocational education, and other buildings used mainly by men. The absence of these facilities can then be used as a reason to bar women from classes. Thus, while it may appear that women voluntarily avoid entering male-dominated areas in education, this may often be motivated by a realization of the actual barriers to their entrance into these fields in the occupational world.

Besides this sex segregation in educational programs, women may face discrimination in financing their education. This involves an assumption that men's education is more important than women's and reflects the cultural assumption that men's major social role is in the economic world, while women's major social role is in the family. Thus, traditionally, families will invest in their daughters' education to ensure that they find suitable husbands and thus provide them with a secure future. Families will invest in sons' education to ensure directly their occupational and economic success. Because the male's economic role is central, families and educational organizations tend to invest more heavily in his education. Explanations of sex stratification in education rest upon families' decisions to allocate resources to males rather than females and on females' views of the nature of the opportunity structure in the adult world.

People in our society tend to see education as the key to success in adulthood, and indeed, schools do help prepare people for their adult roles. Many people believe that if we change boys' and girls' experiences in school, they will have greater equality as men and women. Programs designed to end sex stratification then focus on education and promote developing new curriculum materials and new training programs for women. To some extent, this focus occurs because it is probably easier to affect school policies than those in other institutions.* Yet, given that males' and females' experiences and performance in education have always been at least relatively similar, especially when compared with other areas of society, it is ironic that so many change efforts focus on education. Moreover, because sex inequalities in education largely reflect those in other institutions, changes in education are probably neither the most efficient nor the most effective way to alter sex stratification in the total society (Kempner et al., 1979).

If women are to enter male-dominated occupations, the most effective strategy is for business firms to hire them in these posts. Currently, men and women with identical training are hired for different jobs and then paid vastly different wages. Simply giving women additional training is not going to alter the practice of businesses. In addition, if it ever became true that employees in a given field were not chosen on the basis of sex, then a major reason for the different representation of men and women in training programs would have been removed and students will make different choices. Similarly, schools do not encourage families to invest more heavily in their sons' education than in their daughters'. Families make that decision themselves, and they are prompted by the belief that men's major social roles are in the work world and women's in the home. This belief, of course, is buttressed by the fact that men are paid more for their work. Changing this balance of family and work roles is probably the

*This approach has also been used in attempting to combat poverty in general as well as the discrimination that nonwhites face. The discussion that follows also applies to these attempts.

most direct way, then, to alter sex differences in investment in higher education.

Much research shows that increased education promotes tolerance for the roles of others and support for greater equality between women and men (e.g., Mason, et al., 1976; Mason and Bumpass, 1975). That women generally have as much education as men in the United States also no doubt promotes strains for women when they are placed in a subservient role to men and has been an important impetus for the feminist movement. Thus, education is an important tool for promoting equality but it cannot be the sole answer. If sex stratification in social institutions is to end, changes must be made in each of the institutional areas.

SUMMARY

As institutions, both the family and the educational system prepare people for and maintain them in the occupational world. Women generally are highly visible in both of these institutions. Women's major social role is viewed as anchored in the family, and this idea gained currency in the nineteenth century as industrialization progressed. Even if women work outside the home, as about half of all married women now do, their roles as wives and mothers continue to be perceived as central. In contrast, men's roles as husbands and fathers mainly involve providing for the family through work. Many analysts put women's family roles at the heart of their secondary status.

Both women and men attend schools in the United States in almost equal numbers through the master's level. Women usually receive better grades than men and women teachers predominate, especially at the beginning levels. What sex stratification there is in education reflects the sex stratification in the economy. Change efforts that focus on education alone then may not succeed unless the economy itself can be changed. On the other hand, educational curriculum that sensitizes individuals to the sex stereotyping and sex stratification in the economy may stimulate efforts to change the system.

Suggested Readings

BERNARD, JESSIE, *The Future of Marriage.* New York: Bantam, 1973. A readable discussion on the nature of marriage and its effect on women; contains ideas on what can be done about it.

EISLER, RIANE TENNEHAUS, *Dissolution: No-Fault Divorce, Marriage, and the Future of Women.* New York: McGraw-Hill, 1977. Discusses changing laws concerning marital dissolution and their effect upon women.

POTTKER, JANICE, AND ANDREW FISHEL, eds., *Sex Bias in the Schools: The Research Evidence.* Rutherford, N.J.: Farleigh Dickinson University Press, 1977. A collection of research articles all dealing with sex discrimination in education.

KENISTON, KENNETH, *All Our Children: The American Family Under Pressure.* New York: Harcourt Brace Jovanovich, Inc., 1977. An overview of the modern American family and education with special reference to children.

ROSSI, ALICE S., JEROME KAGAN, AND TAMARA HAREVEN, eds., *The Family.* New York: W. W. Norton & Co., Inc., 1978. An interdisciplinary collection of articles on the family that originally appeared in 1977 as an issue of *Daedalus.*

SKOLNICK, ARLENE S., AND JEROME H. SKOLNICK, eds., *Family in Transition,* 2nd ed. Boston, Mass.: Little, Brown, 1977. Collection of articles on changes in the family, with a focus on changing sex roles.

STOCKARD, JEAN, PATRICIA SCHMUCK, KEN KEMPNER, AND PEG WILLIAMS, *Sex Inequality and Education.* New York: Academic Press, in press. Reviews inequality between male and female students and educators at various educational levels and examines legal bases and possibilities for change.

4: Sex Stratification in Modern Societies

The sex stratification in institutions in the United States is not an exception, but part of a general pattern found in all modern countries. Sex stratification appears in and affects women's position in the economy, in education, the family, and the polity in all countries. This sex stratification may be seen in countries that have been industrialized for many years and in those that are just beginning to develop industrially. It may be seen in countries with widely different political forms, in countries with different religious and cultural beliefs, and in countries in all parts of the world. In this chapter, we explore sex inequality in these societies.

THE ECONOMY

Since the first years of this century, and especially in the last few decades, more and more women have entered the labor force in the United States and in other industrialized nations. Yet the proportion of women working varies from one country to another. This variation appears to be influenced by a number of factors, and we cannot make simple generalizations about their impact. In all countries, however, capitalist or socialist, west or east, with or without specific nondiscriminatory policies, the labor force is segregated by sex and men as a whole earn more than women do.

The Labor Force Participation of Women

A large number of women participate in the labor force, both in fully industrialized and in developing countries. Several variables appear to influence the amount of participation. First, if there is a relative shortage of available male workers, as may happen after years of warfare, the demand for workers may lead to women's greater inclusion in the paid labor force. Second, in some countries official policies strongly support women working outside the home, and this generally produces a larger labor force participation rate. Third, apart from official policy, a country's level of development influences the number of available jobs and thus the number of women who are working. Fourth, ideology or attitudes regarding women's proper roles also influence whether women work. Finally, the pattern of male dominance in a society may affect the options open to women and their tendency to work outside the home.

No simple generalizations can be made about the impact of these variables, for their influence may vary from one society to another. For instance, countries with similar levels of development or similar ideologies may have quite different rates of women's participation in the labor force as a result of different official policies or different patterns of male control over women's lives.

Table 4–1 gives the percentage of all women who are employed in several contemporary societies and the proportion of the total labor force in each country that is female. The first figure indicates how common it is for a woman to be employed in that country; the second figure indicates how large a part of the country's labor force women are.

The crude labor force participation rate, or the proportion of women employed in each country, varies widely from close to one-fifth in countries such as Italy, the Netherlands, Spain, Argentina, and Chile to close to one-half in Bulgaria, Romania, and Poland. Women are now less than half of the labor force in all countries. However, they once were more common than men workers in the USSR and East Germany because of the huge number of men killed in World War II as well as official policies promoting women's work.

The proportion of married women in the labor force better reflects the dedication of women to the labor force. Other data indicate that in the Western European countries, married women in Sweden and Finland have the highest participation rates, and participation rates for married women in the Netherlands and Norway are very low (Galenson, 1973:14–19). As in the United States, the proportion of married women with young children who are working has risen rapidly during the 1970s in many industrialized countries, so that in 1975, 60 percent of all women with children under the age of seven in Sweden were employed (Baude, 1979:149).

Because the Eastern European countries explicitly encourage and expect women to participate in the labor force, the highest percentage of employed women found in any Western European country (38.9 percent in Finland) is slightly lower than the average for all the Eastern

TABLE 4–1 WOMEN'S LABOR FORCE PARTICIPATION IN SELECTED COUNTRIES

COUNTRIES	WOMEN'S CRUDE LABOR FORCE PARTICIPATION RATE[a]	PROPORTION OF THE LABOR FORCE THAT IS FEMALE[b]
Western Europe and North America		
Austria	32.5	39.7
Belgium	22.6	30.1
Canada	27.5	32.9
Denmark	34.9	37.2
Federal Republic of Germany	31.7	36.3
Finland	38.9	42.1
France	29.3	35.2
Italy	20.3	27.8
The Netherlands	19.3	25.6
Norway	21.1	28.1
Spain	14.1	20.6
Sweden	32.3	36.6
Switzerland	32.9	33.7
United Kingdom	33.1	36.7
U.S.A.	32.7	37.9
Eastern Europe		
Bulgaria	45.9	43.0
Czechslovakia	44.2	45.1
Democratic Republic of Germany	43.9	46.2
Hungary	40.7	42.2
Poland	48.6	46.1
Romania	49.1	44.6
U.S.S.R.	46.2	49.7
Yugoslavia	32.7	36.2
Other areas of the world		
Argentina	19.8	25.6
Australia	27.3	31.6
Chile	14.7	23.4
Costa Rica	12.6	19.5
Hong Kong	30.9	34.2
India	26.2	32.2
Israel	21.6	29.7
Japan	40.1	39.6
New Zealand	24.1	30.4

[a]The crude labor force participation rate in the first column is the percentage of employed women in the total population of women.

[b]The figures in the second column give the percentage of women in the labor force; the proportion of all employed people who are women.

Source: Table 1, *Yearbook of Labour Statistics*, 1978. Geneva: International Labour Office, pp. 16–47. All figures are for mid-year, 1975.

European nations (43.9 percent). In fact, of all the Eastern European nations, only Yugoslavia and Hungary have lower crude labor force participation rates than any Western European country.

Because official policies in Eastern and Western Europe differ, different variables are required to explain variations in labor force participation within each set of countries. Among the Western European countries, those with lower birth rates, higher divorce rates, lower cost of living, and higher standard of living have a higher labor force participation rate for women. In the Eastern European countries, these family and economic variables are not important. Instead, demographic variables related to development such as greater urbanization, greater per capita growth rate, and greater population density influence increased employment of women. The only variable that correlates with greater participation of women in the total labor force for both the Eastern European and Western European countries is the greater participation of women in the professions (Kronick and Lieberthal, 1976).

Most nations are now developing industrially. With development, the proportion of the labor force engaged in agriculture shrinks drastically and the proportion of the labor force in manufacturing or industry grows. Most of the female labor force in developing countries works in agriculture, including over 90 percent of the female labor force in some African countries and over 80 percent in some Asian countries (Reid, 1977:29). As these nations industrialize, they tend to modernize the agricultural sector by using more machines. Women are often then excluded from employment opportunities. Men take over the mechanized farming jobs, and women rarely can get new jobs in industry. As the developing countries increase mechanization of the agricultural sector, experts predict that the female labor force participation rates in these developing countries will continue to decline in all age groups. As women lose jobs in the agricultural sector, there are generally few employment opportunities for them in the industrial sector (Reid, 1977:29). This happened in the United States in the late nineteenth and early twentieth centuries. After this initial fall in women's activity rates, however, continued industrial expansion will generally produce new jobs for women. For instance, women's labor force participation rates in France fell when mechanization in agriculture began. But since 1962, further expansion in other sectors has led to an increase in women's rate of participation in the labor force (Galenson, 1973:84). Similarly, as we noted in chapter 2, women's labor force participation in the United States has risen drastically as more jobs have opened to them in recent decades.

Besides the impact of official policy and economic development, ideology and attitudes also affect women's labor force participation. The strikingly low labor force participation rates of married women in Norway and the Netherlands illustrate this. Norway has had full employment since the end of World War II with a severe shortage of workers in jobs traditionally held by women. The geographic characteristics of Norway are similar to Finland, indicating similar industrial and occupational possibilities. The Netherlands has historically been one of the world's most advanced countries in tolerating social and political diversity. Yet, in contrast to neighboring countries, less than 10 percent of all married women in Norway and the Netherlands are employed, and the percentage of married women employed appears to have dropped over the years!

Neither men nor women in these countries approve of women's working. A government survey of married women in Norway found that 57 percent of those who did not work and even 38 percent of those who worked opposed employment of married women outside the home. The same groups of women reported that 70 percent and 47 percent respectively of their husbands opposed women working. A similar study in the Netherlands found that a majority of women opposed employment for women with families. These women also indicated that their husbands were more strongly opposed than they were (Galenson, 1973:46–51, 78–79).

It is important to realize, however, that in countries where people approve of women's working, the overall status of women may not be necessarily improved. Although a larger proportion of women in Finland work than in any other Western European country, both Finnish men and women appear to hold more traditional attitudes toward sex roles in the family and in leadership roles in the society than do either the Swedes or Norwegians. Moreover, household tasks are divided more traditionally in Finland than in the other Scandinavian countries, where women work less (Haavio-Mannila, 1971).

Finally, cultures with equally restrictive ideologies may institutionalize male dominance in ways that allow different access for women to alternative work patterns, even when the levels of industrialization are similar. Latin America has had a marked increase in women's labor force participation, while the Middle East, at a similar point in economic development and with similar restrictive attitudes toward women, has had no increase. These differences in labor force participation appear to come not from differences in fertility or marriage rates, but from differences in the institutional structures that enforce male dominance. In the Middle East, the family and kinship system retains total control over women's lives, an arrangement supported by the judicial and religious systems. In Latin America, both the church and the family maintain sway over women, and their demands may not always coincide. This divided control in Latin America may actually provide more options for women and a greater probability of their joining the labor force, even though the ideology is as restrictive as that in the Middle East (Youssef, 1974).

Sex Segregation of the Labor Force

The evidence strongly suggests that sex segregation of the labor force persists in industrial societies cross-culturally. There is some evidence that what we consider in our country to be traditionally masculine occupations, such as pharmacy and dentistry, can be transformed. Indeed, they have been changed to generally feminine occupations in other countries. Yet this transformation involves only a change in the sex of the dominant occupants and not a mixture within the occupation. How people view the profession also differs. For instance, "In country after country, medicine is regarded as an acceptable extension of women's interest in caring for people. Even in Czarist Russia, many girls studied medicine" (Galenson, 1973:24). In most European countries, about one-fifth of the physicians are women. In 1965, 75 percent of the physicians in the U.S.S.R. were women; the corresponding figure for the United States was 7 percent. Similarly, women dentists and pharmacists are much more common in European countries (including Norway) than in the United States. Notably enough, however, medical personnel enjoy extraordinarily high incomes as well as extensive control over the profession only in the United States (Galenson, 1973:25).

Sex segregation in other areas appears to be similar in most countries. For instance, throughout the world the average proportion of administrators and managers who are women is only 10 percent, and this figure does not vary much even in areas that traditionally employ many women (Boulding, 1979). Although one-third of the engineers in Russia are women, the closest figure in the West is four percent in Finland. However, the higher proportion of women in technical fields in the Eastern bloc countries may mainly result from restrictions placed on women's entrance into the field that they first choose (Scott, 1979:187). Throughout the world, women are generally heavily represented in teaching fields, although, as in the United States, they are more commonly found in the elementary schools and in the less prestigious areas of more advanced education (Galenson, 1975:26–27). This occupational differentiation persists in nonprofessional areas. For instance, in Great Britain, only 4 percent of the work force in mining and quarrying are women, while over 75 percent of those employed in clothing and footwear are women. Women workers in Germany are vastly overrepresented in the service, trade, and agricultural sectors. Ninety-one percent of German nurses and 76 percent of the telephonists are women. In Japan, 100 percent of the nursery nurses and household workers, but only 10 percent of the physicians, are women (Pettman, 1975:159).

Because the Soviet Union has explicitly encouraged the participation of women in the labor force, a large proportion of women work, and in contrast to the United States, Soviet women are found in scientific, technical, and industrial occupations. Yet a study of Soviet census materials concluded that "by and large, women predominate in economic sectors and occupations which are low in status and pay, while they are underrepresented in more prestigious and highly rewarding occupations" (Lapidus, 1976b:125). Just as in the United States, women are found disproportionately in the service sector, as secretaries and bookkeepers, and in the garment and textile industries rather than in mechanical engineering or metallurgy. Ninety-one percent of all employees in the trade and public catering categories, 98 percent of nurses, 75 percent of teachers, 98 percent of nursery school personnel, 95 percent of librarians, 96 percent of telephone operators, and 99 percent of typists and stenographers in the Soviet Union are women (Lapidus, 1976b:125–26).

While women have tended to enter some previously male fields in the Soviet Union, "there has been no reciprocal flow of men into these 'female' occupations" (Lapidus, 1976b:126–27). (This is the reverse of the situation in the United States, where as noted earlier, men have tended to enter female fields, especially the more lucrative areas such as administration. These differences can be at least partly accounted for by the different demands for labor in the U.S.S.R. and the United States. The Soviet Union has placed great emphasis on building its technological and industrial capacity and has had a large demand for labor in these traditionally male fields (Scott, 1979). In contrast, in the United States the traditionally male professional fields have become somewhat crowded since the second World War, leading college-trained men to enter traditionally female fields such as teaching and social work (O'Connor, 1977).

Both medicine and education are dominated by women in the Soviet Union, yet sex segregation also occurs within these areas. Women are much more likely to teach younger children than they are to direct schools. Eighty percent of the teachers of grades one to ten are women and 80 percent of the directors of primary schools are women, yet only 31 percent and 27 percent, respectively, of the directors of eight-year and secondary schools are women. Even fewer women teach and administer at higher levels of education. Similarly, while women predominate in medicine, the chief physicians and supervisory personnel are frequently men (Lapidus, 1976b:129).

Wage Differentials

Sex differentials in wages are also found cross-culturally. Almost every European country has ratified the International Labor Office Convention 100, which assures women "equal pay for work of equal value." Many countries have also passed equal pay laws of their own. But, just as in the United States, the net effect of both the convention and the laws has been virtually no change (Galenson, 1973:30). These laws generally have no effect because the sex segregation of the labor force ensures that few men and women are really employed in the same job. Even among those doing similar work, men may be given one job title and women another. Their unequal pay may then be "officially legal." Women may also be prohibited by law from engaging in some work areas or from working at night and receiving overtime pay (Galenson, 1973:30; see also Pettman, 1975).

Very recently, some European countries, most notably Sweden, have lessened the sex gap in wages by minimizing the overall variation in income between job categories. All socialist countries effectively do this when they minimize the wage gap between all workers. This is not a direct attempt to deal with sex segregation of jobs and sexual inequalities, but an indirect attempt to lessen the sex gap in wages by minimizing overall inequalities in wages earned, thus minimizing class inequalities. Sex segregation of jobs persists in these countries, and women consistently predominate in lower-paying jobs.

These facts are shown by the experience of the Soviet Union. Although the nature of Soviet statistics and available data make it difficult to calculate information on the wage gap that can be directly compared to information from the United States, it is apparent that women in the U.S.S.R. do earn less than men do. Soviet wages are based on the economic sector of employment. Table 4–2 shows the average monthly earnings and the percentage of women in each of these sectors. It is clear that even though there is much less total inequality than in many other countries, the sectors with fewer women tend to have higher salaries and those with more women have lower salaries. Swafford (1978) concludes that the sex discrepancy in wages in the U.S.S.R. cannot be explained by various human capital variables and suggests that discrimination is at least partly to blame.

EDUCATION As nations industrialize, more and more people learn to read and write, and both males and females attend school. Yet sex stratification appears in the sense that educational advantages are given first to men and then to women. When the illiteracy rates of males and females are compared, those of females are almost always higher. In a comparison using data gathered by the United Nations in ninety-four countries, only eight countries had a higher illiteracy rate for males than for females. The percentage of all illiterates who are women runs as high as 81 percent, but never lower than 43 percent (Boulding et al., 1976:134–35). Even though females usually have a higher illiteracy rate, males are more often enrolled in literacy classes. In only 25 percent of the

TABLE 4–2 FEMALE PARTICIPATION IN THE LABOR FORCE AND AVERAGE EARNINGS BY ECONOMIC SECTOR IN SOVIET UNION

ECONOMIC SECTOR	WOMEN AS PERCENTAGE OF LABOR FORCE	AVERAGE MONTHLY EARNINGS (RUBLES)
Construction	29	159.4
Transport	24	150.8
Science and scientific services	49	143.6
Industry (production personnel)	48	142.1
Apparatus of government and economic administration and of cooperative and voluntary organizations	63	124.4
Credit and insurance	68	118.0
Education and culture	73	112.7
Agriculture	44	111.8
Communications	68	102.9
Housing and municipal economy	53	99.6
Trade, public catering, materials and equipment, supply and sales, and agricultural procurement	76	99.3
Arts	45	97.5
Public health, physical culture, and social welfare	85	95.5
Nationwide average	51	130.2

Source: Gail Lapidus, "Occupational Segregation and Public Policy: A Comparative Analysis of American and Soviet Patterns," *Signs*, 1 (1976), 133.

countries included in the United Nations data were women more than 50 percent of the students. In some countries, they represent even less than one percent of the students in the class (Boulding et al., 1976:139–40). Whenever there is a choice between teaching males or females to read or write, the nod appears to be given to males.

Sex stratification also appears cross-culturally in higher education. When choices are to be made, men are almost always the ones allowed the opportunity for a higher education. Some developed countries, such as the United States, the Soviet Union, Finland, France, Poland, and Hungary have more than 40 percent of the university population made up of women. Yet 37 percent of the university students in Sweden, 32 percent of those in the United Kingdom, 28 percent in Japan, 27 percent in the Netherlands, and 22 percent in Switzerland are women. In somewhat less developed countries, usually an even smaller proportion of the university students are women, including only 7 percent in Ethiopia, 15 percent in Kenya, 16 percent in Honduras, and 26 percent in Jordan (Boulding et al., 1976:154–55).

Sex segregation also appears in higher education. In many countries the majority of the university students in education are women. Yet in none of the countries covered in the United Nations data do women make up more than 50 percent of the students in law or engineering. They make up slightly more than half of the students in the social sciences in only a handful of countries (Boulding et al., 1976:157–64). Thus, even in countries such as France, where females and males have similar educational levels, they tend to enter widely different occupational fields and have vastly different economic opportunities in adulthood (Juillard, 1976:118).

Sex segregation sometimes begins much earlier than the university level. Many countries have separate schools for males and females from their earliest years. While these schools generally teach the same curriculum, some authors charge that the girls are channeled more into traditionally female fields, while the males receive more training in the traditionally male and more lucrative areas (e.g., Porter and Venning, 1976:94–95). In support of this, an extensive cross-cultural study of mathematics achievement in schools found the largest gap between males and females in countries with extensive patterns of sex-segregated schooling (Husen, 1967). This suggests that girls simply do not receive the rigorous training boys do, even though this may be required by law.

The reasons why this stratification occurs cross-culturally parallel those in the United States. Families tend to invest more heavily in the education of boys than in that of girls, partly because boys can earn more in the future from their advanced education than girls can. Also, however, in many cultures boys, but not girls, are expected to support their parents in their advancing years. Girls are expected to marry, to leave the family home, and to devote themselves to their husband's family (Van Allen, 1976:35).

Even though extensive sex stratification can be seen cross-culturally, education has been a key factor in promoting women's greater equality. For instance, in the last twenty years in Italy the disparity in educational attainment between men and women has greatly diminished. These similar experiences of males and females in adolescence counteract the repression young girls experience in the family and promote similar aspirations and interests in both sexes. Yet marriage still gives men almost total control over their wives (Bielli, 1976:108). This contradiction between women's heightened aspirations and thier subordinate status may have contributed to the recent feminist activism in Italy.

Similarly, after World War II, Japan established coeducational schools and compulsory education. Although this move ran contrary to the traditional patterns of the society, it is now widely accepted. About as many females as males are enrolled in senior high schools, although there are still more men than women in universities. This education of women is seen as an important reason for women's increasing participation in the economic and social world (Koyama et al., 1967:297–98).

The most dramatic changes related to education probably have been in the Muslim world, a culture that totally segregates males and females after puberty and severely restricts women's public lives. Some countries such as Turkey have had compulsory education for women since the 1920s, but others such as Saudi Arabia and Tunisia did not follow such practices until well into the 1950s and early 1960s. With the increase in women's education, the birth rate has declined, polygamy has often been abolished, laws require the consent of the bride before a marriage can be contracted, and women have gained many important political rights (Youssef, 1976). Generally, then, as women become as educated as men, their aspirations change and they are likely to perceive status inequalities with men more sharply. The recent Islamic revolutions in some Muslim countries led to calls for renewed restrictions on women's freedoms. Such attempts will probably meet with resistance because women have become educated.

THE FAMILY Women in all countries balance their work and family roles in a different way than men do. Just as in the United States, perhaps even more so, women in other industrialized countries are responsible for the life of the home. Even though they often work outside the home, their work is generally seen as subservient and supplementary to their roles of wife and mother. Moreover, because of male dominance, men retain greater overall power in the family and there is no indication that the man shares equally in home chores even when the woman works.

That work is seen as subservient to the family and that women often define their role as a wife and mother as central may influence participation in the labor force. For instance, women in Germany appear to follow the pattern common in the United States of lessening their labor force participation when children are born and sometimes entering the work force again when the children are older (Merkl, 1976:135). In other countries, such as Norway and the Netherlands, where the female labor force participation rate is low, women choose to devote most of their energies to the home. In some countries such as Czechoslovakia, women work because national policies urge it and because two paychecks are needed for the family's survival. In fact, a survey in Czechoslovakia found that one-third of the country's working women would quit if they could (Weitz, 1977:210). These patterns may occur at least partly because women value their family roles. But they also may be prompted by the realization that a job outside the home does not mean that the amount of housework they must do inside the home declines.

Extensive cross-cultural studies of family work patterns show that even when women work outside the home, men do not generally increase their participation in household tasks (Boulding, 1976:112–14, citing Szalai, 1972). This occurs even in countries with official policies that call for women's participation in the work force. For instance, even though many women in the U.S.S.R. work outside the home, they are still responsible for the day-to-day duties of cleaning and washing (Coser, 1974).

Similarly, the 1949 Communist revolution in China brought enormous changes in women's status. While traditionally marriages were arranged and wives and their children were under the total authority of the husband's family, women are now granted a voice in marriage and in the political sphere. Yet housework and child care are still viewed as women's work, and it is seen as natural that only women work in the day care centers (Sidel, 1973).

While non-Communist countries generally do not have policies that explicitly promote women's labor force participation, women often work and again hold two jobs instead of one. In France, it was estimated in 1971 that a working mother of two had an average work week of 84 hours. Husbands rarely participate in household chores. A survey of married French women workers found that 54 percent did all their housework alone, and only 14 percent said that their husbands helped (Juillard, 1976:121).

In some societies, such as those in the Arab countries, men's power has been almost absolute. In others, such as some African countries, women have traditionally had certain property and legal rights. Greater industrialization and urbanization changed both situations. Women in Muslim countries have generally gained rights (Stiehm, 1976); those in other regions may, however, have lost power. For instance, although in some areas of Africa women traditionally owned the land, the European colonists brought the notion that men controlled the land and eventually this right was taken from women (Van Allen, 1976:36). Similarly, some authors suggest that women's increasing participation in spheres outside the family in Latin America may actually decrease the formal power women hold within the family (Jaquette, 1976:67).

Care for young children becomes especially important as more women enter the labor force. Many countries have well-planned centers with varied activities and extensive care as part of an overall policy of child development (Roby, 1973). Yet countries vary considerably in the extent to which day care is available, and no country appears to have fully met the large demand for adequate facilities. For instance, even though Norway passed legislation in 1975 that requires municipalities to provide child-care facilities, only 11 percent of the estimated need was met in 1977, and places to cover only 25 percent of the need are expected to be available in 1981 (Holter and Henriksen, 1979). Although Sweden has an extensive program of day care, it was estimated in 1979 that only about 40 percent of the children under the age of seven who needed such care were being served. It was hoped, however, that places for all children needing care would be available by the mid-1980s (Baude, 1979:161). Finally, even though the Eastern European countries have encouraged women's participation in the labor force, government officials became alarmed about dropping fertility rates in the 1950s and by the 1960s had cut back on provisions for day care. Mothers were encouraged to take leaves from work, and the availability of abortions and, at times, even the availability of birth control were drastically limited. Just as in other countries, many Eastern European children who need day care do not have access to these services (Scott, 1979).

More and more detailed studies concerning women's and men's relationships in various countries are being published. Sometimes the assessments appear contradictory because the authors attach different meanings to male dominance. It is particularly difficult to generalize about power in the family where relations are usually more informal. Women's roles remain anchored in the family, but in industrial societies the family is separate from and takes a back seat to the economy, where men prevail.

THE POLITY Even though almost all countries now grant women the right to vote and have legislation supporting equal rights, sex stratification appears in the polity. All but two of the ninety-seven nations included in a United Nations survey grant women political rights on an equal basis with men. New Zealand granted women suffrage in 1893, Norway in 1913, Denmark in 1915, the Netherlands in 1917, and Sweden in 1919. Other countries, however, such as Iran, Kenya, Monaco, Paraguay, and even Switzerland, did not grant women suffrage until the 1960s. At the time of the United Nations survey, Nigeria still gave women no voting rights and the tiny country of San Marino allowed women to vote but not to hold office (Boulding et al., 1976:250–51).

Even where women have and exercise the right to vote as in the United States, they rarely participate in the highest levels of political life. This may result partly from the pressure to fill family roles, but it also undoubtedly reflects cultural assumptions of male dominance, the belief that ultimate authority and power must rest with men. For instance, in Ireland, the proportion of women in the parliament has actually decreased since the founding of the republic and women are not even called for jury duty unless they make special arrangements (Porter and Venning, 1976:94). The proportion of women in the French parliament has also declined since

World War II, and although women do hold some posts, they are concentrated in areas related to education, health, and social welfare (Juillard, 1976:122; Granrut, 1979). Similarly, in Great Britain, with such notable exceptions as Margaret Thatcher, who was the first woman prime minister, women have not been well represented and have generally held posts in stereotyped areas.

Marxist parties have often explicitly called for the participation of women in political life. The most important way to contribute to political life in the Soviet Union is through the Communist party. Yet even though women far outnumber men in Russia, women make up only about 30 percent of all party members. A man's chance of being selected as a member of the party is about one out of eight; a woman's chance, one in forty (Lapidus, 1976a:310).

Women do participate in political life in the U.S.S.R., yet this participation is more common on the local level than in national decision-making positions. Women represent 47 percent of all the delegates in the local governing bodies, 43 percent at the regional level, 35 percent at the next highest level, and 31 percent at the supreme or highest level (Lapidus, 1976a:309). Because, however, they do not hold the important party positions and have a higher turnover rate, they have less continuity and experience and, thus, less influence on decisions. As in other countries, when women hold official posts, they tend to be concentrated in areas concerned with health, trade, food, housing, social insurance, and light-industry areas seen as appropriate female concerns (Lapidus, 1976a:309).

In China, women's political lives also concentrate on the local level. Women actively participate in the local neighborhood committees that make important decisions about everyday life. Yet women are noticeably absent from the policy-making bodies high in the government.

These sex differences in political participation occur despite legal guarantees of equal status for men and women in most countries. Some laws do, of course, support the maintenance of male dominance. For instance, the civil code of Italy requires that the husband be the head of the family and be responsible for his wife's activities, including even her employment. Similarly, while Ireland's constitution provides for equal treatment of all citizens, it also provides that laws may take into account certain moral and social functions and especially notes the importance of the mother's role in the home (Porter and Venning, 1976:83–84).

Yet other laws do promote equality between men and women and have drastically changed women's lives. The passage of divorce laws is extremely important in helping women terminate painful marriages. Similarly, some countries, such as India, did not recognize the right of widows to inherit their husband's property until specific laws were passed (Narain, 1967). China's Marriage Law, passed in 1950, brought enormous changes to women's lives. This law gave women new divorce and property rights. Concubinage, bigamy, child betrothal, and the bride price—all practices that virtually guaranteed men's dominance over women—were abolished (Holly and Bransfield, 1976).

These legal reforms have drastically altered systems of male dominance, but they have not yet ended sex stratification. Most European nations have adopted some form of a law calling for equal pay for equal work, but the sex segregation of the labor force ensures that men and women work in different areas and the wage gap remains. Women are guaranteed free and equal access to the political arena in most countries, but their unequal participation remains a reality.

Some countries, however, most notably Sweden and Norway, have adopted specific policies that promote the lessening of sex segregation and changes in men's as well as women's roles. For instance, Swedish men are encouraged to help care for their children by taking voluntary paternity leaves at nearly full pay when a child is born. Other provisions in their programs allow parents of preschoolers to work shortened weeks at little loss in pay and to take time off to care for sick children. When the program began in 1974, only 2 percent of the eligible fathers took paternity leaves. By 1979, however, 10 to 12 percent of the eligible fathers participated. Unfortunately, however, such official policies that promote institutional changes are not widespread. A study of 400 companies in Great Britain found that only about 8 percent gave any sort of paternity leave, and no national policy promotes this practice (Morgenthaler, 1979; also Baude, 1979, Holter and Henriksen, 1979).

SUMMARY

As in the United States, sex stratification exists in other contemporary countries. Because it is assumed that women should devote their energies to the family, they may face discrimination in the economy and in the polity. Women's lower participation in higher education and their lower literacy rate also reflects the assumption that their major role is supportive and familial. Yet women's lack of higher education and political power also influences their lack of economic power. The various patterns of institutional sex stratification are obviously mutually reinforcing.

It does not appear that increasing women's labor force participation guarantees less sex stratification in a society. Instead, if men do not increase their participation in family roles—and they usually do not—then women simply assume two heavy jobs instead of one. Neither does socialism, at least as it is currently operating, seem to guarantee women's greater equality. While policies that minimize the wage gap among all workers may indirectly affect women by lowering the overall variance in income, sex stratification appears in both the economy and polity of Communist countries and countries with governing democratic socialist parties. The increasing education of women does appear to promote women's equality to at least some extent (see Youssef and Hartley, 1979). With higher education, then, women are more likely to hold professional jobs and laws promoting women's equality become more common. Furthermore, when women are as well educated as their husbands, there will be increasing strain if they are required to submit to his authority. This may have influenced the recent development of feminist movements in some countries. Finally, laws may promote women's equality and many countries have governmental mechanisms designed to promote the equality of males and females (Boulding et al., 1976:248–49). Yet, despite this legal basis, sex stratification remains in social institutions.

Suggested Readings

BOULDING, ELISE, SHIRLEY A. NUSS, DOROTHY LEE CARSON, AND MICHAEL A. GREENSTEIN, *Handbook of International Data on Women.* New York: Sage Publications, Inc. 1976. Usable collection of data gathered from United Nations publications on the status of women in countries around the world.

The following three edited volumes contain articles written by scholars from around the world. Each is a good collection of articles describing the status of women in a particular country or area of the world.

IGLITZIN, LYNNE B., AND RUTH ROSS, eds., *Women in the World: A Comparative Study.* Santa Barbara, Calif.: Clio Books, 1976.

LIPMAN-BLUMEN, JEAN, AND JESSIE BERNARD, eds., *Sex Roles and Social Policy: A Complex Social Science Equation,* 3 vols. Beverly Hills, Calif.: Sage Publications, Inc., 1979.

PATAI, RAPHAEL, ed., *Women in the Modern World.* New York: Free Press, 1967.

PETTMAN, BARRIE O., *Equal Pay for Women: Progress and Problems in Seven Countries.* Washington, D.C: Hemisphere, 1977. Discusses legislation regarding equal pay for women and men in Great Britain, the United States, Australia, New Zealand, Germany, Canada, and Japan, and the progress toward achieving equality.

5: A Cross-cultural and Evolutionary View of Sex Stratification

Although sex stratification is widespread in industrial societies, could it possibly be missing from other, less complex societies? Anthropologists do not totally agree on whether male dominance characterizes all human cultures. While the majority probably do believe that male dominance is universal, some Marxist anthropologists, in particular, argue that certain nonclass societies were once truly egalitarian but have been made nonegalitarian by modern Western influences. If one defines male dominance, however, in terms of the prestige accorded to activities reserved for males and of formal authority in dominant institutions, then even in relatively egalitarian societies some male dominance existed.

Below, we first use evidence gathered by anthropologists in many societies to assess similarities and differences in social roles in human groups. We then use an evolutionary perspective beginning with our nonhuman primate relatives to explore how patterns of male dominance developed and changed as human society became more complex.

A CROSS-CULTURAL VIEW OF SOCIAL ROLES

Every known society has a sexual division of labor. Activities, however, are not always sex-typed in the same way. For example, in some societies women tend fowls and small animals, and in others men do. In some societies, men carry out dairy operations, and in others women do. On the other hand, there are general tendencies reversed in only a few societies. Generally, men are assigned to such tasks as trapping, herding, fishing, and clearing the land for agriculture, while women are more frequently assigned to jobs such as gathering and preserving food, cooking, carrying water, and grinding grain.

A few distinctions seem to be universal. Childbearing, child nursing, and its caretaking extensions are universally assigned to females and hunting has been universally assigned to males. Among the 224 societies studied by George Murdock, an anthropologist who started the Human Relations Area Files, 166 assigned hunting to "men always." Thirteen assigned it to "men usually," but in no society was it open to "either sex" or to "women usually" or "women always." In addition, metal working and weapon making are exclusively male activities. Although women may participate in warfare, war making is male dominated in all societies that make war (D'Andrade, 1966).

Some authors suggest that these different role assignments may be based on physical sex differences. Perhaps warfare can be explained by men's greater strength and size and women's childbearing. But the manufacture of musical instruments is also almost exclusively a male prerogative, which can hardly be explained by sex differences in physical characteristics. Furthermore, in many societies, women, not men, carry the heavy burdens.

Whatever the basis for these different role assignments, the most important phenomenon in the sexual division of labor is that masculine activities of any and all sorts tend to be defined as more worthwhile and necessary than feminine activities. For example, in some parts of New Guinea where women grow sweet potatoes and men grow yams, yams are the prestige food distributed at feasts while sweet potatoes are nothing very special. Among the Iatmul of New Guinea, both men and women fish for food, but women's fishing is considered merely their work, while men's fishing is viewed as an exciting expedition. In many societies, women actually provide the bulk of a group's nutrition; but whatever men's contribution to the food supply is, it is considered the more important and valuable (Rosaldo, 1974). This difference in evaluation may be linked by the distinction between domestic and public areas of life and more specifically to women's kinship roles and their roles as wives.

The Domestic-Public Distinction

Michelle Rosaldo (1974) suggests that the key social factor underlying the universal cultural devaluation of women may be that human societies have two primary types of institutions: domestic and public. Domestic institutions are organized around one or more mothers and their children, while public activities and institutions are broader and generally organize or relate particular mother-child groups. Rosaldo suggests that males' greater prestige is based on their extradomestic or public activities. Ultimately, women's association with childbearing connects them with domestic institutions and underlies their lower status.

In our society, where most work takes place outside the home and where the home is not the seat of production, it is easy to see this domestic-public split. Even when women work outside the home, as they increasingly do, their domestic roles remain central, and men are defined in terms of their extradomestic occupations.

In other types of societies, the domestic-public split may be considerably blurred. In some hunting and gathering societies, both sexes actively secure food and all activities are, in a sense, public. In these societies, women may have more economic leverage than in ours and men's public power may be displayed in religious ceremonies and rituals.

One basic aspect of men's public roles is that domestic units tend to be linked to the larger society through men. One important way in which males link mother-child or domestic networks to the larger society is through marriage outside their own kin group.

Kinship Systems and Male Dominance

All known societies have incest taboos that prohibit marriage among certain kin. This prohibition forces people to seek mates outside their immediate circle of relatives. There are wide variations with regard to which kin come under the taboo. For example, in some societies, a male can marry a first cousin on his father's side but not on his mother's side because kin are counted only through the father.

We tend to think that our own society's kinship system is normal and obvious and reflects the biological facts of kinship. Actually, however, there are many different ways of counting kin, and all of these, including our own, are primarily social, rather than biological designations. All kinship systems stress some biological facts and ignore others, and all serve mainly to organize the social relations of people in that society. For example, in our society, an adoptive father is still a father and has the same duties and obligations as natural fathers. In addition to different ways of counting kin, there are also wide variations in how marriages are contracted, where married couples live, the permissible number of spouses, and even whom one may talk to. Many societies have kinship systems of such subtlety and complexity that they defy analysis, at least in Western terms. Certain generalizations can be made, however, about the relative prevalence of different types of kinship systems and their implications for the status of women. While generally women gain less from a society's kinship arrangements than do men and while kinship systems reflect male dominance, some kin arrangements give women relatively more authority than others.

Ways of reckoning descent may be roughly categorized as patrilineal, matrilineal, and bilateral. When descent is determined through the father, the society is patrilineal. When descent is figured through the mother's line, the society is matrilineal. When descent is figured through both the father's side and the mother's side, the society is bilateral. Our own society is bilateral although names are inherited patrilineally. Cross-culturally, children are linked with their ancestors exclusively through males at least five times as often as they are linked exclusively through females (Harris, 1977). Furthermore, in societies where children belong to their mother's line (matrilineal societies), males still retain authority. However, this authority over the family is vested more in the mother's brother(s) than in the mother's husband. Inheritance of lore and valuables passes from the mother's brother to his sister's children rather than to his wife's children. The opposite pattern does not occur in patrilineal societies. In no patrilineal society does the father's sister control his children.

Residence patterns may be roughly classified into patrilocal, matrilocal, or neolocal, that is, unrelated to either spouses' parents' residence. Again, the most common residence pattern is some version of patrilocality, where the bride moves from her own family to live with her husband's family. In only one-tenth of all societies does the husband go to live with the wife's family. Rarer still is the pairing of matrilineal descent with matrilocal residence. In such societies, women do have considerable power and authority, even though males officially dominate and retain the final and ultimate authority and power.

It is important to distinguish matriliny and matrilocality from matriarchy. The terms *matriarchy* and *patriarchy* refer not to rules of descent or residence, but to the locus of authority in either women or men. Early anthropologists often described matrilineal and matrilocal societies as matriarchal. This, however, was incorrect because women as a group did not, in fact, have greater authority than men. There is no evidence, historical or contemporary, of any society in which women as a group controlled the political and economic lives of men. (Even the mythical Amazon society excluded men; the Amazon women did not directly rule over or dominate men.) It is true that in matrilineal and matrilocal societies the status of women and the direct power wielded by women are quite high. Descent passes through females and nonrelated husbands come to live in the households or villages of women who are related to each other. Yet, within these groups, the ultimate and final authority rests with men.

Patterns of plural marriage also suggest male dominance. Polygyny (plural wives) is much more common than polyandry (plural husbands). Furthermore, while having more than one wife is ordinarily associated with high status and wealth in a society, the pattern of women having more than one husband is associated with female infanticide. It is a way of ensuring that at least one male is at home to assume responsibility for the household in societies where war or hunting require males to travel long distances.

Overall, then, the formal structure of kinship systems more often than not gives greater weight to the male line and to patrilocal residence. Even in the relatively rare situations where kinship is matrilineal and matrilocal, male authority still prevails but is vested in the mother's brother rather in the mother's husband. Plural wives are more common than plural husbands, and male dominance is still found in societies that practice polyandry.

Women as Wives

In addition to incest taboos, except under very unusual circumstances, all societies recognize what the anthropologist Malinowsky called the "principle of legitimacy." According to this principle, "no child should be brought into the world without a man—and one man at that—assuming the role of sociological father . . . the male link between the child and the rest of the community" (Malinowsky, 1974:59). This linkage is ordinarily accomplished through marriage to the child's mother. While many societies allow intercourse outside of marriage, virtually no society desires that children be born outside of socially approved marriage. Marriage, then, is used by societies to legitimate offspring and to place them socially in the wider society.

It is important to understand that the idea of legitimacy has more to do with the social placement of the child than with any specific role the father might be expected to play with regard to the mother or the child. In this society we tend to think of fathers as protectors and providers, but this is not universal. In some societies the father plays virtually no role except the one of giving the child a position in society. It is also not at all necessary that the father be the same person as the biological father. The notion that every legitimate child must have a father who recognizes or claims him or her gives social control of the mother-child unit to the father and a wider group of kin. Thus, it is not the fact that women are mothers that underlies their secondary status but rather the fact that they are wives in the service of male-dominated kinship arrangements.

It is significant that among the various kinship roles that adult women play, it is the role of wife that tends to be least powerful. Within the larger kinship group the roles of mother and mother-in-law may be quite powerful. For example, in the polygynous (plural wives) Tiwi society, where the recruitment of women to the local group is important, the relationship of mother-in-law and son-in-law is particularly crucial. In order to obtain a virgin wife (the daughter of his prospective mother-in-law), the prospective son-in-law must provide food on a long-term basis for the mother-in-law and live in her camp. This pattern can be viewed as expressing how a male's hunting prowess allows him to buy wives. On the other hand, in certain real respects, the mother of the bride is the beneficiary of and gains considerable power in this transaction. The mother-in-law's power does not derive from her age status either, since she may be a generation younger than her prospective son-in-law, who can be contracting for a daughter not yet born.

In contrast to the mother role, in which women have control over their children, women's role as wives places them under the institutional control of men. This may even be seen in relatively egalitarian societies such as the !Kung, a group that lives in the Kalahari Desert. Here the little sexual inequality that exists seems to be associated with marriage. Drawing on a description of !Kung women's lives written twenty years ago, Lamphere (1977:622) described the situation:

> Young girls were betrothed to older boys at a time when they were still prepubescent and would rather have remained playing in the bush. Although many of these early marriages break up, there is considerable pressure on the girl from her parents to accept the new responsibilities of cooking and gathering for her husband and pressure (and even aggressiveness) from the new husband to accept his sexual advances. It is the 13–14 year old !Kung woman who is in the most vulnerable and unequal situation, and it is perhaps in the husband-wife pair bond that domination is a reality.

Similarly, among the African Yoruba, women are relatively powerful because of their trading activities. Yet, as wives, they must feign ignorance and obedience and in approaching their husbands they must kneel to serve the men (Lloyd, 1965).

In many societies, if a woman is expected either to exercise power or symbolize power in her own right, she is not allowed to hold the status of wife. The reason is that the role of wife implies low status. For instance, over forty African populations, especially the Bantu peoples, have the phenomenon of "female husbands." In these groups when a woman moves into an extradomestic status of high prestige, such as political leader or diviner, she must take on the social role of male by becoming "husband" and head of a household. This phenomenon of female husbands shows that the combination of high power and wife is anomalous. The idea that a political leader cannot be a wife is not limited to Africa but can also be seen in England and on the European continent (O'Brien, 1977). While the word *queen* in English most often denotes the wife of a king, it may also refer to a woman who rules in her own right. When *queen* does refer to a woman who actually rules, however, the husband of this woman is not called a king, but is a prince or a prince consort. This prevents the ruler from being a wife by rendering her mate a prince consort rather than a husband. Thus, at a deeper level, it seems that it is not women's role as mothers but their role as wives that relates to their secondary status in all cultures. Through marriage mothers become wives, and this basic element of kinship systems places males in control of women. It is important, then, to study kinship systems directly if we are to understand how male dominance is maintained.

Matrifocal Societies

If then, it is being a wife, more so than a mother, that is related to the secondary status of women, would we find less sex typing and more equality in societies that stress the mother role more than the wife role? This does, in fact, seem to be the case according to an analysis of "matrifocal" societies done by Nancy Tanner (1974). Matrifocal societies, regardless of their particular type of kinship system, stress the mother role and not the wife role. In these societies, women play roles in the public sphere and define themselves less as wives than as mothers. Tanner quotes Raymond Smith, who coined the term "matrifocality" in 1956, as saying recently that "priority of emphasis is placed upon the mother-child and sibling relationship, while the conjugal relationship is expected to be less solidary and less affectively intense. It is this aspect of familial relations which is crucial in producing matrifocal family structure" (quoted by Tanner, 1974:156).

Tanner describes five societies whose kinship systems are characterized by matrifocality: the Javanese, Atjehnese, and Minangkabau (all Indonesian groups), the Igbo of West Africa, and black Americans. In all of the societies, relationships between the sexes are relatively egalitarian and there is a minimum of differentiation between the sexes. For example, Tanner reports "little difference between women and men with regard to initiative, assertiveness, autonomy, decisiveness" (Tanner, 1974:155).

While matrifocal black families in the United States have generally been analyzed as pathological, there is growing evidence that this may simply reflect the patriarchal or phallocentric bias of our culture. What pathology may exist in the black ghetto may be a result of poverty, not of matrifocality. Diane K. Lewis has argued that, in contrast to much that has been written concerning blacks in the United States, "Afro-Americans share a distinct sub-culture in American society and that 'the hard black core of American is African' " (Lewis, 1975:222). With regard to sex roles she states (Lewis, 1975:230):

> Not only is behavior considered appropriate for males in white culture displayed by both women and men in black culture, but behavior which is associated with females in white culture is characteristic of both men and women in black culture. For example, in black families, both males and females display similar styles of child care; they are nurturing and highly interactive

physically with children. Both men and women value personal relationships and are expressive emotionally.

It is significant that "mothering" is a characteristic of both fathers *and* mothers and is deliberately fostered in both male and female children.

EVOLUTIONARY PERSPECTIVES ON MALE DOMINANCE

Over the years, anthropologists have looked at many societies in different stages of technological development and complexity. From these studies, they have developed an understanding of how women's status and roles have changed through time with changes in work and the methods of survival in the environment. These analyses are either implicitly or explicitly evolutionary in nature, assuming that human societies evolved through several stages: hunting and gathering (or foraging), horticultural, agricultural and/or pastoral, and industrial. Each of these stages has different implications for the status of women, but it is extremely difficult to generalize about just what these implications are.

Anthropologists (e.g., DeVore, 1965) and sociobiologists (e.g., Wilson, 1975, 1978) have extended the evolutionary perspective on human development to include the nonhuman primates and the transitional hominids. While humans are primates, they are not directly descended from the nonhuman primates now in existence. Instead, we share a common ancestor with our closest relatives, the chimpanzees, and evolved over the same historical era beginning perhaps as recently as 20 million years ago. Humans are very similar in genetic makeup to the chimpanzees, with one calculation of the genetic difference being equal to that between two "nearly indistinguishable" fruit flies (Wilson, 1978:25). Nonhuman primates and humans are also similar in various social characteristics, including a long period of dependence of the young on the mother.

Of course, humans do differ physically in many important ways from their nonhuman primate relatives, including posture, locomotion, reproductive physiology and behavior, brain size, and intelligence (Wilson, 1975:547–48). More importantly, the nonhuman primates lack the elaborate cultural symbol systems, most notably the religious rituals and elaborate kinship systems of humans. Thus, we cannot directly infer from their social lives to our own and must guard closely against simplistic applications of the results of studies comparing nonhuman primates to human beings. Yet, because primates do have many physical and social characteristics that are similar to those of humans, we can perhaps gain some idea of the starting point for our own earliest social patterns.

Prehuman Groups

Recent long-term observations of nonhuman primate groups provide important observations about sex roles in these early relatives of humans and provide evidence for deducing the basis upon which human groups developed and elaborated their systems of sex roles and male dominance.

Nonhuman primates such as chimpanzees have basic cognitive capacities that are similar to those of humans. They have been taught to use sign language and computers to communicate with others, to the extent that they can even create new words and thoughts. There is no evidence, however, that as a group they have any type of developed symbol system or social institutions as humans do. They do live in social groups, and, like human children, nonhuman primate infants have a long period of dependency upon their mothers. Although there are "roles" of mother, child, and sibling and the behaviors of males and females differ, there appears to be no role of father or wife as humans know it.

Dominance hierarchies exist in primate groups. Both males and females have dominance hierarchies and, in fact, a male's rank is most influenced by the rank of his mother. Eaton (1976:99–100) describes how this begins when juvenile macaque monkeys play roughly:

> One juvenile screams, inciting its mother to run over and bite the other juvenile, who is in turn aided by its mother. The two mothers then fight, and the dominant female and her offspring chase the lower-ranking female, whose son or daughter flees with her. Once this has happened several times, the offspring of the lower-ranking female will run away from those of the higher-ranking female even when she is not nearby. Occasionally a young macaque will be unusually aggressive and will rise above its mother's rank, but that is exceptional.

These findings have shaken the once common assumption that male dominance hierarchies are the primary basis of group relations. Robert Hinde, one of the world's foremost authorities on animal behavior, discusses the problems with this older view. He notes that dominance relations, because they involve aggression, disrupt the group and do little to promote group cohesion. Moreover, observations of primate groups in natural settings rather than in captive groups suggest that aggression occurs relatively infrequently in the wild. In general, Hinde concludes that male dominance hierarchies and battles do little to bind primate groups together (Hinde, 1972:19–20).

Most of the early studies of primate groups were limited to little more than a year of actual observation. Recently, observers have remained in the field for much longer periods of time, approximating the life span of individual monkeys. They have found another "major axis of social organization in monkey and ape societies: the mother-infant bond which ramifies through time into a 'mother-focused' or matrifocal subunit" (Lancaster, 1976:25). We would expect the mother-child relationship to be close in infancy, but these observations document how the tie continues throughout life, extending over several generations and providing the basis of group cohesion.

Interaction patterns reflect this matrifocal core. Grooming is a major way monkeys express and maintain their social patterns. It is pleasurable both to be groomed and to groom. By examining his genealogical records for the colony and his observations of the grooming relations, Sade (1965) found that the mother-young tie is the major factor in choosing a grooming partner. Even during the mating season when mating pairs groom each other, grooming between close relatives continues. Sade found, for example, that one fully mature male directed 40 percent of his grooming activities to his mother whether or not he was also consorting with estrous females.

Because the mother typically has more than one child, she must transfer or share her attention with all of them. The typical pattern for an older child is to groom, rest, or feed with its siblings when the mother is paying attention to another child. A child may develop a relationship with an older male, but there is no social role of "father" and usually this older male is an older brother or a maternal uncle.

Although the matrifocal pattern probably exists in all primate groups, its strength varies from one species to another. In species where it is strong, multigeneration groups are not uncommon and three and even four generation groups have been observed (Koyama, 1970 cited by Lancaster, 1976:30). This matrifocal pattern involves strong emotional attachments between mothers and their offspring, and may be seen not only in the grooming behavior and aid in defense noted above, but also in day-to-day contacts and grief at separation. For instance, Jane Goodall once observed signs of severe depression and grief in a male chimpanzee at the death of his mother. She suggests that the bonds of affection between a chimp mother and her offspring are very similar to those between a human mother and her children (Beyers, 1972; see also Klaus and Kennell, 1976 for an excellent summary of the maternal bonding process in humans.)

Like humans, nonhuman primate groups have a sex-based division of labor. Male members of some nonhuman primate groups also take different roles depending on their rank in the male dominance hierarchy (Eaton, 1976:102). Yet, unlike humans, ape and monkey groups do not have highly developed symbol systems and, so far as we can tell, they do not, and perhaps cannot, value the work of one sex group more than the other.

Like human groups, nonhuman primate groups differ in the extent of the division of labor between the sexes. In some species, there is only the minimal division of work related to child care. Nonhuman females care for infants because they can nurse the babies. As noted above, some young animals become attached to older males after they are weaned. In groups with only one adult male and several females with their young, the male's role may be limited to impregnating the females and occasionally frightening predators. If he should die or disappear, he does not appear to be missed by the others (Lancaster, 1976:41–42).

In most nonhuman primate groups, males and females participate together in food gathering. In some cases, however, females are smaller and can get more of the smaller branches on trees, or the males' heavier jaws will open larger shells. The most important exception are the cases where chimpanzees and baboons cooperate in hunting for meat. These cooperative hunters are usually male (Lancaster, 1976:42–43).

Just as with human groups, nonhuman primate groups exhibit a variety of mating patterns. The most important evidence comes from the long-term studies of various species. Lancaster (1976:36–37, citing Kummer, 1971) summarizes this evidence:

> There are the old cliches of either the promiscuous primate horde or else the aggressive, dominant male who jealously guards his harem or demands first choice of an estrous female. The field data, however, do not fit this description. In fact, there is no one primate pattern but a wide range of variation in form, from extreme promiscuity to highly exclusive harem systems, from casual mating to highly excited, emotional bonding between mating individuals. Perhaps the best generalization that can be made about primate mating systems is that they tend to be compatible with, or even be a mainstay for, the social system which itself is adapted to meet the demands of the environment.

The division of labor within the primate group, in terms of how important the male is to the functioning of the group, primarily influences the nature of the sexual bond. In some groups, only one male is needed for impregnating the females. Most groups of tree-living monkeys consist of the females, their young, and one male. Predators do not threaten the monkeys much, so only one male is enough to preserve the group. Groups that live on the ground and in more open areas, like baboons, usually have more males to provide more protection. The most dominant male in the group may control the sexual and protective activities of males subordinate to him (Lancaster, 1976:37–43).

Yet it is not necessarily true that the mating patterns of a group underlie its cohesiveness. After long and careful study of the Japanese macaques, a group with transitory and seasonal mating patterns, Eaton concluded that ongoing alliances between females rather than sexual attraction between males and females maintain group cohesion. Only rarely do male macaques form such friendships (Eaton, 1976:102).

Some primate groups also have an incest taboo. For instance, Japanese macaque males do not mate with their mothers and sisters. In Eaton's troop, an "old male Bruno 'adopted' Gamma (a female) when her mother died. Bruno groomed, cuddled, and defended her; even now, eight years later, Gamma still runs to him for support." Because Bruno has never mated with Gamma, Eaton suggests that the incest taboo among monkeys "is not genetically determined, but has its source in a developmental process," coming from the contact between the "mother" and the child (Eaton, 1976:102).

Knowledge about early hominids that were the ancestors of contemporary people comes from archeological records, primarily skeletons and artifacts, and the environment in which these records are found. From this evidence, scientists try to piece together ideas about physical behaviors and characteristics of the beings, including their intelligence and walking patterns as well as knowledge about home life such as patterns of group living and permanent camp sites.

A common assumption is that the innovations that led to the development of human life were developed by "man the hunter." However, Nancy Tanner and Adrienne Zihlman (1976), after reviewing the nature of subhuman primate life and the archeological records, developed hypotheses about the evolution of human societies suggesting that the role of females in this transition was very important. Tanner and Zihlman argue that techniques of food gathering advanced markedly with the transitional hominids. The earliest tools were used for women's tasks including gathering plants, insects, and perhaps small animals, but *"not for hunting* large, swiftly moving, dangerous animals" (Tanner and Zihlman, 1976:601, emphasis in original). Tanner and Zihlman also suggest that the matrifocal pattern seen in contemporary nonhuman primate groups characterized the early hominids and that as with chimpanzees, females usually chose their sexual partners. Tanner and Zihlman (1976:606) suggest that the "mothers chose to copulate most frequently with [the] comparatively sociable, less disruptive, sharing males—with males more like themselves." This selection process reduced the large physical and behavioral sex differences and integrated more males into the social group (see also Zihlman, 1978).

From these studies of nonhuman primates and archeological records, it appears that although sex-typed behaviors did exist in such early groups, there was probably no institutionalized pattern of male dominance. If anything, older females, who have lived in a given monkey colony and area all their lives and are the most knowledgable about feeding areas and other life in the environment, have the most influence over group activities (Leibowitz, 1976). The dominant females within a group also decide whether a new male may join. The cohesive core of nonhuman primate groups comes from relations between mothers and offspring as well as between siblings and female friends. There is no social role of father. Division of labor is minimal in most groups, involving only the care of infants. Females are extremely important to the survival of these groups and conceivably even to the transition to human society. Ironically enough, it is in human societies that systems of male dominance may first be seen, along with the social role of father and kinship systems. The hunting and gathering groups are simplest human societies.

Hunting and Gathering Societies

Although the estimates vary widely, human family life that included the use of tools, language, cooking, and a sex-based division of labor probably first appeared between about 200,000 and 500,000 years ago. Life continued to evolve over the centuries. After the last Ice Age, about 10,000 to 15,000 years ago, societies with hunting and gathering technologies were widespread (Gough, 1971, 1975). This has been the main adaptation of *Homo sapiens.*

Societies with this economic form are still found today, primarily in areas where agricultural or pastoral economies are impractical. It is sometimes difficult, however, to know whether a given social pattern represents an adaptation to culture contact or whether the pattern existed before the society was influenced by the outside world. Anthropologists have studied these groups for a number of years, and from their observations we may get clues about the nature of the earliest human divisions of labor between sex groups. Yet hunters and gatherers constitute only about 0.01 percent of the world's population, and all have had some (and usually considerable) contact with modern culture.

To the extent that we can infer from these contemporary hunters and gatherers what the earliest humanoid social organization was like, it is clear that the "man the hunter" model, which posits that men provided for the women, is far from the truth. An extensive study of ninety hunting and gathering societies in various parts of the world found that in the majority of these societies, gathering, not hunting, is the primary activity. Women are almost wholly responsible for gathering. Even in societies where hunting is important, it is always the less predictable activity; therefore, the products of gathering usually compose the dietary staples. Thus, women make a very substantial contribution to production and subsistence in these societies (Martin and Voorhies, 1975).

Neither do the kinship systems of hunting and gathering societies reflect the male dominance that the "man the hunter" hypothesis would posit. On the other hand, they are usually not matrilineal either. The majority of the societies have bilateral rules of descent and count kin on both the husband's and the wife's side of the family. While patrilocal residence is common, matrilocal residence is an option in many of the societies, and evidence suggests that matrilocality as well as matrilineal descent may have been more frequent in the period before contact with Western "civilized" life.

Hunters and gatherers usually live in small, loosely structured bands consisting of several married couples and their dependents. The organization of these groups is very simple, and institutionalized leadership and hierarchy are minimal. Apart from age, the only major permanent social division is between men and women. Most of these societies have a rather sharp division of labor between the sexes, with women gathering and men hunting.

The usual explanation for men as hunters and women as gatherers is that males are physically suited to hunting in that they are larger and stronger, can run faster, and have greater lung capacity and a hormonally based aggressiveness. Friedl (1975) suggests that this explanation is too simplistic. Most local hunting and gathering bands are small and contain fewer than a dozen women of childbearing age. In addition, the infant mortality rate is very high. Thus, in order to maintain the population, which is already low, all the women need to be pregnant or nursing throughout their childbearing years. Freidl maintains that the sex-based division of labor in hunting and gathering bands comes from the fact that women cannot hunt large game and carry or tend to children at the same time. It is hard enough to gather while carrying small children, much less hunt. The need to maintain the group size pretty much rules out the possibility of some women hunting some of the time while other women bear and care for children. Thus, the necessity for reproduction seems to preclude (at least under these circumstances) women hunters, not their inherent unsuitability for the task.

Many authors (Leacock, 1972; Martin and Voorhies, 1975; Friedl, 1975) conclude that in hunting and gathering societies relationships between the sexes are relatively egalitarian. On the other hand, most of these researchers still find some male dominance. The locus of this authority may vary. For instance, it may be embedded in political patterns of authority or it may appear in religious rites and rituals. Nevertheless, male dominance always appears.

Upon what does this dominance rest? According to Friedl, it is related not simply to the fact that men hunt, but rather to the advantages related to the distribution of the products of the hunt. In hunting and gathering societies, kinship and kin roles define the basis for exchanging the products of hunting and of gathering. Theoretically, it would be possible for a group of brothers and sisters along with their parents to constitute the group that both collected and then exchanged food among themselves. The progeny conceived outside the group by the sisters in each group would be considered to belong to the group, but not the progeny sired outside by the brothers. So far as we know, however, no human society follows this arrangement. Rather, humans have invented the idea of marriage, which not only unites two individuals from differing kin groups but also serves to unite the two separate kin groups in a network of reciprocal obligations. In terms of subsistence itself, marriage enlarges the network of kin from whom food can be received and to whom it will be given. Thus, marriage reduces the risk of starvation for any given individual (Friedl, 1975:20).

While the bulk of vegetable foods and small animals that women collect are rarely shared outside the household, big game is distributed more widely throughout the community. Friedl suggests that this extradomestic and public exchange of meat accounts for the dominance of men in hunting and gathering societies. This ability to act publicly as generous hosts also binds others to repay and gives men the edge over women. Women's gathering activities are absolutely essential to the existence of the society, but they are generally confined to the domestic sphere of the society. The extradomestic exchange of meat coupled with the male monopoly of individual and small-group hunts gives men the ultimate advantage. It places men in the public sphere and binds them to other men in ways that women are not bound.

Friedl classifies hunting and gathering societies into four basic types according to the relative importance of hunting and according to the way in which hunting activities are organized. Each type has distinct implications for the status of women. The four types are as follows: (1) Societies in which both men and women engage in gathering—men usually for themselves and women usually for themselves and for their children—and in which males hunt rather little and have little to distribute. The !Kung Bushmen of the Kalahari Desert, whom we discussed earlier, are of this type. (2) Societies in which both sexes from several households engage in collective hunts in which the men actually kill the animals, but the women actively participate in the entrapment. The sexes may also gather collectively. The food is usually shared immediately and the male advantage in meat distribution is minimized by the collective methods. (3) Societies in which men hunt alone or in groups separately from the women who gather nearer the camp. (4) Societies in which large game provided by men is virtually the only source of food for the society. Women depend on men for food.

Relationships are much more egalitarian in societies of types 1 and 2, where men hunt less or have less control over the distribution of the products of the hunt, than in types 3 and 4. This egalitarianism extends to sexual freedom as well as influence in other kinds of decision making. In the first two groups, men and women are equally free to choose spouses, to take lovers after marriage, and to separate when they wish. In type 4, where men totally control the food supply, women have very little control over their own personal destinies (Friedl, 1975:26). Friedl uses the Eskimo as an example of this type of society; among these peoples, both wife-lending as an act of hospitality and female infanticide are practiced.

Hunting and gathering societies, then, are relatively egalitarian. Their very lack of structure may allow both men and women to become personally powerful, the men through hunting expertise and the women through attracting married offspring to live with them as adults. On the other hand, males do enjoy greater dominance than females even in these societies. This dominance seems to derive not from their subsistence activities so much as from their control of the extradomestic exchange of the products of these activities. Thus, if we can deduce the earliest human adaptation from these societies, we may conclude that the male advantage arose not as a result of biological superiority or greater role in production but of greater control of exchange outside the domestic sphere, involving ties with other men. This includes not just exchange of meat and material goods, but also control over the kinship system and particularly over women as wives.

We also learn from examining the variations in these societies that the greater the society's dependence on the products of the hunt for survival, the greater the likelihood that males will exert considerable control. Thus, even though there is imperfect correspondence between women's contribution to subsistence and their status, the contribution of males to subsistence does enhance their status, at least under these arrangments.

Horticultural Societies

In contrast to hunting and gathering societies, horticultural societies depend for their subsistence on domesticated plants cultivated with hand tools. Horticulture probably developed as a gradual elaboration of the gathering activities of women. It made sedentary communities, increased population density, and more complex sociopolitical arrangements possible. These societies stress kinship lineages more than do either hunters and gatherers or the later agriculturalists. Most of the "tribal" peoples anthropologists have studied have been horticulturists.

Martin and Voorhies (1975) examined a sample of 104 horticultural societies and found both patrilineal and matrilineal systems of kinship although patrilineal descent and patrilocal residence predominated. They found that matrilineal descent and matrilocal residence increases the status of women. The combination of matrilineal descent and matrilocal residence seems to appear where there is little necessity for economic competition among local communities. The pattern loses its adaptive value "in the face of expansive competitive or more intensely exploitive techno-economic systems" (Martin and Voorhies, 1975:229). These latter conditions put pressure on the society to keep related males together for potential warfare, always a masculine specialty.

According to Martin and Voorhies, matriliny coupled with matrilocal residence represents one possible adaptation to horticulture, but is only adaptive under rather limited circumstances. Thus, it was probably never a major stage in cultural evolution. These matrilineal and matrilocal societies are intriguing to study, however, because they do allow women to obtain considerable authority as well as power. The Iroquois Indians of New York, who fascinated early theorists such as Frederick Engels (1972), are a good example of a matrilineal, matrilocal horticultural society. In this group, women of the same matrilineage lived together in different compartments of a long-house with their children and imported husbands. They were exclusive cultivators and also controlled access rights to seeds and to land. Iroquois women were not only producers, but were also collectively the owners of the means of production. Thus, women controlled the dispersal of food to men and children both within and outside their domestic units. This right of women to determine how the products of work were to be allocated gave them real political power in the society (Brown, 1975). On the other hand, even this society cannot be considered matriarchal because formal political control and authority were vested in men. Even though men gained and held office only with female approval, the council of chiefs that headed the Iroquois League was male.

The status of women is more variable and less predictable where descent is patrilineal, but generally speaking, women in these types of horticultural societies are under more rigid sexual controls and have less formal authority. Polygyny, the system where a male has more than one wife, is often associated with horticultural societies, but again it is difficult to make a blanket statement about its effect on women. It sometimes gives women advantages and sometimes reduces their status.

In spite of the much greater diversity in the status of women in horticultural societies, it is possible to find some consistencies: although there is considerable variation in who does the cultivating—one or the other sex or both—clearing land and making war are virtually exclusively male tasks. Friedl speculates that men's monopoly on land clearing is related to their monopoly on war. New lands are likely to be on the border of the territories belonging to others and may be in dispute, thus making war possible. She speculates that war is a male activity because a population can survive the loss of men better than it can the loss of women since women are the childbearers. Men, in turn, by virtue of their control of warfare and land allocation (as between populations) become more involved than women in extradomestic economic and political alliances. Thus, men have greater control than women over the extradomestic distribution and exchange of valued goods and services. This, in turn, enhances their power (Friedl, 1975).

Thus, in both horticultural and hunting and gathering societies, it appears that men dominate women because they have greater control over extradomestic distribution and exchange. Among hunters and gatherers men obtain this control through their monopoly on hunting large game. Among the horticulturists, they gain it through monopoly on the clearing of land and its allocation. Behind this pattern, in both kinds of societies, lies women's childbearing. It allows men to hunt game in hunting and gathering societies and to participate in warfare in horticultural societies. The relative power of women increases among hunters and gatherers and among horticulturists if both sexes contribute to subsistence and also have opportunities for extradomestic distribution and exchange of valued goods and services (Friedl, 1975:135).

Agricultural Societies

The development of agriculture depended upon the use of manure, the plow, and irrigation. These farming innovations were developed separately and in combination at different times and locations throughout the world. The immediate spur to their invention was probably the necessity for increased productivity to meet the needs of a particular population. Agriculture did indeed allow for greater productivity, greater population density, and political centralization. Furthermore, in contrast to hunting and gathering and horticultural societies, the majority of agricultural societies have relatively distinct social classes (Blumberg, 1978).

Agricultural societies have a higher incidence of neolocal residence and bilateral descent than hunting and gathering and horticultural societies. Kinship and domestic groups are smaller, and the incidence of polygyny is much lower. Both the matrilineal and patrilineal adaptations to horticulture give way, as families become less lineage conscious. The main effect of the shift to agriculture on men's and women's roles is the removal of women from production. As a society adopts intensive techniques of cultivation, males consistently tend to take them over, probably because they are stronger and have more freedom to be away from camp (Martin and Voorhies, 1975). Martin and Voorhies argue that the male-provider/female-domestic division of labor first arose in agricultural societies. In many hunting and gathering and horticultural societies, even though men generally have public kinship and religious roles, women are very much involved with production. But with the advent of agriculture, the main responsibility for large-scale economic production shifts to men.

This shift to agriculture that put only men in production was accompanied by the development of an ideology that supported a more rigid distinction between domestic and extradomestic labor. Sometimes the ideology was carried to extremes where women had meaning only in terms of work directly connected with the home. For example, the Islamic religion, which began in an agricultural society, places a value on keeping women within the confines of the home and on severely restricting their sexual freedom. While the seclusion of women in Islam may increase women's solidarity with one another (Nelson and Oleson, 1977), male dominance was definitely enhanced as the domestic-public split was sharpened. This further legitimized men's public role and their claim to formal authority.

As agricultural societies gave way to industrialization, they became even more productive and complex in their division of labor. Gradually, production no longer took place where people lived but in factories. After an initial period in which poor women and children were forced to work in factories for even less than men received, a new system emerged in the nineteenth century in the United States and Western Europe. This system removed most women from production far more than they had been in agricultural societies. As industrialization advanced further, however, women entered the paid labor force outside the home in many societies.

SUMMARY

While there are wide variations in the activities assigned to adult males and females in different cultures, hunting and warfare have almost always been assigned to or controlled by males. Males' monopoly on hunting and warfare, however, cannot in itself account for the greater prestige and authority males have in all cultures. Rosaldo (1974) argues that males' greater authority derives from the universal linking of women to domestic activities and of men to extradomestic ones. In all societies, men have tended to have contact with wider groups than women and have tended to control particular mother-child units. All societies to some extent connect marriage with legitimizing births. This societal requirement is an important means for linking mother-child, or domestic, units to men. Through marriage, women and children are connected with the wider society. In all cultures, the status of wife appears to be understood as incompatible with the exercise of independent authority. Lamphere (1977) argues that since kinship organizes both production and reproduction, men's kinship roles, more than their economic roles, give them greater prestige. Just as kinship systems pattern men's dominance in a society, they limit women's freedom more than men's. Matrilineal and matrilocal kinship systems do tend to enhance women's power, but even within these societies men retain the formal and ultimate authority. Finally, regardless of the particular type of kinship system involved, matrifocal societies tend to be relatively equalitarian.

Evolutionary stages of societies depend upon the development of new technologies that prompt changes in the means of subsistence. Each advance allows societies to become more populous and more complex. Hunting and gathering societies have the smallest role differentiation, while modern industrial societies have a wide proliferation of special roles and hence far greater complexity. There is no perfect correspondence between kinship systems and economic systems. For example, matrilineal and matrilocal principles are found only in special circumstances where lack of competition for land allows groups of related males to be dispersed. On the other hand, the isolated nuclear family consisting of mother, father and children is stressed in both the simplest and the most complex societies, while matriliny and patriliny are most often found in horticultural societies, midway in complexity (Blumberg and Winch, 1974). In industrial societies, kinship recedes in importance and the family is pared down to the smallest possible unit.

While prehuman groups have sex-differentiated behaviors, neither male dominance nor the roles of father, husband, and wife are apparent. In the earliest human adaptations, the distinction between domestic and public activities is not very salient since both sexes are usually involved in providing food. Men do have superior status, which comes from their roles as husbands and from their control of the extradomestic distribution of meat. In horticultural societies, kinship relations are highly elaborated, extended, and defined in the public sphere. Only in rare circumstances are these extended kinship systems matrilineal and matrilocal, and even then men maintain authority in their roles as brothers rather than as husbands. In all these horticultural societies, male dominance seems related to males' extradomestic roles, particularly in their monopoly on obtaining and clearing new lands.

The agricultural adaptation greatly sharpens the domestic-public dichotomy, and women are for the first time clearly assigned to domestic roles almost exclusively. Men's sexual control over women increases, and men and women engage in clearly separate spheres of activity. To some extent, women use the rules and symbolic conceptions that set them apart and circumscribe their activities as a basis for forming extradomestic bonds with other women and creating their own public sphere. On the other hand, kinship itself is male dominated and men's formal authority is great.

With industrialization, production in the home becomes less important, but married women continue to be largely identified with the home, not as producers but as consumers. As industrialization advances from producing goods to producing services, more jobs outside the home tend to become available to women. Now many married women work outside the home.

Suggested Readings

BLUMBERG, RAE LESSER, *Stratification: Socioeconomic and Sexual Inequality.* Dubuque, Iowa: Wm. C. Brown, 1978. A slim volume contrasting Marxist and functionalist perspectives on sex stratification.

MARTIN, M. KAY, AND BARBARA VOORHIES, *Female of the Species.* New York: Columbia University Press, 1975. Excellent source for women's roles in kinship and production from an evolutionary perspective.

REITER, RAYNA R., ed, *Toward an Anthropology of Women.* New York: Monthly Review Press, 1975. Compilation of theoretical and empirical articles on women in a wide range of societies; contains many now classic articles.

ROSALDO, MICHELE Z., AND LOUISE LAMPHERE, eds., *Woman, Culture and Society.* Stanford, Calif.: Stanford University Press, 1974. Compilation of excellent articles on women in various cultures integrated around the conceptual distinction between public and private spheres.

SCHLEGEL, ALICE, ed., *Sexual Stratification: A Cross Cultural View.* New York: Columbia University Press, 1977. A collection of articles, with introductory and concluding essays by the author, that deal specifically with sexual stratification.

PART TWO: SEX ROLE DEVELOPMENT

6: Biological Influences on Sex Differences and Sex Roles

With this chapter we begin our analysis of how individuals develop gender identities, sex differences, and their views of appropriate sex roles. Here we examine the influence of biology on sex role development. We describe the range of differences between the sexes that may be affected by biological factors, and we argue that while biology clearly influences many aspects of human behavior, these influences do not make that behavior inevitable or immutable. Biology may provide cues, but what is done with those cues is a social decision. We begin by discussing how sex differences develop in utero and how sex of assignment (based on genital differences) leads an individual to develop a consonant gender identity. As a way of understanding physiological sexual development and the development of gender identity more fully, we also discuss how these processes can go awry. We then describe the nature of physical differences between the sexes before and after pubescence and what the meaning of these differences might be. Finally, we discuss the influence of biology on psychological traits.

Popularized biologistic theories (for example, Goldberg, 1974; Morris, 1970; and Tiger, 1969) claim that one biological factor or another determines other psychological and social phenomena. Usually, these analyses try to justify male dominance and the traditional sexual division of labor on the basis of some male capacity or female incapacity. This misuse of biology has understandably led many feminists to be extremely leery of any biological perspective on sex differences. Actually, biological data need not, and in fact do not, imply that women are inferior to men nor that societal systems of male dominance or female mothering are inevitable.

As feminists and as social scientists, we believe it important to understand as much evidence as possible relating to sex differences, sex roles, and sex discrimination. Just because biology has been misused, we cannot hide our heads, ostrich-like, from all the controversy and new evidence about biological influences. Biological evidence, carefully interpreted, needs to be incorporated into a feminist analysis.

The cultural patterns of male dominance discussed in earlier chapters influence how humans interpret biological sex differences. Some of this involves *sex stereotypes,* unexamined and oversimplified mental pictures of what women and men are and how they differ. Scientists are not immune from the influence of sex stereotypes, for, like everyone else, scientists live in a male-dominated world. Thus, most scientific investigating and reporting occurs within a masculine paradigm and is likely to have a built-in masculine bias. This masculine paradigm assumes that what is related to males is somehow better than what is associated with females. It may influence what scientists choose to study, the questions they ask, and the interpretations they make. For instance, Alice Rossi (1977:16–17) notes that the familiar description of the union of the sperm and ovum is permeated with masculine fantasy. Even scientific descriptions portray the powerful active sperm swimming strongly toward the passive female egg that is waiting to be penetrated. Actually, the transport of the sperm through the female system cannot be accounted for purely by the movement of the sperm as the transition is far too rapid. Completely inert substances such as dead sperm and particles of India ink reach the oviducts as rapidly as live sperm do!

There are obviously biological differences between females and males. There also probably are some psychological sex differences that have a biological base. However, because many studies of these differences have been based on a masculine paradigm, it is important to try to analyze these differences without a masculine bias. At the same time, we must avoid a possible feminist bias, a tendency to distort findings or overlook contradictory evidence because we want to believe certain "congenial truths" (Mackie, 1977). For instance, many feminists have resisted biological evidence concerning the influence of hormones on behavior, preferring to believe that all sex differences in behavior are learned. Our own view is that it is biased to ignore biological findings.

Few people now would argue for the exclusive importance of either nature or nurture in explaining sex differences. Biology by no means fully determines what happens to individuals or to social groups. While physiological variables may prompt individuals to move in certain directions, the social situation, including economic factors, cultural, or individual desires, may overrule or drastically alter these biological predilections. As Alice Rossi (1977:4) puts it: "A biosocial perspective does not argue that there is a genetic determination of what men can do compared to women; rather, it suggests that the biological contributions shape what is learned, and that there are differences in the ease with which the sexes can learn certain things." In other words, biology can help define potential behavior, which can then be influenced to a greater or lesser extent by other factors.

Because of the obvious difficulties of biological experimentation on human beings, much of the evidence we use comes from studies of animals, especially the higher primates. Although humans are not the direct descendants of any of them, these higher primates are closest to humans in the evolutionary schema, both physiologically and sociologically. Although it is always hazardous to make inferences from animals to humans, certainly the most reliable ones are those made from animals most closely related to humans. Most of the information regarding humans that we use comes from studies of people who have experienced some type of genetic, hormonal, or physiological accident related to gender assignment. While we cannot experiment on humans, we can examine the gender and sex role identification of people with physical anomalies of one kind or another and thus gain insights into the role these factors play in development.

THE DEVELOPMENT OF SEX DIFFERENCES IN UTERO

When a baby is born, its external and internal genitalia are fully developed. This differentiation occurs because the sex chromosomes direct the differential development of the sex glands (gonads). These, in turn, produce different hormonal mixes that influence the genital structures of the two sexes. Some evidence suggests that hormones secreted in utero may also affect sex differences in nurturance and aggression by influencing structures in the brain. Below we describe how these differentiating processes normally take place and how they are sometimes altered.

Normal Prenatal Development

Biological gender is first determined when the male's sperm unites with the female's egg to form the zygote. Both the sperm and the egg cell have twenty-three chromosomes. These chromosomes are then paired in the fertilized egg, yielding twenty-three pairs or forty-six individual chromosomes. One of these pairs of chromosomes determines genetic sex. The egg contributes an X sex chromosome; the sperm contributes either an X or a Y chromosome. If the embryo has two X sex chromosomes, it is a genetic female; if it has an X and a Y chromosome, it is a genetic male. Because the female always contributes an X chromosome, it is the male's sperm that determines a child's sex. Scientists estimate that almost 140 XY conceptions occur for every 100 XX conceptions. However, more XY conceptions fail to develop and so, at birth, the ratio of males to females is about 105 to 100 (Money and Tucker, 1975:41–42).

The embryo that develops from the zygote has a bipotential structure. This original structure and the differentiation for females and males are shown in figure 6-1. For the first six weeks after conception, embryos with either an XX or an XY sex chromosome structure appear the same. All embryos have "growth buds" that can develop into male or female organs. Differentiation takes place in stages, starting first with the gonads or sex glands (the ovaries and testes), moving then to the internal reproductive structures and finally to the external genitalia.

If the embryo has XY sex chromosomes, at about the sixth week after conception the bud of the gonads begins to develop into testicles, the male gonads. If the embryo has XX chromosomes, nothing will happen for about six more weeks, when the buds begin to differentiate into ovaries. These will contain many egg cells for reproduction in later life. Scientists now think that the sex chromosomes never again influence sexual development after the testicles and ovaries develop, even though people carry the sex chromosomes in all cells of their bodies for the rest of their lives (Money and Tucker, 1975:44).

The testicles then begin to produce sex hormones: progesterone, androgen, and estrogen. Although we normally think of estrogen as the female hormone and androgen as the male hormone because of the relative proportion of the hormone each sex group produces, it is important to remember that both males and females have all three hormones in their bodies. The proportion of hormones varies both between men and women and between individuals within each sex group. Testicles produce more androgen than estrogen, and ovaries produce more estrogen than androgen (Money and Tucker, 1975:44–46).

Only the hormone mix normally secreted by males is important for prenatal development. At around the third to fourth month after conception, hormones produced by the testicles cause the wolffian structures, which are present in all fetuses, to develop as seminal vesicles, the prostate, and the vasa. These are the internal male genitalia. During this time of prenatal life, the testicles also produce a substance that inhibits or stops the mullerian structures, also present in all fetuses, from developing into female organs. If testicles have not developed and none of these hormones have been produced, female internal genitalia develop. No hormones are needed to prompt the mullerian structures to develop into the uterus, fallopian tubes, and upper vagina, the internal female genitalia (Money and Tucker, 1975:46–47).

Although the male and female internal genitalia develop from different structures, both present in all fetuses, the external genitalia develop

FIG. 6–1 SEXUAL DIFFERENTIATION IN THE HUMAN FETUS

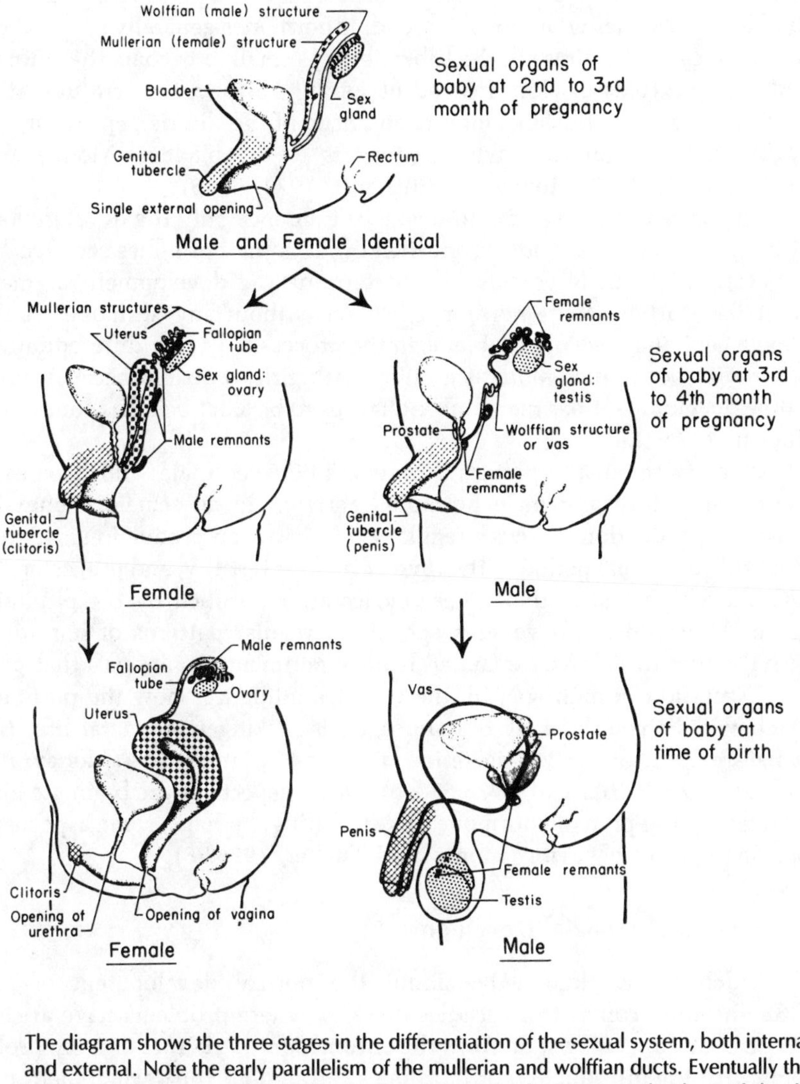

The diagram shows the three stages in the differentiation of the sexual system, both internal and external. Note the early parallelism of the mullerian and wolffian ducts. Eventually the one becomes a vestige and the other develops. (*Source:* John Money and Anke A. Ehrhardt, *Man and Woman, Boy and Girl* [Baltimore, Md.: The Johns Hopkins University Press, 1972], p. 41. Copyright © 1972 by the Johns Hopkins University Press.)

from the same preliminary structure. Again, the hormonal mix determines how the preliminary genital tubercle will develop. If hormones normally secreted by males are present, the tubercle becomes a penis and a scrotum to hold the testicles when they descend. If hormones generally secreted by the testicles are not present, the tubercle stays small to become the clitoris, and the two folds of skin, instead of joining to form the scrotum, stay separate to become the labia minora and head of the clitoris, separating the vagina from the urethra, which connects to the bladder (Money and Tucker, 1975:48–49; Money and Ehrhardt, 1972:43–45).

To summarize, the sex chromosomes influence only the development of male and female gonads. From then on, it is the hormones secreted by the testicles, or male gonads, that determine the development of male genitalia. Without these hormones, in fact without any hormones at all, female genitalia develop. Problems in the process of gender differentiation occur with boys much more often than with girls, probably because masculine development has many more chances to be sidetracked (Money and Tucker, 1976:48).

One of the most important differences between males and females is the cyclic nature of female hormonal activity. In all female mammals, hormone production follows a regular cycle. Estrogen production is higher from the menstrual period to the time of highest fertility, and progesterone levels are higher after that. These cycles are controlled by the pituitary gland. Males do not have such specific or regular patterns of hormonal activity. Scientists have concluded from experiments on animals that prenatal secretion of androgen by the testicles influences how the pituitary gland will behave later. If the androgen is lacking in prenatal life, the female pattern of cyclical secretion develops in later years (Money and Tucker, 1976:66; Barfield, 1976:63–65). Other aspects of the brain are also affected by the prenatal hormone mix including, perhaps, some aspects of personality and behavior (Money and Tucker, 1976:78).

Abnormal Prenatal Development

Much of our knowledge about the normal development of sex differentiation comes from studies of cases where problems have arisen. These conditions may stem from the chromosome structure or from problems with the introduction of hormones throughout the development period. Study of these atypical cases has led to much of our knowledge about the influence of biology on sex role development. While we cannot give a detailed explanation of the many possible abnormalities (for a full account, see Money and Ehrhardt, 1972), we will briefly outline some of the possibilities.

The embryo may have either too few or too many sex chromosomes. In some cases, the second sex chromosome is either missing or defective, and the embryo has an X0 chromosome mixture—or in scientific language, a 45, X, signifying 45 chromosomes plus the X sex chromosome. Children with this mixture develop as anatomic females, but they lack ovaries. Because there are no testicles that secrete hormones, the genitalia develop as feminine. But because no ovaries develop, the child will be sterile in adulthood and will develop secondary sex characteristics only if supplementary estrogen is given at puberty. The condition is known as Turner's syndrome (Money and Tucker, 1975:50).

In other cases, the embryo has one or more extra sex chromosomes. The most common cases are XXX, XXY, and XYY, although other combinations can occur. XXX children are anatomically female and can bear children. Both the XXY and XYY people are anatomically male.

Even if the sex chromosome combination is a normal XX or XY, several anomalies in sex differentiation can occur before the child is born. These may affect the gonads, the internal and external genitalia, and the changes in brain development. Sometimes a fetus will have the normal XX or XY chromosome mixture, but the gonads fail to develop properly. More frequently, the gonads differentiate normally, but the influence of the hormones alters genital or brain differentiation later in prenatal development. Masculine fetal differentiation encounters more problems because not only are male hormones needed to stimulate masculine development, but also an additional hormone is needed to suppress female development. Sometimes the mullerian-inhibiting hormone is not present, and the boy develops a uterus and fallopian tubes along with his functioning male genitalia. The uterus and fallopian tubes will not function because the child lacks ovaries.

In other cases, the embryo has the XY chromosomes and develops testicles, which produce androgen and the mullerian inhibiting hormone, yet it cannot use the androgen. This is called androgen insensitivity, and it is a hereditary trait passed through females and affecting their male children. Since development of the mullerian structures is repressed and the male genitalia cannot develop because of the inability to use androgen, the child has neither male nor female internal genitalia. The mullerian structures are not involved with the external genitalia, and so the child looks like a normal female externally. The child can respond to estrogen, normally secreted by the testes, so at puberty the secondary sex characteristics of a woman will appear. However, the child does not menstruate and as an adult cannot become pregnant, although she can have sexual intercourse. The lack of menstruation often leads to discovery of the condition (Money and Tucker, 1975:52–55).

Sometimes the child will be only partially sensitive to androgen, and the external genitalia will be ambiguous in appearance. In such cases, doctors and counselors recommend rearing the child as a girl. Surgery and hormone therapy can make the external genitals feminine in appearance and suitable for penetration, but the woman cannot bear children. Corrective surgery to produce male external genitalia is much more difficult, and because the boy will never be fully sensitive to androgen, he will never fully develop male secondary sex characteristics such as facial hair, masculine body shape, and a deep voice (Money and Tucker, 1975:55–57).

Because prenatal female differentiation requires no prompting or suppressing hormones, the problems that arise with females involve accidental overdoses of androgen. This may come from tumors of the ovaries or the adrenal cortex, which produce a product closely related to androgen and having the same effects. Other problems can arise from overstimulation from progesterone. Cases of this occurred in the 1940s and 1950s when doctors used progestin, a synthetic form of progesterone, to prevent miscarriage.

The exact effect of these hormones depends on the dosage received by the baby and at what developmental stage. Some babies will look like girls, others will look like boys, and some will have fairly ambiguous genitalia. With surgery and hormonal therapy, these children can function as their assigned sex. Unlike the androgen-insensitivity syndrome, XX babies with an androgen overdose who look like boys at birth can be raised as boys. They are sensitive to androgen and, with hormone therapy, can develop masculine secondary sex characteristics. With their prenatally masculinized external genitalia, they can function sexually as a normal male, except that they are sterile (Money and Tucker, 1975:57–59). There are no known cases of male XY fetuses exposed to excessive amounts of estrogen since large prenatal doses of estrogen almost invariably produce miscarriage (Money and Tucker, 1975:71; Money and Ehrhardt, 1972:46).

THE FORMATION OF GENDER IDENTITY

Remarkable as it may be in view of the complexity of the process of differentiation, the vast majority of individuals have unambiguously male or female genitals at birth. Ordinarily, too, the vast majority of people develop in the first few years after birth an unambiguous *gender identity,* a "gut level" conviction that one is male or female. No one is quite sure yet how this gender identity develops, but we do know that the most important factor is the assignment of a gender to an individual by others at birth. Children who have been assigned a gender that is not consonant with their biological or chromosomal gender actually grow up thinking and feeling that they belong to their assigned gender. Although one is assigned to a gender by the appearance of the genitals, it is not biology that produces the cognitive phenomenon of feeling masculine or feminine. Rather, it appears that communications of the parents and others in the child's environment have a virtually irreversible effect on the child's gender identity.

The Early Plasticity of Gender Identity

A case involving male identical twins illustrates the flexibility of gender identity in the early months of life. In the 1960s, a young couple took their seven-month-old twin boys to a hospital to be circumcized. Money and Tucker (1975:91–2) describe what happened:

> The physician elected to use an electric cauterizing needle instead of a scalpel to remove the foreskin of the one who chanced to be brought to the operating room first. When this baby's foreskin didn't give on the first try, or on the second, the doctor stepped up the current. On the third try, the surge of heat from the electricity literally cooked the baby's penis. Unable to heal, the penis dried up, and in a few days sloughed off completely, like the stub of an umbilical cord.

The local doctors were able to give no aid or suggestions to the distraught parents. Finally, they found a plastic surgeon who had heard of the pediatric endocrine clinic at The Johns Hopkins University Medical Center and suggested that the child be reassigned as a girl. The parents began to call the child by a girl's name and ceased dressing her in boy's clothes. When the child was seventeen months old, they went to Johns Hopkins. After extensive counseling, the child had surgery to remove the testicles and construct external female genitalia. Later, a vagina could be constructed and female hormones given.

The child had just begun to talk when the decision about reassignment was reached. The reassignment has been termed a total success, largely because of the open and careful attitudes of the parents along with the yearly counseling and follow-up examinations from the medical center. The child thinks of herself as a girl, pursues feminine activities, and talks of her future as an adult woman. The boy twin pursues masculine activities and goals. The girl has "tomboyish" traits, but her core gender identity, what she thinks she is, is feminine (Money and Ehrhardt, 1972:118–23; Money and Tucker, 1975:91–93).

This example of alternative gender identities for children with identical chromosomal structures most convincingly illustrates the plasticity of gender identity in early years and the powerful influence of sex of assignment in establishing this identity. Still other examples of children matched with regard to the nature of their biological abnormalities support this thesis. These stories also illustrate the deep-seated nature of gender identity and the fact that it develops relatively early in life.

Money and Ehrhardt (1972) present cases of matched pairs of genetically female individuals with the adrenogenital syndrome, that is, the malfunction of the adrenal glands that causes excessive male hormones to be secreted. At birth, both members of each pair had ambiguous external genitalia, but one was assigned to be a female and the other a male. The assignment was usually a function of the judgment of the professional personnel attending the birth and counseling the parents shortly thereafter.

In one matched pair, the child raised as a girl had corrective surgery at the age of two but was pronounced a girl and seen as such from the age of two months on. She had a fairly normal girlhood, although as is typical of girls with this syndrome, she exhibited "tomboyish" traits. She also projected her romantic interests with boys into the future, concentrating on her academic interests during adolescence. The member of this pair assigned as a boy had an unhappier experience. A series of operations designed to masculinize his genitalia ended in failure. At the age of three, he was again admitted into the hospital and was terrified by his thought "that a nurse would cut off his wee wee" (Money and Ehrhardt, 1972:155). It was decided to let the child continue to live as a boy, and surgery succeeded in making masculine genitalia. His family life was not happy, he was an underachiever at school, and he tended to become a rebel later. All his romantic interests were directed toward girls, even though he was continually afraid that his penis would be too small for intercourse.

The two children in the second pair experienced hormonal sex changes at age twelve that did not correspond to their gender identity. The child who thought herself a girl found her body masculinizing with her voice changing and facial hair appearing; the boy found his body feminizing with enlarging breasts. Both children were extremely upset with their condition, and after diagnosis they underwent surgery and hormonal therapy to bring their bodies in line with their gender identities. Both children reported romantic interests in the sex group other than their assignment, and they engaged in activities typical of their assigned gender. Clearly again, the sex of assignment outweighed biological factors in determining gender identity and role.

The Importance of Gender Identity

Some cases are not as clear-cut. This most often occurs if the parents are at all ambiguous about the child's gender. The results are extremely unpleasant for the children involved. A third matched pair that Money and Ehrhardt (1972) discuss involves two children who requested a sex reassignment in their tenth and eleventh years. In both cases, the parents had not been clearly told the sex of the child at birth. Furthermore, there had been no corrective surgery at that time, follow-up treatments, or counseling. Both cases were referred to Johns Hopkins when school authorities became alarmed about the children's refusal to communicate with others. In each case, medical and psychiatric personnel conferred with the children and their parents both separately and together. The possibility of sex reassignment was openly discussed with the children. Each child opted for a sex reassignment, both choosing to write notes rather than verbalize their desires. The note of the child wishing to change to a boy dramatically illustrates the urgency these children felt. She wrote, "I got to be a boy." After the sex reassignments and corrective surgeries, both children blossomed. They began to talk to others, became much more proficient both academically and socially, and began to date. The boy is sexually interested in girls exclusively, and the girl is married.

Most people simply take their assigned gender for granted and do not question it. Yet because one's gender identity is established early at an unconscious level, it becomes a basic anchor in the personality. The difficulties of changing gender identity once it has been established corroborate this. Robert Stoller (1974) reports a case of a genetic female with masculinized genitalia who was raised as a boy until the age of six when she precociously entered puberty, not unusual in such cases. The pediatrician recommended that the parents change the child's gender, buy her girl's clothes, and fix her hair as a girl's. Stoller reports that the results were disastrous. In later years, the girl was "unable to progress in school, with a severe speech defect, no friends, clumsy, and grotesque-appearing in girl's clothes" (Stoller, 1974:347). The age of six was apparently far too late to attempt to change the child's gender identity.

Money and Ehrhardt (1972:176–79) suggest that the process of gender identification may parallel the process of imprinting in animals. There may be only a short period within the child's life where it is possible to establish or alter the child's core gender identity. Thus, whenever there is a question about a child's gender, doctors try to decide gender assignment as soon after birth as possible.

Transsexualism

In recent years, adults whose gender identity does not match their biological gender or their social sex role or even the gender they usually display have become more prominent in the public eye. These people have one biological gender both internally and externally, yet feel that they are actually a member of the other sex. That is, they have the one biological sex and the other gender identity. Such people are called transsexuals, and they are not transvestites nor homosexuals. Unless they are psychotic or delusional, transsexuals recognize their assigned gender and often can act successfully in that role (Green, 1974:327; see also Person and Ovesey, 1974). They feel that they are "women trapped in men's bodies" or, much more infrequently, "men trapped in women's bodies." (Only one female wants to become male for every three to six males who want to become female.) They typically have a body characteristic of their assigned sex group, but are extremely unhappy with it.

James Morris, a famous and daring reporter who once climbed Mount Everest, elected to become Jan Morris. He wrote a book describing this experience. He says, "I was born with the wrong body, being feminine by gender but male by sex, and I could achieve completeness only when the one was adjusted to the other" (quoted in Money and Tucker, 1975:31). Richard Raskind, a topnotch men's tennis player, a well-respected opthalmologist, and a married man with children, shocked the sports world when he became Renée Richards and sought to play tournament tennis as a woman. Richards also reported the agony she felt in her presurgery dilemma. "As a child . . . I would pray every night that I could be a girl. I knew then I wanted Renée as my name. It means reborn" (*People,* 1976:18).

Richards and Morris along with several thousand other people were medically given new female bodies. While the transition from a female to a male body is more difficult and not requested as often, it too is possible. Before agreeing to a professed transsexual's request for a sex change operation, reputable medical centers require many hours of psychological examinations and counseling. The individual is required to live successfully for at least a year as a member of the desired sex group before final changing surgery is performed. For male to female transitions, feminizing estrogens are administered, and the masculine external genitalia are transformed surgically to feminine genitalia. Surgeons, of course, cannot create the uterus and ovaries, but they can form a vagina. Although the process is surgically more complex and less satisfactory, female to male transsexuals follow the same pattern by receiving male hormones and transforming surgery. Although the sex change operations do not solve all of the transsexual's problems, most transsexuals who have the operation are reported to be very happy over the results and few regret their decision (Money and Tucker, 1975:32–33). On the other hand, evidence from a follow-up study begun in 1971 indicates that transsexuals who have a sex change operation do not differ significantly in their life adjustment from those transsexuals who weather an identity crisis without having an operation (Meyer and Reter, 1979).

Scientists still do not know why transsexuals develop gender identities contrary to their biological sex. A number of people are examining physiological, psychological, and sociological explanations. We do know that transsexuals are not unique to our culture and that there have been examples of such people throughout the ages. Robert Stoller (1968, 1974), a psychiatrist who founded the Gender Identity Clinic at UCLA, suggests that unusual experiences in the early years of life and, especially for males, difficulties in separating their own identity from their mothers', may contribute to later conflict in gender identification. Persons and Ovesey (1974) have conducted intensive clinical interviews with a number of transsexuals over a period of several years. They conclude that while transsexualism may take a number of forms, it does involve extreme separation anxiety regarding the mother and fantasies of fusion with her. At this time, then, it appears that problems in gender identity development begin early in life and can be traced to particular family situations. However, more work remains to be done, and as transsexuals become more open about their experiences, we may learn more about their unique situations and about the nature of gender identity in general.

Some feminists suggest that transsexualism is simply "the result of the stereotyped sex roles of a rigidly gender-defined society" (Raymond, 1977:12) and that "transsexualism is most basically the result of normative definitions of masculinity and femininity" (1977:15). Raymond suggests that "counseling which incorporates elements of 'consciousness-raising' " is preferable to sex change operations (1977:22). Because gender identity forms a core part of self-identity, it is likely that neither sex change operations nor counseling can totally undo its importance to individuals.

The basis of male dominance probably does not lie in the fact that people have a gender identity tied to biology, but rather in the identification or association of greater power and prestige with males. The solution to male dominance, then, lies more with changing this valuation than with eliminating gender identity itself. In later chapters, we will show that, in fact, a secure gender identity—not the elimination of this identity—will be most important in eliminating male dominance.

THE NATURE OF PHYSICAL DIFFERENCES

Physiological differences between the sexes continue to appear and develop after birth. Some of these differences, primarily involving traits such as skin sensitivity and strength, first appear at birth. Others become important only at puberty when sex differences in hormonal levels again occur. Below, we discuss differences in size and strength, susceptibility to illness and disease, postpubescent development, and perception.

Size and Strength

At birth, boy babies tend to be slightly longer and weigh slightly more than girl babies. Females' lungs and hearts are proportionally smaller than those of males, and females have a lower percentage of their body weight in muscle, but a higher percentage in fat (Barfield, 1976:66). Despite these size differences, females mature more rapidly than males. This difference first appears seven weeks after conception. By the time of birth, the female is four weeks ahead of the male baby. Females learn to walk and talk and are toilet trained more quickly than males. They also reach puberty and full physiological maturity earlier (Barfield, 1976:67).

At birth, male metabolism is faster than female, although the difference may not be statistically significant. From the age of two months, males consume more calories than females. Adult males also have a lower resting heart rate, higher blood pressure, greater oxygen-carrying capacity, and more efficient recovery from muscular activity (Barfield, 1976:69–70). These physiological characteristics are one basis of male superiority in strength. Females may certainly develop their strength and endurance through exercise programs. In recent years as more funds have been devoted to training women athletes, they have rapidly improved their athletic performance. However, it is not yet known whether they will match men athletically.

Illness and Disease

A well-known sex difference that appears even prenatally is the male's greater susceptibility to illness and death. As we noted in the previous section, many more male than female fetuses are conceived, but the sex ratio is almost equal at birth. After birth, males also tend to be more susceptible to both disease and death. In this country, one-third more males than females die before their first birthday. Even as life expectancy in a society lengthens, the benefits accrue faster for women than for men, although this may result from the decline of female deaths associated with pregnancy and birth (Barfield, 1976:67). Figure 6-2 shows the change in the relative death rates of females and males during this century. From 1900 to 1970, the female death rate has become consistently lower than the male rate. This drop is especially noticeable in the childbearing years, a result of the rapid advances in maternal health care.

Males are susceptible to physical difficulties that pass females by. Such well-known problems as color blindness, hemophilia, and even baldness result from the males' XY chromosome structure. These inherited conditions arise from genetic information on the X chromosome that the child receives from the mother. Girls may also receive this condition-carrying X chromosome. But because the gene related to hemophilia or color blindness is recessive, the corresponding gene on the girls' other X chromosome can prevent the appearance of the condition in the female. The boy has no other X chromosome to block this effect and thus exhibits the defect. The

FIG. 6–2 FEMALE DEATH RATE AS PERCENTAGE OF MALE DEATH RATE BY AGE GROUP IN 1900, 1940, AND 1970 (Age Adjusted to Total U.S. Population, 1940)

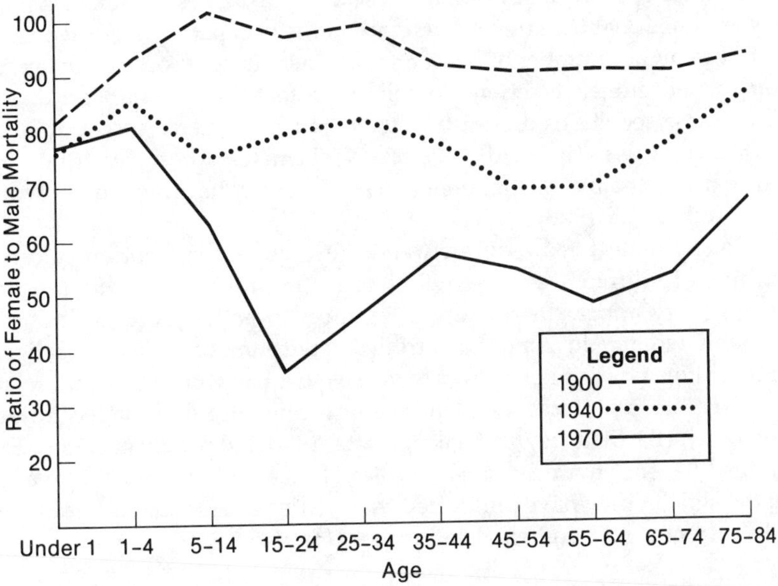

Source: Data from Metropolitan Life Insurance Corporation, "Sex Differentials in Mortality," *Statistical Bulletin,* 55 [August 1974]. Graph provided by Walter T. Martin, Department of Sociology, University of Oregon.)

girl remains a carrier and can pass the characteristic on to her offspring (Barfield, 1976:67).

Some disorders may develop more often in males than in females because males are developmentally behind females. These problems include greater proneness to speech defects such as stuttering and language disorders, reading disabilities, limited vision, impaired hearing and deafness, and mental retardation (Barfield, 1976:67–68). Studies of school children consistently note that boys are much more likely than girls to be referred for almost all learning disorders (e. g., Mumpower, 1970).

The incidence of other disorders may be influenced by our culture. Both males and females have physiological reactions to stress. But in our culture men more often develop peptic ulcers and skin disorders, and women exhibit headaches, migraines, backaches, and insomnia.

Finally, some sex differences in physical vulnerability may come from environmental and activity differences. A higher proportion of male deaths than female deaths result from accidents and injuries. Males also smoke cigarettes more and die from lung cancer more than females. However, as women become more involved in dangerous activity and as they increase their smoking, their death rate in these areas also rises. While it is popularly assumed that the stresses men face in the occupational world contribute to the higher number of heart attacks, there is now some evidence that women's hormonal secretions somehow protect them from heart disease. When these secretions diminish at menopause, women's susceptibility to heart disease rises (Barfield, 1976:68–69). Females' lower death rate may also be promoted by their tendency to seek medical help more quickly than men (Verbrugge, 1976).

Not all male-female differences in disease and susceptibility can be attributed to differences in activities or environments. The differences in susceptibility appear before any differences in activity occur. Studies of men and women in similar controlled environments, such as religious communities where men and women have similar work tasks and related pressures, sleep patterns, diet, and medical care, also find longer lifespans for women (Barfield, 1976:69, citing Potts, 1970 and Madigan, 1957). Even so, the different environments and roles of men and women before entering the cloister may have influenced these differences, and it is hard to ever fully rule out environmental influences (Harrison, 1978).

Perception

There is evidence of sex differences in sense perception. Some of the evidence is contradictory, however, and some differences appear only in adulthood, indicating that adult hormonal levels may contribute to their development. Females do appear to be more sensitive to tastes, with female infants perhaps responding more to sweet tastes and female adults discriminating bitter tastes more readily than males. While there seem to be no sex differences in the sense of smell in infancy, by adulthood women are more sensitive to odors. This seems to be related to the increased estrogens in the body after puberty. Although the evidence is contradictory, there is some indication that female infants are more sensitive to touch than male infants. In adulthood, women can detect painful stimuli more quickly than men. The two sex groups do not tend to differ in responses to auditory or visual stimuli in infancy or for the most part in later life (Maccoby and Jacklin, 1974:19–35; Barfield, 1976:70).

There does appear to be a sex difference in visual-spatial ability. Maccoby and Jacklin have reviewed the many studies in this area and conclude that more males have this ability than females. Tests used to measure spatial ability usually involve comparing one object with a number of others rotated in different planes and matching the two that are alike, looking at systems of gears and finding which gear moves a specific part, or looking at a two-dimensional picture of a three-dimensional surface and telling how many surfaces are on the figure (Maccoby and Jacklin, 1974:91–94). For many years, psychologists thought that spatial perception was a psychological trait linked to analytic reasoning skills. They now realize that it is a simple perceptive ability unrelated to intellectual capacity (See discussion in chapter 7).

Maccoby and Jacklin (1974) suggest that boys' greater spatial ability may have a biological base. They summarize three theories that purport to account for this. The first is a genetic explanation, the second involves hormones, and the third involves hemispheres in the brain. None of these theories has been proved, and further research is needed to understand the physiological source of spatial perception (see also Lambert, 1978).

While there is considerable evidence that biological factors are involved in visual-spatial ability, several researchers have shown that the ability can be improved by training, especially in girls (e. g., Connor et al., 1978). That training helps girls' scores more than boys' suggests that boys may already have been trained in some way for this ability. For instance, activities such as model construction and block building may encourage the development of spatial visual skills (Sherman, 1967).

One interesting finding in this area is the negative association of males' "masculinity" with their visual spatial ability. Boys with more masculine physical characteristics, including large chest and biceps along with pubic hair, tend in these studies to have lower scores of spatial ability. Conversely, boys with less masculine bodies have higher spatial ability. Similar results have come from various personality measures of masculinity. Obviously, masculinity is a complex phenomenon. Even though biology may influence both processes, what makes a good football player is not necessarily what makes a good mechanic.

Postpubescent Differences

At puberty, physical differences between the sexes triggered by hormones appear for the first time since before birth. From birth through about eight years of age, boys and girls have similar hormone levels and they grow at about the same pace. Boys are slightly, but insignificantly, bigger than girls until age five. From then until females begin to grow as they enter puberty, around eleven years of age, boys and girls grow at about the same pace. At puberty girls only initially grow faster than boys (Money and Ehrhardt, 1972:195).

Scientists do not yet understand exactly why or how puberty begins when it does. They do know that at around eleven years of age in girls and thirteen years in boys, the pituitary gland secretes gonadotropic hormones that prompt the gonads to secrete sex hormones. Pubescence is accompanied by a growth spurt and the development of secondary sex characteristics such as female breast development, male voice changes, and the growth of pubic hair in both sexes (Money and Ehrhardt, 1972:196–97). It is at this time that females' distinctive pelvic shape develops (Katchadourian and Lunde, 1975:95).

The age of puberty has steadily declined over the last 150 years. Some suggest that better nutrition and public health accounts for the change. This is supported by a study that found that body weight correlates with the timing of the growth spurt and onset of menstruation in girls, both signs of pubescence. Girls with different timings of puberty all had the same body weight when it began, whether menstruation and the growth spurt were early, on time, or late (Frisch and Revelle, 1970 cited by Money and Ehrhardt, 1972:197–98).

Many sex differences in body shape and proportion come from the differences in growth at puberty. Males continue their growth spurt longer than females and end up taller than females. Women have lighter skeletons, wider pelvises, different shoulder and pelvis proportions, and different socket shapes at the shoulder and pelvis than men. These differences are, of course, functional in childbearing. They also contribute to the different throwing and running styles of men and women, and to women's better ability to float and lower overall strength.

Summary Comment

In general, sex differences in physical characteristics appear at birth or develop at puberty. Males are larger and stronger, and they have well-developed visual-spatial ability more often than females. Females mature more quickly, are less susceptible to disease, live longer, and may be more sensitive to taste, smell, and touch than males are. While women have a regular pattern of hormone secretion after puberty, no regular pattern has yet been found in men.

While these physical differences generally appear cross-culturally, the meaning given to them varies from one society to another. For example, in this society, we have tended to stress women's relative lack of strength and men are expected to be the burden carriers. In other societies, relative strength is apparently unimportant and women carry the heavy loads. Biological differences are also used to justify differential evaluation of the sexes, but here again the connection is by no means obvious. If one focuses on endurance and freedom from physical defect, one could argue for the natural superiority of women. If one focuses on size and strength, men might be called naturally superior.

PHYSIOLOGY AND PSYCHOLOGICAL SEX DIFFERENCES

In chapter 7, we thoroughly review psychological sex differences that seem substantiated by research evidence. Some of the differences we think of as "psychological," however, may have a physiological base, including sex differences in nurturance, aggression, and mood change.

Nurturance

We use the term *nurturance* to describe the "giving of aid and comfort to others" (Maccoby and Jacklin, 1974:214–15). Nurturant behavior often involves responding to bids for help and comfort from others who are younger, weaker, or for some other reason in a dependent position (Maccoby and Jacklin, 1974:215). Nurturant care of the young is essential for the survival of the human species, for human young depend totally on others for their care for a number of years.

Sex differences in the propensity to nurture appear in studies of adolescent animals and in studies of humans. Field studies show that young male langurs and baboons mainly play with other males and that young females spend a great deal of time with adult females and help take care of infants (Jay, 1963 and DeVore, 1963 reported in Ehrhardt, 1973:103). Similar results have also been observed with human children in a wide cross-section of cultures (Whiting and Whiting, 1975; see also chapter 7). Similarly, experimenters who gave young monkeys to preadolescent pairs of male and female monkeys found that the preadolescent females were four times as likely as the males to act maternally toward the young monkeys. The males were ten times as likely as the females to exhibit hostile behaviors (Chamove et al., 1967 cited by Maccoby and Jacklin, 1974:218).

Prenatal hormones and nurturance The major studies involving humans are Anke Ehrhardt's (1973; also Ehrhardt and Baker, 1974) reports of young women who received excessive doses of androgen prenatally and, in some cases, continued receiving them postnatally. These are carefully planned and well-supervised studies. In the main research at Johns Hopkins University, three groups of young women with various genetic or prenatal hormonal abnormalities were matched one to one with normal young women. The matching variables included age, race, socioeconomic status of the family, and intelligence. The three groups of children with abnormalities included ten girls who had received large doses of progestin during prenatal life when their mothers were given drugs to prevent miscarriage; fifteen girls who had the adrenogenital syndrome and were treated with corrective surgery and cortisone to counteract the overactivity of the adrenal glands; and fifteen girls with Turner's syndrome, who typically have a missing sex chromosome and no gonads at all. The last group experience no hormones at all during prenatal life. At the time of the 1973 report the children ranged from four to sixteen years of age. Although social scientists generally try to have more subjects than the eighty children in this study, the small sample is inevitable when the various conditions are so rare.

All the children and mothers in both the control groups and the experimental groups were interviewed and given various sex-role preference tests. Because many of these children did have abnormal genitalia at birth and, in the case of the adrenogenital syndrome, must continue to take cortisone to counter the masculinizing hormones, it is conceivable that their parents reacted to them in ways different than the mothers of the children in the control group. Ehrhardt and her colleagues examined this possibility, but could find "no consistent difference in parental attitude toward their daughters' behavior between patient and control groups" (Ehrhardt, 1973:114). In-depth inverviews with parents in one study showed that most of them "had little persistent concern about the genital abnormality [of their daughters] at birth, and their daughters' behavior [discussed below] was not seen as related to the genital abnormality" (Ehrhardt and Baker, 1974:49).

Ehrhardt's 1973 study found striking differences between the groups with fetal masculinization and their control groups (Ehrhardt, 1973:107). The children with the adrenogenital syndrome displayed the most differences. They were less likely than their matched counterparts to anticipate their marriage or wedding in play or daydreams; more likely to give greater priority to a career than marriage in their future plans; less likely to daydream or fantasize about pregnancy and motherhood; as likely to like boys' toys, such as cars, guns and trucks as much as or more than dolls; less likely to be interested in caring for small children; more likely to like to play with boys; and more likely to have high physical energy. The girls who had experienced doses of prenatal progestin differed from their controls by more often placing greater priority on a career than on marriage and preferring toys usually liked by boys. Even with the small size of the sample, these differences were statistically significant. The girls with Turner's syndrome showed no differences from their control group except for a slight nonsignificant tendency to be even more interested in small children and in becoming a mother than their matched counterparts.

To check the accuracy of the findings with the children with adrenogenital syndrome, Ehrhardt and Baker (1974) replicated the 1973 study with a different sample. This time they used same-sex siblings as a control group. With the exception of no significant difference between the groups in the tendency to see a career as more important than marriage, they found the same differences as in the previous study.

It is important to remember that all of the girls in the studies have a feminine gender identity and appear to be heterosexual. It is also important to realize that these results do not mean that all young women who were tomboys during childhood had high prenatal doses of androgen or progestin. Excessive prenatal hormonal doses occur only rarely. Most tomboy behavior can probably be adequately explained by social influences. In fact, in this society tomboyism in girls is very common. What these results do indicate is that even though there were no differences in their gender identity, the girls who received excessive doses of prenatal progestin or androgen are more often tomboys and less often interested in caring for young children than girls who did not receive these hormones.

Although evidence on the adult lives of these women will not be available for a number of years, some data do exist on genetic females with the adrenogenital syndrome who were born before the discovery in the 1950s that cortisone could control the condition. Data are also available on adult patients with the androgen insensitivity syndrome: genetic males who cannot respond to the androgen their bodies secrete and develop female external genitalia and secondary sex characteristics, but no internal genitalia (Money et al., 1968). The majority of the adult women with the androgen insensitivity syndrome want to become full-time wives and to have children by adoption (Ehrhardt, 1973:112). They report frequently daydreaming about a family and are strongly attracted to the care of infants. In contrast, while over half of the women with the late-treated adrenogenital syndrome had married and some had had children, only a minority wanted to be a full-time wife with no outside job or career. It is important to note that the adult behavior of women with both syndromes corresponded with their childhood play behavior. Those with the adrenogenital syndrome showed little interest in dolls as children, while those with androgen insensitivity enjoyed doll play and infant care. Thus, it does appear that prenatal secretions of hormones influence interest in caring for infants, but not the individual's gender identity.

Postnatal influences on nurturance While aggressiveness seems to interfere with their maternal behaviors, male mammals can display nurturance. It appears that postnatal situations also affect nurturance. Male rats frequently attack and eat new litters. Yet, after eating several litters, they do exhibit maternal or nurturant behaviors (Rosenblatt, 1969; Rosenberg et al., 1971). Similarly, male monkeys may also kill young monkeys, but will eventually respond in a nurturant manner to an infant's demands. Harlow, a pioneer in experiments with monkeys, reported that when an infant is caged with a male monkey, the infant "will persist in its attempts to achieve ventral contact despite repeated rebuffs, and that eventually the male will permit the contact and spend a good deal of time holding the infant close to his body" (Maccoby and Jacklin, 1974:218). Other researchers (Mitchell et al., 1974) left an infant monkey in a cage alone with an adult male, who took over all the parenting functions. The babies are apparently indistinguishable from other adult monkeys when grown, although their tie with their male parent tends to strengthen, rather than diminish, over the years and they engage in more rough play with the male than they would with a mother. These studies show that all animals can display some level of maternal behavior that is not related to hormonal balance, although it is possible that the male's aggressiveness may interfere with this behavior at some points (cf. Maccoby and Jacklin, 1974:216).

The hormones produced during pregnancy and parturition also enhance nurturant behavior. Experiments with animals show how the hormones of pregnancy help produce the nurturant behaviors females show toward their young. In separate studies, researchers have injected blood plasma from pregnant rats or combinations of hormones that appear during pregnancy into virgin female rats. These injected females respond much more quickly to new litters than do untreated females (Rosenblatt, 1969 cited by Maccoby and Jacklin, 1974:215; see also Moltz et al., 1970).

Other studies with animals suggest that female responsiveness to young increases during pregnancy. This does not occur if her ovaries, which produce the hormones, have been removed. As the hormones associated with the pregnancy and parturition gradually disappear after birth, the nurturant behavior diminishes. When postparturient females are continually given new young litters their amount of "mothering" behavior lessens (Rosenblatt, 1969, cited by Maccoby and Jacklin, 1974:215–16; see also Trause et al., 1976).

Although biological factors influence nurturance, other factors also play an important part. With both lower mammals and humans, there appears to be an important period right after birth when the amount of mother-child contact influences later maternal responsiveness. Apparently, early physical contact between the mother and child is important in prompting and cementing the learning of maternal roles. Leifer and associates (1972) compared human mothers of premature infants who had been separated from their babies for three to twelve weeks after birth with mothers who had always been with their full term child. The mothers with the continuous experience exhibited more affectionate touching, smiling, and close holding behavior with their children at both one and four weeks after the premature infants had left the hospital. Leifer (1970) also compared two groups of mothers of premature infants. One group was allowed to touch and handle their premature newborn, while the other group was only allowed to peer at the child through a window in the hospital corridor. There was some indication that the mothers who touched their infants showed a stronger attachment to their offspring than the other mothers when all the infants were at home. Recent studies of full-term deliveries also indicate that less sedation of the mother, greater participation in the delivery, and immediate contact between the mother and child after birth help cement the affectional mother-child bonds (Klaus and Kennel, 1976).

Evidence also indicates that greater participation in the experience of childbirth and early contact with the child influences the attachment of fathers to their children. Fathers show the same kind of engrossment with their infants that mothers do (Klaus and Kennell, 1976), and the experience of delivery and postbirth contact seems especially important in stimulating this attachment.* It should be noted that the attachment and nurturant behavior develop as parents and child interact and communicate with each other. Extensive sedation at delivery interferes with this process because the child and mother are often too groggy to communicate.

While the prenatal hormone doses males receive may hinder their interest in nurturing young children, they by no means eliminate their capacity for nurturing as shown by experiences of fathers of newborns. Even among young boys, those with younger siblings at home show more nurturance in doll play than other boys. Girls show nurturance whether or not they have younger siblings (Maccoby and Jacklin, n. d., cited in Ehrhardt and Baker, 1974:38).

While hormones secreted during pregnancy may help prompt women's nurturant behavior, the social experience of birth also may enhance women's and men's nurturance. Thus, hormonal influence helps prompt the appearance of and interest in nurturant behavior, but social situations and interactions also exert an influence, making it possible for males as well as females to nurture. Thus, just because research findings on animals and humans indicate some hormonal basis for nurturance, we need not conclude that this means women must nurture and that men cannot.

Aggression

Males exhibit more aggressive behavior than females in all known societies. Children exhibit these sex differences early in life, and there is little evidence that adults have "socialized" or encouraged males to increase these behaviors. Male nonhuman primates also exhibit more aggression than their female counterparts (Maccoby and Jacklin, 1974: 242–43). Certainly, aspects of these differences are socially learned. Most important, the patterns of aggressive behavior that individuals exhibit depend on the

*G. H. Peterson, L. E. Mehl, and H. P. Leiderman, 1977: Personal Communication.

social and cultural context. For instance, young boys may wrestle and fight during school recess, but they know that such behavior is not permitted in the classroom. Brawls and fights may occur regularly in some areas of town, but almost never in others.

Yet there is evidence that physiological influences also affect this difference between the sex groups. This evidence comes both from studies of nonhuman mammals and from studies of human beings. As with influences on nurturance, this may involve both the prenatal influence of hormones and postnatal hormonal differences.

Prenatal influences In experimental situations, researchers have administered high dosages of androgens to pregnant monkeys. Their female children exhibit "male-like play patterns, including elevated levels of rough-and-tumble play" (Moyer, 1974:367; also see Young, Goy, and Phoenix, 1964). Other studies with rodents show that prenatal testosterone, an androgen, in female rats increases their fighting in adulthood (Edwards, 1969).

While one may generalize from such animal studies to humans only with caution, studies with humans do suggest some connection between prenatal hormone doses and later aggression. Some direct evidence comes from the studies reported in the previous section of genetic females who received abnormal hormone doses in prenatal life. Compared with their matched counterparts, the girls with excessive doses of prenatal hormones (either progestin or androgen) seemed to have a higher level of energy and preferred boys' toys and activities, including outdoor sports and games (Ehrhardt, 1973). In the study (Ehrhardt and Baker, 1974) comparing youngsters with the adrenogenital syndrome with nonaffected siblings of the same sex (and for the girls with the mother), similar results occurred. Both girls and boys with excessive prenatal androgen doses were rated by themselves and other family members as expending a much more intense physical energy than the comparison groups. This was not unfocused hyperactivity; it involved a high degree of rough, outdoor play. There was also a trend, which was not significant, for the female subjects to instigate family fights more often than either the sisters or mothers in the comparison groups.

It is important to realize that the girls with excessive prenatal hormones had relatively normal hormonal dosages in postnatal life. They look like other girls, they are no bigger than other girls, and they have definite female gender identities. The boys with adrenogenital syndrome also experience excessive prenatal androgen doses, but look like other boys at birth. They are given cortisone treatments to prevent the early onset of puberty. The behavioral differences between the groups are thought to come from the prenatal influences of the hormones on the brain.

The increased activity of the children with excessive hormonal doses may not be the same as aggression, which is usually defined as action with intent to hurt another (see discussion in chapter 7). It may be that in acting out a female gender identity, these girls learn to pattern their activity in nonaggressive ways. This finding suggests that since the feminine role does not include aggressiveness, hormones cannot produce it. The hormones do influence the young women, but the influence is expressed in ways compatible with a feminine identity.

Ehrhardt and Baker (1974) did not find that the genetic boys who had received unusually large doses of androgen during fetal life were behaviorally different from their unaffected brothers except for the increased energy level. This suggests that a certain level of prenatal male hormones is needed for "masculine" behavior but that excessive amounts will have little effect (Maccoby and Jacklin, 1974:245).

Postnatal influences At puberty, the differences in hormone levels of the two sexes widen greatly. Girls begin to secrete more estrogens, and boys to secrete more androgens. Some studies of animals link the level of androgen in the body with the level of aggressive behavior. For instance, injections of testosterone led to vast increases in aggressive behaviors in juvenile male macaques (Kling, 1968, cited in Moyer, 1974:344). Furthermore, some studies show that levels of aggression can be greatly lowered in a number of animals by castration, which removes the source of testosterone, and then heightened again by artificially administering the missing testosterone (Moyer, 1974:345). Antiandrogens, which block the effect of androgen, have been given to men in some countries who were convicted of sexual offenses. The blocking of the testosterone effect appears to have a calming influence. While the treatment does not change the nature of their sexual predilections, it can "reduce or inhibit the sexual reaction" (Laschet, 1973:317). Once this sexual reaction is reduced, the men may learn new behavior patterns.

Hormonal levels can fluctuate markedly as a result of changes in the social environment. Evidence from studies of monkey groups indicates that the more dominant animals have higher androgen levels than the less dominant animals (Rose et al., 1971). Also, when low dominance monkeys in an all-male group are moved to a group with females whom they can dominate, their androgen levels rise (Rose et al., 1972 cited by Maccoby and Jacklin, 1974:246). However, administering testosterone to castrated macaques in one study did not alter their position in the already established group hierarchy (Mirsky cited by Moyer, 1974:345). A position of dominance may influence testosterone levels, but hormonal levels may not be sufficient impetus to alter already established social patterns of dominance.

Under certain conditions, females are aggressive. Maternal aggression is found in many different species (Moyer, 1974, 1976). This behavior, whether involving attacks toward strangers or just general irritability, is usually directly related to pregnancy, parturition, and lactation. Among the primates, this aggression appears to be elicited largely by the distress of the young and is shown by others as well as the mother. Males in a primate troop and other females besides the mother may display strong defensive reactions for the young (Moyer, 1976, citing DeVore, 1963, and Hamburg, 1971).

In some cases animal mothers kill their young. However, this probably arises from a different endocrine base than maternal aggression, including an abnormally high level of androgen (Moyer, 1976:182; also see Davis and Gandelman, 1972).

Mood

Advertisements of medications to combat women's "premenstrual tension" or the "monthly blues" commonly appear in magazines, newspapers, and on television. Sixty percent of all women report that they experience discomfort or changes with their monthly menstrual period (Ramey, 1976:139). Some of the shifts in mood that women experience may result from negative attitudes toward the bodily functions, but some may result from the influence of different hormonal levels within the body. All living creatures experience cyclic changes. Sleep, pain tolerance, and cell division all appear to vary in regular cycles. Yet, among humans, women's mood changes during the monthly menstrual cycle have usually received the most research and popular attention (Parlee, 1976:125, citing Luce, 1970).

The female secretes hormones in a fixed pattern, corresponding with the menstrual cycle. During the first half of the menstrual cycle, after menstruation, the secretion of estrogen rises. Midway through the cycle, ovulation occurs, as an egg is released from a follicle in one ovary. Estrogen secretion then drops, but begins to rise again about the twentieth day of the cycle and finally drops quickly just before menstruation. Progesterone, also called the pregnancy hormone, increases after ovulation and peaks around the twentieth day of the cycle. Its function is to prepare the body for pregnancy in case sperm fertilizes the egg. Just before menstruation the level of progesterone production falls markedly. There is some evidence that testosterone, a type of androgen, is secreted more heavily just before menstruation and also at ovulation (Bardwick, 1974:29; Money and Ehrhardt, 1972:222; Barfield, 1976:70–71).

Hormones travel through the blood stream and thus can potentially affect all parts of the body (Money and Ehrhardt, 1972:222). A number of studies document how women's periodic hormonal cycle affects mood fluctuations. Measures have included women's self-reports of moods, analyses of the content of their conversations, and observations of their behavior. Although some women have much wider mood changes than others, a good deal of evidence indicates that hostility, anxiety, and depression appear more during the premenstrual stage than in other parts of the cycle. Self-esteem and self-confidence seem to be highest in midcycle at ovulation (Hoyenga and Hoyenga, 1979:145–53). Bardwick (1974) suggests that not only the high level of testosterone present premenstrually, but also its interactive effect with the low level of estrogen and progesterone produce the increased assertiveness and hostility before menstruation. The high level of testosterone at midcycle along with the high level of estrogen might influence the greater feelings of self-esteem then (Bardwick, 1974:35). In spite of the large amount of work that has been done, this area requires further research before we can understand fully the association between hormonal levels and mood. It must also be noted that not all women experience mood fluctuations that correspond to the menstrual cycle. It has been suggested that the women who are most likely to show overt behavioral changes are those who are genetically most sensitive to hormone changes or those who are experiencing physical or psychological stress (Hoyenga and Hoyenga, 1979:152).

Some people suggest that men as well as women experience cycles of hormonal secretions and mood. Estelle Ramey (1976), an endocrinologist, has been especially influential in promoting this view. She reports a study of male factory workers that showed regular variation of emotions over each twenty-four-hour period and over a regular period of four to six weeks. A sixteen-year study in Denmark found a thirty-day rhythm in the hormones men secreted (Ramey, 1976:139). On the other hand, Doering and his associates (1974) found wide fluctuations in the testosterone levels of young male subjects tested over several months. No regular pattern in the fluctuations was apparent. On the average, individuals' levels of testosterone throughout a two-month period did not correlate with their reported levels of hostility, anger, and depression. However, individuals who had higher average levels of testosterone over the two-month period did report a higher average level of depression. It appears, then, that though men may have cyclical changes in mood and other body functions, individual fluctuations in hormones are probably not related to these changes. Certainly, however, much more research is also needed in this area.

Whatever may eventually be found with regard to hormonal and mood fluctuations in men, we can say now that the attention given to these matters in women has often been used to disparage them. Both women and men have fluctuations in mood from one time to another. Yet, to say that women should not hold responsible positions because their monthly changes in hormonal secretions affect their moods is akin to saying that men should not hold responsible positions because of their biologically based aggressiveness!

Summary Comment

In general, biological influences appear to affect psychological traits by increasing the likelihood that certain behaviors such as aggression or nurturance will appear. It is probably easier to prompt women to nurture and men to be aggressive because of prenatal hormonal influences and hormonal changes later in life. Yet under certain circumstances both women and men can nurture and both women and men can be aggressive. Hormones are neither necessary nor sufficient for these behaviors. Thus, that nurturance and aggression are influenced by biology does not mean that the social assignment of mothering to women and warfare to men is inevitable.

Although both men and women are subject to changes in mood, women's moods are somewhat more predictable than men's because they are more clearly influenced by cyclic hormonal changes. It is a masculine bias to assume that these cyclic changes are in themselves bad.

THE INFLUENCE OF BIOLOGY ON SEX ROLES

Social scientists and feminists have often avoided biological explanations of sex differences. Yet in actuality, the findings concerning biological differences between the sexes do not degrade women and, in fact, indicate little or no basis for the patterns of male dominance found in human societies.

The findings reported in this chapter, as well as in chapter 5, indicate that there may be biological influences on sex differences in social roles, including child care and food gathering; on psychological traits such as nurturance and aggression; and on physical differences, such as strength, susceptibility to disease, and perceptual ability. From an evolutionary viewpoint these sex differences have been functional for the preservation of the human species. For example, women's hormonal impetus to nurturing is functional, since extended periods of nurturance are vital for the development of the child's ability to relate to others. On the other hand, the physiological prompting of this nurturant response in women does not mean that men should not nurture. In fact, the power of infants themselves to evoke nurturant responses in both sexes means that men, too, can nurture, and this provides additional guarantees for the well-being of the child.

Because they cannot lactate and physically provide milk for the young, males are not essential for the care of infants. Thus, men could be biologically prepared to fight off intruders and to capture game to supplement the regular food supply. The physical prompting of aggressive tendencies as well as males' greater strength and visual-spatial perceptual ability could enhance their skills in this area. As we saw in chapter 5, however, the basic reason why males were the warmakers and hunters in the earliest human societies was most likely that they were simply more expendable than women (Friedl, 1975). Even females' lower susceptibility to illness and death may help contribute to group survival, because the presence of females who can nurture and bear children is more important to the group's ultimate survival (cf. Rossi, 1977; Leakey and Lewin, 1977). It does not follow from all this, however, that a greater division of labor between the sexes indicates better life possibilities.

Many popular writers who point out the biological impetus behind certain sex differences imply that this can explain all social phenomena. They also imply that these differences cannot be altered and that the status quo is inevitable and immutable. In contrast, social scientists and feminists correctly argue that humans are quite capable of structuring social situations and social roles to minimize the impact of physiological sex differences. Certainly too, members of one sex can learn to perform roles usually assigned to members of the other sex. Biology may give cues for social roles, but it does not determine them.

Some writers also contend that male dominance itself can be explained by biology. Yet the activities and roles toward which females are biologically prompted are more important to the long-term survival of the group than those of males. For example, the affectional bonds between mother and young and between female members of primate groups promote group cohesion and survival much more than dominance and aggression. While biology can help explain the social role divisions between women and men, it cannot explain why men's activities are valued more highly than women's. In order to explain this, one must look for theories that take into account the unique capacity of humans to imagine, to interpret, and to create meaning from their physical and social world.

SUMMARY

Physical differences between females and males first develop before birth. Although all embryos have a bipotential physical structure, the presence of either the XY or XX sex chromosomes prompts the development of the testes or the ovaries. In males, the testes produce the sex hormones that prompt the development of male genitalia. Without the hormone mix normally secreted prenatally by males, the fetus will develop female genitalia.

At birth, a child is pronounced female or male. This social decision is the basis of gender identity, a person's conviction that he or she is a male or a female. This gender identity develops very early in life and is virtually impossible to change after a young age. Transsexuals form a gender identity that does not match their genitalia. Although this condition is very rare, some transsexuals have had surgery to transform their bodies to match their gender identity.

Males and females do differ physically. Differences occur in size, strength, incidence of illness and death, perception, and of course reproductive functions. Physiological differences between males and females may also be related to sex differences in nurturance, aggression, and changes in mood.

While some of these physical differences have probably been important in the maintenance of human society and the preservation of the species, none of the physical differences can account for the maintenance of male dominance.

Suggested Readings

FRIEDMAN, RICHARD C., RALPH M. RICHART, AND RAYMOND L. VANDE WIELE, eds., *Sex Differences in Behavior.* New York: John Wiley, 1974. Collection of research articles dealing with the development of physical sex differences and physiological influences on personality.

GREEN, RICHARD, *Sexual Identity in Children and Adults.* New York: Basic Books, 1974.

HOYENGA, KATHERINE BLICK, AND KERMIT T. HOYENGA, *The Question of Sex Differences: Psychological, Cultural, and Biological Issues.* Boston, Mass.: Little, Brown, 1979. Textbook that includes an up-to-date, but rather difficult, review of literature regarding biological influences on sex differences.

KLAUS, MARSHALL H. AND JOHN H. KENNEL, *Maternal-Infant Bonding.* St. Louis: C. V. Mosby, 1976.

MONEY, JOHN, AND PATRICIA TUCKER, *Sexual Signatures: On Being a Man or a Woman.* Boston, Mass.: Little, Brown, 1975. Well-written explanation of the development of physical sex differences and gender identity.

MOYER, KENNETH E., *The Psychobiology of Aggression.* New York: Harper & Row, Pub., 1976. A complete review of the physiological basis of aggression.

TEITELBAUM, MICHAEL, ed., *Sex Differences: Social and Biological Perspectives.* Garden City, N.Y.: Anchor Books, 1976. Readable collection of articles that includes, among other topics, a discussion of sociobiology, physical sex differences, and social patterns in nonhuman primate groups.

7: Psychological Sex Differences

In part because of the feminist movement, psychologists' interest in sex differences has been rekindled. Fortunately, now there is a new awareness of sex stereotyping and of the relationship of these stereotypes to male dominance. We are also more aware of the ways in which some research findings of difference have been exaggerated and how differences that do exist have been conceptualized in terms of a male bias.

In this chapter, after discussing sex stereotyping, we will review cross-cultural research and the major evaluative work of Maccoby and Jacklin (1974) along with new material in order to assess similarities and differences between the sexes in personality characteristics and abilities. We shall also review evidence concerning the causes of these differences and try to assess the relative influence of genetically and hormonally induced brain differences, differences in training or experience, and differences in social roles.

In the last part of the chapter after a discussion of attempts to measure individual differences by M-F tests, we shift our focus from specific differences in traits and abilities to a discussion of attempts to generalize about how traits are organized in the personalities of the two sexes. Here we discuss qualitative typologies that seek to capture in a global way basic differences in orientation between the sexes.

In discussing the ways in which the sexes are psychologically the same and the ways in which they are different, we are not trying in any direct way to explain male dominance, but simply to get a picture of what exists. Getting that picture is an ongoing process, and all the evidence is by no means in. Nevertheless, while the sexes probably differ less than we once thought, they do differ, and in order to construct a more egalitarian society we need to take these differences into account. So far, our society has tended toward the view that women should be more like men. Some of the findings and interpretations in this chapter suggest the reverse.

SEX STEREOTYPES AND MALE BIAS

In the early 1970s a group of researchers in the northeast United States conducted a series of studies on sex stereotyping of personality characteristics (Broverman et al., 1972). These researchers began their work by asking a group of undergraduate men and women to list all the ways they thought men and women differed psychologically. They then listed all the traits which the students mentioned at least twice, placing them in a bipolar form on a continuum ranging from one extreme to the other with sixty points in between. Using a number of other samples of men and women from seventeen to sixty years of age, they asked respondents to indicate the extent to which each item characterized adult men and adult women. For instance, on the item ranging from "not at all aggressive" to "very aggressive," respondents would indicate the closeness of the typical adult man or typical adult woman to each pole.

Broverman and her associates found extensive agreement on the nature of these stereotypes and on the values attached to them. Men were consistently characterized as more aggressive, independent, objective, dominant, active, competitive, logical, worldly, and ambitious than women. Men were also stereotyped as less emotional, excitable, and dependent than women. Women were stereotyped as more talkative, tactful, gentle, religious, neat, and sensitive to others than men. These researchers suggest that, in general, males are perceived as more competent than females and females as more warm and expressive than males. The researchers also found that more of the traits stereotyped as masculine than those stereotyped as feminine were perceived as desirable; that is, both male and female respondents considered the masculine poles of the various items socially desirable more often than the feminine poles.

Another version of this finding came from a study of sex stereotypes held by mental health professionals (Broverman et al., 1970). Clinical psychologists, pychiatrists, and psychiatric social workers were asked to indicate which pole of the pair of items was more descriptive of a "mature, healthy, socially competent" adult. They asked the question with respect to "an adult man," "an adult woman" and "an adult person." The professionals' judgments of the desirable characteristics for an adult person and an adult male were quite similar. In contrast the professionals saw a "mature, healthy, socially competent adult woman" as more submissive, less independent, less competitive, and more emotional than either the adult male or the adult person. Here we have a clear indication that these professionals are operating within a masculine paradigm that equates adult human with adult male and makes the male the standard by which feminine traits are judged.

Studies such as these suggest that in addition to the importance of finding out whether psychological differences actually exist between the sexes, it is important to recognize that social science professionals as well as the general population are likely to evaluate any differences in favor of males. Even when the differences themselves cannot be readily interpreted as favoring males, the author's exposition may make it seem that males "win out." As an example, Garai and Scheinfeld (1968), in a review of findings concerning sex differences in verbal and mathematical abilities, display a systematic male bias in their interpretation and reporting. Mary Parlee documents their bias by calculating that in the seventy-six comparisons Garai and Scheinfeld make between the abilities of females and males, they use some form of the word *superior* ("male superiority has been shown on . . .") to characterize 46 percent of the comparisons where males scored higher but use it in only 27 percent of the cases where females' scores were higher. This gives the impression that males performed considerably better than females in the experiments reviewed, while actually a simple count of the findings shows that females scored higher in the majority of the comparisons (Parlee 1975:128).

In this instance, male bias does not show up in the appraisal of traits but in overuse of such terms as *superior* and *surpassed* to characterize male scores. Recent attempts to summarize findings on sex differences are much more sensitive to male bias in the assessment of differences and have moved to correct them.

CROSS-CULTURAL STUDIES The work of Margaret Mead, especially her *Sex and Temperament in Three Primitive Societies* (1935), is the classic refutation of the idea that sex differences are the same the world over. In comparing the Arapesh and the Mundugamor peoples in New Guinea, Mead showed that many of the characteristics Americans classify as typically male or female are classified differently in these cultures. Among the Arapesh, both men and women are nurturant, gentle, and compliant. Relations of husband and wife are patterned after those of mother and child, and the Arapesh husband speaks of "growing" his much younger wife. According to Mead, the personalities of males and females in this society are not sharply differentiated by sex. Both boys and girls learn to be cooperative, unaggressive, and responsive to the needs and demands of others (1935:279). In contrast, the Mundugamor are head-hunters and cannibals, and both males and females are aggressive, highly sexed, and nonnurturant. Thus, among the Arapesh, both sexes would seem feminine to us, while both sexes among the Mundugamor would seem exaggeratedly masculine. Neither the Arapesh nor the Mundugamor makes aggressiveness or nurturance specific to one sex. These sharp contrasts with our society indicate that culture may play a powerful role in shaping the personalities of both sexes.

Perhaps the most interesting group Mead studied was the Tchambuli. This society virtually reverses our own sex roles and stereotypes. The women are brisk, efficient, managerial, impersonal, and unadorned, while the men are decorated and vain and spend their time carving, painting, and practicing dance steps. This marked contrast again shows the power of culture, "that a culture can select a few traits from the wide gamut of human endowment and specialize these traits either for one sex or for the entire community" (Mead, 1935:289).

Even though male and female personality traits are similar among the Mundugamor and Arapesh and reversed among the Tchambuli, sex roles and sex status are differentiated in all three societies. Among the Mundugamor, the women provide the food while the men are the much admired head-hunters. Among the Arapesh, during certain rituals, the wife is required to act like an ignorant child, clearly subordinate to her husband. Finally, even though Tchambuli women are traders and have considerable economic power, they still must engage in a tribal ritual that marks them as inferior to men in knowledge and morality. All societies have some cultural mechanism, whether it be religious, political, or economic, that marks females as inferior to males.

Although sex typing takes different forms and may be maximized or minimized within a given culture, some fairly constant sex-linked characteristics appear in children in a wide variety of cultures. Some knowledge about cross-cultural variations in personality sex differences come from reviewing ethnographic observations of anthropologists in many different cultures over the years (Barry et al., 1957). Other more systematic knowledge comes from careful observations of children in different cultures such as those described by Beatrice and John Whiting (1975). The Whitings and their associates observed boys and girls from six cultures who were between the ages of three and eleven. They observed them in carefully chosen time sequences at home, at play, and at assigned tasks.

In all the cultures the Whitings studied, girls touch others and seek help more often than boys, while boys seek dominance and attention more often than girls. The Whitings suggest that these behaviors are alternative styles for getting others to satisfy egoistic dependency needs. Girls also more often show nurturance by offering help and support than boys. Boys more often engage in aggressive behaviors including assaults, insults, and horseplay. There were no sex differences in sociability, including tendencies to make a friendly response, engage in activities together, and to cooperate for the sake of social interaction. Neither are there sex differences in prosocial behavior including reprimanding others and making responsible suggestions. While girls' help seeking and touching decreases with age and their nurturance increases, boys' behaviors do not change significantly over time.

It is not unreasonable to assume that the earliest appearing sex differences in personality are more likely to be innate or influenced by biology than later appearing ones. The largest sex differences in the youngest age group occur in the touching and help-seeking behaviors, which are most common with the girls, and in the aggressive behaviors, which boys display more often (see Whiting and Whiting, 1975:138). Beatrice Whiting and Carolyn Edwards (1973) argue that these touching and horseplay behaviors are most likely to be innate and that they constitute alternative ways that boys and girls seek and offer physical contact. Sex differences in nurturance and dominant-dependent behaviors appear only later and probably result from later differences in socialization experiences as children begin to learn adult roles.

Sex differences in the socialization experience involve different interaction situations, different role expectations, and also different behaviors of the children themselves. The others with whom one interacts help influence behavior. Infants evoke nurturance, and parents tend to inhibit aggressive behavior and evoke more intimate touching and help-seeking behavior. The reason for the greater nurturance of girls and their lesser aggressiveness may be that they interact with infants and parents more than boys do. On the other hand, this cannot explain all the sex differences in personality because some sex differences remain in all interactional settings (Whiting and Whiting, 1975:183–84).

At least some of these differences seem to be prompted by children's own actions. Boys may tend to avoid adults because adults usually squelch aggressiveness, at least towards themselves. By avoiding adults, boys may reinforce their propensity for aggressiveness and their own dominance. By staying closer to adults and adult women in particular, girls may develop nurturant skills and minimize aggressive tendencies as they participate more in interactions with an older generation. This may also involve an element of role modeling as the girls try to emulate their mothers' behaviors.

Finally, assignment of responsibilities or social roles also helps explain sex differences in behavior. The Whitings found that in all six cultures girls care for infant siblings more often than boys. Girls, then, are expected to be nurturant. Barry, Bacon, and Child's (1957) large study of sex differences in socialization practices in 110 cultures also found differential role expectations for boys and girls. Pressure toward nurturance, responsibility, and (less clearly) obedience are most often stronger for girls, whereas pressures toward achievement and self-reliance are most often stronger for boys. The Whitings' findings suggest that the sexes do not differ on prosocial behavior that may be similar to acting responsibly but they do differ with respect to nurturance. If one can equate the seeking of dominance and attention with achievement, then boys in the Whitings' study do, in fact, emphasize these behaviors, and perhaps socialization pressures influence this emphasis. On the other hand, these behaviors appear early and do not change with age, suggesting that socialization may not be a major influence.

Clearly, more cross-cultural studies are needed if we are to increase our confidence in our knowledge about sex differences. Most of what we know comes from data collected on middle-class children in the United States and England. But as we shall see, the Whitings' cross-cultural findings on social behaviors parallel quite closely those obtained from the large number of studies done in the United States.

SIMILARITIES AND DIFFERENCES IN TRAITS AND BEHAVIORAL TENDENCIES

To write their *Psychology of Sex Differences,* Maccoby and Jacklin (1974) took on the time-consuming and painstaking task of summarizing, categorizing, and interpreting approximately 1600 studies concerned with psychological sex differences. They report not just some, but insofar as is possible, all of the findings, both those showing differences and those showing no differences between the sexes in a given area. This complete coverage is an extremely important safeguard against the tendency to accept "congenial truths," that is, to examine and note only the findings compatible with one's biases.

Looking at all the studies in an area also helps combat what Maccoby and Jacklin call the "primacy effect" in beliefs about scientific truths. It may take an overwhelming amount of negative evidence, not just a preponderance, to refute an original erroneous impression, especially if it involves an exciting positive finding. For example, a study on thirteen-month-old infants' behavior in the face of an obstacle indicated that while girls tended to cry, boys tended to try to move the barrier or go around it (Goldberg and Lewis, 1969). This was obviously a truth congenial to those with a masculine bias. A number of feminists also tended to accept it and explained the behavior differences in terms of socialization: mothers must have somehow encouraged their daughters in dependency and their sons in active mastery. At any rate, all assumed that findings from this one study settled the matter. Actually, Maccoby and Jacklin found a number of studies that contradict these findings, and they conclude that there is insufficient evidence concerning sex differences in dependency for a clear-cut answer at this time (Maccoby and Jacklin, 1974:181–82). While it is tempting to cite a study in detail and then generalize about the findings, it is clearly better to look at the total array of relevant studies before coming to conclusions.

But this procedure, too, involves some difficulties. In the first place, not all of the studies are equally well designed or even accurate. For example, observations of actual behavior may contradict self-ratings of behavior. Findings of no difference between the sexes are also less often reported than findings of statistically significant sex differences. On the other hand, in studies not specifically dealing with sex differences, a sex difference that appears may not be reported simply because the editor of the journal publishing the research cut the article to its stated essentials to save space. In fact, many of the findings that Maccoby and Jacklin used are accidental or incidental to other scientific concerns.

Frequently the nature of sex differences varies with age. Maccoby and Jacklin wisely restrict their survey to studies of the early childhood years, although they include some data on college students. In general, the younger the child, the less likely differences are to be found. When one studies young adults, one is likely to discover a great many differences in social roles revolving around work, marriage, and child care rather than basic differences in orientation and capacities. If one is interested in understanding sex differences in basic orientations and capacities, it is probably best to observe young children.

Finally, we must remember that when we speak of psychological sex differences, we are never dealing with categorical differences, but with central tendencies. Individuals from each sex group will always overlap considerably, and the within-group differences may be greater than the between-group differences. For instance, the difference between the most aggressive girl and the least aggressive girl in a group may be much larger than the difference between the average aggressiveness of the girls and the average of the boys. Furthermore, the most aggressive girl will probably be more aggressive than a large number of males.

Using Maccoby and Jacklin's categories, but including newer studies as well, we review sex differences and similarities in four major areas: temperament, social approach-avoidance, power relationships, and mental abilities and achievement.

Temperament

Temperament refers to both general activity level and emotionality. Activity level is not a consistent characteristic of individual children from one time to another during the preschool years. Rather, it responds to a number of emotional states and to other people in the environment. Because of this instability, Maccoby and Jacklin believe it inaccurate to describe males as generally more active than females, even though in those studies showing sex differences, the males are usually more active. More important, the studies consistently show no differences in the activity levels of infants and very young children. In spite of the stereotype that male infants are more active, the truth is that given a room full of infants under two years of age, it would be impossible to identify males and females by activity level. The lack of a higher level of male activity at birth has important implications for those who see masculine aggression or adult achievement as resulting from an initial higher activity level.

Although there are no early differences, it is true that studies on older children tend to find boys more active. In a review of a number of studies, including nine that were not included in Maccoby and Jacklin's survey, Jeanne Block (1976) found that males were more active in 41 percent of the studies and females in only 5 percent. It is especially significant that a reliable elicitor of greater activity in boys is the presence of other boys. Greater activity is not elicited in girls by the presence of other girls or by the presence of boys.

While in many situations girls are less active than boys, the findings do not justify calling girls passive. Helene Deutsch (1944) defines female passivity as "activity turned inward," and it would seem that only in this sense could girls be called passive. While boys are running around, girls may be concentrating.

In contrast to the stereotype of women as emotional and easily frustrated, Maccoby and Jacklin conclude that the sexes probably do not differ in the first year of life in the frequency and duration of crying. There is some evidence, however, that boys after the age of about eighteen months have more outbursts of negative emotion in response to frustration. This does not necessarily lead to constructive action and may in some cases impede such action. A little later, it appears that the sex differences in frustration responses are caused not so much by boys increasing the frequency and intensity of their emotional reactions as by girls decreasing theirs at a faster rate than boys. Thus, the sex differences found here contradict the stereotype, with boys displaying more frequent and intense emotional outbursts than girls.

With respect to fear and timidity, teacher ratings and self-reports indicate that girls are more timid and anxious than boys. In contrast, observational studies usually do not show such a difference, especially when young subjects are studied. The self-report and teacher-rating data may simply indicate differences in willingness to admit to certain behavior and sex stereotypes. Since most of the data on fear and timidity come from self-reports and since researchers have used few physiological measures of these responses, Maccoby and Jacklin feel that they can reach no firm conclusions on this subject, and they speculate that the answer may turn out to depend on the particular stimulus situation. Girls may be more afraid of some things and boys more afraid of others.

In summary, these findings indicate that there are sex differences in temperament, yet they do not create a picture of generalized masculine activity, impulsiveness, or bravery. All of these traits are situation specific, and males' activity level particularly may depend on the presence of other males.

Social Approach-Avoidance

Perhaps no stereotype of females is as pervasive as the belief that women are dependent. No one questions that many females are economically dependent on males, but does economic dependence mean psychological dependence? Much of the contemporary work on sex roles assumes that it does, and then argues that women are somehow socialized to be dependent. Maccoby and Jacklin argue, however, that dependency, defined as seeking nurturance, help, or care, does not represent a single identifiable cluster in the social behavior of young children. Rather, there are proximity-seeking behaviors and attention-seeking behaviors, as well as sociable behaviors and social skills. Furthermore, the tendency to direct these behaviors toward adults is relatively independent of the tendency to direct them toward age mates.

Maccoby and Jacklin suggest, then, that dependence may involve proximity-seeking behaviors and a broader category of behaviors that include social responsiveness, social interests, and social skills. They include here also attention-seeking behaviors (which boys engage in more than girls).

Proximity seeking Using both experimental data and some cross-cultural data, Maccoby and Jacklin conclude that there are no firm sex differences in the tendency to seek out contact with others. This conclusion holds whether the objects of attachment are adults or other children.

In five of the six cultures that the Whitings studies describe (Whiting and Whiting, 1975), girls between the ages of three and six were more likely to touch and hold others than boys. Maccoby and Jacklin are aware of these and other cross-cultural findings. They argue, however, that they may simply occur because children are often assigned by their elders to different settings because of their sex. Thus, girls may be assigned roles that keep them nearer the home and, hence, nearer others. Boys' opportunities to seek physical contact may be reduced because they are assigned tasks away from home. In studies of boys and girls in the same settings, sex differences in proximity-seeking do not consistently appear.

Sociability One of the more firmly entrenched ideas about sex differences has been that girls are more social than boys and that boys are more task oriented than girls. For example, Garai and Scheinfeld (1968:270) state that: "In psychological development, from earliest infancy on, males exhibit a greater interest in objects and their manipulation, whereas females show a greater interest in people and a greater capacity for the establishment of interpersonal relations." Maccoby and Jacklin, on the other hand, argue that this broad social-nonsocial distinction does not differentiate the sexes in early infancy or even in later years.

As proximity-seeking behaviors give way to more complex forms of sociability, boys and girls remain very similar in the amount of friendly interaction they have with nonfamily adults. Boys are even more likely than girls to engage in positive interaction with their same-sex peers, but girls (at a somewhat later age) are more likely to report that they "like" the people with whom they interact. The size of groupings the two sexes join also differ, with boys playing in larger groups than girls. But these differences appear to involve patterns of sociability, not sociability itself. Maccoby and Jacklin also find that girls have no greater sensitivity to social cues and are not more "empathetic" than boys. In fact, they suggest that the social judgment skills of males have been "seriously underrated."

Maccoby and Jacklin point out that this conclusion does not contradict an earlier book of Maccoby's (1966), in which she also surveyed the literature on sex differences. Here, she indicated that women and girls showed more interest in social activity, in personal appearance, and attractiveness and became interested in the other sex sooner than boys. She also reported that girls' and women's tastes in books and magazines were "more oriented toward the gentler aspects of interpersonal relations and less toward aggression, 'action' and science than was true for boys" (Maccoby and Jacklin, 1974:214). Maccoby and Jacklin do not now deny these earlier findings but warn about overgeneralizing from them. Their point is that neither sex has greater general social ability or social sensitivity. Both sexes are social and respond to social cues, but the contexts and occasions in which they do so vary in ways that are sex typed.

In this conclusion, Maccoby and Jacklin have made an important conceptual clarification. Their finding that both sexes are equally social but in different contexts can be used to combat a very damaging image of women stemming from the stereotype that males are task oriented and females are people oriented. This dichotomy can suggest that women are motivated externally by a desire to please, are more dependent on social rewards, and lack inner motivation for action. Men, by contrast, sound principled, autonomous, and even immune from social constraints. In fact, neither sex is exempt from the rules governing social interaction, neither sex is free from the effects of social rewards or social punishment, and neither sex is unsocial.

Nurturance While there is much evidence on older children and adults to suggest that women and girls do, in fact, nurture more than men and boys, Maccoby and Jacklin prefer to leave open the question of whether the sexes differ with respect to nurturance. They do so because there are so few studies concerning nurturance behaviors in young children and because evidence indicates that men are nurturant when given the opportunity. While men's nurturing may be impeded by both male hormones and by definitions of proper masculinity, there is every indication that men and boys have the capacity to be nurturant.

It is interesting that those who consider women to be passive usually fail to consider that the nurturance they often also attribute to women has a very active character. As Maccoby and Jacklin suggest in another context, "Training a girl to be 'feminine' in the traditional nonassertive, 'helpless' and self-deprecatory sense may actually make her a worse mother" (1974:373). For, in caring for the child, she has total control over the child's well-being. In fact, dependency needs are likely to be the greatest danger to successful motherhood (Escalona, 1949:34).

Summary From all of the studies relating to the issue of social approach-avoidance, it appears that both sexes are highly sociable and responsive to social cues. The difference does not lie in degree of sociability, but in the specific patterning of the social interactions. One important difference in these patterns is that boys tend to play in larger groups while girls tend to have more intimate friendships in twos or sometimes threes. Maccoby and Jacklin suggest that large groups more often have a dominance hierarchy, while twosomes can easily function on an egalitarian basis. This leads us to a discussion of how males and females differ in power relations, both in same-sex and in cross-sex groupings.

Power Relationships

War has always tended to be the province of men. Both the seizing of territory, possessions, or governments by force and the forceful resistance to such attempts have been male activities. Males also engage in person-to-person combat much more than females do. There is much to suggest that males are naturally aggressive. In this section, we will explore the research evidence on gender differences in aggression, competition, and dominance and try to understand the complex relationships among them.

Aggression Although they are usually concerned with classifying behaviors, not motives, Maccoby and Jacklin define aggression as consisting of both actions and motives whose central theme is the intent to hurt (1974:227). They also speak of aggression as the expression of hostile feelings. Actually, it would be almost impossible to define aggression without taking intent into account. For example, even some very careful behavioral studies employ an operational definition of aggression that is designed to measure intent. Omark, Omark, and Edelman (1973) define aggression as "pushing or hitting without smiling." Not smiling (unless, of course, the push was accidental) would indicate the individual was not kidding and intended to hurt. These researchers have done extensive observations on school playgrounds in the United States, Switzerland, and Ethiopia and find a greater incidence of hitting without smiling among boys in all three countries.

Maccoby and Jacklin believe that the evidence strongly indicates that males are more aggressive than females. While almost everyone is convinced that boys are physically more aggressive than girls, some argue that girls are more verbally aggressive than boys and that while boys aggress directly, girls aggress indirectly. According to this hypothesis, the two sexes are equally aggressive in their underlying motivation, but characteristically show aggression in different ways. Although some studies do indicate that boys are more likely to aggress physically than verbally, there is also evidence that verbal aggression is not so much an alternative to physical aggression as it is a prelude to it. Anyone who has heard boys shouting insults to one another before the fists start flying can attest to this possibility. Even the studies that treat girls' propensity for "tattling" and "excluding" as evidence for aggression do not provide clear-cut evidence that girls make up for more overt aggression by these means. For example, in a study (Feshback, 1969) often cited in support of the hypothesis that girls and boys express aggression in different modes, girls in two-person groups tended to ignore, avoid, and exclude a third person initially more than boys. However, this behavior only lasted for about four minutes before the girls warmed up. Maccoby and Jacklin also question whether it is legitimate to call initial lack of acceptance of a newcomer aggression in the sense of intent to hurt, especially since girls usually play in two-person groups and boys do not.

It is true that girls have more anxiety about aggression than boys. Some have interpreted this to mean that girls have aggressive tendencies equal to those of boys, but repress them out of fear of punishment or retaliation. Maccoby and Jacklin suggest, however, that if this were so, surely the aggression would come out in some attenuated form. What actually happens, though, is that boys act out aggressive impulses in play as well as in reality. In addition, boys are more likely than girls to aggress in the presence of weakness in another male. Girls do not respond to weakness in either boys or girls with aggression. Surely, if girls were repressing great amounts of aggression, they would take it out in a disguised form or on a nonthreatening person. But they do not. In summary, then, Maccoby and Jacklin argue that males really are more aggressive than females—both physically and verbally, directly and indirectly, and in a wide variety of settings.

A review of the experimental literature on aggression (Frodi, Macaulay, and Thome, 1977) argues that women may act as aggressively as men under certain experimental conditions. These conditions involve a situation where the women do not emphathize with the victim and in which they feel the aggression is justified. One such justification that cannot be very well tested on humans is a threat to their offspring. It is possible that we rarely see aggresion in human females simply because they are rarely faced with a direct threat to their children. On the other hand, of all the traits discussed, aggressiveness does appear to be most clearly a generalized trait that characterizes males far more than females and that probably has a biological base. (See also the animal studies discussed in Chapter 6.)

To say that aggression is biologically based, however, does not explain its social patterning—how it appears in social roles—nor does it in itself explain the greater prestige given to males. It is important that readers be aware of their own biases regarding the value of aggressiveness. In a society governed by a masculine paradigm, aggression is likely to have desirable connotations. In the public mind, it is often associated with competitiveness, single-mindedness, or strong will. Steven Goldberg, in his *The Inevitability of Patriarchy,* uses the assessment that males are more aggressive than females to construct a theory to explain the universality of male dominance. Goldberg argues in effect that because of their innate aggressiveness, males "try harder." Goldberg argues that feminists agree with him that aggressiveness explains male dominance and says that the only difference between him and feminists is that the latter claim that masculine aggressiveness is learned and not innate and that, therefore, women could learn it too (1974:263). Some feminists might take this position, but they are operating within a male paradigm that sees aggression as a desirable characteristic. In contrast, Maccoby and Jacklin do not define aggression as a positive trait and argue that it is as likely to interfere with constructive activity as it is to underlie it. Their definition of aggression as the intent to hurt emphasizes its antisocial nature.

Competition The evidence regarding sex differences in competitiveness is not as clear-cut as the evidence on masculine aggressiveness. Maccoby and Jacklin note that almost all the research on competition has involved situations contrived to make competitiveness maladaptive to eventual success. For example, research using the prisoner's dilemma game for measuring cooperation has not consistently shown males to be more competitive. It is likely that if studies were designed so that competitiveness led to individual success or dominance, males would more clearly show up as more competitive than females. While masculine aggression may reinforce greater masculine competitiveness, this does not mean that females are born to lose because they are less motivated to compete. Rather, it seems that while constructive behaviors among males may be motivated by aggressive competitive motives, constructive behaviors among females may have different underlying motives. As we shall see in a later section, boys' achievement efforts and imagery in many spheres are enhanced in a competitive situation while girls' are not. Girls are motivated to achieve, but not necessarily by competitive or aggressive motives.

Dominance As in other areas, the findings concerning sex differences in dominance behaviors depend in part on how one defines the concept of dominance. If toughness (giving out and taking physical abuse) is the criterion, then boys win hands down. Although there is some overlap, boys are considered tougher than girls as early as nursery school age. On the other hand, if dominance is defined broadly enough to include moral leadership, behavior that is in fact controlling, or behavior in which one resists the control of others, then women too may dominate others. Maccoby and Jacklin use this broader definition.

While young boys often use direct aggression in their dominance attempts, they do so less and less as they grow older. The status hierarchy in human societies seldom reflects prowess in physical aggression. Nowadays it is brains not brawn that is rewarded, and there remains only a symbolic connection between fighting and success. Raw aggression is more of an impediment than a help to making it in the higher circles of power. Thus, if aggressive and dominance needs motivate adult males to work and achieve, these needs must undergo considerable socializing in the life history of the individual.

As with aggression, dominance struggles tend to occur between males, not between males and females. In childhood, the sexes tend to play in segregated groups, thus preventing direct confrontation. In the adult occupational world, much the same thing seems to happen. Occupational segregation prevents direct competition between males and females and indirectly between husbands and wives. To say that girls do not seek dominance, however, is not to say that girls are submissive or have a need to comply. Maccoby and Jacklin find little evidence that girls are generally submissive or compliant. What they do find is that "girls conform more readily than boys to directives from parents" (1974:272). The other side of this point is, however, that boys may conform more readily than girls to peer group norms.

Like aggression, the term *dominance* tends to have a positive meaning in a society controlled by a masculine paradigm. Such a paradigm defines the issue as "dominate or be dominated." A feminine paradigm, on the other hand, might deny the necessity for either dominance or submission. Resistance to domination would be desirable, but not domination itself. Maccoby and Jacklin's conclusions regarding sex differences in this area tend to confirm this view.

Mental Abilities and Achievement

There are no differences in measured intelligence between boys and girls, in part because test items that differentiate between males and females are discarded in establishing norms for these intelligence tests. There are some sex differences in special academic skills, and girls generally receive better grades than boys. As we have seen, this appears in the early years of school, continues through junior high and high school, and still appears in college. On the other hand, as earlier chapters also showed, men are more often found in the prestigious and lucrative occupations and are more likely to obtain graduate and professional degrees than women. It would be easy to assume that women's failure to attain these positions is related to deficiencies in their mental capacities, but this is not supported by the evidence.

Analytic ability Analytic ability involves the ability to break a problem down into its component parts in order to reach a solution. It requires a capacity to restructure and to inhibit a previously established set toward a problem. While there may be other ways to solve a problem than through analytic ability and there may be kinds of problems that do not lend themselves to solution through analytic ability, in modern Western society analytic ability is highly valued and is ordinarily thought to be more characteristic of males than of females.

Actually, the question of sex differences in such abilities cannot be answered with a simple yes or no since different kinds of tests measure what appear to be different facets of this ability. We do know with considerable certainty that at a very general level it is not true that girls are better at rote learning and simple repetitive tasks and that boys are better at tasks requiring higher-level cognitive processes and inhibition of previously learned responses (Maccoby and Jacklin, 1974:350). We also know that while men are better than women at tests measuring visual-spatial ability, such as the Rod and Frame Test and the Embedded Figures Test, these are not tests of any general ability to think analytically, but measures of a much more specific perceptual skill.

A better measure of analytic ability are tests that measure the ability to break set or restructure. Males are rather clearly better than females on such tests when they involve set breaking in a quantitative context. On the other hand, Maccoby and Jacklin argue that females may be slightly more adept than males at set breaking in a verbal context where the task is to recombine letters to make words, as in anagrams. Block (1976) argues, however, that anagram studies are not true measures of insight since the subjects are explicitly instructed to make as many words as possible from the letters while in the other insight tests, subjects are not explicitly instructed on how to proceed, and thus must arrive on their own at the insight that restructuring is needed.

While Block is technically correct that the test instructions are different in anagrams than in other insight tests, Maccoby and Jacklin are correct in arguing that there may be different kinds of insight and that all kinds need to be considered before coming to the conclusion that males are better at set breaking in general. To make this point, they used anagram tests that involve set breaking to make words. The results show that women often do better than men in these tests. It would also seem important to construct tests of analytic ability that involve socioemotional or human relational problems. So far, this has not been done.

Verbal and mathematical ability Maccoby and Jacklin conclude that boys excel in mathematical ability and girls have greater verbal ability. Although these differences become most apparent in later years, in this country girls' better reading skills usually appear by the first grade (Gates, 1961). While boys and girls with equal scores on reading readiness tests appear to achieve equally well in reading in the first grade (Balow, 1963), more girls than boys seem to be ready to read and boys do not quickly catch up with girls in this area.

Females' greater verbal fluency begins to appear strongly at about age ten or eleven and continues through high school and college. Sex differences are most apparent in measures of specific skills. These include spelling and punctuation, but also high level skills such as "comprehension of complex written text, quick understanding of complex logical relations expressed in verbal terms, and in some instances, verbal creativity" (Maccoby and Jacklin, 1974:84). There is some evidence that girls' greater verbal skills may help explain their higher grades, even in traditionally male areas such as the sciences (Goldman and Hewitt, 1976:53).

Although generally these verbal differences become more pronounced at adolescence, there is some evidence that sex differences in favor of girls are more common in younger children (between age three and adolescence) in disadvantaged populations than in advantaged groups. Maccoby and Jacklin (1974:84–85) suggest that this could result from the fact that boys are much more susceptible than girls to the hazards of pre- and postnatal poor nutrition.

Sex differences in quantitative ability also appear most strongly after puberty. Girls learn to count sooner than boys do, yet during the early school years, boys and girls generally score equally on tests of arithmetical computation (Maccoby, 1966:26). Differences begin to appear around adolescence, when boys start to do better in mathematics achievement tests, although girls continue to receive better grades. Boys also begin to show more interest and better performance in science areas at adolescence. Females' generally better performance in verbal areas and males' superior performance in math and science continue into college and adult occupational lives as males and females major in different academic areas and enter different occupational fields.

Several explanations for these sex differences are possible. Three of these involve characteristics of students: Boys and girls may have different achievement patterns because they take different courses, because they have different skills, or because they have different interests including an interest generated by the sex typing of an area as masculine or feminine.

A large data base was used to test the hypothesis that boys have higher math achievement scores because they take more math courses than girls do. This hypothesis was not supported. Boys and girls who had taken the same number of math courses showed the same sex differential in test scores found in the total sample (Maccoby and Jacklin, 1974:85–91).

It is possible that boys' greater math ability is related to their greater visual-spatial ability. The sex differences in math scores appear in adolescence at about the same time that sex differences in visual-spatial ability first appear. Moreover, a study of scores on physics achievement tests given to a large sample of high-school students showed that "on the portions of the test calling for visual-spatial skills, the male physics students did better; on verbal test items, female physics students obtained higher scores" (Maccoby and Jacklin, 1974:89–91).

While there is some evidence that spatial-visual ability may be inherited in a sex-linked pattern, this does not appear to hold for verbal ability. Studies, including those of twins separated at birth, show that verbal ability has significant heritability. This means that at least part of people's verbal ability can be traced to the verbal ability of their ancestors. However, there does not appear to be any sex linkage in the inheritability of verbal traits. Thus, while sex differences in mathematics achievement may be at least partially explained by inherited skill related traits, this may not account for the sex differences in verbal ability (Maccoby and Jacklin, 1974:120–21). Nevertheless, there is increasing evidence that females' superior verbal ability may have a biological base. One of the most promising theories involves sex differences in functioning of the brain hemispheres (Goleman, 1978).

A number of studies indicate that students' attitudes and interests may affect their academic achievement. This association is apparently stronger for boys than for girls. Generally, children tend to see school and school related objects as feminine. Some parts of school, however, are more masculine than others, and evidence exists that it is in these more masculine areas that boys choose to pursue and excel. Studies indicate that boys' and girls' perceptions of certain academic areas as feminine and others as masculine coincide with growing differences in math and science skills. A study of second, sixth, and twelfth graders in New York public schools found that their perceptions of artistic, social, and reading skills as feminine and spatial, mechanical, and arithmetic skills as masculine became more defined as the students got older (Stein and Smithells, 1969). Another study (Hilton and Berglund, 1973) found that the changes in students' mathematics achievement from the fifth through the eleventh grades paralleled the changes in interest. The boys became more interested in mathematics at the same time that they saw it as helpful in their future occupational lives, and they became more proficient than the girls as shown by achievement scores.

Importantly enough, it appears to be the sex-typed definition of a subject area that most influences academic achievement. Dwyer (1974), in a study of second through twelfth graders, found that children's perceptions of areas as appropriate for their own sex group influenced their achievement more than how much they liked the subject or even whether they were male or female. The impact of perceived sex typing was much stronger for boys than for girls, and boys were more likely than girls to label an area as appropriate for only one sex group. Moreover, boys are more likely to pursue math if their *fathers* define it as a masculine activity (Hill, 1967).

In general, then, it is not clear that the amount of course work influences sex differences in mathematics achievement. While inherited skills may influence sex differences in mathematics achievement, it appears that students' interests in general subject areas, in particular curricular materials, and, most important, their perceptions of areas as either masculine or feminine influence achievement in both verbal and mathematical areas. In sum, then, while there may be some biological basis for the sex differences in verbal and mathematical performance, these areas are also clearly influenced by social interest and sex-typed expectations.

Adult achievement None of these findings concerning sex differences in abilities, however, can directly account for the fact that, in comparison to women, adult men hold the prestigious jobs and make achievements that are recognized and rewarded. A number of researchers have explored the possibility that women are not psychologically motivated to achieve, that they have less achievement motivation than men do. While the original works tended to focus on psychological motivations underlying achievements, later reinterpretations have used social role analyses.

The classic work in this field was done over twenty years ago by David McClelland and his colleagues (1953). Most of their work was with men, but a few of their studies did include women. They tried to measure achievement motivation with a projective test by showing subjects a picture, asking them to tell a story about it, and then counting the number of achievement related themes in the story. Sometimes, the picture was shown under an arousal situation supposedly designed to make the subjects want to achieve even more. Usually, the arousal situation involved tasks that the subjects were told would measure their leadership potential. Usually, boys were shown pictures of boys and under the arousal situation (but not the normal situation) would show high achievement motivation. Girls were usually shown pictures with girls and gave fewer achievement related themes in their responses in both conditions. Based on these results, McClelland and his associates concluded that girls have a lower achievement motive than boys.

Other researchers have expanded on McClelland's work and tried to modify the rather harsh conclusion that women are not motivated to achieve. Veroff (1977) suggests that males tend to emphasize the "impact" of their achievements including what they accomplished and how they compared it to the work of others, while females emphasize the process of achievement including whether they accomplish a task alone and try as hard as they can. From empirical studies, Veroff and associates (1975) concluded that women may be less likely to structure a situation in terms of achievement, but that once they are in an achievement setting, they are more likely than men to anticipate success. Similarly, Lois Hoffman (1972) suggests that females tend to achieve to attain social approval, while males are motivated to strive for excellence in achievement apart from approval.*

These results are based mainly on studies that showed only pictures of girls to girls and only pictures of boys to boys. A more complete research design finds that when shown pictures of males, both girls and boys show a high level of achievement imagery. In this case, females' level of achievment imagery is high whether or not it is an arousal situation; males seem to require an arousal situation to show a high level of achievement imagery. Neither females nor males show as high a level of achievement imagery when shown pictures of females (Maccoby and Jacklin, 1974:138).

*This is another version of the social/nonsocial distinction which Maccoby and Jacklin criticize.

That an individual's measure of achievement motivation may vary with different stimuli suggests that achievement themes reflect not as much an inherent psychological motive to achieve as much as an understanding of actual social roles. Because achievement, as it is usually defined, is a male area, both males and females give a larger number of achievement related themes in stories regarding males than in stories regarding females.

It is also possible that, instead of females not achieving or even tending to achieve to gain social approval as Hoffman suggests, females see the successful use of social skills as achievement in and of itself. The traditional area for women's achievement involves interpersonal sensitivity and responsibility. Studies do show that women, but not men, increase their achievement (not affiliation) imagery with arousal treatments that stressed social acceptability and skill. This is especially true for women who value women's traditional roles. Also females are more responsive than males to social approval when the task is nonsocial (Stein and Bailey, 1975:152–53). It may well be, then, that females express achievement motivation in activities that are culturally defined as feminine. They attempt to resolve the conflict between achievement desires and prescriptions for the feminine role by transferring achievement to a feminine context (Stein and Bailey, 1975:153). In the same way that we suggested in chapter 1 that women respond to male expectations of role segregation and devaluation, women may deal with conflicts regarding achievement by staying only within traditional female areas or redefining an achievement activity as feminine (cf. Stein and Bailey, 1975:153–55).

Another attempt to explain women's apparent lack of achievement is what Matina Horner calls "the motive to avoid success" (Horner, 1968, 1970, 1972). Building on the earlier work of McClelland and his associates and hoping to clarify earlier findings regarding sex differences in achievement motivation, Horner devised a technique to tap women's conflicts regarding success. She hypothesized that because women "expect negative consequences (such as social rejection and/or feelings of being unfeminine) as a result of succeeding" they may expect more negative consequences from success than men would (Horner, 1972:159). To test this she asked subjects to write stories about members of their own sex who were described as being successful in the traditionally male area of medical school. She then used the number of unpleasant themes in these stories as a measure of the subject's motive to avoid success. As she expected, the females in the study showed much more of this motive to avoid success than the males did. Somewhat paradoxically, the women who were high in the motive to avoid success tended to perform better on a task designed to measure actual achievement in a noncompetitive setting than in a large, mixed-sex competitive setting.

Since Horner's original work, many people have continued to explore the motive to avoid success hypothesis in both males and females and with many different story cues than in the original studies. David Tresemer (1977) reviewed these studies and concluded that in general females do not show a higher motive to avoid success than males do. While a number of studies have also examined the association of imagery indicating a motive to avoid success with actual behavior, Tresemer concluded that the results were not consistent enough to support firm conclusions.

Horner's original work focused on psychological motives. Other researchers have reinterpreted the studies in this area using a social role analysis in a way that helps to make at least some of the conflicting results more understandable. In her original work, Horner repeated the practice in McClelland's early studies of having respondents tell stories only about people of their own sex. Condry and Dyer (1976) note that later studies show that *both* males and females tend to give more negative responses to stimuli regarding women and fewer negative responses to stimuli regarding men. They suggest that what Horner and others interpret as a psychological motive to avoid success may actually be realistic interpretations of the experiences women may have in settings that are generally defined as masculine. Both males and females may realize that by violating traditional sex role expectations, females may face negative reactions. In support of this interpretation, detailed analyses of the fear of success stories written by males and females show that males tended to write stories with negative consequences stemming from achievement because they tended to question the value of success itself. In contrast, females' stories regarding negative consequences especially involved expectations of negative sanctions from other people (Hoffman, 1974, 1975; see also Schnitzer, 1977). While men receive positive sanctions for achievement, women are often socially punished for it and are called pushy and unfeminine. This reflects the even more basic fact that adult social roles are structured so that a wife gains in prestige from her husband's achievement while her own achievement is likely to be considered a threat to him.

In 1966, Maccoby suggested that girls' lesser achievement might result from their greater dependency. In the 1974 book, Maccoby changes her position since she did not find girls to be either more dependent or more approval seeking than boys. Ultimately, then, the explanation for the relative absence of women in prestigious adult roles does not lie in dependency or lack of motivation for high attainment, but in the masculine definition of what constitutes high attainment and in definitions of appropriate sex roles which support occupational achievement for men and work against it for women. (See also chapter 11.)

Summary and Conclusions

Psychological studies generally show few sex differences, especially among young children, in psychological traits and behavioral tendencies.

With regard to temperament, although many studies show males to be more active, males cannot be described as generally more active across all situations than females. Certainly females cannot be called passive. The findings also cast doubt on the idea that girls are more emotional than boys. No differences in either activity level or emotionality are found in infants.

Studies relevant to social approach and avoidance yield no clear-cut sex differences. The bulk of evidence indicates that the two sexes are remarkably similar in dependency by almost any definition: attachment, affiliation, sensitivity to and interest in social cues, interpersonal relations, or empathy. Both sexes are highly sociable, and the cliché that boys are task oriented while girls are people oriented is simply false. Evidence on male-female differences in nurturing behavior is too scanty for firm conclusions, but new evidence suggests that, if given an opportunity, males can nurture almost as well as females.

In contrast, with respect to power, Maccoby and Jacklin find males consistently more aggressive than females—both physically and verbally, directly and indirectly, and in a wide variety of settings. They suggest that this aggressiveness, defined as the intent to hurt another, is rooted in biology but is socially patterned. While males may not be more dominant than females in all ways, boys clearly make more overt and direct attempts to dominate others than girls.

With regard to intellect and achievement, there is no evidence that males have more general analytic ability than females, although males do have greater spatial ability and are better at most nonverbal insight problems. Although the sexes do not differ in how they learn generally, girls excel verbally and boys excel mathematically. The causes of these differences are by no means clear, and both biological and social factors may be involved. Sex differences in adult achievement patterns cannot be explained directly by differences in talents and capacities or motivation, but must be explained in terms of differing adult social role expectations.

Some professionals disagree with Maccoby and Jacklin's conclusions. Jeanne Block (1976), a specialist in the psychology of sex differences, feels that Maccoby and Jacklin underestimate and minimize the number and extent of sex differences. As she points out, Maccoby and Jacklin's findings are not only contrary to stereotypical views, but also contrary to conclusions in previous surveys of the literature on sex differences. For example, most earlier surveys concluded that females were more social than males. (For these reviews, see Terman and Tyler, 1954; Tyler 1965; and Maccoby, 1966.)

As we have indicated, Maccoby and Jacklin reached these conclusions of fewer differences mainly by reconceptualizing some of the key dimensions they used to interpret the available data. For example, they concluded that both males and females are equally social by defining sociability broadly. This is correct because it makes clear that both males and females are equally responsive to social sanctions, even though women may have more social interests in the narrow sense. In a number of other instances, they report no differences or inconclusive evidence because they interpret categories such as activity and dominance very broadly. The general picture they build up by this reconceptualization is that, with the clear exception of aggression, a socially undesirable trait, both males and females share basic human capacities and propensities. This emphasis seems generally useful and can act as a salutary antidote to the earlier masculine bias in studies of sex differences.

MEASURING MASCULINITY, FEMININITY, AND ANDROGYNY

Sometimes researchers try to measure individual differences in psychological traits considered characteristic of males and females. They have devised so-called M-F tests to rank individuals in terms of the degree of their masculinity or femininity. These tests are constructed empirically rather than theoretically; that is, by choosing the test items on the basis of whether they actually do differentiate between males and females, regardless of why they might do so. For example, Gough's Femininity Scale (Gough, 1952), a widely used M-F test on the California Personality Inventory, is an empirical scale of fifty-eight items chosen because women typically answer the items differently than men. The items were selected from batteries of other test questions that were not originally intended to measure masculinity-femininity, but these items did tend to differentiate the sexes. An individual's score on the test is based on the number of items answered in the manner most typical of women. The following three items are illustrative:

"I become quite irritated when I see someone spit on the sidewalk."
"I always like to keep my things neat and tidy and in good order."
"I like to go to parties and other affairs where there is lots of loud fun."

Women tend to answer yes to the first and second items and no to the third. Although the feminine answers to these may seem obvious once they are pointed out, it is doubtful if anyone would have made up these items in an effort to tap masculinity-femininity. Even within a given item, it is difficult to know what element makes it feminine. For instance, the word *tidy* in item two is a word that men tend to avoid. Perhaps simply the presence of this word, rather than a lack of neatness among men, accounts for their answering no.

Other well-known M-F tests besides Gough's include: Terman and

Miles's Attitude-Interest Analysis Test, a 1936 test that set the pattern for subsequent tests; Strong's M-F scale of the Vocational Interest Blank; the M-F scale of the Minnesota Multiphasic Personality Inventory (MMPI); and the Guilford Masculinity Scale built on a factor-analytic technique. Another frequently used test is the Franck and Rosen Drawing Completion Test. In contrast to the other tests, this projective test purports to measure unconscious masculinity-femininity. It was also developed by empirical methods, by assessing how the drawings of most men and most women differ. Finally, there is the IT Scale for Children. This is a sex role preference test, but it is often used as if it measures psychological masculinity-femininity.

Criticisms of M-F Tests

Although M-F tests do to some extent differentiate between men and women and some tests even do so cross-culturally, it is hard to interpret the meaning of an individual's score. In the first place, to the extent that M-F tests are based on sex role stereotypes, it is possible for individuals to fake their answers or to simply fall into stereotypic responses. To complicate matters, only some items are based on stereotypes. Nichols (1962) analyzed items drawn from M-F tests and concluded they are of three types: subtle items that do differentiate between the sexes, obvious items that differentiate, and stereotypical items that in fact do not differentiate. All of this complicates enormously the meaning of the scores obtained.

Another questionable aspect of M-F measures is that the scores vary by the social class, education, geographic location, and age of the subjects. For example, more highly educated males score more feminine than less highly educated ones, while more highly educated females score more masculine than less educated women. This systematic variation certainly calls into question the assumption that the tests are measuring some stable personality trait.

A more important problem with M-F tests, however, is that they imply that masculinity-femininity is a single bipolar dimension and that an individual can be ranked on this dimension in terms of a single score. In fact, considerable evidence suggests that on all of the M-F tests, more than a single dimension is involved. Thus, for example, both high-school boys and adult engineers may receive a rather high masculinity score, but the test items that cause these high scores are different for the two groups (Lewis, 1968:69–71). In addition to the different dimensions within each test, the tests themselves do not all measure the same dimensions (Constantinople, 1973).

Another criticism of M-F tests is that they tend to distract us from the more important fact that the traits and interests making up masculinity-femininity constitute a relatively small proportion of all personality traits and interests. Furthermore, there is some evidence that the personality traits that do differentiate the sexes are on the average relatively secondary (Pleck, 1975:165). Finally, attempts to measure masculinity-femininity imply that somehow it is "good" to be high in the characteristics of one's own sex group. Sandra Bem (1974) challenges this assumption explicitly.

Bem's Androgyny Scale

Bem (1974) devised a test to measure the degree to which an individual is both masculine and feminine, that is, androgynous. The Bem Sex-Role Inventory (BSRI) treats masculinity and femininity as two unrelated dimensions rather than as two ends of a single dimension. The test consists of a list of twenty stereotypically masculine characteristics (e.g., "independent," "assertive"), twenty stereotypically feminine characteristics (e.g., "childlike," "tender"), and twenty neutral characteristics (e.g., "happy," "sincere"). The items used to measure masculinity and femininity do not correlate with each other negatively or positively. Subjects are asked to indicate on a seven-point scale how well each characteristic describes themselves. A person who has the masculine items to a high degree and the feminine items to a low degree would be said to have a masculine sex role. A person who has the feminine traits to a high degree and the masculine traits to a low degree would have a feminine sex role. A person who scores high in both stereotypically masculine and stereotypically feminine traits is considered androgynous (Bem et al., 1976).

Bem's can hardly be called a subtle test since the items she uses are blatant stereotypes, but it does provide a simple and understandable argument against the bipolar assumption of most M-F tests. It also attacks the implication in the bipolar assumption that women should be feminine and men should be masculine. In research using the scores on this test, Bem shows that androgynous people are more likely to respond appropriately to a greater variety of situations than people who rate themselves as stereotypically masculine or stereotypically feminine (Bem, 1975). Combining the results of two separate experiments, she found that while nonandrogynous males did well only when the behavior was congruent with their self-definition as either masculine or feminine, the androgynous male does well in both the feminine domain and the masculine domain. Matters were a bit more complex with the females. Bem found that feminine women by her measure were so passive that they were competent in neither sphere while both masculine and androgynous women engaged in both masculine and feminine behavior. Findings using Bem's scale are difficult to interpret, however, since the measures of masculinity and femininity used in the scale are based on stereotypes that describe the actual characteristics of men and women with at least partial inaccuracy.*

QUALITATIVE DESCRIPTIONS OF MASCULINITY AND FEMININITY

Efforts such as Maccoby and Jacklin's to assess systematically sex differences in traits and tendencies do not consider possible sex differences in patterns of relationship between traits. Many of the studies Maccoby and Jacklin report as showing no sex differences in a certain behavior have actually found striking sex differences in the pattern of relationships between a certain trait and other personality variables (Block, 1976). For example, a study might conclude that there are no differences between the sexes in helping responses but might also find that helping behavior correlates positively with several other variables in boys and correlates negatively with those same variables in girls. Indeed, the differences in the linkages between traits in the personalities of males and females may be more important than the differences in average scores (Tyler, 1965:264).

Some scholars have sought to understand these sex differences in patterns and linkages of traits by using qualitative typologies that delineate broad differences in orientation between the sexes. By using broad, qualitative descriptions, they hope to capture the principle of organization by which specific traits may be patterned within each sex. Some hope that the qualitative approach may help us see femininity in a more positive way and overcome the tendency for researchers to study males more than they study females (Carlson, 1971). This final section reviews some of the theories that attempt to delineate the essence of masculinity and femininity including our own argument for the instrumental-expressive distinction.

Transcendence and Immanence

Well over a quarter century ago, Simone de Beauvoir (1953) sensitively discussed a distinction between masculine and feminine orientations that was based on the existential notions of transcendence and immanence. She believed that people attain liberty and meaning in life through exploits and projects, an acting on the world that leads to transcending one's immediate situation. Even though women as human beings are free and autonomous, de Beauvoir explained that they live in a world where men have defined them as objects, as the Other, as a group apart. Because of this, women find

*Garnets and Pleck (1979) suggest that to measure androgyny we also need a measure of the extent to which sex typing ceases to be salient to a person.

it difficult to transcend their situation. Thus, while men's situation is one of transcendence, where they may act on and move beyond their present state, women remain in immanence, a situation of restriction and confinement that they are unable to transcend.

While de Beauvoir recognized how a male dominant society can constrain women's actions, her descriptions of feminine nature are always colored by her dedication to transcendence. She saw this latter as the morally superior stance involving not so much self-interest as self-determination and autonomy. She saw immanence as static and unfree. As a result she tended to define femininity only in relation to masculinity and did not see positive aspects in femininity itself. More recent attempts to theoretically distinguish masculinity and femininity have tried to counter this masculine bias and see positive aspects in their conceptions of both masculinity and femininity.

Allocentric and Autocentric Ego Styles

David Gutmann (1965), a psychoanalytically oriented theorist, directly attacks the masculine bias in the concept ego strength. He argues that the criteria used to assess ego strength, such as impersonality and objectivity, are masculine in nature and irrelevant to women's situation and their ego development in this society. He uses the terms *autocentric* and *allocentric* to describe feminine and masculine ego styles. For Gutmann, the allocentric masculine ego tends to objectify others and to experience its own separateness from others. With the autocentric feminine ego, the distinctions between self and others and self and environment are blurred, and thus, ego boundaries are more permeable. For example, males characteristically approach the Thematic Apperception Test (TAT cards depict ambiguous figures and situations about which the subject must tell a story) by distancing themselves from the cards and making it very clear that they are imagining the story, using the pictures as cues. Women seem to experience the pictures they see in the cards as real events and get into their stories more than the men.

Gutmann also suggests that the autocentric (feminine) and allocentric (masculine) ego states differ in their perceptions of space and time, constancy and change, self and others. An empirical test of this formulation that analyzed the words, approaches, and constructs used by college students in written exercises supported Gutmann's theory. The researcher found that "males represent experiences of self, other, space, and time in individualistic, objective, and distant ways, while females represent experiences in relatively interpersonal, subjective, immediate ways in responding to a range of common tasks" (Carlson, 1971:270–71).

Gutmann suggests that these differences may arise because the sexes grow up in different "maturational milieux," or environments. For instance, he argues (1970) that some middle-class male youths have feminine egos that alienate them from the competitive struggles of the business world. These feminine egos developed from very strong ties to autocentric mothers. While Gutmann himself believes that this may be maladaptive for our society, these more feminine egos in middle-class males may actually presage a change toward more androgynous sex roles in our society.

Agency and Communion

Although Gutmann's formulation helps portray differing qualities of masculine and feminine ego functioning, it does not allow for both masculine and feminine qualities in one individual (Carlson, 1971:271). David Bakan's (1966) more generalized concepts of agency and communion offer this possibility. Bakan saw these concepts as dynamic principles interacting with each other. The terms are defined at a very high level of abstraction (1966:15) and characterize

> two fundamental modalities in the existence of living forms, agency for the existence of an organism as an individual, and communion for the participation of the individual in some larger organism of which the individual is a part. . . . Agency manifests itself in the formation of separations: communion in the lack of separations. Agency manifests itself in isolation, alienation and aloneness; communion in contact, openness, and union. Agency manifests itself in the urge to master; communion in noncontractual cooperation.

Bakan believes that both agency and communion are necessary qualities within any organism. If societies or individuals are to be viable, agency must be combined with communion.

Jeanne Block (1973) uses Bakan's agency and communion to describe sex role changes over the life cycle precisely because it allows for one principle to be tempered with the other. In Block's view, the earliest stage of development for children of both sexes is unmitigated agency. At this impulse-ridden and self-protective level, children are concerned with "self-assertion, self-expression, and self-extension." In a slightly later stage of development when sex roles diverge, communion is emphasized for girls and discouraged for boys. At the adult level, as their emotional maturity increases, both sexes may eventually arrive at an integration of both orientations, although males will specialize in agency and females in communion. Empirical work supports the thesis that males express slightly more agentic themes than females in reporting significant emotional experiences. Moreover, females have been found to have both agentic and communal orientations more often than males (Carlson, 1971).

Bakan's distinction is important in defining overall orientations, yet it can also be confusing. The concepts involved are so global and all-inclusive that their specific meaning is difficult to pin down. For example, the term *agentic* describes highly disciplined, self-oriented striving in the occupational world as well as the impulse-ridden self-assertion and self-extension of the infant. Such a remarkable equation may more confuse than clarify.

Instrumental and Expressive Orientations

A less global formulation that also allows for both masculine and feminine orientations in the personality and does not denigrate women is Talcott Parsons's instrumental-expressive distinction. The instrumental-expressive distinction is not a single dimension. Rather, it refers to two aspects of behavior, both distinctly social, each with a positive and negative pole. Drawing on distinctions running throughout several of Parsons's theoretical works, we (see Johnson et al., 1975) define an action as expressive if it involves an orientation toward the relations among the individuals interacting within a social group. Instrumental action involves an orientation to goals outside the immediate relational system. Instrumental actions are directed toward attaining some product as a means to a desired objective; expressive actions are concerned with the emotional quality of the group, controlling tensions, and motivating other group members. Individuals employ both instrumental and expressive modes of relating and within a given situation may act in both an expressive and an instrumental manner at different points in the interaction.

While both instrumental and expressive actions are socially rewarded and emotionally gratifying, the rewards differ. The rewards for expressive actions are more reciprocal and emotionally direct. For example, someone responds to a friend's support with gratitude and love, and the reward for loving is often being loved in return. The rewards for instrumental action, on the other hand, tend to be impersonal. For example, a student who successfully explains a difficult topic to a seminar is probably rewarded with respect and approval by the instructor, symbolized by a high grade. Both rewards for instrumental and for expressive behavior might be socially and emotionally meaningful to the recipient. Thus, the instrumental and expressive distinction is not between nonsocial and social behavior or between nonemotionality and emotionality. Instead, it involves distinctions in role behavior and goals of action.

Both instrumental and expressive actions are necessary for social systems to function, and both kinds of orientations are present in both sexes. Instrumental actions relate individuals and groups to the wider environment; expressive actions relate individual units within a group.

Many feminists and social scientists have avoided attributing expressiveness to women for fear that it will be used as a scientific justification for keeping women in the home and implying that they are emotional, incompetent, and dependent. However, these characteristics are not inherent in the definition of expressiveness, and a derogatory view of women need not result from use of the term. In fact, the distinction can point to the very positive aspects of women's roles and personality organization.

While expressiveness does engage socioemotional skills, it is misleading to view it as simply being emotional. It is true that women are penalized less for expressing emotion than men; indeed, women are even expected to express it on occasion. But more generally, women are expected to understand and deal with emotion, more than simply being subject to it. Women may resonate with, respond to, cope with, and even define emotions for others, but it seems incorrect to equate these acts with being emotional. Men are potentially as emotional as women, but they are discouraged from expressing emotion and from being sensitive to their own or others' emotions on pain of being considered unmasculine (Balswick and Peek, 1971). Expressiveness, then, is an interactive capacity, not a subjective state.

The contention that expressiveness implies lack of instrumental competence results in part from the unnecessary assumption that the instrumental-expressive distinction is a single dimension. This implies that a woman who is a pleasure to be with must be incapable of instrumental competence and the women who is a success in instrumental terms must be an unpleasant person in interpersonal interactions. Actually, the instrumental-expressive distinction is two dimensions, each with a positive and negative pole.

The assumption that women are more passive and dependent than men is so pervasive that it has often been either explicitly or implicitly read into the instrumental-expressive distinction. As we noted earlier, everyone clearly depends on the responses of others; we all ultimately seek social rewards. In this respect, men are no more independent than women. The instrumental-expressive difference lies, then, not in autonomy versus dependence, but in the nature of the rewards sought. Expressive rewards are direct and personal; instrumental rewards are indirect and impersonal. Neither is expressiveness tied to passivity. Expressiveness does not mean doing what others want one to do; it may just as well involve getting others to do what one wants *them* to do.

Empirical studies have demonstrated the usefulness of this conceptualization. For instance, our study using self-ratings of college students found that men and women differed considerably more in their scores on the expressive dimension than they did in their scores on the instrumental dimension. Women saw themselves as more positively expressive (e.g., sweeter and kinder) and less negatively expressive (e.g., quarrelsome and unfriendly) than men saw themselves. On the other hand, women did not see themselves as any more dependent or negatively instrumental (lazy or quitting) than men (Johnson et al., 1975). An earlier analysis of sex differences in self-attribution had similar results, with the researchers reporting that "the major differences in the self-concepts of the sexes is that women conceive of themselves as being much richer in the positive qualities of social warmth and empathy" (Bennett and Cohen, 1959:125). Men defined themselves in terms of not being too warm and empathetic, or, in our terms, of not being too positively expressive.

Empirical evidence also shows that expressive behaviors in females do not correlate with passivity. For instance, a careful observational study of nursery-school children (Fagot, 1978) found that only two of seven categories of behavior were sex typed. Fagot's aggressive masculine category is similar to what we call negative expressiveness. It includes such acts as taking an object, hitting, pushing, shoving, and playing with transportation toys. The other factor is labeled feminine. It includes playing with dolls and dancing, which could be related to expressive behaviors, to the extent that doll play involves behavior similar to nurturance. These feminine behaviors were strongly negatively correlated with passive nontask behaviors. That is, the so-called feminine behaviors were associated with the absence of passivity. Similarly, our study of college students (Johnson et al., 1975) found that women associated positive expressiveness with feelings of independence. The men in the sample, on the other hand, tended to relate independence to both positive instrumental traits and negative expressive traits. The women in the sample, then, incorporated positive expressiveness, positive instrumentalness, and independence in their self-pictures, while the men generally did not include positive expressiveness with independence and instrumentalness. Both Heilbrun (1968) and Brim (1958) also report that positive expressive and positive instrumental traits may be found together in females but not in males. These different patterns of traits in the two sexes support the theory that the development of masculinity involves the rejection of femininity. Males express independence by not being too expressive. It may be that male aggressiveness, especially as Maccoby and Jacklin describe it in younger boys, reinforces negative expressive behavior as boys display hurting rather than helping behavior and disrupting and disobeying behavior rather than integrating tendencies.

Because men reject femininity, women as well as men have sometimes questioned the value of expressiveness. This probably reflects the masculine bias that influences our thinking. Our own view is that expressiveness is a common human orientation that one might hope could be fostered in both sexes. Certainly, the pressure men are under to eschew positive expressiveness in order to prove their masculinity is no reason to devalue it.

Many feminists fear that if women lay claim to expressiveness, it will be used against them in the job market to justify assigning them helping and other low-level jobs. To some extent, these fears have been justified. However, the answer for women is probably not to deny expressiveness in their fight for inclusion, but to insist that an expressive orientation can operate along with instrumental orientations and that expressiveness might, in fact, enrich instrumental activities.

SUMMARY

This chapter has canvassed attempts to specify sex differences in generalized traits and behavioral tendencies, to measure individual differences in masculinity, femininity, and androgyny, and to define sex differences in orientation and in the organization of traits within the personality. There are virtually no sex differences among infants, and the major psychological difference between the sexes that appears to be biologically based is that males are more aggressive than females. However, this greater male aggressiveness by itself cannot explain male dominance or male achievement. It is essentially an antisocial trait that may reinforce males' greater negative expressiveness. A number of theorists discuss orientational differences between the sexes. We argue that the most useful distinction suggests that males see themselves as less expressive than females and tend to relate psychological independence to negative expressiveness. Females, on the other hand, relate expressiveness to independence and instrumentalness. These findings support the theory that the development of masculinity involves the rejection of femininity.

Suggested Readings

ASTIN, HELEN, ALLISON PARELMAN, AND ANNE FISHER, *Sex Roles: A Research Bibliography.* Washington, D.C.: Department of Health, Education, and Welfare Publication Number (ADM) 75–166.

KAPLAN, ALEXANDRA G., AND JOAN P. BEAN, eds., *Beyond Sex-Role Stereotypes: Readings Toward a Psychology of Androgyny.* Boston, Mass.: Little, Brown, 1976. Collection of articles focused on transcending sex differences.

LLOYD, BARBARA, AND JOHN ARCHER, eds., *Exploring Sex Differences.* New York: Academic Press, 1976. Articles on psychological sex differences from various disciplines.

MACCOBY, ELEANOR E., AND CAROL N. JACKLIN, *The Psychology of Sex Differences.* Stanford, Calif.: Stanford University Press, 1974. The most recent comprehensive review of psychological sex differences and similarities.

MEDNICK, MARTHA T. F., SANDRA S. TANGRI, AND LOIS W. HOFFMAN, eds., *Women and Achievement: Social and Motivational Analyses.* New York: Halsted Press, 1975. A collection of articles related to women's achievements in the occupational world and their psychological motivation for achievement.

TRESEMER, DAVID M. *Fear of Success.* New York: Plenum Press, 1977. An analysis of writings regarding the motive to avoid success from a number of years ago to the present.

WHITING, BEATRICE B., AND JOHN W. M. WHITING. *Children of Six Cultures: A Psychocultural Analysis.* Cambridge, Mass.: Harvard University Press, 1975. A summary of systematic research done on sex differences in children from six cultures.

8: Becoming Sex Typed: Theories from Psychology

Even though one can find few sex differences in infants, behavior is clearly sex typed in some respects by the time children reach nursery school age. Boys are more disruptive, and boys and girls play with different toys and engage in different types of activities. By the age of four children's play choices clearly reflect adult activities. Furthermore, boys "starting at about the age of four, become increasingly more sex-typed than girls, in that they are more likely to avoid sex-inappropriate activities, and more likely to accept (prefer) the activities associated with their own sex role" (Maccoby and Jacklin, 1974:284). These differences are present even in nursery schools where the personnel try not to encourage sex typing (Joffe, 1971).

How do these differences come about and why do they persist even in neutral environments? While biological factors may play a part, learning is also involved. But how does this learning occur? Are children rewarded for sex-typed behavior by their parents? Do they learn it by observation and imitation? Or do they find out what sex they are and then figure out how to behave accordingly? These questions roughly represent the three theoretical positions in psychology known as social learning theory, modeling theory, and cognitive developmental theory. We investigate all three in this chapter.

None of these theories was specifically developed to explain sex-typed behavior. Rather, they are general theories about human learning and development that should be applicable to sex-typed behavior as well as other kinds of behavior. Although the differences among them are more than just a matter of emphasis, the three theories do not represent absolutely different perspectives. Social learning theory and modeling theory are particularly close to one another—in fact, modeling theorists usually consider themselves social learning theorists. Furthermore, proponents of both modeling and social learning theory recognize that cognitive understanding (the basis of cognitive developmental theory) is distinctly involved in learning. For its part, cognitive developmental theory recognizes that reinforcement and modeling take place but sees them as secondary to cognitive processes.

We will evaluate each of these theories in terms of their adequacy in explaining sex typed behavior. We use the word *evaluate* advisedly. There is no way that one can actually empirically test a theory. All one can do is examine the evidence for and against certain hypotheses that one might develop on the basis of a particular theory. When a particular hypothesis fails to hold up, one may question the theory itself. Yet frequently the fault does not lie with the underlying theory, but with the particular hypotheses derived from it. The phenomena predicted by the theory may indeed exist, but not exactly in the way specified in a concrete hypothesis. If we fail to see evidence, for example, of reinforcement of sex-typed behaviors, two explanations are possible: Either reinforcement does not adequately account for sex typing (in which case one must look for other explanations), or sex-typed behavior is actually being reinforced, but in a different way than stated by the particular hypothesis.

Beyond assessing the theories in terms of how well each can explain sex typing, we will also be concerned with their adequacy in dealing with the phenomenon of male dominance itself. Each of these theories implies something about why males have greater prestige and power than females.

SOCIAL LEARNING THEORY

Social learning theory originally grew out of stimulus-response theory, or behaviorism. The original idea of behaviorism was that a behavioral repertoire is built into the individual on the basis of the rewards or lack of rewards coming from the external environment. Since rewarded behavior is repeated and nonrewarded behavior is extinguished, behavior is shaped in terms of a schedule of reinforcements. Behaviorists, then, are not primarily concerned with the internal mental states of individuals, in part, because these are subjective and cannot be objectively observed. They are more concerned with the individual as an organism who can be conditioned to behave in a certain way.

Social learning theorists have modified the extreme forms of this behavioristic view considerably and would no longer say that each and every little bit of behavior has to be directly rewarded to be learned. Social learning theorists such as Walter Mischel (1970) and Albert Bandura and R. H. Walters (1963) also recognize that cognitive processes do intervene between stimulus and response and that individuals are capable of generalizing from a specific case to other similar cases. They are also capable of observational learning, such as perceiving what happens to others who display a certain behavior and inferring what the consequences of such an action would be for themselves. They can remember past outcomes and thus predict future outcomes and act accordingly. Thus, while social learning theorists continue to believe that behavior patterns are maintained through reinforcement, they have moved away from the view that cognitive processes are irrelevant.

Social learning theorists also believe that the reinforcements that maintain behavior patterns are primarily social, and many of them share with psychoanalytic theory a belief in the importance of early childhood experience. Because of its dependency, the infant is especially sensitive to the mother's reactions. As the primary nurturer, she becomes an important shaper of the infant's behavior.

There is considerable variety in the reinforcement variables examined by social learning theorists. Investigations of naturalistic antecedents or causes of sex typing have tended to involve very general parental variables such as permissiveness, affection, and punitiveness. Researchers who study behavior in the laboratory usually examine more concrete reinforcement contingencies. Regardless of the level of abstraction at which they study reinforcement, though, social learning theorists assume that the sexes are treated differently by parents and other socializing agents and that this differential treatment produces or maintains sex-typed characteristics.

Differential Reinforcement by Parents

Maccoby and Jacklin (1974) summarize findings about parental behavior toward boys and girls. Using the same procedure as in their analysis of sex differences, they list all the studies relevant to a particular kind of parental behavior and base their conclusions on the findings of a majority of the studies. The general picture given by Maccoby and Jacklin is that parents (remembering that we have much more data on mothers than on fathers) do not treat the sexes very differently when they are young in terms of such broad areas as amount and type of interaction, affection, automony granting, and responses to dependency and aggression.

This seems to be true even though parents have sex-stereotyped *expectations* concerning even infants' behavior. For example, studies suggest that people attribute different emotions to infants depending on whether they think the child is a boy or a girl. In an ambiguous experimental situation, an infant crying, the boy was seen as angry and the girl as afraid and the boy was considered to be more active and potent than the girl. Male students more often rated behaviors differently on the basis of sex than female students did (cited in Birns, 1976:244). Moreover, real parents of newborns show the same perception, again with fathers being more extreme in their stereotyping of males and females than are mothers (Rubin et al., 1974). Even though parents do expect boy and girl infants to be different, Maccoby and Jacklin argue that this does not necessarily lead them to reinforce differences if and when they appear.

Certainly sex role expectations are differentiated cross-culturally, yet the issue in evaluating social learning theory is narrower. Do parents actually reward sex-differentiated behaviors especially in very young children and if so, how? Maccoby and Jacklin argue that while there are a few clear-cut ways in which parents do differentiate their behavior toward the sexes, it is not clear how these reinforce sex typing. Sometimes, indeed, parental behaviors seem to work against sex typing rather than for it.

Amount and kind of interaction In general, boy and girl infants seem to receive the same amount of physical handling from their parents, but boy infants are handled more roughly than girls. The particular way in which gross motor behavior is reinforced in boys varies with the child's age but a continuing theme is that girls are treated as though they are more likely to be hurt than boys. It is possible that this more gentle handling is elicited in the parents by the greater tactile sensitivity of infant girls. Whether boys ask for it, girls object to it, or parents simply do it, this greater roughness with boys exists and it does seem important. The rougher treatment may be related to the greater frequency of rough and tumble play and aggression found among boys.

Most of the studies show no difference in the amount of verbal interaction boys and girls receive, although there is some evidence that middle-class mothers may vocalize more to girls, especially if they are first-born. Boys and girls also appear to receive the same amount of parental warmth, but there may be subtle differences in the particular form the affectional contact takes. There is some evidence (Lewis, 1972) that while mothers are more likely to hold girl infants in a face-to-face position, they tend to place boys on their lap facing away from them. Michael Lewis (1972) speculates that this is the beginning of the masculine external orientation. On the other hand, another study reports that black parents tend to hold both male and female babies in their laps directly facing them (D. Lewis, 1975). We cannot assume that middle-class white parents represent all parents.

When only the evidence with regard to fathers is examined, more clear-cut differences in the treatment of the sexes are found, perhaps especially after early infancy. For instance, Lamb and Lamb (1976) report that while fathers do not interact differently with sons and daughters during the first year of life, in the second year they become more than twice as active in interacting with their sons as with their daughters. Mothers remain equally active with children of either sex during these two years (1976:382). The similarity in amount of interaction with their mothers is probably related to the fact that the mothers' activities mainly involve caretaking while the fathers' activities more often involve play (Lamb and Lamb, 1976). These differences also appear with somewhat older children. Observations of parents in a teaching situation with their children showed that fathers differentiated their teaching strategies according to the sex of the child more than mothers (Block et al., 1974, described in Hoffman, 1977).

Responses relating to independence and dependence The preponderance of data indicates that mothers do not make sex distinctions in the amount of freedom they grant or the amount of self-help they expect of their children. Indeed the studies that have found differential treatment of boys and girls reveal that in many instances girls are actually given more autonomy than boys (Maccoby and Jacklin, 1974:316). This may have to do with the parents' expectation that boys are wilder and hence need more control. The only area where girls are likely to experience greater parental control is chaperonage, because of the fear that girls will be sexually molested. One study found that at about age seven, parents began to be more concerned about the whereabouts of their girls than of their boys (Newson and Newson, 1968).

Although it has been widely assumed that dependency is tolerated or even rewarded by parents and teachers in girls more than in boys, the findings are not as clear cut as most people think. While some studies have found that parents do not differentiate at all, others show that mothers are more likely to respond positively to a boy's dependency bids and fathers more likely to respond positively to such bids from girls (Rothbart and Maccoby, 1966; Baumrind and Black, 1967).

Just as with the differences found in studies of interaction patterns, these studies of dependency show that fathers differentiate more between boys and girls than mothers do. Fathers are especially likely to comfort girls more than boys, either in everyday interactions or when a girl is seen as upset (Block, 1973, in press).

Children's requests for help are sometimes seen as an aspect of dependency. A study by Beverly Fagot (1978) on first-born toddlers illustrates the complexities involved in interpreting the meaning of requests for help. Fagot found that toddler girls asked both parents for help three times more often than boys and that parents were more likely to react positively when girls asked for help than when boys did. Does this mean that girls are more dependent than boys and that parents reward this dependency? This question cannot be precisely answered from Fagot's data, but she does suggest some alternative interpretations from her interviews with parents. She notes that parents would often spontaneously mention that their daughters appear more competent than same-aged sons of their friends. Is it possible then that girls' requests for help indicate competence and interest rather than dependence? Similarly, parents may be more willing to respond positively to girls' requests because they could actually help them and helping them would lead to pleasant interaction and increased competence. As Fagot suggests, the failure to respond to the males' requests for help may be because the parents feel that they are merely seeking attention or that it is useless to try to help toddler boys.

Fagot's study illustrates a general problem in interpreting research findings. It might be tempting to use this observational study of help seeking on such young children to "prove" that two-year-old girls are more dependent than boys and that this dependency is unwittingly reinforced by parents. But help seeking may not mean dependency at all.

Responses to aggression Since we have argued that males are indeed more aggressive than females, it is especially important to examine research on parental behavior to see if reinforcement can account for greater male aggression. Do parents do something to encourage or even produce it? Some early findings reported by Sears, Maccoby, and Levin (1957) suggest that this might happen. Mothers of sons said they allowed more aggression toward the parents themselves and other children than did mothers of daughters. Maccoby and Jacklin feel, however, that more recent research "calls for reevaluation of the question of differential parental reinforcement of aggression in the two sexes" (1974:323). These studies suggest that fathers, mothers, and teachers more often reprimand boys strongly for aggression (or temper) than girls.

Perhaps as with other variables, the term *aggression* is too broad and unspecific. It may be, for example, that fathers tolerate insolence and hostility toward themselves more from girls than from boys (at least in the middle class) (Rothbart and Maccoby, 1966; Lambert et al., 1971), yet fathers would expect their sons to defend themselves against other boys (Tasch, 1952). It would be necessary then to differentiate the target and perhaps also the nature of the aggressive acts.

Toy choices and play preferences It has been widely assumed that children play with sex-typed toys and engage in sex-typed activities because their parents insist upon it. On the other hand, parents may buy their children sex-typed toys because they request them. This may result from the influence of media on children. Very likely, all of these influences are present, and it is very difficult to find the first cause. However, we should not too readily assume that the sex typing of toy choice results from parental and other adult pressure. For example, Jacklin and her associates (1973) found that the toys mothers chose to offer their thirteen- and fourteen-month-old children in a free-play session did not differ according to the sex of the child but that the children's toy choices did. The results would have been more impressive if the possible choices had included dolls, however.

Fagot (1978) found that two-year-olds showed marked differences in their toy and play preferences. Girls preferred dolls and soft toys, and boys preferred to play with blocks and manipulate objects. She also found, however, that parents did, in fact, reinforce these behaviors. They gave boys significantly more positive responses when they played with blocks than they did girls and gave girls significantly more negative responses when they manipulated objects. They gave more positive responses to girls than boys and more negative responses to boys than girls for playing with dolls. Fathers more than mothers gave negative responses to boys when they played with dolls and when they played with other kinds of soft toys. Interestingly enough, the parents themselves did not consider manipulating objects inappropriate for girls, yet they were, in fact, discouraging it. Fagot concludes that while parental responses cannot explain the initial appearance of the differing dispositions toward toys, parents do reinforce them once they appear.

What is perhaps more significant in the study of toy choices, and this seems to apply in all areas of sex typing, is the finding that boys receive more social pressure against "inappropriate" sex typing than do girls. This ranges from parents being more disturbed at a boy's inappropriate toy choice (Hartup and Moore, 1973; Fling and Manosevitz, 1972; Fagot, 1974, 1978) to the fact that homosexuality is considered more reprehensible in males than in females (Lehne, 1976). Again it appears to be fathers who are most concerned that their sons not choose the wrong toy (Lansky, 1967) and that they not be sissies (Goodenough, 1957). Fathers also seem to encourage a kind of flirtatious male-oriented femininity in their daughters more than mothers do (Goodenough, 1957). In this connection, Fagot (1978) reports that while mothers encouraged their daughter's attempts to help, fathers in particular encouraged their daughter's proximity.

Punishing and rewarding responses A very clear difference in the early socialization of the sexes shows up with regard to child punishment. Both observational and interview studies over a wide range of ages show that boys receive more physical punishment and are the objects of more power assertion from their parents than girls. Is this explained by a prohibition on hurting girls (found in studies by Taylor and Epstein, 1967 and Block, 1973), or is it because boys need more punishment? As we have seen earlier, boys are less likely than girls to comply with adult requests. Is it possible that they receive greater punishment because they fail to comply? Minton and others (1971) found that parents increase their coerciveness in the face of noncompliance and that noncompliance in one episode increases the likelihood that the parent will use coercive methods more quickly the next time. Thus, the effects of boys' noncompliance or negative expressiveness are cumulative, producing more and more scolding and punishment. Serbin and others (1973) report similar phenomena in the nursery school.

Regardless of the precipitating cause, the greater punishment that boys receive has been used to explain other features of sex typing in boys. For example, Minton and others (1971) report that children who had been punished at home remained a greater distance from their mothers in an experimental situation two weeks later. Thus, boys' lesser interest in being close to their mothers may be accounted for by the greater punishment they receive. While Sears and others (1965) suggest that a punitive atmosphere in the home tends to "feminize" both boys and girls, modeling theorists suggest that the greater punishment received by boys serves to make them more aggressive, because they copy the aggression directed toward them. Still other theorists suggest that punishment is frustrating and, according to one hypothesis, frustration leads to aggression. Which one of these hypotheses may be true or how in different ways they may all be true is not easily determined. Maccoby and Jacklin tend not to attach a great deal of significance to the greater punishment received by boys, but many other theorists find this to be an important explanation for the greater aggressiveness found in boys.

Perhaps Maccoby and Jacklin do not stress the role of punishment in the sex typing of boys because considerable evidence indicates that boys also receive more rewards or positive feedback than girls. For example, Spaulding (1963) observed in twenty-one fourth to sixth grade classes that teachers gave more approval, instruction, attention by listening, and disapproval to boys than to girls. This would suggest that boys are not generally more frustrated than girls, but simply get a heavier input of attention, both positive and negative. Possibly because boys assert masculinity through negative expressive behavior, they may require both more punishment and more praise to keep them in line. The findings of greater punishment and rewards for boys also may directly reflect male dominance, the idea that boys are more important than girls and thus receive more attention of all types.

There is some evidence that fathers, more than mothers, account for the greater physical punishment received by boys and also for the greater rewards. An observational study on fourteen families with a boy and a girl showed that while there were no differences in the responses by mothers to their sons and daughters, fathers provided almost twice as many positive responses to their sons as to their daughters (Margolin and Patterson, 1975). Fathers are also more likely to physically punish boys than girls.

Mothers tend to use indirect or more psychological methods on both sexes (Bronfenbrenner, 1961; Sears et al., 1957; White House Conference, 1936).

Assessment—Fathers versus Mothers

Social learning theory would broadly predict that sex-typed differences result from differing reinforcement contingencies for the two sexes, that children learn sex-typed behavior through reward and punishment. Social learning theory would then predict that parents respond differently to boys than to girls, especially in areas of behavior seen as sex typed. In general, we have found that while parents do respond differently to the sexes in some respects in early childhood, these instances are rather few and specific. The more general picture suggests that mothers, at least (since they are the ones most often studied), do not treat the sexes very differently.

Several processes besides direct reinforcement might explain the specific differences in the treatment of boys and girls. It may be that the greater punishment administered to sons can be explained by boys' greater resistance to complying with commands. We also suggest that girls may receive more gentle handling because they "elicit" it by their own qualities and responses. In these cases differential treatment might arise because of differing eliciting qualities of boys and girls. It may be that the child differentially reinforces the parent rather than vice versa or at least that the parent and the child differentially reinforce each other equally.

We also cite some evidence that a parent's differentiated responses to boys and girls depends on the parent's own sex. Thus, we find some tendency for fathers to be more lenient with girls and mothers to be more lenient with boys. Maccoby and Jacklin point out, however, that this conflicts with simple reinforcement theory in that the parents of any given child would work at cross-purposes with each other.

We must also consider the possibility that some of the reinforcement contingencies manipulated by parents actually inhibit rather than produce sex-typed behavior in children. Many parents do not attempt to sex-type their children, but rather assume that their children's behavior is already sex typed and attempt to socialize children of both sexes in terms of the same major goals (Maccoby and Jacklin, 1974:326). We know that is true at least of middle-class white mothers and working-class black mothers in the United States.

None of the above considerations should necessarily make us abandon social learning theory altogether as a viable explanation of sex typing. However, many further specifications will have to be made beyond simply saying that parents shape their children into masculine and feminine behaviors.

One approach to specifying how reinforcement may work involves showing how very specific concrete reinforcements given early in life may have far-reaching effects on later behavior. Fagot (1978), for example, agrees with Maccoby and Jacklin that complex behaviors, such as aggression and affection, of which parents are conscious are not reinforced differentially, but she argues that parents do unwittingly reinforce certain simpler behaviors. An example would be their responding to toddler girls' requests for help more favorably than to boys' requests. On the other hand, as we have seen, it is not always clear just what more complex behaviors these differential responses are reinforcing. Neither is it clear how far one can generalize from studies of white middle-class parents. For example, remember that specific methods of holding children vary between blacks and whites.

Another way of specifying how reinforcement might work is with the idea that mothers, who have been studied far more than fathers, do not reinforce sex typing as much as fathers. While the behavior of at least middle-class fathers and mothers does seem to work against sex typing in some respects, it is also true that fathers do reinforce sex-typed behavior more than mothers. Since Maccoby and Jacklin's assessment, more studies have included fathers, and all of these studies have consistently found that fathers with children of every age level are more concerned about sex typing than mothers and differentiate their behavior toward the sexes more than mothers do.

MODELING THEORY One social learning explanation of how we acquire behaviors is modeling, imitation, or identification. Social learning theorists suggest that through these processes, complex and elaborate behaviors, which are not directly and specifically reinforced, come to be part of the child's behavior. Several hypotheses have been offered concerning the models imitated by children. Some writers hypothesize that children will imitate the most nurturant model, others that children will imitate the person who controls resources that the child needs or wants. These hypotheses suggest that the parents will likely serve as models. However, neither of them can directly explain differential sex typing, since mothers are usually the more nurturant parent for both boys and girls, and after infancy, fathers may be perceived as the controller of resources for both sexes. Both these hypotheses have a distinct bearing on sex typing, but in a complex way. First, we will examine two more straightforward hypotheses that address directly the question of why children would imitate and identify with the same-sex model, but not the cross-sex model.

The model availability hypothesis suggests that children are more frequently exposed to same-sex models than to cross-sex models. This is patently untrue in the middle class, where both male and female infants and children usually see their mothers more than their fathers and generally see women more than men. The likelihood of significantly greater exposure to one sex over another as siblings is also low. Cultures may differ in the sex of the persons with whom a child spends the most time. However, it is generally true that infants of both sexes are cared for primarily by women. This coincides with the hypothesis that the most nurturant person is likely to be the model, but again this cannot directly explain sex typing, since it predicts that both sexes would model after the mother.

Another hypothesis is that same-sex models will be imitated more than other-sex ones because children tend to imitate models whom they perceive to be similar to themselves. While there is some evidence that selective attention and imitation do occur in older children and adults, it is difficult to see how very young children who have not established a concept of their own sex could know which parent they were more similar to. One solution is to suggest that while young children develop sex-typed behaviors through simple reinforcement, older children acquire more complex sex-typed responses by modeling after the parent of the same sex (Goldberg and Lewis, 1969).

Modeling Parents

Certainly we could strengthen our confidence in the modeling hypothesis if we had some evidence that a child does actually resemble the same-sexed parent. While finding similarities between parent and same-sex child would not prove that they occurred through modeling, finding little similarity would give us reason to seriously question the modeling hypothesis as an explanation of sex typing. In fact, correlation studies of parent-child similarities find that children are not especially similar to their own parents, and that it is not at all clear that girls are more like their mothers and boys are more like their fathers. This is true for both young children and young adults, and for both non–sex-typed and sex-typed behavior. With regard to sex typed preferences, several studies have found that the femininity of girls is not related to their mother's femininity (Hetherington, 1965). Mussen and Rutherford (1963) also found that girls who showed the most "feminine" preferences on the IT Scale for Children were no more likely to have very feminine mothers than other girls. Interestingly enough, what this study did find was that the fathers of the most feminine girls "tended to be more masculine in interests and orientations (score lower on the Femininity Scale) than the fathers of the other group" (1963:601). This finding would suggest that sex typing may be learned through role complementarity or role complementation; in other words, one may learn a role by playing opposite someone rather than by copying.

Other studies have found no relation between the masculinity of boys and that of their fathers, nor between the masculinity of boys and the masculinity or femininity of their mothers (Angrilli, 1960; Heller, 1959). It may be that complementarity works best with fathers and daughters. At any rate, correlational studies give no support to simple modeling theory.

Another contradiction to modeling theory is that direct observations of preschool or grade school age children indicate little consistent tendency to select same sex models. Studies of imitation where models are not the child's parents greatly outnumber studies of the child directly with his or her own parents. Neither kind of study, however, shows any strong tendency for children to imitate same-sex models.

Since Maccoby and Jacklin's summary appeared, David Lynn (1976) designed an observational study of children's modeling behavior that allows comparison of a child's tendency to model the same-sex parent's behavior versus a same-sex stranger's behavior. This is an important distinction in Lynn's own modification of modeling theory. Lynn (1969) argues that it is easier for a girl to acquire her sex-typed characteristics by imitating her mother than it is for a boy to get his sex-typed characteristics by copying his father. The reason is that mothers are both more salient and more available than fathers. As Lynn puts it, the father as a model is an outline lacking most details, whereas the mother as a model is a detailed map.

Lynn reasoned that if the father was a general model of masculinity rather than a detailed map of himself, the son might be just as likely to imitate any man as his own father. On the other hand, he predicted that a boy would not be just as likely to imitate any woman as his own mother, but might imitate his mother because he knew her capacities as a total person well.

Lynn's results confirmed his hypotheses: about as many boys imitated the male stranger as their own father and the number of boys imitating the father was not greater than those imitating the mother, while twice as many boys imitated the male stranger as the female stranger. Lynn interprets these findings to mean that boys are motivated to imitate a masculine figure over a feminine one, but that the mother is not perceived by the boy as representing femininity. Rather, she is seen as a generally competent person with whom the boy is familiar. The conclusion would have been further strengthened if he had included a fourth group involving a choice between the child's mother and a female stranger. Lynn asserts that when a boy chooses to imitate his mother over his father, it "represents motivating factors other than masculinity and femininity." Lynn's findings imply that the mother identification is a less sex-typed identification than the boy's father identification.

Lynn (1969) within academic psychology and many others with a more psychoanalytic orientation (Johnson, 1963, 1975; Parsons and Bales, 1955; Chodorow, 1974; and Stoller, 1974) stress the importance of the mother as an object of identification for both sexes in early infancy. The theory that children identify with the more nurturant parent would also imply that both sexes will initially model after or identify with the mother. The model availability hypothesis would also lead us to expect this because mothers are more available for identification than fathers. If indeed this happens, it poses a problem for modeling theory alone as an explanation of sex typing. As Maccoby and Jacklin point out, if boys initially imitate their mothers and then switch to male figures, girls (who do not have to switch models) should be more sex typed than boys. In fact, quite the opposite is the case. Existing research using behavioral measures indicates that boys of preschool age are more clearly sex typed than girls (Maccoby and Jacklin, 1974:284).

Boys may be more sex typed than girls precisely because they are "leaning over backward" to counteract their initial identification with, or disposition to model, the mother. Once they recognize that the mother is of a different sex and that they as boys are expected to be masculine, they begin to react against femininity. Some of the negative expressiveness characteristic of boys may stem from this reaction.

Models from Television

While modeling theory in and of itself when applied to children and parents does not explain the acquisition of sex typing very well, it may be more effective when applied to the mass media and especially to television. Here, larger than life stereotypes are presented for children to copy. Many studies show that television viewers do pay more attention to characters that are members of their own sex group than to those that are members of the other sex (e.g., Sprafkin and Liebert, 1978). At least two studies directly examine the influence of television on sex-typed attitudes of children. Frueh and McGhee (1975) found that children who watch more hours of television are more likely to have traditional sex role attitudes than less frequent TV watchers. Televised portrayals of occupational and play roles have been shown to influence children's definitions of the sex appropriateness of those activities, with less sex-typed portrayals leading to a greater willingness to accept these roles as possible in reality (Atkin, 1975).

In an interesting and unique study of adolescents, Cynthia Quattelbaum (1977) explored exactly what characteristics of television characters young people consciously model. She found that over half of both the boys and girls in her sample reported that they modeled television characters and that they would like to be similar to a television character when they grew up. The boys mentioned thirteen characters they would like to resemble in the future with Starsky (of "Starsky and Hutch" fame) receiving the most votes. The females identified sixteen characters, with Mary Richards (Mary Tyler Moore) the most popular choice. Interestingly enough, both the boys and girls said that they wanted to be like these characters because they "helped people." The girls also wanted to model Mary Richards because she was independent and had a career. In this case, then, the modeling may counteract traditional sex stereotypes in some respects.

Assessment—Modeling People or Modeling Roles?

While modeling does provide children with a wide repertoire of potential behaviors, exactly how children come to display sex-typed behavior is not directly explained by modeling theory without additional assumptions. One reason that modeling theory does not seem to adequately explain how young children acquire sex-typed behaviors is that it assumes that children copy specific individuals or specific behaviors rather than social roles. John Finley Scott (1971) points out that if one looks at the acquisition of sex typing in the child in terms of the learning of appropriate age and sex roles, the modeling of specific persons, especially the parents, becomes totally inadequate as an explanation. After all, mothers are not six-year-old girls, yet it is the role of child and girl that must be learned. While Scott does believe role learning entails reinforcement and modeling, he sees it as involving "less the modeling of persons [and] more the learning of roles" (1971:149). While Scott shares with the reinforcement and modeling theorists an emphasis on external reinforcements, his views suggest that these perspectives need to be supplemented by Kohlberg's cognitive developmental theory and more sociological theory focusing on family roles (see chapter 10).

DEVELOPMENTAL THEORY

Lawrence Kohlberg's (1966) explanation of sex-typed behavior emphasizes the child and its understanding rather than parents and their reinforcements. According to Kohlberg, the child categorizes himself or herself as a male or a female and then seeks to act and feel like one. Thus, a girl does not act like a girl because she is rewarded for doing so, but because she knows she is a girl. Kohlberg describes the difference between his theory and social learning theory this way (1966:89, our arrangement):

> The social-learning syllogism is:
>
> "I want rewards,
>
> I am rewarded for doing boy things,
>
> Therefore, I want to be a boy."

The cognitive developmental syllogism is:

"I am a boy,

Therefore I want to do boy things,

Therefore the opportunity to do boy things (and to gain approval for doing them) is rewarding."

While social learning theory stresses the learning of specific sex-typed behaviors, Kohlberg's theory emphasizes the acquisition of gender itself. For Kohlberg, gender identity is a cause of sex role learning rather than a product of it.

Sex Stereotyping in Terms of Physical Differences

Kohlberg's theory of sex role development derives, in part, from Jean Piaget's work on general processes of cognitive development in children. Basically Kohlberg thinks that gender identity or self-categorization as a boy or a girl is the primary organizer of sex-role attitudes and that basic universal sex role stereotypes develop from the child's conceptions of body differences, which are given further support by visible social role differences. Only after masculine and feminine values have been acquired on the basis of these stereotypes does the child tend to identify with same-sex figures, especially the parent of the the same sex.

For Kohlberg, gender identity formation is essentially based on the cognitive capacity to perceive objects as constant, independent of their surroundings. Understanding that one is a girl or a boy and that this cannot be changed is fundamentally the same process involved in the general stabilization of constancies of physical objects that Piaget describes. The ability to grasp these constancies is related to mental maturity. By the third year the child usually knows its own sex and later learns to label the sex of others correctly.

After forming this identity and learning that gender and genital differences cannot change, the child wants to adopt sex-typed behavior. Kohlberg argues that this sex typing is not obtained directly by adopting the actual behaviors of parents and siblings because the ideas of young children about sex typing are more, not less, stereotyped than those of adults. He thinks children build up these ideas mainly from perceiving sex differences in bodily structure and capacities that are usually supported by clearly discernible differences in the social roles the sexes play. For example, they perceive that mothers take care of children and that fathers are often away. He cites studies indicating that while children aged four or five remain confused about genital differences they clearly stereotype the sexes in terms of size, strength, aggression, and power at this age (1966:104).

According to Kohlberg, "the stereotype of masculine aggressiveness has a body-image basis because it is linked to the child's belief that males are physically more powerful and more invulnerable than females" (1966:101). In this connection he reports that almost all the twenty-four children in a first-grade class agreed that boys fight more than girls. When they were asked why girls don't fight like boys, the most frequent response was that girls "get hurt" more easily than boys (1966:101). Children are also exposed to masculine aggression through learning that it is males who usually play potentially violent roles such as policeman, soldier, or robber.

In the child's concrete thinking, social power derives from physical power which derives from physical size. A number of studies indicate that by the age of five or six, children of both sexes attribute greater power, strength, competence and status to males. Although children do award a number of superior values to females, including nurturance, attractiveness, and niceness, basic power and prestige values are primarily awarded to males. Kohlberg feels these tendencies to attribute superior power and status to the male role are universal. As we saw in chapter 5, the greater prestige given to males does appear to be universal but this does not necessarily prove that it is based on body image.

Children from five to eight increasingly view sex-stereotyped behavior as morally required even though it may not be stressed by their middle-class parents. At this stage children do not distinguish between conventional social expectations and moral laws and duties. They see acting out one's gender identity as a moral obligation. For example, a child of five to seven is likely to say, " 'God made her a girl and she has to stay a girl, that's what God meant her to be' " (Kohlberg, 1966:123).

Identification Phenomena

In Kohlberg's view, the specific attributes of the child's own parents may inhibit or facilitate sex typing but do not cause it. "There seem to be 'natural stereotypes of paternal power which facilitate the boy's competence-motivated identification with masculine and father-role attributes. If family reality is extremely or grossly discrepant from these stereotypes, the boy's masculine values do not develop strongly' " (1966:161). In support of this he cites studies that show less sex typing in boys from homes in which the mother is dominant. In addition, he concludes that while maternal warmth has no effect, paternal warmth facilitates masculine sex typing because it helps reduce the "naturally threatening" aspects of the father image and makes it easier for the boy to identify with masculinity.

Kohlberg summarizes his discussion of four- to eight-year-old boys' modeling of their fathers with the following bedtime conversation of a five-year-old boy and his father (1966:136, italics Kohlberg's):

"Oh, Daddy, how old will I be when *I can go hunting* with you? We'll go in the woods, you with your gun, me with my bow and arrow. Daddy, wouldn't it be neat if *we could* lasso a wild horse? Do you think we could do it? Do you think I could ride a horse backward if someone's leading me like you?"

Here we see the boy clearly motivated to be competent in concrete stereotypical masculine activities. He is getting support from his father in carrying out these activities, definitely feels his father could do these activities, and categorizes himself with his father. This fantasy "has little to do with the father's actual interests and abilities [the man was a college teacher], and much to do with the concrete masculine sex-role stereotypes of children" (1966:137).

As usual, the research findings with respect to identification or modeling behaviors in girls do not neatly parallel the findings in boys. While modeling the father goes along with boys' developing sex-typed behavior, it is not at all clear that modeling the mother goes along with girls' developing sex-typed behavior. In the first place, mother identification does not positively correlate with measures of general social adjustment in girls, whereas father identification correlates with measures of social adjustment in boys. Also, girls who come from mother-dominant homes are not more identified with the feminine role than girls from homes where the mother is not dominant. Finally, girls as well as boys at about the age of four become more father oriented. Thus, girls do not simply remain tied to the mother, but turn away from her and seek a relationship with the father.

According to Kohlberg, identifying with or modeling parents does not itself create sex-typed behavior, but the quality of a child's relationship to the parent can affect sex-typing, especially the quality of the relationship to the father. The quality of the relationship of a boy with his father causes him not so much to model him as to use him as a supportive figure in learning to become masculine. The quality of the relationship of a girl with her father causes her not to copy him but to use him as a sounding board as she figures out what it means to be feminine.

Cognitive Stages

On the basis of interviews with children from six to eighteen, Dorothy Ullian (1976) suggests that as children grow older they qualitatively shift their views of sex roles. While children at first see sex differences as coming from biological and physical differences between the sexes, as they get older children move into a societal orientation rather than a biological orientation toward sex roles. They do not challenge the role definitions of the social system, but simply believe "that a proper match exists between one's acquired traits and abilities, and one's future role in the familial, occupational, and social system" (Ullian, 1976:38).

For instance, Ullian asked a ten-year-old boy the question, "Would it be wrong if (a) man wore jewelry?" The boy responded, "Well, women wouldn't just go wearing men's things. You could, it would be right, but everyone would say, 'look at him,' and he would not get a job if he wanted to and nobody would accept him; they would think he was a weird guy" (Ullian, 1976:39).

While adolescents are aware that sex roles are to some extent arbitrary, they tend to elect to stick with them for psychological reasons related to their anticipation of heterosexual dating.

Assessment—
Is There Room for Change?

Kohlberg argues that sex typing occurs in the process of cognitive maturation. Reinforcement and modeling may take place, but they essentially operate after the child has already acquired very stereotyped views of appropriate gender behavior. These stereotypical ideas develop from the child's perception of gross physical and social role differences between the sexes. Generally speaking, Kohlberg is not as concerned with explaining a child's behavior as he is with explaining a child's conceptions of his or her own and others' sex roles. The child's ideas are not innate, nor do they magically appear solely because of mental maturation. Rather, they develop out of the individual's own mental equipment interacting with the outside world.

As Maccoby and Jacklin point out, it is difficult to test Kohlberg's cognitive developmental theory directly. His own major argument for his theory is that the child's level of mental maturity (holding chronological age constant) predicts her or his sex role attitudes better than other variables, such as similarity to the parent of the same sex (Kohlberg and Zigler, 1967). Kohlberg also shows that much of the available data on modeling and reinforcement is at least consistent with his theory. Maccoby and Jacklin are correct in calling Kohlberg's theory one of self-socialization, in that he explicitly states that children's basic concepts of sex roles are their own and that these concepts result from their "active interpretation of a social order which makes use of sex categories in culturally universal ways" (Kohlberg, 1966:108). Thus, from Kohlberg's standpoint, the answer to the question we posed at the beginning of the chapter about why nursery school children already appear to be sex typed is that it happens in the course of normal cognitive development. What then are the implications of Kohlberg's theory for change?

Kohlberg wrote his main essay on the development of sex typing in children in 1966. At that time he did not deal with the issue of the desirability or nondesirability of sex typing in adults. Ullian's (1976) work suggests, however, that although children's notions are grounded in biological differences at first and tend to be strongly stereotyped, these ideas are clearly modified (not merely elaborated) as children mature. Older children stop basing their conceptions of sex roles on physical differences and explain them in sociological and psychological terms, which leads them to see that sex role conceptions can be modified by individuals and groups. Kohlberg (1966) notes that while strong sex typing is associated with high intelligence in young children, it is associated with low intelligence in adolescents. Thus, later on, less stereotyped conceptions of sex roles appear to be part of cognitive growth.

Kohlberg's theory is a stage theory in the sense that an individual must develop one mode of understanding before proceeding to another. Several other investigators have also used the stage theory approach and conclude that less rigid and more flexible and adaptive ideas concerning proper sex roles are associated with greater moral or ego development. For example, Jeanne Block (1973) sees the highest stage of ego development as involving an integration of both masculine and feminine traits and values. The rigid sex typing of young children then may be merely a phase rather than an end product. Rebecca, Hefner, and Oleshansky (1976) suggest that sex role development proceeds through three main stages: an undifferentiated conception of sex roles; a polarized, stereotyped, either-or view of sex roles coinciding with Kohlberg's "conventional" stage; and, finally, a flexible dynamic transcendence of sex roles. They believe that most people and institutions, including social scientists today, are at the second or conventional stage and that this is a major cause of sex discrimination. All of these models are hierarchic; they imply that at any one time there is only one characteristic level for each person. They also imply that not all people will reach each stage; some will be less "mature" or "developed" than others.

Ullian's and Kohlberg's cognitive approach and Block's and Rebecca and her associates' ego psychology approach focus on different correlates of sex role development. Ullian and Kohlberg stress the relation of cognitive development to views on conformity to sex roles, while Block focuses on the association between personal maturity and conceptions of sex roles.

Joseph Pleck (1975) criticizes Kohlberg's theory on the grounds that it cannot account for the observed drift in sex role norms over time toward more androgynous conceptions. While it is true that Kohlberg did not address himself specifically to the question of why cultures differ or how they change, nothing in his theory denies cultural differences and cultural change. All Kohlberg's theory implies is that adults, because of their greater cognitive maturity, are probably ahead of children in making these changes.

While Kohlberg's theory does imply that all humans need and must have a sense of gender identity to function at all, his theory predicts that children will become less rather than more rigid concerning sex roles as they mature. In fact, a secure gender identity may actually be associated with being less rigid about what one's gender identity means for what one can do and be in the world. If one is very certain that one *is* a male, then one might not fear breaking the rules about what males are supposed to be like.

A SUMMARY INTERPRETATION In summary then, what can we say about the utility of social learning, modeling, and cognitive development theory in explaining the sex-typed behavior of young children? As we have seen, middle-class parents, at least, reinforce broad categories of sex-typed behavior far less than most people think, and when clear sex differences in specific reinforcements are found (such as help-seeking requests), it is difficult to know precisely what, if any, sex-typed behavior is being reinforced.

Beverly Fagot, a psychologist, has studied sex typing by observing very young children, their parents, and their nursery school teachers for many years. She concludes that the only way that teachers and conceivably parents could possibily influence children's conceptions of sex roles through different reinforcement contingencies would be if they were to get down on the floor and actively play with them and intervene in their conversations and behaviors. Even then, based on other attempts with experimental interventions, she doubts if the effects could be generalized to other settings. Children learn sex roles and develop sex-typed behaviors very early, and they base their learnings on their interpretations of the world and expectations of others. Thus, parental or educational interventions in the form of behavior programming will probably have only a short-term and very specific influence (Fagot, 1979).

We have also seen that parental modeling is questionable as an explanation for sex typing since the degree of a child's sex typing does not correlate with the degree of sex typing of his or her same-sexed parent. If we must choose between the three theories, then, Kohlberg's makes the most sense. This theory suggests that children are self-motivated to become sex typed as their maturing cognitive capacity interacts with the sex-typed environment.

If we look at reinforcement and modeling phenomena within a cognitive developmental framework, we can see how social reinforcements may actually operate even though they are not captured by the specific studies that have been conducted. From a cognitive developmental standpoint, social expectations communicated in the form of attributions may serve as powerful reinforcers. If a child knows he is a boy, he tries to act like one, and confirmation that he is doing so will be a positive reinforcement. For example, if a male child resists the commands of adults and overhears that he is "all-boy," even as he gets a spanking for his disobedience, he is likely to be pleased and conclude that he has been successful in finding out and displaying the attributes really expected of boys. Thus, even though parents do not reward behaviors such as dependency and aggression that they see as sex typed, parents (especially fathers) do indeed think the sexes differ. Children pick up on this and act accordingly.

Similarly with modeling, children see others as representing sex roles and thus get their ideas of how men and women, boys and girls, are supposed to act by observing the roles they play. Precisely because the cognitive development of young children is too immature for subtleties, their notions of what behaviors are appropriate to each sex may actually be more stereotyped than those of their parents. In general, modeling theory works better with respect to television models than parental models. In television, children can see gross images of the masculine model, larger than life as it were. While a middle-class child may not know what his father does at his law office, he does know that cowboys are always males. While TV does offer readily available stereotypes, children would probably create them with or without the help of television because cognitive immaturity causes children to simplify and concretize the phenomena they see.

The findings concerning reinforcement and modeling do suggest that fathers play a stronger part in sex typing their children than do mothers. As we saw, fathers are more likely to reinforce sex-typed behavior than mothers. Some of the evidence we presented on modeling suggests that both boys and girls may model the mother as a person in terms of general competence, but that fathers and other males are more relevant where sex typing is concerned. David Lynn suggests that boys view their fathers and other men as representing masculinity and that their identification with them is a positional rather than a personal identification. The findings that a girl's femininity is more closely related to her father's masculinity than to her mother's femininity suggests that girls may learn about at least the flirtatious and directly male-oriented aspects of femininity (as opposed to the motherly aspects) more from playing a role complementary to their fathers than by modeling their mothers. Thus, while these findings suggest that more than parental modeling is involved in sex typing, they also suggest that fathers, more so than mothers, are the focus of this sex typing.

Finally, what are the implications of the three theories for explaining male dominance itself? Clearly, we differ from those who use the social learning approach to argue essentially that male dominance occurs because women are reinforced in passivity and dependence and, thus, are rendered incapable of competing with men. In the first place, there is little evidence that women are passive and dependent (though as adults, women may admit to self-doubts more than men). There is also little evidence that reinforcement of passivity and dependency as such takes place. There is little evidence, too, that women become passive and dependent by modeling their mothers, especially as they model the mother role, which can hardly be called passive. These explanations of male dominance seem more than anything else to blame the victim and are unjustified by the empirical evidence.

While reinforcement and modeling do operate, they need to be understood within a framework that takes social roles and social meaning directly into account as cognitive developmental theory allows us to do. Then, we see that girls may be reinforced in playing certain roles and they copy certain roles rather than learning actual traits. Finally, these roles themselves may be part of the system of male dominance.

Little in cognitive developmental theory in and of itself allows us to explain male dominance. That is, while cognitive developmental theory is important to our analysis because it allows us to talk of such things as a masculine paradigm, it is not very helpful in analyzing why we have that paradigm. Neither cognitive developmental theory nor social learning theory nor modeling theory can explain, for example, why it is considered worse for boys to act like a girl than for a girl to act like a boy or why males are more concerned with sex typing than females. Cognitive developmental theory tells us that children think males dominate because they are bigger and stronger, but these are the views of children and change as children become more sophisticated. In human society, where culture dominates biology, there must be other reasons why we tend to be governed by a paradigm that tells us males are better. In order to explain this, we turn in the next chapter to psychoanalytic theory and its several interpretations.

SUMMARY

Three theoretical approaches from academic psychology have been used to explain how children acquire sex-typed behaviors. Social learning suggests that boys and girls are rewarded for different behaviors by their parents. Modeling theory is a variation of social learning theory that suggests that children learn sex roles by imitating their parents and others. Cognitive developmental theory posits that children first understand that they are boys and girls and then adopt the behaviors that they believe are appropriate for their sex.

Cognitive developmental theory appears to have the most support, although both modeling and social learning may be seen to operate within a cognitive developmental framework. While these theories can help account for how sex differentiated behavior is learned, none of them can directly explain the higher valuation all societies give to males.

Suggested Readings

DENMARK, FLORENCE L., AND JULIA SHERMAN, eds., *Psychology of Women: Future Directions of Research.* New York: Psychological Dimensions, Inc., in press. An edited book containing many important new articles on the psychology and socialization of women.

DENMARK, FLORENCE L. AND RHODA K. UNGER, eds., *Woman: Dependent or Independent Variable?* New York: Psychological Dimensions, Inc., 1975. Book of readings on sex differences relevant to chapters 6, 7, and 8.

LYNN, DAVID, *Parental and Sex-Role Identification.* Berkeley, Calif.: McCutchan Publishing Corporation, 1969. A summary of the author's theories regarding children's identification with their fathers and mothers.

MACCOBY, ELEANOR E., AND CAROL N. JACKLIN, *The Psychology of Sex Differences.* Stanford, Calif.: Stanford University Press, 1974. The most recent summary of studies concerning sex differences and early socialization; contains an annotated bibliography.

WEITZMAN, LENORE, *Sex Role Socialization: A Focus on Women.* Palo Alto, Calif.: Mayfield Publishing Company, 1979. A short review of socialization studies that analyzes children's books as well as family studies.

9: Psychoanalytic Explanations of Sex Role Development and Male Dominance

While biological influences can explain some sex differences in psychological traits and social roles, they cannot account for the greater value given to male roles. Similarly, theories from academic psychology help explain how children learn sex roles and self-conceptions but they cannot account for the importance of gender in people's lives, the intense feelings people have about sex roles and sex differences, or the greater value accorded male roles. To help account for these phenomena and for male dominance itself, we turn now to psychoanalytic theory.

This field, more than any other discipline, is explicitly concerned with sex differences, sexuality, gender identity, sexual preference, and their development. While academic psychologists accustomed to controlled experiments have generally rejected psychoanalytic theory, it has been used by some anthropologists and sociologists concerned with the family, kinship, socialization, and the perpetuation of cultural patterns.

THE PSYCHOANALYTIC PERSPECTIVE

Psychoanalysis was founded by Sigmund Freud and remains an active discipline. While a number of Freud's theories have been modified, challenged, and even discarded by his followers over the years, the basic concepts and ideas that he introduced are still central to the discipline and have been widely accepted by others in the social sciences. These include his concept of the *unconscious,* the idea that we have thoughts and ideas not available to our conscious selves that affect our

Parts of this chapter originally appeared in "The Social Origins of Male Dominance," by Jean Stockard and Miriam M. Johnson, in *Sex Roles,* 5 (1979), pp. 199–218, and are included here with the permission of Plenum Publishing Corporation.

behavior, feelings, and physical well-being. This unconscious mental activity is not something simply unnoticed but something actively *repressed* (although not consciously so) because it is too threatening, painful, or unmanageable. Furthermore, psychoanalysis postulates that we unwittingly carry over, or *transfer,* attitudes born in old relationships into new relationships (cf. Dyrud, 1976:23). Psychoanalysis, then, explicitly acknowledges that people attach meaning to their experiences. In infants and young children these meanings are very primitive and global. The basic themes of these early fantasies and interpretations, which may later be repressed, reflect or represent relatively consistent themes in human sociosexual relations. A central theme that Freud focused on was the conflict set up in individuals between the near universal social taboo on incest and children's natural love for their parents. The psychologist Gardner Lindzey (1967) attributes the great impact that psychoanalysis has had in the behavioral sciences to the fact that it grounds itself on this universal human conflict.

The original intent of psychoanalysis was to understand how people's experiences and interpretations could create neuroses or mental illnesses. Psychoanalysts believe that when people understand the reasons for their obsessions and delusions they can then deal with their illness. Freud reminded his readers "that psychoanalytic investigations have no more bias in any direction than has any other scientific research. In tracing back to its concealed source what is manifest, psychoanalysis has no aim but that of disclosing connections" (Freud, 1963b:66). In exploring people's psychic lives psychoanalysts developed complex theories concerning the nature of masculinity and femininity, why most men become masculine and most women feminine.

The terms used by psychoanalysts have changed over the years. Freud built his theories from the assumption of certain underlying drives or instincts in human beings. While he also discussed the importance of object relations—the social associations of an individual with others—his writings tend to emphasize this biological basis. To a large extent other psychoanalytic writings through the 1930s shared this emphasis. By the 1940s, however, object relations theorists were arguing that the child's social relational experience from infancy rather than its fixation on various bodily zones determines psychological development and personality formation. Children *internalize* these object relations through *introjection* and *identification* processes and thus come to feel toward themselves as they imagined the parent to be and feel. Different parental images occur at different stages of the child's development. (For an excellent summary of the object relations school see Chodorow, 1978.)

With a few notable exceptions, until very recently, most feminists have been hostile to psychoanalysis. For example, Pauline Bart, a contemporary sociologist and feminist, writes (1976:9):

> Psychoanalysis has been a malignant influence on American society, more benign than the Ku Klux Klan, but more harmful than the Republican party. As the Klan was an instrument of social control, keeping uppity blacks in their place, psychoanalysis, particularly in the fifties, was used as an ideology to symbolically destroy uppity women. . . . Psychoanalysis was to sexism what the Klan was to racism.

Bart sees practitioners in the field as intent on keeping women in their place and of justifying this with a mystifying ideology about the perils of penis envy and the glories of true femininity. Unfortunately, in this country, this accusation has often been justified in the sense that psychoanalysts prescribed that women adjust to male dominance and the feminine role to achieve mental health (see "Report of the Task Force on Sex Bias," 1975).

Another reason for feminists' antipathy for Freud was the fear that he was a biological determinist. Although it is true that Freud put much stress on the anatomical differences between the sexes and once made the statement that "anatomy is destiny," it is not true that he felt that sex typing came about completely automatically. That he made parent-child interaction so central suggests that he thought learning was involved. Although one may argue about the extent to which Freud thought gender-related behavior instinctual, it is very possible to view psychoanalysis as a theory of the social creation of masculinity and femininity.

More basically, many social scientists (both feminists and nonfeminists) have questioned psychoanalysis's claims of truth. These scientists argue that psychoanalytic ideas are not so much wrong as they are impossible to prove wrong, because the concepts and their connections with behavior are vague and untestable in controlled experimental situations. This is not a devastating criticism, however, since many of the phenomena that social scientists deal with are not amenable to experimental testing. The only appropriate way to refute psychoanalytic theory would not be in an experiment but by means of an alternative theory that more convincingly explained the behaviors it is concerned with.

In spite of the intense reaction against Freud by many feminists and experimental scientists, it is important to study his work and that of other psychoanalysts precisely because they, more than the members of any other discipline, deal with the very matters that concern feminists. As feminists themselves have delved deeper into the basic factors underlying the secondary status of women, they have concluded that Freud's analysis of the child's developing sexuality within the family and the consequences of the incest taboo is highly relevant. Even though Freud himself may have been guilty of sexism, a psychoanalytic perspective need not endorse male dominance. In fact, it can point toward important ways of altering that system.

Furthermore, even though psychoanalysis has been criticized for not being verified empirically, this does not mean that these theories do not have an empirical basis. Freud first developed his theories about psychosexual development by analyzing his own memories and dreams and those of his patients. Many of his patients were adults, but some were children. His students and followers added to the theories through their own observations and analyses of their patients. Some of these theorists, most notably Freud's own daughter Anna, and Melanie Klein, extensively observed and analyzed children, often using play sessions in which they encouraged children to talk about their fantasies and imaginary creations. In more recent years, psychoanalysts (e.g., Galenson and Roiphe, 1974) through their observations of children have added much to our knowledge of how gender identity is formed. Anthropologists have also observed the development of children in other cultures. While the nature of the various developmental stages and processes psychoanalysts discuss may depend to some extent on who fills family roles (for instance, a maternal uncle may fill the functions in some matrilineal societies that a father does in patrilineal societies), these comparisons have also informed and generally confirmed the theories that we discuss below.

Despite agreement on basic concepts and purpose, psychoanalysis, like any ongoing discipline, has been rife with controversies and alternative approaches to various issues. The controversy regarding the development of masculinity and femininity began very early, and the two trends of thought that first appeared in the 1920s are still visible today. While in our discussion we separate these two general approaches, they were first developed as a series of articles often written in response to each other.

Feminists have used insights derived from both schools of thought in their analyses of how gender identity forms and of how male dominance is reproduced. The phallocentric school, as we shall call it, is represented by Freud himself and stresses the Oedipus complex and the father in gender differentiation. The gynocentric school of thought corrects Freud's lack of emphasis on the impact of children's earliest relationship with the mother before the Oedipal period on the development of gender identity.

THE PHALLOCENTRIC VIEW While Freud began developing his phallocentric view early in his career, a number of other writers have also contributed to the approach. Helene Deutsch (1944) especially clarified the analysis of feminine development and modified some of Freud's most sexist views.* She also dealt more concretely with how the father influences the girl's adoption of some aspects of femininity. The work of Erik Erikson, a contemporary psychoanalyst, also fits into the phallocentric framework but modifies Freud's analysis by attributing more value to feminine orientations and traits than Freud did. Contemporary feminists have used Freud's phallocentric theory to analyze women's secondary status, and these analyses of the basis of male dominance are reviewed in the last part of this section.

Developmental Stages

The sexual instinct, or eros, is most important in psychoanalytic theories of sex role development. Sexual life to Freud included "the function of obtaining pleasure from the zones of the body"(Freud, 1940:9). Thus sexuality is not located just in the genitals, but can and does involve other areas of the body. Libido is the energy of eros, the driving force to unite with others and receive pleasure. For Freud, sexuality and sexual manifestations start very soon after birth.

Freud's theory of self-development is a theory of gender socialization because he recognized that males and females have different experiences in the parental family in their formative years. He suggested that childhood development occurs in several stages, each involving a different focus of sexual energy. These developmental stages are analytic concepts, and they may not be clearly demarcated in an individual child. Freud believed that they can overlap and in fact often occur simultaneously.

Freud suggested that the child's sexual life first focuses not on the genital area, but on other areas of the body that bring and produce pleasure. The first erogenous zone is the mouth. Babies seek food and are satisfied by the mother or other person who feeds them. This act is obviously pleasurable, not just in satisfying the basic need for nourishment, but also in providing contact with the mother's body. Freud believed that both boys and girls experience this first stage in essentially the same way, although the girl may develop a greater dependency on the mother in both this and the second stage (Freud, 1963a). The second stage of development is the anal, or the sadistic-anal, phase. Pleasure in this stage comes from excretory functions and from aggression against others. Both libidinal and destructive urges exist at this stage of development.

*Helene Deutsch's work shows elements of both perspectives that we discuss here. While she was a student of Freud's (as was Ernest Jones) and followed his analysis of developmental stages, she also used some of the work of gynocentric theorists in discussing the nature of penis envy and in emphasizing the importance of the mother in development. This illustrates how much the two perspectives are part of the total discipline of psychoanalysis and how the writings show mutual influences.

Only at the third developmental stage did Freud suggest that males and females begin to develop differently. In this stage children expand their awareness to the genital area of their body. Freud called this the phallic stage, and it is at this stage that children experience the Oedipus complex and become aware of the incest taboo.

Freud came to believe that even very young children have some idea of the nature of sexual acts. In his self-analysis of the late 1890s he found the core of the Oedipus complex. He discovered in himself and later in both his male and female patients an early desire to possess the mother and a corresponding jealousy of the father. For the boy this desire is thwarted when he perceives that he cannot possess her, for she belongs to the father. The boy also fears retribution from the father in the form of castration if he should act on his desires, so he gives up his desire for the mother in a massive act of repression and identifies with the father.

It is important to understand that Freud always assumed that both males and females have a bisexual potential. A male child not only has a wish to actively possess his mother, but he also has a feminine wish to be passively possessed by his father. When the boy becomes aware in the phallic period of the anatomical fact of having a penis, he increases the active masculine desire for the mother. At this point the boy also makes a strong connection between the degradation of women and their lack of a penis. The realization of the possibility of castration, the undesirable results (becoming like a woman), and the fear of this possibility lead to the resolution of the boy's Oedipus complex. He renounces his claim for the mother in deference to the father. His desires for the mother become sublimated and in essence destroyed. He also represses his jealousy of the father and identifies with him and takes over the father's prohibitions into his own psyche in the form of a conscience, or superego.

Freud did not see the girl's experience as a mirror image of the boy's and did not approve of Carl Jung's use of the term *Electra complex* to describe the girl's experience. Freud believed that the resolution of the phallic phase was different and more complex for girls than for boys. In the phallic stage, just as the boy discovers his penis, the girl discovers her clitoris. Because stimulation of the clitoris brings her pleasure, it functions for her like the penis does for the boy. Thus Freud believed that her orientation at this point is masculine and that she too wants to actively possess the mother. But Freud assumed that in comparing herself to little boys, the girl feels that her organ is inferior, that she has been shortchanged. Although she believes at first that her clitoris will grow to match the boy's penis, she later decides that while she once had the larger appendage, it was removed. She has been castrated. This is the girl's castration complex. Freud believed that while the boy fears castration, the girl thinks that she is castrated and accepts the "fact" of her castration. Freud called the girl's hope that she could regain the penis *penis envy.*

As a result of her castration complex, Freud suggested, the girl gives up clitoral masturbation and enters the Oedipal phase. The realization that she does not have a penis makes her turn from the mother as her love object to the father in the hope that he can give her a baby to replace her lost penis. The girl transforms her desire for a penis into a desire for a child. The core of the Oedipus complex for the girl is the hope that the father will give her this child (penis). Because she gradually realizes the father will not do this, Freud believed that she abandons the Oedipus complex only slowly and always remains to a certain extent suspended in a dependent relationship with both her mother and father.

Later Modifications of Phallocentric Theory

Freud's idea that females are mutilated males and that females deeply envy males' genitalia is obviously sexist and unsupported by evidence. Both Helene Deutsch and Erik Erikson, while retaining major aspects of Freud's analysis, have tried to alter the concept of penis envy. Helene Deutsch (1944:vol. 1, 231) accepted the view of the gynocentric theorists (see below) that what appeared to be penis envy is not a deep seated phenomenon, but simply a rationalization or defense mechanism against emotions regarding the mother. Deutsch also suggested that penis envy is only half of a genital trauma for young girls that results from giving up the clitoris without yet being in a position to use the vagina. In other words, Deutsch suggested that penis envy is only part of a larger genital trauma that arises because girls have no conspicuous genital organs on which to focus their energies.

Erik Erikson goes a step beyond Deutsch's formulation by focusing on the positive elements of both males' and females' genitalia rather than only on those of males. Erikson once asked a large number of children to create "an exciting scene from an imaginary moving picture" using a collection of toys and blocks. Through this method he hoped to understand more about how they saw themselves and the world around them. Both he and independent researchers observed that the girls tended to create peaceful interior scenes with people in sitting or standing positions. Their scenes had low walls and occasionally an elaborate doorway with dangerous intruders. Boys tended to build scenes with high towers, walls with protrusions, and people outside the enclosures and moving about. The boys' scenes often displayed accidents and dangers of collapse and ruin (Erikson, 1968:268–71). Using this play as an indicator of psychic life, much as Freud used the memories of free association, Erikson suggests that the scenes portray important characteristics of male and female development and outlook. While not concentrating on the obvious interpretation of the males' displays of protrusions and activity, he explores the possibility that the females' constructions suggested a theme of inner space. Erikson proposes that psychoanalysis make "a shift of theoretical emphasis from the loss of an external organ to a sense of vital inner potential; . . . from a 'passive' renunciation of male activity to the purposeful and competent pursuit of activities consonant with the possession of ovaries, a uterus, and a vagina" (1968:275). In short, Erikson modifies Freud's view of penis envy by focusing on what he sees as the positive aspects of women's genitalia and psyche. He believes that this perspective can provide a new way of examining the development of women without necessarily seeing them as wounded men.

Recently Paula Caplan (cited in Goleman, 1978:53) replicated Erikson's study using much younger children and concluded that there are no sex differences in the scenes they constructed. Caplan tried to control for the possible influence of the objects used by first giving the children blocks only, then all the toys except blocks, and finally the blocks and toys together. She concluded that Erikson's subjects' sex-typed constructions could have resulted from their tendency to use different objects in their constructions rather than from any difference in the way boys and girls saw the world. Because the children were only two-to-four-year-olds, Caplan's subjects may also have been too young to have reached the phallic stage. In any case, while the discrepant findings of the two studies remain to be explained, the thrust of Erikson's argument need not rest on the illustrative experiment.

Development of the Superego

For Freud the different ways in which boys and girls resolve the Oedipus complex lead to important characterological differences between the sexes. In boys the castration complex promotes a prompt and sure resolution of the Oedipus complex and the development of the superego. The superego is the conscience, the moral authority, and arbiter within the individual. It enforces the rules of society on the individual, most especially the incest taboo. Freud believed that when the Oedipus complex succumbs to the threat of castration, the boy firmly establishes the superego. "This new psychical agency continues to carry on the functions which have hitherto been performed by people (the abandoned objects) in the external world: it observes the ego [the rational part of the self], gives it orders, judges it, and threatens it with punishments, exactly like the parents whose place it has taken" (Freud, 1940:62).

Freud believed that for the girl, however, the Oedipus complex can never be fully resolved. For Freud castration is a foregone fact that produces the girl's Oedipus complex instead of motivating its resolution. The Oedipus complex can only gradually disappear; and, because it cannot be totally resolved, Freud believed that women never develop the strong superego that men develop (1963c:193):

> Their superego is never so inexorable, so impersonal, so independent of its emotional origins as we require it to be in men. Character traits which critics of every epoch have brought up against women—that they show less sense of justice than men, that they are less ready to submit to the great necessities of life, that they are more often influenced in their judgments by feelings of affection or hostility—all these would be amply accounted for by the modification in the formation of their superego which we have already inferred.

Obviously some feminists have been outraged and many psychoanalysts embarrassed by the devaluation of women implied in Freud's characterization of their weak superegos. Within the psychoanalytic community itself, Helene Deutsch, David Gutmann (chapter 7), and Erik Erikson have tried to counteract Freud's view by giving women's characteristics the same value as men's.

Freud's theory of sex role development obviously has a masculine bias that assumes the physical superiority of the penis and the moral superiority of males' psyches. While he admitted (see especially Freud, 1933) that he could not fully explain female development and looked to the writings of others for explication, Freud never renounced the basic phallocentric nature of his work. Women for Freud tended to be deprived males. He believed that their initial impulses were masculine and that motherhood for women was not a basic superiority or even an equivalent capability, but a circuitous route for women to get a penis for themselves. Deutsch and Erikson have attempted to alter some of the more objectionable parts of Freud's work, but have retained his general phallocentric emphasis.

EXPLANATIONS OF MALE DOMINANCE USING FREUD'S PHALLOCENTRIC THEORY

Juliet Mitchell and Gayle Rubin are feminist theorists who hold to Freud's own analysis because they see it as an essentially accurate description of the symbolic ideas held by both males and females in a male-dominated society. They look at the incest taboo that arises from the resolution of the Oedipus complex as the key element of kinship systems. Because kinship arrangements are made possible by the incest taboo and always seem to involve male dominance, Mitchell and Rubin suggest that somehow the source of male power may lie within the resolution of the Oedipus complex itself.

The Oedipus Complex and Male Dominance

Juliet Mitchell interprets the girl's resolution of her Oedipus complex as representing "her acceptance of her inferior, feminine place in patriarchal society" (1974:366). She sees Freud as documenting that women at first are active and masculine but are forced to give up and reconcile themselves to femininity. Mitchell does not accept Shulamith Firestone's (1971) notion that penis envy in the female child simply recognizes the social fact that males really do have power. Neither does she think that women literally envy the male organ in an anatomical sense. Rather, both she and Rubin suggest that women envy the penis because in patriarchal culture the phallus (a term meaning the erect penis and which Freud used on occasion to mean the symbolic penis) is seen as a symbol for male dominance. In male-dominated cultures the phallus *is* considered to be of great value. According to Mitchell and Rubin, following the French psychoanalyst Lacan, the organ itself is neither good nor bad, worthy or unworthy, powerful or powerless, until it is given a cultural definition. The presence or absence of the phallus stands for both the categorizing of humans into two basic types and also for the dominance of the type with the phallus, namely males.

Mitchell and Rubin suggest that the Oedipal phase is the time when gender identity is organized according to the kinship rules of the culture. If the boy gives up his mother to his father during the Oedipal crisis, his father will validate the phallus in his son (accept him as a male and not castrate him). The little girl lacks this symbolic token that can be exchanged for a woman. She never gets the phallus. She can get it in intercourse or in the form of a child but only as a gift from a man. Thus the resolution of the Oedipus complex for the girl means accepting castration, becoming feminine, and giving in to male dominance. Rubin and Mitchell suggest that it is no wonder some women refuse to give up and envy the phallus, because accepting femininity involves accepting a secondary status.*

Kinship and Male Dominance

Both Mitchell and Rubin use the arguments of Claude Levi-Strauss (1969), the noted contemporary French anthropologist. He suggests that men's dominance is reflected not only in the extradomestic exchange of

*Juliet Mitchell, especially, has tended to be almost totally uncritical of Freud's work. Her *Psychoanalysis and Feminism* (1974) suggests that Freud's own analysis is far superior to those theorists who have attempted to revise his work. Nancy Chodorow (1978) takes issue with Mitchell's unquestioning acceptance of Freud. She argues that while sometimes Freud was describing how women do in fact develop in a patriarchal society, at other times he was simply making assertions about women's reactions that are not supported by clinical evidence. She would argue that even though the phallus is a valued symbol, it is pure male fantasy to assume that the instant a little girl sees a boy's penis she wants one. According to Chodorow, it does a disservice to psychoanalysis as a theory of personality development to adopt Freud uncritically, even as a description of psychosexual development in a male-dominant society.

gifts and goods, but more importantly in the extradomestic exchange of women themselves. According to Levi-Strauss the institution of marriage involves essentially the exchange of women by men. Levi-Strauss argues that the taboo on incest is a social invention that forces the exchange of women outside the immediate kin group to which they belong. This establishes social ties and obligations between kin groups. The incest taboo then is not simply a prohibition of marriage with close relatives for biological reasons. It has a social function: requiring that groups give marriage partners to outsiders. The act of exchange and the resulting reciprocal relationships create alliances between kin groups and make a wider community possible. Thus, the existence of society itself depends on the incest taboo.

More important, according to Levi-Strauss, it has always been men who exchange women and not vice versa. This can be seen in our own society in the custom of the father giving the bride away in marriage ceremonies. Thus Levi-Strauss notes (1969:115):

> The total relationship of exchange which constitutes marriage is not established between a man and a woman, but between two groups of men, and the woman figures only as one of the objects in the exchange, not as one of the partners. . . . This remains true even when the girl's feelings are taken into consideration, as, moreover, is usually the case. In acquiescing to the proposed union, she precipitates or allows the exchange to take place, she cannot alter its nature.

Rubin succintly summarizes the importance of this insight (1975:175; italics ours): "It suggests that we look for the ultimate locus of women's oppression within the *traffic in women,* rather than with the traffic in merchandise." Levi-Strauss focuses our attention on kinship structures rather than economic relations. Rubin stresses that Levi-Strauss's exchange of women thesis should not be taken too literally, however. She suggests that the term is "shorthand for expressing that the social relations of a kinship system specify that men have certain rights in their female kin, and that women do not have the same rights either to themselves or to their male kin" (Rubin, 1975:172).

Neither Freud nor Levi-Strauss directly addresses the question of why men exchange women instead of women exchanging men or the more general question of why male dominance exists. Yet their theories suggest that the answer to the origin of male dominance in human societies may lie in men's roles in kinship systems rather than in their roles in the production and exchange of goods. Levi-Strauss goes on to argue that since there are very few universal aspects of the division of labor between the sexes apart from tasks related to child care, there must be some reason besides biological capacity for the sex-based division of labor found in every society. He proposes that the division of labor is a societal device to create "a reciprocal state of dependency between the sexes" (cited in Rubin, 1975:178). In essence, assigning sharply different roles to males and females makes them depend on one another and thus motivates marriage or relatively permanent bonding between the sexes.

Rubin goes beyond Levi-Strauss's idea that the division of labor between the sexes necessitates marriage and suggests that heterosexuality and gender identity itself are also socially imposed. She suggests that "far from being an expression of natural differences, exclusive gender identity is the suppression of natural similarities. It requires repression: in men, of whatever is the local version of 'feminine' traits; in women of the local definition of 'masculine' traits" (Rubin, 1975:180). Even in societies that allow homosexuality under certain circumstances, heterosexuality is always the predominant norm and homosexual relationships tend also to be defined in terms of mutual dependencies.

To illustrate Rubin's general point, a number of primitive societies provide for the possibility that some individuals find it very difficult to fit into the gender role prescribed for their biological sex. These societies create additional gender categories or statuses (supernumerary sexes) for those who cannot fit into the ordinary gender categories. Both the Mohave and the Chuckchee, for example, recognize only two biological sexes but generate four rather than two gender statuses. Among the Mohave Indians, centered in what is now California, biological females were allowed to adopt a masculine-like role and were called *hwame,* and biological males could adopt a feminine-like role and be called *alyha.* Most individuals who chose to do this underwent a ceremonial initiation into their new status at puberty. Individuals in each category could marry persons of the same biological sex, but they took a role similar to that of the other sex (Martin and Voorhies, 1975). Thus the resulting union between two males or two females was socially defined as a heterosexual union of social female and male. These practices suggest that societies insist upon complementary gender statuses for reasons other than biological propensity, specifically as a way of defining social order. The presence of supernumerary sexes does not really challenge the division of labor between the sexes because there is always a tendency to assimilate the supernumerary sexes to one or the other sex group.

Thus, according to Rubin, human sexuality is organized in the interest of kinship organization, which rests upon the incest taboo and heterosexuality. The incest taboo forces marriage outside the immediate kin group, and obligatory heterosexuality reinforces marriage itself. Mitchell and Rubin suggest that the Oedipal phase is the time when gender identity is organized according to the kinship rules of the culture.

Mitchell's and Rubin's analyses suggest that the secondary status of women is very deeply rooted indeed. They argue that for change to occur the Oedipus complex itself must be attacked. Since the Oedipus complex rests upon the internalization of kinship rules, Rubin claims that "feminists must call for a revolution in kinship" (1975:199). Neither Rubin nor Mitchell, however, gives a very clear picture of how this may occur. Rubin suggests that males' sharing child-care responsibility with females may be important in that it could make individuals bisexual. She implies that somehow both gender identity and obligatory heterosexuality would have to disappear before the whole Oedipal structure that oppresses women could collapse. Mitchell argues that the family is actually unnecessary in capitalist societies and suggests but does not develop the idea that the key for change may lie in the contradiction between the irrelevancy of kinship exchange in capitalist society and the societal demands that it be preserved.

In the last analysis, neither Mitchell nor Rubin offers much hope for change. The possibility or even desirability of eliminating human kinship systems altogether as a way of ending male dominance seems highly questionable. Also it is questionable if one can eliminate gender identity totally, as Rubin seems to imply, since it does have a body image basis. Mitchell and Rubin both repeat Freud's practice of including in the concept of gender identity not only the self-definition of a person as male or female, but also sexual preference. As we shall show later, it is important to keep these two factors separate since they may have separate sources.

Summary and Interpretation

For phallocentric theorists, femininity is problematic. Freud saw the route to masculinity as rather straightforward, ending with identification with the father. Girls by contrast arrive at what he called "mature femininity" by a very circuitous route in which they are induced to give up their active masculine strivings and become acquiescent and passive. Mitchell and Rubin, feminists who accept the phallocentric emphasis, interpret the difficulty of becoming feminine as referring to the fact that in a male-dominant society, women are oppressed by femininity and resist taking it on. Phallocentric theorists stress, however, that the phallocentric emphasis in our society and in all societies is a cultural, not a biological phenomenon. In male-dominated cultures the phallus is valued.

Mitchell's and Rubin's analyses seem important in focusing our attention on human kinship systems and on the fact that within them women are secondary to men. Their analyses can be linked to a theme we have stressed previously: Women's secondary status seems more related to their role as wives than as mothers. The wife role is a kinship role par excellence because it is marriage between unrelated individuals that makes kinship systems possible. In phallocentric cultures, women are defined in relation to the phallus. They are seen as wives, or sex objects, primarily and as mothers, or people, secondarily. They serve the kinship system.

The gynocentric theorists do not deny that we live in a phallocentric culture, but they ask why this occurs. While phallocentric theorists focus on the phallic period and the Oedipus complex, gynocentric theorists focus on the pre-Oedipal period as the source of males' apparent need to dominate. They point to the universal phenomenon of women's mothering as the source.

THE GYNOCENTRIC VIEW In the decade from 1925 to 1935 psychoanalysis focused a great deal of attention on masculine and feminine development, and the different theories were first developed. Ernest Jones, Freud's student and biographer, gave the most definitive articulation of the different approaches and tried to arbitrate the dispute. The work of Melanie Klein and Karen Horney, two early feminists, was most important in Jones's formulation, and the later writings of Helene Deutsch, Ronald Fairbairn, and Nancy Chodorow have contributed further ideas. The various issues raised have never been fully resolved but have reappeared in different forms to the present day.

All the writers we discuss, while approaching the question of childhood development in a different way than Freud, accept his ideas of the unconscious, of repression, and of the importance of sexuality in human society. The changes in emphasis in the gynocentric perspective over the years involved a move from biological and physical descriptions by the early writers to an emphasis on social relations and the development of the ego in later years. While the descriptive terms and emphases change, the gynocentric basis of the analysis remains the same.

The gynocentric position turns Freud's conception around and stresses that a feminine orientation predominates for both males and females in the first stage of life. The gynocentric basis of this position is obvious. The mother is the first person to whom the children relate. Moreover, the first primary orientation of children toward the world around them is seen as feminine. These theorists view castration anxiety as only a secondary manifestation. In contrast to Freud's own view, the gynocentric theorists do not see femininity as a secondary phenomenon, but as part of the child's first orientation toward the world.

The Pre-Oedipal Stages

For gynocentric theorists the first stage in life involves a feminine orientation. Based on her analyses of children, Melanie Klein emphasized the importance of the oral-incorporative stage and the child's close relationship with the mother in early infancy. Although Freud associated destructive urges with the anal stage, Klein believed that sadistic or destructive urges are also found with the oral-incorporative stage. While these urges are first directed toward the self, they become deflected outwards against the mother, the primary object in the child's world.

Helene Deutsch (vol 1., 1944) also emphasized that children's first object relation is with the mother figure. She feeds, cleans, and directs them through the first years of life. Deutsch stressed that it is only natural that children develop not only intense affective attachments to the mother, but also dependencies. The quality of this first-love relationship between the mother and child is the basis of all subsequent development (Fairbairn, 1952). The relationship is a "primary identification, the precursor of object love" (Fliess, 1961:121) and is necessary for the formation of the ego, or self. This strong attachment applies to whomever cares for the child, but because the person is generally a female, this primary identification is feminine in nature in all known cultures.

Most of these theorists agree with Freud that this pre-Oedipal period is largely similar for boys and girls. But while Freud thought a masculine orientation predominates, the gynocentric theorists think a feminine orientation prevails. Both boys and girls identify with the mother and "definitive differentiation" between the sexes occurs later (Deutsch, 1944:vol. 1, 287–88; Klein, 1960). Yet mothers, because they have once been the daughters of mothers, may identify more with their girl children than with their boy children. The tie between a mother and daughter may be stronger than that between the mother and son because the mother tries to repeat "her own mother-child history" (Deutsch, 1944:205).

The Girl's Oedipus Complex

While Freud believed that the phallic phase represented a basic masculine orientation in girls, gynocentric theorists (e.g., Klein, 1960; Jones, 1935) suggest that the phallic phase really only manifests attempts to deal with deep-seated anxiety about aggression against the mother and guilt associated with the Oedipus complex. Karen Horney, for example, talked about a "fictitious male role" to which girls retreat in order to deny their incestuous desires for the father (Horney, 1967b:64).

Because the phallic stage or penis envy is not really a stage but a defensive position, it is never fully overcome. Instead, as the girl grows older, the need for this defense lessens. She develops other defensive postures and realizes that her wish for a penis is an unsatisfactory solution to her anxiety and desire to be separate from the mother. Her femininity, which has always been present, is then more visible. Thus, according to gynocentric theorists, the girl does not revert to femininity because she cannot have masculinity. Femininity is the basic identity.

The gynocentric theorists do not accept Freud's view that the resolution of the Oedipus complex leads to a weaker superego for girls than for boys. They agree with Freud that the superego is based on the incorporation of the parental figures. However, they suggest that this incorporation begins in the first stages of life.

The gynocentric theorists with an object relations orientation and interest in ego psychology stress that the Oedipus crisis involves breaking the primary identification and dependence on the mother that was established in earlier stages. The father assists in breaking these ties. Fairburn suggested that the resolution of the Oedipus complex is a key element in the move away from infantile dependence on the mother. For him, "the 'overcoming of the Oedipus complex' . . . is clearly the struggle to repress an elaborate unresolved infantile dependence on parents, and ultimately on the mother, under the pressure of the need to adjust to the demands of outer life on an increasingly grown-up level" (Guntrip, 1961:357).

Resolution of the Oedipus crisis involves both transformation of the first primary identification with the mother and breaking the intense ties of dependence formed in early infancy. Helene Deutsch (1944) and Nancy Chodorow (1978) note how the father helps break the girl's dependent ties with the mother. They suggest that older women also help widen the girl's social world and encourage her independence from the mother. The daughter has both strong affectional ties and also hostility toward the mother, especially as she grows older, because she sees her mother as keeping her as a child. This vacillation and dependence on the mother continues to at least some extent throughout life and one can never fully break this dependent tie (Deutsch, 1944; Chodorow, 1978).

Nancy Chodorow (1978) stresses particularly the significance of the girl's pre-Oedipal tie to her mother in her resolution of the Oedipus complex. Daughters, according to Chodorow, do not feel inadequate because they have no penis. Rather they, along with boys, feel inadequate because of the mother's omnipotence. Unlike the male child, the girl does not have a penis to help her feel separate and independent from the mother, and also the mother herself feels differently toward her daughter than toward her son. Penis envy in girls then, according to this view, develops, not because girls wish to become men, but because they want to liberate themselves from the mother and become "complete, autonomous *women*" (Chasseguet-Smirgel, 1964:118).

These authors also suggest that a girl might develop penis envy because she needs the mother's love. This need coupled with her perception that the mother prefers men may cause the girl to feel she needs a penis in order to win her mother's love. Here it is the girl's love for her mother rather than her hostility toward her that explains penis envy.

Both these explanations have the advantage of not positing some biologically given heterosexuality in explaining the girl's turn toward the father. Both suggest that the girl's turn to the father is not because she already is heterosexual but rather because of the nature of her relationship with her mother and because of her mother's own attitudes. While the father encourages the girl's male-oriented femininity, the girl's identity as a woman is developed in her first, early identification with the mother.

The Boy's Oedipus Complex

The early gynocentric theorists stressed that the first orientation of boys, as well as girls, is feminine. As with the development of girls, the gynocentric theorists see male castration anxiety (the fear of castration) as only a secondary manifestation of the resolution of the phallic phase. The theoretical explanation of the process is extremely complex and involves fantasies the boy creates to deal with his anxiety regarding his desires for the mother and his fears of both parents (see Jones, 1933; Klein, 1960).

Later writers in the gynocentric vein emphasize how changes in social relations prompt the resolution of the boy's Oedipus crisis. Helene Deutsch again saw the father as helping to promote the boy's independence from the mother. In a man-to-man relationship the father encourages the boy's independence from the mother and even supports his devaluation of the mother. The nature of this father and son relationship varies from one family to another and affects the boy's later life.

While the father helps promote a boy's gender identity—his conviction that he is male—this process is more difficult for males than for females because their first and primary identity was feminine. The boy must replace his early feminine identification with the mother with a masculine identification, usually based on the father or other males. But adult males tend to be remote from the world of children and are not available for identification. The boy's identification with the masculine role then tends to be more diffuse, an identification with a position or a fantasized image rather than with a person. Because what he knows most intimately is feminine, the boy comes to define masculinity as that which is not feminine. Internally he rejects his early attachment to and dependence on the mother. Externally he devalues what is feminine and denies his attachment to the feminine world (Chodorow, 1974).

Both because the male's sex role identity is built upon a negative basis, only knowing what it is not, and because there are few actual males with whom the boy can identify, his sex role identity is more ambiguous and unstable than the girl's. Chodorow (1978) suggests that boys' and girls' different experiences of identification contribute to their later life orientations. The girl may continue her personal identifications with others, primarily with her children and other women. The boy, however, less often has personal identifications, having neither close relationships with children nor in many societies personal affective relationships with other men. The recent work with transsexuals (see chapter 6) supports this thesis that males' first identification is feminine and that difficulties in breaking this tie produce problems in gender identification.

Summary

In contrast to Freud's phallocentric approach, the gynocentric theorists assert that children's first orientation is feminine. The castration anxiety and penis envy Freud noted are seen by these theorists as secondary manifestations that result from anxiety regarding the Oedipus complex and hostility toward and fear of the mother. The Oedipus complex is seen as both the time at which children develop greater independence from the mother and the point at which their gender identity becomes fixed. Because the child's basic identity is feminine, the boy's gender identity is less stable than that of the girl, yet the girl may maintain a closer relationship to the mother. This perspective on sex role development is especially helpful in understanding motives underlying male dominance.

GYNOCENTRIC EXPLANATIONS OF MALE DOMINANCE

Two basic themes, both of which arise from the emphasis on the pre-Oedipal period of intense mother-child contact, are important in the gynocentric analysis of male dominance. One involves the unconscious fear and envy children of both sexes, but especially males, feel toward the mother. The other concerns the problems males encounter in establishing a secure sense of masculine gender identity. The earliest gynocentric theorists tended to emphasize the fear-and-envy hypothesis. Later ones, who used an object relational analysis, emphasized identity problems of males. None of the early theorists was primarily concerned with explaining male dominance but some did point to how the early primacy of the mother is related to a tendency of males to devalue females and femininity. Below we trace each of these themes and explore their implications for change.

Fear and Envy of Women

The early gynocentric theorists stressed how the mother's power over the child in its early years contributes to the child's unconscious fear and envy first of its mother and later of women in general. This stems from the child's total dependence on the mother and the child's hostility and ambivalence that arise at the Oedipal period. While both female and male children experience this fear and envy, the female can counter it later with the fact that she herself is a female. The male child has no such relief, and the envy and dread may be repressed and later expressed collectively in legends, artwork, and ceremonies and sometimes individually in dreams and neuroses. Below we note examples of how this fear and envy is shown in the actions of individuals, in stories and art, and in collective ceremonies and customs and how it relates to individual and group efforts to devalue the activities and nature of women.*

Karen Horney reported a small experiment conducted in a children's clinic in Germany that she interpreted as confirming the strength of males' symbolic fear of the vagina (1967a:137–38):

> The physician [who conducted the experiment] was playing ball with the children at a treatment center and after a time showed them that the ball had a slit in it. She pulled the edges of the slit apart and put her finger in, so that it was held fast by the ball. Of 28 boys whom she asked to do the same, only 6 did it without fear and 8 could not be induced to do it at all. Of 19 girls, 9 put their finger in without a trace of fear; the rest showed a slight uneasiness but none of them serious anxiety.

Horney linked men's general fear of women to the boy's fear of being rebuffed by the mother and the subsequent loss of self-esteem. In turn she saw this fear as prompting men's compulsion to prove their manhood. This compulsion is linked to the desire to conquer or possess many women, "the propensity to debase the love object"—that is, to love only women who are seen as less than equal to them, and the tendency to "diminish the self-respect of the woman" (Horney, 1967a:145–46).

Fear of women and of female genitalia may be seen in both myths and written history in widely varying cultures. This fear may be masked, however, by outward glorification of women. For example, a medieval statue when viewed from the front appears to be a peaceful serene woman, but from the back it is literally "covered with sores, ulcers, worms and all manner of pestilence" (Lederer, 1968:37). Hays (1964, 1972) specifically argues that social institutions in societies from the most primitive to the most modern have been designed to defend men against their fears of women by circumscribing, regulating, and containing women.

In addition to fear, however, there is an element of envy and even awe in men's attitude toward women. Margaret Mead argues that men envy

*Freud himself noted men's dread of women's genitals in his analysis of "The Taboo on Virginity" (Freud, 1963d:76–79), but he later dropped this in favor of men's fear of castration by the father or his representatives. The gynocentric theorists, however, developed this idea in their own work. Ernest Jones suggested that the boy believes his own genitals are inferior in size to his mother's vagina and that this influences a boy's castration fears at the time of the Oedipus crisis (1933).

women's procreative powers and interprets some initiation ceremonies and puberty rites of primitive tribes as attempts to give this mysterious power to men. In the parts of New Guinea she studied, "it is men who spend their ceremonial lives pretending that it was they who had borne the children, that they can 'make men' " (1974:97). According to Mead, men in New Guinea also tell stories about how their mythical man-making powers were invented by a woman and stolen from her by men.* Other groups in this area have initiation ceremonies in which boys are taught to make their noses bleed in imitation of female menstruation (Lidz and Lidz, 1977).

Horney and Mead both suggest a probable link between men's envy of women and their cultural productivity, their creation of material and cultural goods (Horney, 1967b:61) and their need for achievement (Mead, 1949). This may be seen in the Biblical account of creation in Genesis, where the woman Eve is in effect born of the man Adam. Also, primitive initiation ceremonies of boys are conducted by older men, suggesting the idea of boys being reborn, this time of men. Thus the initiation of males by males along with some of the symbolism can be taken as an acting out of the repressed male wish to give birth. "He [the boy] still carries his knowledge of child-birth as something that women can do, that his sister will be able to do, as a latent goad to some other type of achievement. He embarks on a long course of growth and practice, the outcome of which, if he sees it as not only being able to possess a woman, but to become a father, is very uncertain" (Mead, 1949:166).

These writers focus on how males' fear and envy of women prompt their need to separate their activities from women's and to devalue women's role. Recently, Dorothy Dinnerstein (1976) has argued that both women and men agree to let males have the power in the adult world because this power is less of a psychological threat than the power the mother had over them as infants. She emphasizes that both males and females fear the power of the mother and suggests that we give males authority because it appears to be a refuge from female authority. Female rule is more threatening because it is more primitive and more all encompassing—"the relatively limited despotism of the father is a relief to us" (1976:189). Thus "both men and women use the unresolved early threat of female domination to justify keeping the infantilism in themselves alive under male domination" (Dinnerstein, 1976:191; see also Stannard, 1977).

*This idea has been attributed to Bruno Bettleheim, who devotes a chapter to it in his book *Symbolic Wounds* (1954). Mead notes that Bettleheim used her own discussion of these activities, which she published in *Male and Female* in 1949, without acknowledgement and then speculated on "why men said they had stolen their supernatural imitative feminine powers from women" (Mead, 1974:97)!

Tenuous Masculine Identity

While unconscious fear and envy of the mother's power may prompt men to separate their own activities from women's and to elevate their own power, the tenuous nature of males' gender identity also contributes to this motive. Cultural ceremonies illustrate men's need to break with the world of women when they enter adulthood. For men all initiation ceremonies signify passage into the adult male role. Initiation ceremonies are much more common for males than for females, suggesting that it is males who need an extra push into masculinity. Initiation ceremonies for young men are also more common in father-absent societies, whose sleeping patterns and residence arrangements emphasize and exaggerate the mother-son bond (Burton and Whiting, 1961). Other evidence from our own society indicates that in cultural groups where the father is only rarely involved in childhood socialization young males tend to develop their own initiatory rites, such as gang or club membership, to demonstrate their departure from the world of women.*

Moreover, just as Margaret Mead suggests that males' fear of women influences their achievement needs, so does their need to separate their own identity from women's. In a great number of human societies, men's sureness of their sex role is tied up with their right or ability to practice some activity that women are not allowed to practice. Their maleness, in fact, has to be underwritten by preventing women from entering some field or performing some feat. Here may be found the relationship between maleness and pride, a need for prestige that will outstrip the prestige accorded to any woman. There seems no evidence that it is necessary for men to surpass women in any specific way. Rather, men do need to find reassurance in achievement. Because of this connection, cultures frequently phrase achievement as something that women do not or cannot do, rather than directly as something that men do well (Mead, 1949:168–69):

> The recurrent problem of civilization is to define the male role satisfactorily enough—whether it be to build gardens or raise cattle, kill game or kill enemies, build bridges or handle bank-shares—so that the male may in the course of his life reach a solid sense of irreversible achievement, of which his childhood knowledge of the satisfactions of child-bearing have given him a glimpse. . . . If men are ever to be at peace, they must have, in addition to paternity, culturally elaborated forms of expression that are lasting and sure.

*Clearly, initiation ceremonies have multiple meanings and functions. By discussing their possible psychological significance for masculinity we do not mean to imply that these are their only function.

Each culture—in its own way—has developed forms that will make men satisfied in their constructive activities without distorting their sure sense of their masculinity.

This tenuous identity influences males' devaluation of women. Nancy Chodorow (1974:50) stresses that the boy's "attempt to gain an elusive masculine identification . . . explains the psychological dynamics of the universal social and cultural devaluation and subordination of women." The boy, in order to deny his attachment and deep personal identification with his mother, does so "by repressing whatever he takes to be feminine inside himself, and, more importantly, by denigrating and devaluing whatever he considers to be feminine in the outside world." Beyond this, Chodorow suggests that in the social world "he also appropriates to himself and defines as superior particular social activities and cultural (moral, religious, and creative) spheres."

Summary and Implications

Gynocentric theories suggest a psychological explanation of male dominance that rests on the universal social assignment of mothering to women. To escape from the power of the mother and the intensity of their first feminine identification, males create ways of coping that deny this identity in themselves and establish their own independent power. Societies value the phallus because it symbolizes males' separate identity from the mother and their greater power. According to this perspective, males' psychic need for individuation—that is, for separating themselves from the mother—requires that they devalue, and segregate themselves from, the activities that represent her world and the time when they were totally dependent on and identified with her. Females, because their first identity is feminine, have no such need to segregate and devalue the actions of males.

If the source of the fear and envy of the mother as well as males' tenuous masculine identity is the close mother-child contact in infancy, an obvious way to alter this would be for both males and females to nurture infants. In contrast to Rubin's suggestion (1975) that this would obliterate gender identity, it would probably facilitate a less problematic gender identity for both males and females and minimize males' psychic need to disparage women. Such a move would also minimize the division of roles within the family. In contrast to Mitchell's suggestion that the family could be eliminated, the extension of child-care tasks to both males and females would facilitate a less oppressive family situation, for both adults and children.

Thus, while the phallocentric analysis describes how the male-dominant culture continues to be reproduced and stresses the role of phallic symbolism in feminizing women, the gynocentric perspective describes how the masculine motive to dominate is reproduced. The social role analysis discussed in the next chapter clarifies these views and helps point toward change.

SUMMARY

A psychoanalytic explanation of sex role development focuses on early associations within the family and can help account for the motivational bases of male dominance. Two threads of psychoanalytic thought may be distinguished. The phallocentric perspective follows Freud's early outline and assumes the basic superiority of males and that girls accept femininity only when they realize that they cannot be males. This analysis has been used by contemporary feminists to show how the maintenance of male dominance is linked to human kinship systems, the incest taboo, and the resolution of the Oedipus complex. The gynocentric perspective, while using basic concepts and understandings of Freud, stresses the early and basic feminine orientation of both males and females. Theorists with this perspective suggest that because of this early feminine orientation and early associations with the mother, it is more difficult for males than females to establish their gender identity. Feminist theorists use this perspective to analyze the origin of the psychological motive behind male dominance.

Suggested Readings

DINNERSTEIN, DOROTHY, *The Mermaid and the Minotaur: Sexual Arrangements and Human Malaise.* New York: Harper & Row, Pub., 1976. The author's version of the theory that male dominance is a result of women's mothering.

FREUD, SIGMUND, *Sexuality and the Psychology of Love,* ed. Philip Rieff. New York: Collier Books, 1963. An easily available volume that includes most of Freud's writings that deal with sex role development.

The International Journal of Psychoanalysis. The best way to understand psychoanalytic writings is to read the original sources. Most of the early articles by such people as Ernest Jones, Helene Deutsch, Karen Horney, Melanie Klein, and Sigmund Freud and many later ones were published in this journal.

MITCHELL, JULIET, *Psychoanalysis and Feminism.* New York: Vintage, 1974. Reviews and interprets theories of others and presents Mitchell's own psychoanalytic view of the basis of male dominance.

STROUSE, JEAN, ed., *Women and Analysis.* New York: Grossman, 1974. A collection of older and contemporary psychoanalytic writings on women.

10: Parents, Peers, and Male Dominance

In this chapter we focus on role interaction between parents and children in the family and interaction in sex-segregated peer groups. From this we can see how institutionalized roles within these groups contribute to the development of sex-differentiated personalities and the reproduction of male dominance.* This social-role perspective on personality development will help us integrate many of the findings from psychological and psychoanalytic studies reported earlier. We begin with a discussion of how fathers and mothers affect the sex typing of their children and then turn to a discussion of adolescence and how the male peer group contributes to and reinforces attitudes of male dominance and female devaluation. We also discuss the deviant phenomena of incest and rape, as they are both consequences and distorted versions of family relations and male peer-group relations respectively.

PARENTAL ROLES AND SEX TYPING

While Talcott Parsons's (1955, 1970) model of sex role socialization in the family does not attempt to analyze male dominance, his model of interaction in reciprocal roles is a useful starting point in analyzing the development of sex-differentiated personalities and male dominance in social systems. In essence Parsons's model recasts psychoanalytic ideas on development into terms compatible with social learning, modeling, and cognitive developmental theory and puts them all into the framework of

*We prefer the word *reproduce* to *transmit* because, as Christopher Lasch (1977:93) points out, the latter implies a cultural determinism we wish to avoid. The word *reproduce* implies that social relations produce social relations, and this more closely represents our meaning.

social role theory. He suggests that through interactions in the family in reciprocal roles the child learns both what it is to be human and what it means to be male or female.

Parsons suggests that the processes Freud referred to as identification and social learning theorists refer to as modeling can best be understood not so much as learning to become like another as learning to play a social role with another person. A role defines the expected behavior for an individual in a given status. Roles are complementary or reciprocal because they make no sense without the related actions of others. For example, the husband role is complementary to the wife role, and the mother role is complementary to the child role. Social learning, then, takes place through interacting in complementary or reciprocal roles in terms of a shared system of meaning or values. Common meanings and understandings are established in the interaction. In learning to play social roles with their parents, children are not only integrated into a social interaction system, but also their personalities are in large measure formed by this social interaction. Sex-typed personalities then are reproduced in children by interacting in family roles.

According to Parsons, in spite of enormous cross-cultural variations in kinship systems and family structure, all societies have two basic structural regularities that underlie the uniformities we find in sex role acquisition: A child's first human contact tends to be with a nurturing female or females; the father or other male(s), who is not primarily nurturant, enters both the male and female child's psychological world at a later time. This does not mean that fathers do not nurture, but that cross-culturally the mother role is more associated with nurturance than the father role. The concept *mother* may mean different things to different people and in different cultures, but cross-culturally nurturance is at least one of its meanings. Parsons's model does not refer to the structure of any particular concrete family; rather, he describes the family in terms of sex and generational roles. Obviously many children can and do grow up without mothers or fathers, but they do not grow up without a conception of what mothers and fathers are supposed to be like.

Parsons suggests that through interaction with the mother in a dyadic role relationship infants of both sexes learn to respond to the attitudes of others and to love. This first interaction of the infant with its mother is not sex typed. Both male and female infants learn how to feel nurturant as well as how to be nurtured in interaction with the mother.

According to Parsons's role-oriented version of Freud, the Oedipal stage has two functions: to promote the internalization of sex role categorization, and to break the child's dependent relationship with the mother and integrate him or her into the role system of the family as a whole. This is the meaning that Parsons gives to Freud's superego concept. In Parsons's view, both sexes (not just males) must achieve independence from the mother and join the wider social system. As he puts it, "The childhood level of dependency is just as unsuitable for either sex beyond a certain point" (1970:41). Thus, while sex role adoption and breaking dependency ties with the mother occur closely in time, they are distinct conceptually. Parsons believed that Freud did not adequately distinguish the two (1970:41–42).

When the child moves into the larger social system of the family as a whole, two major differentiating axes—age and sex—become important. The boy learns that he cannot adopt his mother's role because of his sex categorization; on the other hand, he cannot adopt his father's role with the mother because of the generational difference. Like the boy, the girl breaks her dependent attachment to the mother and enters the wider social system of the family. In so doing she identifies again with the mother because of their common gender, but she cannot take over the mother's relation with the father because of the generational difference. In essence, Parsons sees the incest taboo as reflecting and preserving the difference between generations and of emphasizing the responsibility of the parent for the child as a person. Parsons himself does not explain how sex categorization is learned, nor does he give any special role to the father in the process other than noting that the father is the representative not only of masculinity but also of the family as a whole. In Freud's account, the boy acquires a superego when he identifies with, or introjects, his threatening father. The girl, by contrast, is left to acquire what superego she can through more gradual means. Unlike Freud, Parsons sees both sexes as acquiring a superego by internalizing the role structure of the family, including its sex-differentiated roles and incest taboos.

Parsons's model is more a conceptual framework in whose terms further analyses can be made than an empirical analysis in and of itself. Because the model is so general, it can serve as a baseline for developing specific hypotheses to interpret empirical data on parental roles and the development of sex typing in children.

Johnson (1963) suggests as an implication of both Freud's and Parsons's theories that given women's earlier primacy for children, the father role might be more crucial than the mother role in reinforcing masculine and feminine behaviors and orientations in children of both sexes. This view of the father as the focus of sex-differentiated behaviors has since received considerable empirical support (see chapter 8) and can help specify more concretely how sex differentiation and male dominance are reproduced.

Much of the confusion about whether and how mothers and fathers might foster sex typing in their children can be clarified if we make a distinction within the so-called feminine role between its nurturant aspects and its heterosexual aspects. Both sexes learn nurturance from being nurtured, usually by the mother. Acquiring the heterosexual aspects of femininity (and also of masculinity), on the other hand, appears to be more associated with interactions with the father and is also tied in with male dominance. The heterosexual aspects of sex roles (the wife role for women and the husband role for men) involve an element of masculine superiority. As we discussed earlier, the husband role, is culturally defined as more powerful than the wife role because of male dominance in the society. The term *feminine* in our culture more often refers to the heterosexual than to the nurturant or maternal aspects of the feminine role. (Johnson, 1975).

The Mother Role and Learning to Be Human

In the maternal role as opposed to the wife role, the mother has considerable power over her offspring throughout their lives. The reciprocal of the mother role is the child role, and the mother is more powerful than the child because of the generational difference. The strong mother-child bonds developed in infancy continue throughout life, and mothers may retain emotional and psychological influence over their children until death.

In the first few years of life, infants learn in their interactions with their mothers to relate in nurturant and expressive modes—to respond to and be aware of the social needs of others. In the reciprocal role relation with the mother, the child learns both its own responsive child role and that of the nurturant mother. Both boys and girls relate to the mother in this manner and develop their basic human qualities, their capacity to relate to other people, to care for and care about other people.

Research indicates that the degree of a child's self-control is related to the warmth and responsiveness of his or her early caretaker. For example, researchers once found that the development of obedience and then internalized controls in infants is related to the "sensitivity of maternal responsiveness to infant signals, but not to frequency of commands or forcible interventions" (Stayton et al., 1971:1067). Another study reports that one of the most consistently replicated findings in child-rearing studies is the positive association between ratings of maternal warmth and ratings of conscience in children of both sexes (Yarrow et al., 1968:103). (Unfortunately, we know of no studies that correlate paternal warmth and internalized control of infants. Such studies are undoubtedly rare because fathers spend little time in early child care.) All of this supports Parsons's view that the early influence of nurturant and maternal love helps establish internal controls.

Social learning and modeling theorists also suggest that the mother is the major source of moral learning. Kohlberg (and to some extent the gynocentric psychoanalytic theorist Melanie Klein) suggest (contrary to Freud) that the mother's moral role leads girls to have stronger consciences than boys. However, the relationship both boys and girls have with the mother comes before sex differentiation becomes salient and before the Oedipal period. Thus, we see no reason to assume that one sex is more socialized or moral than the other. Both sexes learn to respond to social sanctions in connection with the pre-Oedipal mother relationship (Johnson, 1976).

Some authors in the psychoanalytic tradition suggest that this early emotional relationship with the mother is more intense for daughters than for sons. According to Chodorow (1978), because the mother and daughter are the same sex the mother experiences and treats girls differently from boys. She contends that these differences are too subtle to be captured by the psychological studies Maccoby and Jacklin evaluated when they concluded that mothers treated the sexes remarkably alike. Chodorow argues that on a deep emotional level, quite apart from a level of role expectations and even physical contact, mothers experience daughters as less separate from themselves than sons. In fact, Chodorow suggests that these differences in maternal relations produce the sex differences in personality organization described in chapter 7. She sees females as less separate and differentiated from others than males are.

In support of her argument that mothers experience and treat their pre-Oedipal girls and boys differently, Chodorow relies on evidence from psychiatrists treating patients rather than on the kinds of experimental evidence that Maccoby and Jacklin used. She notes that there are many more clinical accounts of pathological mothers who deny separateness and refuse to allow their daughters to individuate than accounts of mothers who do the same with sons. She maintains that these cases reflect in exaggerated form the differences in normal tendencies. Hence she says that girls retain their pre-Oedipal attachment to their mothers and continue to define and experience themselves as continuous with others.

Chodorow's description of women feeling more continuous with others and less individuated than men obscures several important distinctions. Her description implies that mothers' treatment of daughters makes them both more dependent and more expressive than males. We have argued that women are no more dependent on others' responses than men but they are more expressive. Both males and females learn from the mother how to nurture and to deal with others in expressive modes, but men later deny this capacity in their effort to establish a separate identity. Chodorow argues that mothers "mother" their female infants more than their male infants and thus reproduce mothering in females.

We argue that both sexes learn the maternal role from the mother but males are later constrained to deny this capacity. Both boys and girls must become more independent as they grow older (Johnson, 1975, 1977; Stockard and Johnson, 1979). Because of the early primacy of the mother in all societies, fathers or other males tend to represent independence from the mother to children of both sexes. The father helps both boys and girls achieve freedom from depending on and merging with the mother. In fact, Chodorow suggests that the strength of the girl's involvement with the father is proportional to the degree to which she was formerly attached to her mother.

The Father Role and Learning Sex-Typed Interaction

Many accounts of the Oedipal period tend to assume a symmetrical process in which girls love their fathers and copy their mothers, while boys love their mothers and copy their fathers. In fact, from a psychological standpoint, the mother in the Oedipal period does not play a role toward her son that is symmetrical to the role the father plays toward his daughter (Johnson, 1963, 1975). In a male-dominant society the male's learning to be masculine by interacting with his mother introduces a contradiction, because in this relationship she, the mother, is the dominant figure. The relationship between mother and son reverses the usual power position between the sexes. As a consequence, the son cannot very well use the complementary relationship of mother and son as a model for learning adult heterosexual relations, for these involve the sexual control of women. Thus, while mothers and sons may interact sometimes in a way that mimics adult heterosexual relations, the mother-son relationship is not the prototype of these. In the father-daughter relationship, on the other hand, the father is dominant both because of his generation and because of his sex. Therefore, this relationship does mimic more closely adult heterosexual relationships.

The anthropologist Serge Moscovici (Brogger, 1976) argues that because the mother-son relationship involves female dominance, the fundamental reason for the incest taboo is to end this relationship and install male dominance. He says, essentially, that if sons were allowed to stay with (or marry) their mothers, women, not men, would be the dominant group. Moscovici argues that the only true incest taboo is that between mother and son (and indeed this is by far the strongest and most universal taboo) and the fear of this type of incest is inspired by the fear of female dominance.

In a very different way, Maccoby and Jacklin in their discussion of how males learn masculinity also recognize that the mother-son relationship is not the prototype of adult male-female relationships (1974:306, first italics authors', second ours):

> *Each parent transfers to his children some of the behavior he is accustomed to displaying toward adults of the two sexes.* In some cases this amounts to outright sexual attraction and seduction of the opposite sex child. . . . Most commonly, of course, there are simply discreet elements of flirtation with the opposite sex child. Dominance-submission relationships, as well as sexual ones, may generalize to children. If a woman is accustomed to taking a submissive stance toward her husband and other adult men, the hypothesis says that she will be more likely to behave submissively toward a son than a daughter. Clearly there are instances in which the role demands of parenthood (especially *motherhood*) are not consistent with habitual male-female interaction patterns.

This emphasis on the mother role is needed as an important qualification to the assumption that males learn the heterosexual masculine role from interacting with their mothers as girls learn the heterosexual aspects of the feminine role from interacting with their fathers. Since the mother role carries more power than the son role, a seductive relation between mother and son, if not counteracted by some other factor, may actually be more of a threat than a spur to the son's masculinity with its overtones of male dominance.

The different feelings and emotions involved in the father-daughter and mother-son relationship in the middle class were once commented on by Mike Nichols in an interview: "Women, girls, live very comfortably with the fact that they want to sleep with their fathers. Right from the beginning they make jokes about it. They sit on Daddy's lap. Everybody knows it and it's sort of nice. Not us. Lots of edginess. Lots of 'Oh mother puhleeze!' I think the discomfort stays with us always" (Goldsmith, 1970:143). While Nichols is describing a middle-class phenomenon and may have exaggerated the overt sexuality in the father-daughter relationship, his perception that males somehow must resist their mothers seems correct. Males feel this uneasiness because the mother's dominance over the child is incompatible with the expected dominance of the male over the female. Although males may develop heterosexual urges as well as learn how to nurture and love from their mothers, they do not learn to take women as sex objects from their mothers. In a patriarchal world, growing up for the male involves overcoming the power of the mother and gaining independence. It also involves learning that males should be dominant over females and learning to take the sexual initiative with women. Males learn this largely through interaction with other males. They protect themselves from female dominance through their interactions with their fathers and within the male peer group.

Fathers and sex-differentiating behaviors As we saw in chapter 8, Maccoby and Jacklin (1974) conclude that in spite of a few widely cited studies showing differential maternal treatment, generally researchers have found that mothers distinguish little in handling their male and female children. In contrast, the few studies on fathers all suggest that they do differentiate between the sexes and have differing expectations for the future of their boys and girls. The classic study was done by Evelyn Goodenough (1957) on upper-class parents of nursery-school children. Goodenough found that mothers were not nearly so concerned with sex typing as fathers. Furthermore, she reported that fathers seemed to be actively and personally involved in sex typing while the mothers were aware of it but did not actively implement it.

Those few studies where the behavior of fathers and mothers can be compared provide evidence at least in the middle class (where most of these studies were done): that fathers are more concerned with their children being "appropriately" sex typed than mothers; that fathers respond to children on the basis of their sex more than mothers; and that fathers differentiate their role toward other-sexed children more than mothers. We cited evidence for these assertions in Chapter 8.

Studies of older children and adolescents show much the same thing. A national survey once asked, "What kind of person would you want your son to become?" and "What kind of person would you want your daughter to become?" Among the parents with at least one child, 21 percent of the fathers answered in terms of career or occupational success for sons while only 14 percent gave this answer for daughters. Mothers were also more likely to mention career success for sons, but made a less marked differentiation between expectations for sons and daughters (Hoffman, 1977:651).

Fathers also differentiate between boys and girls more than mothers in their treatment of and interactions with their children. Urie Bronfenbrenner once reported in a study of adolescents that "generally speaking it is the father who is especially likely to treat children of the two sexes differently. . . . Girls receive more affection, attention and praise than boys —especially from their fathers—whereas boys are subjected to greater pressure and discipline, again mainly from their fathers" (1961:249).

Yet, impressive as this evidence is, most of it comes from studies of the American middle class and it cannot be generalized to all cultural settings or even to the working class in this country. For example, there is evidence that working-class fathers may be very punitive toward their daughters (Droppleman and Schaefer, 1963), while middle-class fathers are more overtly affectionate (Bronfenbrenner, 1961). While fathers differentiate their behavior toward the sexes in both classes, the form of this differentiation may vary. In addition, working-class mothers may be more likely to make sex differentiations than middle-class mothers (Kagan, 1972).

Although some of the findings we cited in chapter 8 regarding attitudes and expectations may turn out to be specific to the middle class, we might predict that the father's role toward the girl, whatever its specific form, is more directly related to control over her sexuality and concern with it than is the mother's role toward the boy. In other words, the father affects the heterosexual, not the maternal aspects, of sex role behavior. The heterosexual aspects of the feminine role reflect and support male dominance, while the maternal aspects actually work against it. So when we say men are more concerned with sex typing than women, we mean that the core of this concern has the effect of creating and maintaining men's sexual dominance over women.

Fathers and the heterosexual aspects of sex roles If we maintain the distinction between the maternal and the heterosexual aspects of femininity, the data do suggest that males are more concerned with the heterosexual aspects of sex roles than females are and that the father role is more involved in the process by which individuals become heterosexual. Males are more likely than females to support the double standard of sexual behavior for males and females. Obviously, both fathers and mothers are concerned with the morality of their sons and daughters, and both fathers and mothers do tend to be more concerned for their daughters than for their sons. Yet college students appear to perceive that their fathers are much less disapproving of male premarital intercourse than mothers are. Reports show fathers differentiating between males and females more than mothers in that they disapprove less of premarital sex for males. The same pattern appears with reports of the attitudes to brothers and sisters (Kaats and Davis, 1970). Similarly, a survey of high-school students' occupational choices reported that females more often than males believed that having a "sexually moral" job was important to their parents. Many more young women attributed this concern to their fathers than to their mothers (Johnson, 1977).

Of course, this evidence does indicate that mothers also support the double standard, though less so than fathers. Both sexes are operating within the masculine paradigm, but because it *is* masculine its main tenets are held, under most circumstances, more strongly by males than by females.

Seymour Fisher (1974) conducted a five-year study using the verbal reports of 300 middle-class housewives on their frequency of orgasm. He found that virtually the only factor that differentiated the women with low orgasm rates from the women with high orgasm rates in marital coitus was the reported quality of their early relationship with their fathers. If a woman perceived her father as not having invested serious or dependable interest in her, she was likely to report orgasmic difficulties. On the other hand, he found no correlation between orgasmic consistency in marital intercourse and attitudes toward the mothers.

In a similarly unanticipated finding, Mirra Komarovsky (1976) reports from her study of college men that the most significant factor differentiating students who were still virgins in their senior year from the majority of students who had had sexual intercourse was "unsatisfactory relationships with fathers." Komarovsky remarks that this finding is contrary to the usual opinion that the mother-son relationship is important in accounting for the sexual problems of males (1976:124).

Fathers and sexual preference Perhaps the clearest test of the hypothesis that the father is more involved in children's adoption of the specifically sexual aspects of sex roles than the mother comes from data on the factors influencing sexual preference. Sexual preference refers to whether individuals prefer to relate sexually to members of their own sex or to members of the other sex. Increasingly, sexual preference is coming to be seen as distinct from gender identity. Most homosexuals (individuals who prefer same sex sexual partners) identify with their own biological sex. While it is important not to dwell on the causes of homosexuality as if it were a disease, it is also important not to ignore existing data comparing the backgrounds of heterosexuals and homosexuals for what they can tell us about social factors affecting sexual preference.* While clearly there are multiple routes by which an individual might arrive at a given sexual orientation, in contemporary society where families tend to be nuclear, isolated from each other, and privatized, the impact of parents on their children's sexuality might be expected to be great. As it turns out, data concerning the parental relationships of both female and male homosexuals strongly suggest that the father relationship is more crucial than the mother relationship (Johnson, 1979).†

*Much of the research on homosexuality is flawed methodologically because the subjects have come from patient populations and the findings cannot be taken as representative of normally functioning homosexuals. Even the studies on nonpatients do not represent the actual distribution of homosexuals in the population. Also the supposedly heterosexual controls in these studies may have actually contained some homosexuals or bisexuals since researchers usually assume heterosexuality if individuals do not explicitly define themselves as homosexual. Finally, these studies are retrospective rather than longitudinal and we must assume that individuals' present perceptions of their past are accurate. Because of these difficulties, research on the causes of homosexuality is rightfully suspect. On the other hand, imperfect research is better than no research at all if it is used with discrimination.

†We do not wish to reject out of hand the possibility that sex object choice has a biological component. But this biological component must be expressed and developed in a social context. Thus, the analysis of the relation to the father would not be invalidated if such a biological influence could be substantiated.

Psychoanalytic theories concerning male homosexuality generally posit that homosexuals are likely to have had close-binding mothers and hostile or distant fathers who did not counteract the mother's seductiveness. This left the male child forever tied to the mother and unable to seek relationships with other women. In general, however, the studies of male homosexuals compared to heterosexuals (whether researchers used patients or nonpatients as subjects) have actually found a close-binding mother far less consistently than they have found a hostile or detached father (Johnson, 1979).

While many psychoanalytic theorists tend to relate homosexuality to an overly close mother relationship, Irving Bieber and others (1962) theoretically account for why the father relationship might be especially important. Bieber argues that under ordinary circumstances all males would be heterosexual (especially in a world that values heterosexuality), but homosexuals have rejected heterosexuality out of fear not of women but of other men. Bieber's idea is that homosexuals fear that they will be in some way punished for showing an interest in women by aggressive males who "own" these women. They therefore turn away from heterosexuality and seek sexual relations with men who are perceived (perhaps because they are themselves not heterosexual) as nonthreatening.

This fear of males develops during the Oedipal phase when the child fears the father's punishment for his sexualized attachment to the mother. Ordinarily, the fear is resolved when the boy learns to relinquish the mother and joins the world of male peers, finally becoming sexually attached to another woman with his father's blessings. But when the father fails to form a solidary relationship with the child, the child continues to fear the father's intervention in his sexualized relationship with the mother. He finds it hard to join his male peers and repeats this fear in relations with other women in whom he may become interested sexually. Thus, to the extent that women may be phobic to male homosexuals, the women are perceived as belonging to a fear-inspiring man.

Bieber's analysis fits with Kohlberg's idea that adult men in general are perceived by boys and girls alike to be more threatening than adult women. These ideas are based on the gross physical differences between the sexes such as men's greater size and strength, their deeper and louder voices, and their larger physical movements. Thus, men project a greater potential for violence than women do and, in fact, men are more aggressive than women. It would follow that if the father or some other male does not ally himself with the child to mitigate this perception and to indicate to the child that men are not fearsome after all, the child (especially if he perceives himself to be unlike other males his age) will probably feel unable to join the world of males in general. This helps explain why some male homosexuals actually did have violent and frightening fathers, while many others simply had fathers who were passively hostile or indifferent to them. In both of these cases, there was no solidary relationship between father and son and no way to mitigate the sons' early impression that masculinity is formidable.

In arguing that the father is more critical than the mother with respect to influencing sexual preference, we do not mean to imply that many other factors are also not important or that Bieber's explanation covers all instances of homosexuality. Neither do we wish to imply that homosexuality is undesirable. We focus on parental relations not in order to cure homosexuality, but because it has significance for our general analysis of male dominance. Bieber's work is significant for us because it suggests that while superficially homosexuals appear to reject women, at a deeper (perhaps unconscious) level, it may be that many homosexual males are attempting to cope with male dominance. Certainly one important implication of this analysis is that it is not the supermasculine father that would be conducive to heterosexuality in his son (if heterosexuality remains a desirable goal), but a male who would mitigate the image of the threatening male who "owns" women.

With regard to lesbians some psychoanalytically oriented theorists posit a reversal of the male situation and suspect a hostile and distant mother and a close-binding father. Still another theory is put forth by the psychiatrist Charlotte Wolff (1971), who argues that mothers "are the strongest force in the development of lesbianism" by virtue of their rejection of the daughter and preference for men. In Wolff's view, what the father is like is relatively inconsequential. Again, however, when we examine all the research comparing lesbian women with heterosexual women, we find that where a comparison can be made the groups differ much less with respect to their relationship with their mothers than with regard to their relationship with their fathers (Johnson et al., in press).

Majorie Leonard (1966) gives clinical examples of how fathers can deter daughters from being heterosexual in various ways—by not being there enough to provide a realistic image of men, or by being too overwhelmingly seductive and causing the daughter to flee from him and males in general. Some feminists (Chafetz et al., 1977) also see lesbianism as a rejection of male-dominated heterosexual relationships.

Harvey Kaye and his associates in a study of lesbians modeled after the Bieber study found, contrary to their expectations, that the mothers of lesbians did not differ markedly from their counterparts in the control group. The authors report that fathers, however, are "an alien breed in contrast to the control fathers" (1967:629). They state that the fathers "tend to be puritanical, exploitative, and feared by their daughters, although the fear is not that of being physically abused. He is overly possessive and is subtly interested in his daughter physically, yet tends to discourage her development as an adult" (1967:634). Another study found that four of the ten items on a family relations test that suggested fear-invoking behavior by the father showed significant differences between lesbians and nonlesbians. None of the fear-invoking items for the mother showed differences. Another study comparing lesbians and nonlesbians (Johnson et al., in press) found the same lack of difference between the groups concerning the mother, but showed that lesbians were likely to see their fathers as repressive and especially as intolerant of expressions of anger. While the mother herself probably does affect the girl's perception of the father and men in general, the father image, however this image developed, appears to be most important in influencing the daughter's views of men and her later sexuality.

In our view, homosexuals in general do not constitute a vanguard against male dominance, since they may be as much involved in sexist role-playing as heterosexuals. On the other hand, many homosexuals, especially lesbians, are using their refusal of heterosexuality as a way of protesting male dominance in heterosexual relations. Heterosexuality per se does not necessarily have to involve male dominance, however, nor does heterosexuality explain male dominance. Fathers could help boys and girls survive in a male-dominant society, while also trying to change it by affirming the gender identity of each sex without defining male dominance and female submission as a part of sexual identity and heterosexuality.

Incestuous fathers Only recently has the phenomenon of incest received much public attention, and this discussion perhaps accounts in part for the marked increase in reported cases. While both father-daughter and mother-son incest are tabooed in our society, incest between mothers and sons is extremely rare compared to incest between fathers and daughters. This fact is yet another indication of male dominance. As we noted earlier, mother-son incest would constitute a reversal of male dominance if the boy were young, while father-daughter incest fits the paradigm of dominant male and subordinate female. (Father-son incest is not unheard of, but is very rare compared to father-daughter incest.)

Judith Herman and Lisa Hirschman interpret father-daughter incest as "an abuse which is inherent in a father dominated family system" (1977:741). Using Freud's categories, they say that the taboo against father-daughter incest does not carry the same force as the taboo against mother-son incest because there is no punishing father to prevent father-daughter incest as there is to prevent mother-son incest (1977:740). In the Freudian account of the Oedipus complex, the boy gives up his incestuous desires for the mother out of fear of the castrating father, who has rights in the mother. On the other hand, the mother does not have comparable rights in the father. Herman and Hirschman contend that for every family in which incest is actually consummated, there are likely many more with essentially similar if less extreme psychological dynamics, including such things as flirting and sharing of sexual secrets.

Clinicians, social workers, and academicians who deal with incest cases generally find that the incestuous father is not crazy or otherwise deviant and that sexual abuse may occur situationally, such as times when the mother is ill or refuses sexual relations (Armstrong, 1978; Meiselman, 1978). It often appears that fathers simply do not see anything seriously wrong with incest because they conceive of themselves as owning the child. One mother of an incest victim whose husband is now in therapy said he had been a very authoritarian person: "He didn't see our daughter as a person. She was *his.* He didn't see it as incest" (quoted by Armstrong, 1978:56). While the father himself is not an authoritarian in all cases, father-daughter incest does involve the exploitation of a dependent child.

Father-daughter incest differs from rape because it occurs in the context of a family relationship in which the parent is supposed to care for and about the child. The victim of rape is not socially or psychologically dependent on the rapist and is thus free to hate him. The daughter of an incestuous father, however, cannot hate her father because she depends on him for protection and love. While she may feel repelled in one way by his sexual demands, at the same time she may feel that this is the only kind of love she can get and may prefer it to no love at all (Herman and Hirschman, 1977:748). Thus, incest victims may be psychologically affected more deeply and adversely than rape victims because their own self-image and sense of worth is more involved.

The precise harm done to incest victims varies. Herman and Hirschman found that their cases almost uniformly reported an inability to feel and communicate. They tended to think of themselves as witches, bitches, and whores and as undeserving of love. They usually did not hate their fathers and in fact overvalued men and got into masochistic relationships with them. They tended to hate themselves and their mothers far more than they hated men. In a larger study of women who had been outpatients in a mental health clinic, Karen Meiselman (1978) found that orgasmic dysfunction was strikingly more characteristic of the women who had been incest victims than of the women in the control group of patients who had not experienced incest.

The mothers of incest victims have often been themselves blamed for colluding in the incest. This has in part come about because the victims almost uniformly report poor relations with their mothers. Generally, the mothers of incest victims have been weak in some way or other, did not respect themselves or their daughters, and thereby "allowed" incest to occur. Both the behavior of the mother and the incest victim and the behavior of the father himself ultimately reflect a patriarchal system. The mother sees herself as not having the power to defend the daughter against the father, and the father sees himself as having a right to his daughter.

Herman and Hirschman argue that the best therapy for incest victims is perhaps consciousness raising about the prevalence of incest and its relation to male dominance. They see efforts to reintegrate fathers into the world of children as a positive development, but only "on the condition that they learn more appropriate parental behavior." As they put it, "A seductive father is not much of an improvement over an abandoning or distant one" (1977:756). At several points we have argued that fathers should take a more nurturant role within the family. The problem of incest reminds us, however, that by nurturance we do not mean seductiveness. The nurturing father needs to form a genuine coalition with the mother on the basis of their equality, not on the basis of his authority in the family. In this coalition with the mother, the father cares for and about his children as children, not as sex objects.

Summary

Children of both sexes learn nurturant and maternal attitudes and behaviors in their earliest interactions with a maternal figure. In this relationship with the mother, both sexes learn to respond to the attitudes of others, to love and to be loved. This relationship is not the prototype of male dominance, and it is not markedly sex differentiated. Male dominance appears to be reinforced by fathers more than by mothers. Evidence suggests that fathers are more concerned about sex typing and are more differentiating in their behavior toward each sex than are mothers.

The child's relationship with the father seems especially related to adopting the heterosexual aspects of sex roles. Studies of various aspects of heterosexual behavior indicate that the father relationship is a more important influence than the mother relationship. One analysis suggests that heterosexuality in males is effected through minimizing the child's fear of other males. Thus while males in general in a male-dominant society reinforce male dominance, individual male parents in a male-dominant world can help mitigate this fear.

The far greater prevalence of father-daughter incest than mother-son incest reflects male dominance. Fathers who do use their daughters as sex objects usually assume that this is their privilege as the father and that the mother will not interfere because of her lesser power. Mothers are far less likely than fathers to make their male children into sex objects.

To some extent in this society, heterosexual relations are characterized by male dominance and are governed by a masculine paradigm, but heterosexuality itself does not necessarily imply or explain male dominance. The psychological motive that may underlie males' devaluation of women arises not as much from boys' assuming the heterosexual aspect of masculinity but more from their repressing the maternal aspects of femininity. This repression also occurs at the time of the Oedipus complex, when children begin to enter the world beyond the mother-child dyad and seek to become independent from the mother.

THE REVOLT FROM THE MOTHER

In chapter 9 we reviewed the work of the gynocentric psychoanalytic theorists and their view that boys' and girls' first identification is with the mother, their primary caretaker. Because mothers or other females are the early caretakers of infants, it is more difficult for boys to establish masculinity than for girls to establish femininity. Parsons (1954) analyzes male sex role development in the United States as the gynocentric theorists do by suggesting that in establishing masculinity boys must reject their first identification with and attachment to the mother. He also notes that males in attempting to gain independence from the mother also tend to reject what they see as the goodness of the mother. The mother in the middle class tends to represent rules and conformity in her capacity as primary guardian and caretaker of the child. In revolting against the mother or rejecting his identification with her, the boy unconsciously identifies goodness with femininity and "being a 'bad boy' becomes a positive goal." Thus, Parsons suggests that the boy's need to reject the identification with the mother not only leads to an identification of himself as unlike her in a psychic sense, but in the tendency of boys toward antisocial role behavior (1954:305–7). This is also the source of the boy's rejection of positive expressiveness for negative expressiveness. Expressiveness represents the mother and goodness, and the boy fears retaining this if he is to be a "real male" (Johnson et al., 1975).

Leslie Fiedler (1968), describes what is essentially "the bad boy pattern" as a pervasive theme in American literature. He cites numerous works of fiction from Mark Twain's stories up to Ken Kesey's *One Flew Over the Cuckoo's Nest* as sagas in which men (or boys) seek to escape from a world dominated by female morality. In almost all of this literature one's sympathy is with the bad boy. As Parsons points out, mothers themselves seem to love the bad son more than the good son who tries too hard to please her. Thus, it seems to be almost understood by all of us that somehow boys must be bad to be unquestionably masculine real boys. Girls, on the other hand, feel no need to reject the mother and establish alternative role patterns (Parsons, 1954b:306).

Boys' tendency to resist what they perceive to be feminine can also help explain the different attitudes boys and girls hold toward school. Many studies show that girls like school more than boys and usually make better grades than boys. Girls' greater liking of school appears to be associated with children's tendency to define school and school objects as feminine (Kagan, 1964).

Males' difficulties in becoming masculine not only play into the bad boy pattern but also and more importantly are related to the devaluation of women. Ruth Hartley (1959) reports from a study of eight- to eleven-year-old boys that they seemed to bolster themselves in assuming expected masculine attributes by taking a very negative view of women. These boys described girls as limited and restrained and adult women as weak, afraid, easily tired, in need of help, squeamish, inadequate in emergencies, making an undue fuss over things, not very intelligent, and demanding and jealous of their husbands. These preadolescent boys tended to see the masculine role as extremely demanding, yet their very negative image of the feminine alternative impelled them to assume masculinity. One must be masculine in order not to be such a pitiful specimen! Hartley implies that the greater prestige of masculinity helps induce males to take on the responsibilities (and freedoms) that go with it.

In contrast to males, females do not need to reject the first identification they have with their mothers, although they do need to become less dependent. They do not have a need for greater glory as an inducement to be feminine. In fact, even though girls increasingly realize that males do receive more prestige, they continue to remain feminine. Kohlberg in surveying the research literature on this reports that "girls continue to prefer feminine objects and activities at all ages, and their own preferences seem to be even more feminine than their more objective and stereotyped judgments of value" (1966:121). This strongly suggests that girls are feminine in a way that boys are not masculine and that they remain feminine in spite of the prestige that accrues to masculinity. It seems that in breaking their dependency ties with their mothers girls are more likely to become hostile toward their own mothers than to reject the maternal role itself.

As we discussed in chapter 9, fathers are likely to form a kind of coalition against mothers with children of both sexes. In our society where the mother-infant tie is so exclusive, this coalition may help the child become less emotionally dependent on the mother, but it may also lead, in the case of the father-son relationship, to a devaluation of women.

PEER GROUP INTERACTION One important way males handle the threat of being unable to separate themselves from women and femininity is through male peer groups. As we have seen, males very early show an interest in other males and tend to bond together in "homosocial" fellowship. While there is competition in male groups, the basic ambiance seems to be one of solidarity based on being masculine. Hanging out with the boys, a male can be comfortable, protected from the judgments and the anger of women and most importantly from the danger of femininity itself. In doing this, however, the male peer group can also be a powerful promoter of the sex objectification of women, making women not human beings but objects to be possessed and used sexually. These attitudes toward women in fact are more likely to be fostered in the male peer group than by fathers.

While women also bond together, in some societies more than in others, the emphasis on the nuclear family and the heterosexual bond in our society paradoxically works against women's being close to one another. To the extent that women depend on men economically, they are in part constrained to give men their primary loyalty.

Growing Up Male

Cross-culturally, the solidarity among boys is ordinarily not duplicated among young girls, who tend to mix more with adults than boys do. Male groups involve a mixture of both dominance struggles and camaraderie. Young boys in most societies tend to play in larger groups than girls and, partially as a function of the larger size of these groups, they tend to develop dominance hierarchies in which boys jockey and compete for position. These groups also involve a certain amount of friendly aggression such as bopping, tripping, wrestling, and exchanging of verbal insults. The intimate exchange of insults is epitomized by the practice called "doin' the dozens" among ghetto black adolescents (Udry, 1974:73).

At first, the validation of masculinity involves avoiding what is feminine in the literal sense. Boys in elementary school are likely to exclude girls from their activities. Our concern here, however, is what happens in early adolescence as children begin to anticipate adult roles and boys begin to learn their heterosexual role in the context of both competition and solidarity within the male peer group.

Competition in sexual capacity In early adolescence, masturbation may become an occasion for exhibition and comparison among boys. Kinsey and his associates (1948:168) found that 60 percent of the preadolescent boys they interviewed had engaged in sexual exhibition or other sex play with other boys. Kinsey comments that this behavior in the young boy "is fostered by his socially encouraged disdain for girls' ways, by his admiration for masculine prowess, and by his desire to emulate older boys. . . . The anatomy and functional capacities of male genitalia interest the younger boy to a degree that is not appreciated by older males who have become heterosexually conditioned."

Günter Grass (1961) in his novel *Cat and Mouse* graphically describes an exhibition of masturbation among a group of young adolescent boys on a deserted ship monitored by a lone girl. One particular male was acknowledged to be the clear winner of the rather disorganized competition not only on the basis of the size of his penis, but also on the basis of his speed (duly timed by a watch) in reaching ejaculation and on his ability to repeat this performance several times in rapid succession. The episode suggests how readily sexuality can be assimilated to a competitive format essentially unrelated to one's own pleasure, much less that of a partner.

Competition in heterosexual prowess While virtually all boys masturbate, intercourse with a female is usually considered far preferable, and among many groups of boys, especially in the working class, masturbation is considered positively unmanly. Thus, sooner or later, heterosexual prowess becomes the basis for competition. While males' first sexual encounters are less likely to be with prostitutes than they once were, they are still likely to be with girls or women with whom they do not have a sustained relationship. These first encounters do not involve the idea of relating emotionally to a female human so much as the idea of validating one's status as a male among males. To actually have intercourse with a girl becomes an important rite of passage (usually publicly affirmed) in the male group. This demand may occur quite early. Bill Cosby (1975) in an article that first appeared in *Playboy* describes how he, as a preadolescent, had no knowledge of the basic mechanics of intercourse, but did know that it was important to "get pussy" from a girl—however this was done. After visiting a willing girl and doing very little, he was able to parry the questions of his friends concerning the details of his experience with the inspired explanation that they had "done it, the regular way." At the same time he hoped to find out what the regular way was! This episode illustrates nicely how important in the male peer group it is to be sexually experienced, so experienced that one dare not reveal ignorance of basic sexual information.

In our society fathers ordinarily do not give sexual information to their children. The heart-to-heart talk a boy is supposed to have with his father is indeed a myth. Most fathers' difficulties in talking to their sons about sex may stem from their own ambivalent attitudes toward women. Does the father talk to his son as the husband of his son's mother or as a fellow male who has had his share of fun chasing women? Are women equal partners in a marriage or are they sex objects? From whatever cause, all the studies that have been done on boys show that over 90 percent learned about contraceptives, prostitution, and coitus from their peers, not their parents. A study of sexual behavior in the 1970s indicates that both males and females under twenty-five years of age were almost as likely to report they received their sexual information from peers as did people who are now fifty-five and over (Hunt, 1974:125).

Male sexuality, then, develops in the context of status striving in the male peer group. The focus at adolescence tends to be on "getting it from" or "doing it to" girls, with the reactions of the latter of little concern beyond securing their minimal cooperation (Udry, 1974:71). Many men, then, learn to become aroused sexually in a context in which sexual excitement is associated with defining women as objects of conquest (Litewka, 1974:45). While men undoubtedly vary considerably in this respect, at least part of the explanation of why men are prone to consider women sex objects is that they become sexual in the context of competition with other males.

Sex as a direct expression of male dominance While in the male peer group sex may become an occasion for competition, sex is sometimes also used by men as a direct expression of aggression or dominance. Men may use sex directly as a way of controlling uppity or threatening women. At the peace demonstration in Washington, D.C. in 1969, when an attractive radical woman was speaking concerning women, the male radicals expressed their resentment by sexualizing her and all that she said: "Take it off! Take her off the stage and fuck her!" They yelled and guffawed at statements such as "We must take to the streets," making her reference to a march into a reference to prostitution (Hymowitz and Weissman, 1978:348).

The association between sex and dominance is seen even more clearly in situations where males use sexual relations to express dominance over other males. This appears most graphically in reports of male homosexual behavior in prisons. In prison, "fucking" another male is symbolic of establishing dominance over him, of humiliating him. Part of the explanation for the humiliation is that the one who is penetrated becomes symbolically like a woman. Men who sexually assault other men in prison do not define their behavior as unmasculine or homosexual because it is understood as an expression of dominance associated with masculinity. This dominance is dramatically expressed in the movie *Deliverance,* where a trespasser from the city is humiliated by being sodomized (anally penetrated) at gunpoint in front of his friends by one of the local males.

Penetration as dominance is not confined to heterosexual males. Blumstein and Schwartz quote a bisexual male: "There are four kinds of men: men who screw women, men who screw men and women, men who screw men, and then there are the queers (i.e., the ones who get screwed)" (1976:19). Many slang words, used to describe sexual intercourse also connote dominance and aggression. To get "fucked," "screwed," "reamed," or "had" implies that one has been victimized. While this is not the typical male view of intercourse, there is within the masculine paradigm a symbolic association between sexual initiative and aggressive dominance. The association of sex with love is more a part of a feminine paradigm and males as they "grow up" and form long lasting alliances with women begin to share this view.

It is significant that male homosexual behavior in prison contrasts sharply with homosexual behavior among female prisoners. In female prisons, homosexual relationships are usually patterned after traditional heterosexual marriages. Establishing these relationships between a "stud" and a "femme" involves no physical coercion, and the relationship resembles an ordinary heterosexual marriage with the partners calling each other sometimes "mommy" and "poppy" or "my old lady" and "my old man." This seems important evidence that women tend to assimilate sexuality to at least relatively egalitarian relationships more readily than men do. While women without men assimilate sexuality to a family, men without women assimilate it to a dominance hierarchy (Giallombardo, 1966).

Male bonding and women as sex objects The competitive aspect of male sexuality should not be overemphasized. As Richard Udry points out, sexual competition among males, with females the objects of conquest, provides a set of experiences that cement them as a male group (1974:72–73). Boys may egg each other on to make sexual attempts with girls ("It's tonight or never"), but this is not so much competition as peer pressure to *be* heterosexual. The male peer group's conception of heterosexuality, however, distinctly does not mean liking or loving girls in the sense of allowing them to have power over one. Instead, it means making girls into objects.

Jean Lipman-Blumen (1976) argues that men do not make women sex objects but that women make themselves sex objects in order to entice males away from their homosocial self-sufficiency. While women do emphasize their specifically sexual qualities in order to attract men, the making of women into sex objects has psychological roots within men themselves. If males' self-doubts are related to their need to separate themselves from their mother, who was to them as a child a powerful feminine figure, then what better way to quell those doubts than to define women as mere objects? Making women into sex objects becomes a way of reinforcing masculine gender identity by rendering women harmless. If a woman is a "cunt," a "piece," a "skirt," or if one looks at women as assemblages of "asses," "tits," and "beavers," then the male is in control of them, and not the reverse. Among male peers, becoming involved in a relationship with a woman is often explicitly condemned. For instance, in traditional Muslim societies, love has been thought to downgrade men because it robs them of their masculinity (Safilios-Rothschild, 1977:61). According to the recent testimony of some men in a men's consciousness raising group (1975:195), going steady was considered bad because it put one in danger of being "pussy whipped," of letting a woman get the upper hand. When a male does get married or forms a serious relationship with a woman, he is viewed somewhat as a deserter from the male group or he may be commiserated with as having been hooked or trapped. Some homosexual males pride themselves on their supermasculinity, which, they feel, is attested to by the fact that they would never let themselves be trapped by a woman. Heterosexuality, then, as it is fostered in the male peer group, is of a sort that defines women as objects of male conquest who are not to be taken seriously. The pursuit of women becomes a game that knits heterosexual males together more than it divides them.

This does not mean that men do not fall in love or become seriously emotionally committed to women. Such emotional involvement for men, however, may signify a sharp break with the male peer group that does not occur when women fall in love, mainly because women in their peer groups do not compare heterosexual encounters or objectify the other sex in the same way that men do.

The motive for rape To some extent the motivational dynamics behind rape can be explained in terms of male peer group phenomena. Susan Brownmiller (1975) and Susan Griffin (1975) argue that the motives of rapists primarily involve male violence and male bonding. The most clear-cut examples are the rapes that occur during wars. Men show solidarity against enemy males by raping their women. Even though women are the victims, to some extent they represent the enemy males. Rapes in war are usually gang rapes, which increase the solidarity of the males involved. In the U.S., gang rapes or rapes by pairs of buddies are usually planned beforehand and have little or nothing to do with sexual seduction or temptation by a woman. The victim or the place of the attack is often picked in advance. Gang rapists are ordinarily not mentally disturbed; they are engaging in an act of violence and male solidarity at the expense of a woman. Here the idea of ownership by enemy males is transformed into the idea that all unprotected women are fair game.

Actually most rapes, apart from war-connected rapes, involve only one man. But, from the statistics of the sociologist Menachem Amir (1971), Brownmiller contends that those who rape alone are of the same mentality as those who rape in groups. Even those who rape alone see themselves as one of the boys. The motives for rape, then, derive from males' identification with other males, whether or not they are present at the time, an identification that turns women into objects of sexual conquest. This is the reason why Griffin calls rape the all-American crime.

Certainly most men are not rapists nor do most men condone rape. Certainly, too, most women will live out their lives without being raped.

On the other hand, while only some women are actually raped (255,000 per year), almost all women from an early age are aware of the possibility of rape and fear it (Brownmiller, 1975:175). As we noted earlier, one of the few ways middle-class parents treat males and females differently is greater chaperonage for girls. The fear of rape becomes an important mechanism by which the total system of male dominance is reinforced. In coping with this fear women often restrict their activities or depend on a male protector. The courts themselves in trying rape cases reinforce the idea that women should restrict their own freedom (including their sexual freedom) in order to avoid rape. This assumption is rarely made in the case of a person who is the victim of a nonsexual assault or robbery. Thus, to an extent, both men and women accept the idea that while men rape, women cause it. The victim is blamed for rape, and the threat of rape becomes a way of restricting women's freedom.

The laws on rape and their enforcement are changing. Most especially, the traditional definition of rape not as a violation of a woman's integrity but as a violation of her chastity is being questioned. For many years courts questioned a rape victim's prior sexual behavior and expected her to prove her chastity by struggling against the rapist. The view behind this practice is also related to the opinion that a husband cannot rape his wife because in effect he already owns her chastity. Until recently, the law reflected the general Victorian view that women are either good or bad, pure or impure, chaste or fair game. This view, while appearing to help good women, in fact defines all women in terms of their sexuality and its patterning, rather than as human beings who, just as men, need freedom to live in the world without fear.

Griffin and Brownmiller both point out that an important exception to the pervasiveness of rape cross-culturally and historically is the absence of rape among the peace-loving, nonviolent Arapesh described by Margaret Mead. As we have seen earlier, this is a society where there is a strong tradition of male nurturance. Certainly, rape and the motive to rape should be minimized in situations where violence, male bonding, and the sex objectification of women are minimized.

Is the male peer group declining? Men counteract the initial power of the mother through their interaction in male peer groups in which women as objects of sexual conquest are rendered psychologically harmless. In stressing, perhaps overstressing, the extent to which women become sex objects for the male peer group, we underscore the argument that when males are among males, they are most constrained to denigrate women. To the extent that the male peer group is a prime reinforcer of women as sex objects, it becomes important to assess whether its power is increasing or declining. In our society cross-sex interaction in all age groups appears to be increasing. More and more children, adolescents, and adults are interacting more and more frequently in mixed-sex groups. The most significant trend of all is that since the 1960s there has been considerable cross-sex interaction in elementary schools in all types of communities (cited in Udry, 1974). The early emphasis on couples that this involves, acts to break up the male peer group well before adolescence.

It is not entirely clear what the content of this early heterosexual interaction is like. Apparently it began in the 1960s as a kind of adult-fostered premature dating in which the children aped the stereotypes of coy-female/gallant-male, but this seems to be less the case now. The dating pattern itself is on the decline in all age groups, replaced by more serious going-steady relationships, which are more like friendships than courtship relationships. Heterosexual cohabitation among older adolescents also has this same quality of friendship even though a sexual relationship is involved.

The increase in cross-sex interaction may also be seen in the fact that almost all colleges now are coeducational and dormitories and off-campus rentals frequently house both males and females. Traditional men's clubs, which usually exclude women, have declined markedly since as early as World War II. On the other hand, fraternities are beginning to thrive again and it is not clear to what extent this reflects a renewed defensive male bonding.

Growing Up Female

While the significant biological event initiating adolescence for boys is ejaculation, the significant biological event for girls is menstruation. Unlike ejaculation, menstruation is not directly connected with genital sexuality, but is rather an event testifying to the possibility of motherhood. It may be more of an inhibitor than a spur to masturbation. Kinsey and his associates reported that by age twenty, 92 percent of all males had masturbated to orgasm, while only 33 percent of females had (1953:173). Apparently girls in adolescence do not generally see themselves as sexual beings, and very few girls report feeling sexually deprived during adolescence. Nevertheless, both boys and girls are sexual beings. In contrast to boys, whose budding sexuality is often painfully obvious, girls' sexuality may be less conscious and insistent. For instance, the avid interest many young girls show in horses and bike riding may stem at least partially from the sexual stimulation these activities provide. Moreover, many ways of sitting adopted by young girls can be stimulating.

Girls' lesser tendency to masturbate in adolescence may have a social rather than a physiological cause. It seems important that while a majority of boys learned to masturbate from conversation and printed sources, girls who masturbated learned about it through self-discovery (Kinsey et al., 1953:173). This suggests that many girls simply are unaware of masturbation as a possibility for them unless they discover it on their own. Alix Shulman (1973), for example in her *Memoirs of an Ex-Prom Queen,* recounts that for a long time she thought that she alone possessed a special "joy button," as she called her clitoris. Recently, girls are likely to have become more aware of masturbation through reading. Morton Hunt, in a study somewhat comparable to Kinsey's larger and more rigorous study, reports that 60 percent of the women in his sample aged eighteen to twenty-four were masturbating (1974:85). It is not clear what percentage of younger girls masturbate, but surely the figure has increased to some extent. Generally, however, women are more likely to masturbate after, not before, they have experienced intercourse.

While the incidence of masturbation has at least doubled in the last generation among girls, their rate is still considerably below that of boys. Nevertheless, this increase in masturbation does indicate a greater potential interest in the physical aspects of sex among females than they were previously thought to have.

Men as objects Men's sex objectification of women may have a parallel among women. Safilios-Rothschild (1977) suggests that women make men into objects too, not objects of sexual conquest but objects to support them. Men are then objectified by women as money-making machines. Certainly men have taken this view—witness the turn of the century jokes about women as golddiggers. Women as sex objects to men was taken for granted, and then men complained that women used their sexuality to get what they wanted. While women sometimes do calculate with regard to men and thus use them in that sense, the parallelism between men's objectification of women and women's objectification of men should not be allowed to obscure the basic asymmetry of the situation. Because men do, in fact, control most of the resources in the wider society, women are constrained to use their sexuality as a way of gaining access to the money, prestige, and power men control.

That women do calculate with regard to men is evidenced by the differences in men's and women's attitudes toward marrying for love. Kephart (1967) asked college men and women the following question: "If a boy (girl) had all the other qualities you desired, would you marry this person if you were not in love with him (her)?" Sixty-five percent of the males answered that they would not marry if they were not in love, but only 24 percent of the women were equally sure that they would not. The great majority of the women (72 percent) answered that they were undecided on this question. One young woman remarked that it was hard to give a clear-cut answer to this question because, she said, "If a boy had all the other qualities I desired, and I was not in love with him—well, I think I could talk myself into falling in love!" (Kephart, 1967:473). This young woman was prepared to do what Arlie Hochschild (1975a) calls emotion work. She would try to make herself feel what her calculation tells her she needs to feel.

As Willard Waller (1951) pointed out years ago, when a man marries, he chooses a companion and a helpmate but a woman chooses a companion and also a standard of living. Therefore, "it is necessary for a woman to be mercenary" (quoted in Z. Rubin, 1977). Shulamith Firestone (1971:140) agrees and argues that women unlike men are in no position to love freely. Women are not so financially dependent on men as they were 50 or 100 years ago. Yet one can still make sense of all the findings reported on differences between men's and women's love patterns in terms of two principles: first, marriage is more important to women than to men; second, courtship is less under women's direct control, and women are not expected to initiate relationships.

Contrary to stereotype, men fall in love more easily than women and are more devastated if a relationship ends (Z. Rubin, 1977). Men, as it were, can afford to be more emotional and less calculating than women. Women, whose life chances depend a great deal on whom they marry, yet who cannot initiate courtship, are thus constrained to work on their emotions more than men. They learn how to manipulate their own emotions to make them fit with their choice of a man. Women also learn how to manipulate the emotions of the man they want in order to cause him to fall in love with them.

From young person to sex object The necessity of attracting men in order to gain a measure of power over them makes women's experiences in growing up very different from men's. Simone de Beauvoir in her now dated but insightful chapter on "The Young Girl" in *The Second Sex* describes the conflicts girls experience as they learn to transform themselves from active child to false object. In order to attract men, the girl must lie. "But, above all, the lie to which the adolescent girl is condemned is that she must pretend to be an object, and a fascinating one, when she senses herself as an uncertain, dissociated being, well aware of her blemishes. Make up, false hair, girdles, and 'reinforced' brassieres are all lies. The very face itself becomes a mask: spontaneous expressions are artfully induced" (1953:357–58).

While the nature of the artifices changes through time, the woman and her body remain on display. The conception of women as display objects to be evaluated has been continuously reinforced by the practice of selling all kinds of products from bathtubs to cars with the image of the sexy, attractive, partially undressed woman (Israel and Eliasson, 1971). Good-looking women are also used to enhance sports events. Cheerleaders are now a prominent part of not only scholastic but also professional football games. Beauty contests, of course, are another example of women as display objects.

Because they are display objects, women learn to look at themselves as such. They learn to look at their faces and figures objectively and then deliberately work at making the best of them, disguising them or transforming them to fit the current image. The psychological effect of viewing oneself as an object in this way can be alienating and makes it difficult for women to gain a sense of themselves as real people. Boskind-Lodahl (1976:343) suggests that the pathological starving or gorging pattern found almost exclusively among adolescent girls may be understood as an obsession with self-defeating attempts to change their bodies to fit an ideal image.

The further irony of women transforming themselves into sex objects is that the very qualities of attractiveness to men are often also the qualities men use as the reason for refusing women legitimate power. Thus a man may say, "How can I take you seriously when you are so beautiful," or "You're so cute when you're mad." Fortunately, most men's and women's consciousnesses have been raised with regard to the most blatant forms of this tendency to objectify and then patronize women. Yet it remains true that physical appearance is more important for women than for men.

Female bonding In past times and in some contemporary situations involving relationships with extended kin, women have formed strong solidary bonds with one another. Carroll Smith-Rosenberg (1975) studied the correspondence and diaries of men and women in the late eighteenth and nineteenth centuries and found that friendship and love between women was of great importance in the lives of both sexes. Married and unmarried women visited each other, wrote to each other, and helped each other in crises. The close emotional attachments women had with each other partially competed with their attachment to their husbands in empathy and depth of commitment. At present in areas where extended kin live close to each other, mothers and their adult daughters may interact frequently in their daily lives and are closer to each other than they are to their husbands (Young and Willmott, 1973). Even today, in a situation where extended kin are less important, deep friendships and loyalties between individual women continue to exist.

These female friendships, however, differ from male friendships in important ways. Male bonding is more impersonal and is related to reinforcing masculinity, while female bonding is more personal, empathetic, and familistic. Men use their interest in women as a basis for bonding together as men in pursuit of women. With women, matters are very different. While occasionally (and increasingly) women may talk together about men as sex objects ("What a hunk!"), generally women do not bond together on the basis of their common physical interest in men except as a kind of protest. More important, women cannot bond together on the basis of their interest in men as money, power, and prestige machines because the initiative lies with men. They must be chosen by a man. Thus, women become separated from one another in the pursuit of men. Alix Shulman recounts how her sorority sisters turned on her because they thought she was beautiful and thus had an advantage over them in the competition for men. "*Surely I must be beautiful if she hates me for it!* Well let her hate me then, what do I care? Obviously this hatchery is not the world" (1973:58). Generally, the informal rule among women is that all is fair in love and war. It is considered impolite to congratulate a bride precisely because it points up the truth that women compete for men. In a male-dominated society, heterosexuality then has tended to break up the bonds between women, while to some extent it has been used to solidify the bonds between men. To the extent that our society makes it necessary for a woman to become attached to a man in order to survive socially and economically and to the extent that men define the nature of women, the bonds that women might have with women necessarily become tenuous.

Directions of change We noted in the last section that the male peer group may be declining and with it the tendency to make women sex objects. A decrease in male bonding would set the stage for more genuine and egalitarian relationships between men and women. While feminists urge women to learn to like women and to bond together, it is not clear that this is actually taking place on any broad scale. Women do seem to be bonding more with each other in situations where sexual competition is minimized. It is true that at least young women seem less committed to marriage than they once were since singleness is increasing and age at marriage is increasing. As a number of factors coalesce to make women less dependent on men financially and men less threatened by women as independent people, the ground is being laid for cross-sex interaction with less distinction between the sexes. Males and females may now be more able to interact with each other in a way that parallels a friendship relationship rather than in a money-machine/sex-object relationship that is mutually exploitative.

SUMMARY

In this chapter we have used a role-oriented version of psychoanalytic theory to describe how gender roles and male dominance are reproduced within the family and within male peer groups. The central elements in this process are that both males' and females' first interaction tends to be with a maternal figure and within this interaction infants of both sexes are hooked into social roles and become responsive to social sanctions. The meaning of the Oedipal phase in part is that children cease to interact in merely dyadic relations and instead internalize the rules and roles in the family system as a whole. This involves learning sex differentiated roles, including heterosexuality and male dominance.

Sex roles may be differentiated into maternal and heterosexual aspects. The maternal aspect is learned in nurturant interactions in the early years of life. Because females are responsible for early child-care in all cultures, this first reciprocal role interaction is ordinarily with a female, a maternal figure who holds great power over the child. Because we live in a male-dominant society, this early stage of female dominance cannot be the prototype for adult heterosexual relations. Specifically, sex typing becomes important at the Oedipal stage, when the father enters the child's world. Fathers are more concerned with sex typing of their children than mothers are. Males are also more concerned with maintaining the sexual double standard than females are. This is because ending the double standard would directly challenge patterns of male dominance.

At the Oedipal period, as boys develop their identity as males, they repress their earlier identification with the mother and tend to reject the nurturant and maternal aspect of their personalities. To reinforce their sense of masculinity males strongly stress segregation of sex roles, devalue women and make women sex objects. The husband-father role, then, as the adult male role within the family, is the role that introduces the sex differentiating principle into the family. The woman's status as a sex object is first played out in relation to her father, and the boy learns to be dominant from his father and other males.

On the other hand, daughters of fathers do not become total sex objects because of the incest taboo. Fathers are more likely to break the taboo than mothers, but within the family wives and daughters have more equal status and are less likely to be merely sex objects to husbands and fathers than they are outside the family. It is within the male peer group that males are most likely to define women as objects of conquest and to devalue them. These groups tend to have a dominance hierarchy and function to reinforce a system of male dominance in the wider society. They are more prominent among adolescents than among older men in the United States, and some of the grosser aspects of males' devaluation of females may be mitigated by marriage.

Suggested Readings

BILLER, HENRY, *Father, Child, and Sex Role: Paternal Determinants of Personality Development.* Lexington, Mass.: Heath, 1971. Summary of research on the relationship of the father to sex typing.

BROWNMILLER, SUSAN, *Against Our Will: Men, Women, and Rape.* New York: Simon & Schuster, 1975. The classic case for the relevance of rape to understanding women's situation.

CHODOROW, NANCY, *The Reproduction of Mothering: Psychoanalysis and the Sociology of Gender.* Berkeley: University of California Press, 1978. A psychoanalytic and sociological interpretation of why women are more oriented to mothering then men are.

DAVID, DEBORAH S., AND ROBERT BRANNON, eds., *The Forty-Nine Percent Majority: The Male Sex Role.* Reading Mass.: Addison-Wesley, 1976.

MEISELMAN, KARIN C., *Incest.* San Francisco, Calif.: Jossey-Bass, 1978. Reviews research concerning father-daughter incest and also reports the author's carefully done research.

PARSONS, TALCOTT, *Social Structure and Personality.* New York: Free Press, 1970. Contains essays on sex role development in the family and later socialization.

PETRAS, JOHN W., ed., *Sex Male/Gender Masculine.* Port Washington, N.Y.: Alfred Publishing Co., 1975. Good collection of readings on the male sex role.

SAFILIOS-ROTHSCHILD, CONSTANTINA, *Love, Sex, and Sex Roles.* Englewood Cliffs, N.J.: Prentice-Hall, 1977. A brief look at modern views on love, sex, and marriage with some predictions for the future.

11: Sex Roles throughout the Life Cycle

Any given individual ordinarily has a number of statuses, each with a corresponding set of role expectations. These statuses tend to be hierarchically ranked; some are more important and controlling than others (McCall and Simmons, 1978). For example, as we have seen, even when a woman in our society works at a very demanding job outside the home, the role obligations attached to her family statuses are expected to take priority: She is to be wife and mother first and jobholder second. For the man, on the other hand, the status of worker is considerably more salient in people's minds than his status as father and husband. These different *status sets* (Epstein, 1974:370) of men and women are anticipated in adolescence, become most important during young adulthood, and ordinarily decline in importance during the later years of life.

Life cycle changes may be classified differently in different cultures. For instance, Chippewa Indians divide a woman's life into four categories: birth to walking; walking to puberty; puberty to birth of first granddaughter; and first granddaughter to first great granddaughter. People in our culture generally distinguish childhood and adolescence, young adulthood, middle age and finally old age. Whatever the specific classification used, however, life stages generally reflect not only physical changes but, also and more importantly, changes in the social statuses an individual holds.

There are no strict age norms for entering a given stage; instead, there is a span of years in which a given behavior is considered appropriate. The vast majority of the men and women in a middle-aged and middle-class sample agreed that the best age for a man to marry was between twenty and twenty-five years of age and that the best time for a woman was between nineteen and twenty-four years of age (Neugarten, Moore, and Lowe, 1968:24). Yet there is a wide range of times at which people may actually enter one stage or another. For instance, women are capable of bearing children from their teens into their forties. In general, middle-class people tend to enter various life stages at an older age than working-class people. Middle-class women and men marry, have children, and also have grandchildren at older ages than do working class men and women (Neugarten and Moore, 1968:7). Nevertheless, life events typically do occur in a given order—for example, finishing school, starting work, and then marrying—and some evidence indicates that altering this order can adversely affect individuals' lives and happiness (Hogan, 1978).

Each life stage has its own rewards and its own problems as individuals face different role expectations and demands. Sociologists tend to focus on the role strains that people experience, usually because of the different emphasis given to the various statuses that they hold. Psychoanalytic theorists also discuss developmental crises, ranging from the Oedipal crisis in early childhood through the identity crisis in adolescence to concerns about generativity and continuance of life in older years. In the following sections we discuss each of the life stages after childhood, looking at the different experiences of males and females. Because of the available data, much of our discussion will focus on middle class whites in the United States. Also, much of our discussion will necessarily focus on typical experiences of individuals in each life stage rather than the broad range of exceptional behaviors that are possible.

ADOLESCENCE

Adult role expectations begin to exert a strong influence on the sexes at adolescence, the time between childhood and adulthood. The length of the adolescent period varies from one culture to another, and in some cultures it is not socially recognized at all. In the United States its length also varies among subgroups and tends to be longer for middle-class children than for working-class children.

By the end of adolescence, sex segregation that foresees adult roles is widely apparent. Both males and females are beginning to move out of their family of orientation and to form their identities—boys centering on their status as workers, and girls centering on their status of spouse and parent. Boys' and girls' different academic interests begin to parallel the occupations available to males and females, and especially middle-class girls avoid extreme academic success that may threaten boys' areas of competence. The young women and men perceive the roles that will be available to them in the years to come and adjust their interests and plans largely to fit these possibilities.

Social Roles in Adolescence

During adolescence young people begin to disengage themselves from their parents and siblings and to develop greater individual autonomy. Girls appear to begin to make this shift somewhat earlier than boys, and the time of the most dramatic changes in orientation tends to coincide with puberty (Bowerman and Kinch, 1959). This shift does not involve a sharp break from home, but instead a gradual increase of autonomy. Probably because jobs such as baby sitting are more often available to them, girls start earning money away from home earlier than boys do. Also, probably because of the earlier onset of pubescence and the pattern of dating older boys, girls start dating earlier than boys. Yet, they do not reject their parents, and a nationwide study indicates that girls are more likely than boys to spend some leisure time with their parents in middle adolescence (Douvan and Adelson, 1966:40–50).

As adolescents move away from their orientation to their family and their status as children, their friendships with their peers become more and more important. While friends are very important to both adolescent boys and girls, girls more than boys want their friendships to contain elements of intimacy, support, and understanding. As we would expect from our discussion of sex differences in personality development, boys do not seem as interested in these affective qualities and emotional ties as they are in congenial companions with whom they can engage in activities (Douvan and Adelson, 1966). Boys also tend to develop emotional autonomy from the family more quickly than girls (Douvan and Adelson, 1966:40–50), perhaps as part of their rejection of the positive expressiveness involved in intimate ties. The boys do not necessarily, however, reject their parents' values (Offer, 1969:60–61).

As would be expected, adolescent males and females pursue different leisure activities. A study of students in high schools in the Midwest found that the boys prefer outdoor activities such as sports, boating, or going around with their friends, while girls prefer being with their friends, watching movies or television, reading, and listening to records (Coleman, 1961).

In recent years sexual activity among adolescents has generally increased. Yet while young women are apparently more knowledgeable about birth control than they were a few years ago, they do not use it consistently, probably because they feel guilty about their sexual activity (Fox, 1976). As a result, more than a million adolescent girls get pregnant every year and about 60 percent of these have babies. The vast majority of these young women then keep their infants (Fosburgh, 1977:29). This situation illustrates the intense problems that can come with the too-rapid acquisition of new statuses at adolescence. Marriages of adolescents tend to break up quickly, and, if the young woman remains single (as many do), the father of the child rarely contributes to its support. The young woman then usually becomes dependent on her parents or the welfare system and rarely finishes her schooling (Forsburgh, 1977:30). This can place a heavy burden on the young woman's mother who, as we will see below, is generally ready to put childrearing behind her and concentrate on other areas of life.

While the acquisition of the status of parent in adolescence is rather rare, all adolescents appear to anticipate their future roles as worker and as spouse. Girls' anticipation of the wife role is clearly shown in changes in their grades at adolescence. In a male-dominant society women tend to seek the status of wife indirectly and in anticipating this role appear to try to minimize any direct competition between themselves and their future mates. One way to do this is to avoid male-dominated work areas. The academic classroom, however, involves direct competition. Here, even though girls still maintain higher average grades than boys, they begin to hold down their achievement so that they do not appear to be "too brilliant." In fact, a large study of students in Midwestern high schools conducted by the sociologist James Coleman found that while boys and girls start out their high-school careers feeling quite similarly about the designation of "brilliant student," by the end of the four years the best girl students are "*less* likely . . . to want to be remembered for their scholastic achievements, and the best boy students [are] *more* likely to want to be remembered in this way" (Coleman, 1961:251). Coleman suggests that "for many a girl, the solution to the dilemma of being 'good, but not aggressively brilliant' is an ingenious one: she gets good grades, but she is never extremely outstanding. She is neither better than the best boy student nor poorer than the worst" (Coleman, 1961:252–53). This strain may be greatest on the brightest young women. The girls in Coleman's sample had an average intelligence quotient that was higher than the boys. Yet, among the students who got the best grades, the boys had higher IQs than the girls, indicating that, in contrast to the boys, the girls with the greatest potential were not using it.

Sex differences in approaches to academic life may vary with the social class composition of the school. In middle-class schools, which tend to reward academic achievement more highly, Coleman found that the boys were more likely to want to be remembered as brilliant students than in working-class schools, where rewards for academic achievement were low. However, just the reverse occurred for the girls. Girls attending schools that rewarded academic achievement were less likely to want to be remembered as brilliant students than girls in the schools where academic achievement was less rewarded. Moreover, in the middle-class schools, where boys and girls are closest in grades, girls are most likely to hide their scholarly success. Similarly, boys in working-class schools are more likely than boys in middle-class schools to describe a scholarly girl positively.

Coleman suggests that these patterns reflect the greater sex role differentiation in academic expectations in the working class than in the middle class. Working-class girls can legitimately achieve academically, while boys have other areas for achievement. In contrast, in the middle class both boys and girls are expected to be concerned with academic success. When a middle-class girl does well academically, she enters the boys' province. She perceives that this would not tend to make her more attractive to boys, and thus she may be motivated to limit her competition with the boys if she is to obtain the status of wife.

Developmental Crises in Adolescence

The anticipation of adult statuses and roles produces strains and conflicts for adolescents. Psychoanalysts describe the difficulties adolescents face in developing their identity and intimate relations with others as they anticipate these new roles. Erik Erikson (1959, 1968) popularized the idea of an identity crisis in adolescence. While a person's identity has of course been present since childhood, adolescents become crucially aware of the possibilities open to them and may become obsessed with the issue of who they are.

Because males and females face sharply different role expectations in adult life, the nature of the identities they develop at adolescence differ. From their nationwide survey of adolescents Douvan and Adelson conclude that "For the boy, identity revolves around the questions, 'Who am I? What do I do?' The nature of his occupation plays a crucial defining role in a man's identity. The girl, on the other hand, depends on marriage for her critical defining element; she will take her self-definition, by and large, from the man she marries and the children she raises" (Douvan and Adelson, 1966:24).

As late as 1975, Lowenthal and her associates reported similar results in their sample of mainly middle- and working-class high-school seniors (1975:16). All of the girls saw marriage and family as central in their life plans, with those who planned to attend college anticipating marriage after college. The boys in this sample only mentioned marriage and families if they had already settled on their work plans. In general, future work careers are central to the boys' view of themselves. Yet, Gisela Konopka (1976) suggests that even though girls generally do anticipate getting married and having children, most want to have "done something" in the work world first.

Boys face a more concrete task than girls of actively deciding what route they will pursue after finishing their schooling, for their future identification largely centers on their occupational role. The process of identity formation for girls is more ambiguous because most women still see their major adult statuses as wife and mother. What these statuses will actually entail largely depends on whom they marry. Unsurprisingly, studies find that while girls tend to have a sharp discrepancy between their fantasies for the future and their plans for reality, boys usually do not. Boys' dreams of the future and their actual plans are relatively similar and center on their future occupations. Like boys, girls tend to concretely plan for the period before marriage—their educational decisions and occupational plans. But, in contrast to boys, in their fantasies they focus on personal attractiveness, popularity, and their marital future (Douvan and Adelson, 1966).

YOUNG ADULTHOOD

Both women and men usually hold at some time in young adulthood the statuses of worker, parent, and spouse. Yet the balance they have between these roles differs more markedly at this stage than perhaps at any other. Women are more involved in roles associated with wife and mother; men are more involved in work roles. These different balances contribute to the strains found in their young adult lives and the nature of their search for individual meaning in life.

Family responsibilities during young adulthood have undergone dramatic alterations over the years, partly because the childbearing period has been greatly compressed and adult women's life expectancy has greatly increased. Between 1800 and 1900 the total fertility rate among whites was cut in half as the average number of children born to a white woman surviving menopause fell from 7.04 to 3.56 (Hareven, 1976). The birth rate in this century rose somewhat in the 1950s and 1960s from a low in the Depression of the 1930s, but it now has dropped considerably. Furthermore, fewer children are spaced closer and closer together, and age at marriage has also decreased. At the turn of the century the typical woman married at twenty-six, had her last child at the age of thirty-three, saw her last child married when she was fifty-six, and died herself in another ten years or so. By contrast the typical woman now marries at twenty-one or twenty-two and has her last child at twenty-six and is around forty-seven when that child leaves home. She can then expect to live thirty more years (Giele, 1978; Hareven, 1976:107).

The Status Sets of Men and Women

When viewed from a life-span perspective, the role of "only a housewife" for women seems to be largely disappearing. In the past women have been least likely to be in the labor force when they have young children in the home and most likely to reenter the labor force when their children are grown. In recent years the number of women in the labor force has increased, and the largest growth has been in the category of women with young children. In fact, the labor force participation rate for women without children under eighteen is lower than that for mothers of school-age children.

Do these statistics indicate a change in the work patterns of women throughout the life cycle? Probably this pattern is being modified somewhat from its earlier form, but the statistics confound differences between generations with differences in life cycle stages in women's labor force participation. Women are still prone to lessen their labor force participation when their children are young. However, fewer women follow this pattern now than a few years ago. More young women either are not stopping work or are returning while their children are still preschoolers. We suspect that as women who are now young reach the stage where their children are old enough to leave home, they will be more likely to reenter the labor force than were women who are now middle aged. At that time the proportion of women without children under eighteen who are in the labor force should be much higher than it is now. Some support for this view comes from data we have gathered. Only 11 percent of the young women college students we surveyed in late 1973 said that they would choose to work when they had small children at home; 75 percent predicted that they would work after their children left home. In contrast, in 1976, 50 percent of the college women we surveyed said that they would always work after marriage. Komarovsky (1974:530) reported similar findings.

There are a number of ways in which women balance the demands of home and work, and their stage in the family life cycle largely influences the type of balance they make. In the newlywed stage, after marriage but before children are born, most young women work outside the home. In a cross-sectional study of middle- and lower-class people in California, Lowenthal and her associates (1975:19) found that 84 percent of the women who had been recently married worked outside the home. However, most of these women viewed their working as helping out until they could get more settled and their husbands had finished school. Most of them planned to lessen their work commitment in later years. Even though newlywed women do not yet have families, Lowenthal and her associates suggest that they anticipate motherhood, both in their temporary attitude toward work and also in their active life style. They suggest that women in the preparental stage tend to stress activity and to be involved in a wide variety of activities because they foresee the role constriction that will come with motherhood (Lowenthal et al., 1975:17).

As we noted above, women with preschool children are generally less likely than those in any other life stage (except old age) to be in the labor force. There are a number of reasons for this. If mothers of small children are to work outside the home, they must find child care for their small children, which is often difficult to find or so expensive, given women's low wages, that the mother pays almost as much for child care as she earns. In addition, with each child that enters the family, the mother's workload in the home increases. One estimate is that with each child added to the family, the required load of housework increases five to ten hours a week, depending on the child's age and birth order. More specific statistics suggest that with no children in the family, about 1,000 hours of housework a year are needed to keep a household running. With no children under six about 1,500 hours a year are required. With children under six, about 2,000 hours a year are needed, twice the amount of work required when there were no children in the home (Bernard, 1975a:116). Thus, the workload may be so great that a young mother cannot manage physically to work outside the home. Husbands rarely give substantial help with this work, so a working mother essentially may have two full-time jobs. Because of the restrictions involved with young children, women at this stage may be more similar to each other than at any other stage (Lopata, 1971:36). Indeed, fewer women are working at this stage. Most of them are concentrating their energies within the family.

As a woman's children grow older, she enters what Lopata (1971) calls the full house plateau, a time where there is an "increasing diversity of life styles." Housework becomes less of a burden, and, as the children's interactions outside the family increase, child care also becomes less burdensome. More women return to work as their children enter school, although Lopata notes that some may return only sporadically. Middle-class women may devote themselves more to community affairs and volunteer work. Other women may settle into the housewife role and see the rest of their lives as involved with family relations and their children and eventually their grandchildren. Lopata finds that the housewife only role is more common among older, urban, lower-middle-class women (Lopata, 1971:38). Apart from the women who are free to enter and leave the labor market, try out volunteer activities, or stay in the home, an increasing number of women enter the labor market at this stage out of financial necessity. As children get older, economic strains on the family increase, and a number of women return to work to help out with the family's finances (Oppenheimer, 1974). Because they have been out of the labor market for a number of years, however, they often face even greater discrimination than women with continuous work histories. Their wages may be quite poor and their jobs unfulfilling.

While women are likely to be involved in both family and work roles, men are more likely to be committed to work roles than to family roles. Lopata asked the housewives she interviewed about the roles that were most important to them. Over and over the housewives saw their roles associated with the status of mother as most central in their lives, and the working women saw the roles associated with wife as most important (Lopata, 1971:48). When asked about the most important role their husbands played in the family, the women were most likely to respond that it was as "breadwinner" (Lopata, 1971:91; see Lowenthal et al., 1975:17 for similar results). Because men's work roles do not vary as their children age they do not experience the changes women do at various stages of the family life cycle (cf., Kline, 1975).

Strains at Young Adulthood

The different foci of men and women at young adulthood result in strain for both sexes. First, our society expects that a mother should be solely devoted to her child, and the isolated nuclear family increases the probability that a woman will be the only person involved in infant care. Second, the father is often heavily involved in his own work activities and other pursuits. He may be launching a career when the children are born, and he may have little time to spend with his family. Jessie Bernard (1975b) points out that our society is unusual in the isolation and stress placed on young mothers. Fathers generally provide only a minimal amount of help with infant care, and there are rarely others such as relatives or servants who can help. Young mothers experience considerable stress from the increased responsibility as well as from their isolation from the adult world.

While many women follow the pattern of marriage and motherhood, an increasing number of young women devote themselves exclusively to their careers in young adulthood. This pattern is more common among women in the professions than among women in other areas. Even though they avoid the parent and sometimes the spouse status, these young women do not escape role strains. Instead, it appears that as they get older, many of them reevaluate the course of their lives as they realize they have only a few years left in which they may biologically bear a child. This appears to be a developmental crisis in the psychoanalytic sense as the women balance and evaluate the ways to find fulfillment for themselves and to contribute to the development of the next generation. Some of these women decide to have families and to assume the status of parent; others decide to remain devoted to their work-related roles (Gould, 1972; Sheehy, 1977). Because the male is expected to focus his energies on work, his life tends to become divided not between work and family but between work and leisure and tends to specialize in a narrow range of interests that limit the possibilities of true communication with others. The man's focus on the often instrumental world of work deprives him of the more human and expressive qualities found in nurturant roles within the family (Parsons, 1954a).

This lack of positive expressiveness in the male role can create intrapsychic strains for men to the extent that it involves a tendency to avoid self-disclosure and a desire not to expose areas of weakness or vulnerability. According to Sidney Jourard (1971), a clinical psychologist, it is hard and stressful work to be continuously guarding against exposure—work that is unhealthy. Jourard suggests that one major hazard men run from this lack of sensitivity to themselves is that they may literally "go till they drop." For instance, many ambitious men literally work around the clock and have jobs that involve a good deal of stress. Such blind devotion to work and continual stress have been cited as two of the reasons underlying men's high rate of cardiovascular disease. Perhaps if men were more aware of what Jourard calls "all-is-not-well-signals" in themselves, they could avoid some of the catastrophic illnesses that beset them.

Yet men's reluctance to disclose themselves may function as a way of maintaining dominance. The lack of self-disclosure that characterizes the male role in this society is not just an unfortunate cultural trait, but may be a device that men use to maintain and exert power. If a man lets people know how he really feels—that he is hurt, that he is afraid—he may lose power (Sattel, 1976). Thus, men in the last analysis may be reluctant to give up their shields against self-disclosure even though they endanger their health.

MIDDLE AGE

Middle age appears to occur when the person perceives that middle age has begun. In her studies of older men and women, Bernice Neugarten found that men and women have different perceptions of when middle age occurs (1968b:96):

> Women, but not men, tend to define their age status in terms of timing of events within the family cycle. For married women, middle age is closely tied to the launching of children into the adult world, and even unmarried career women often discuss middle age in terms of the family they might have had.
>
> Men, on the other hand, perceive the onset of middle age by cues presented outside the family context, often from the deferential behavior accorded them in the work setting. . . . The most dramatic cues for the male . . . are often biological.

For both women and men, middle age involves physical changes, developmental crises, and role strains, although the changes in roles may be more stressful for females than for males.

Physical Changes

Neugarten suggests that men look for signs of aging in the health of either themselves or their friends. In contrast women do not "body-monitor" or look for illness in themselves as much as they look for such signs in their husbands, perhaps in preparation for widowhood that they will probably face in the future. Yet both women and men show physical signs of middle age and aging. Their appearance changes as their bodies begin to age.

Unlike other primates and unlike men, women live past the period when they can reproduce, entering menopause (Williams, 1977:358). From about forty-five to sixty years of age the ovaries decrease their functioning and ovulation stops. Gradually a woman is no longer able to bear children. While almost all women recognize physical symptoms at this time, only about 10 percent are "obviously inconvenienced" (Katchadourian and Lunde, 1975:102). The possible symptoms include the hot flush or hot flashes—a "brief episode of feelings of warmth and flushing, accompanied by perspiration"—as well as dizziness, insomnia, headaches, tingling sensations, and anxiety (Williams, 1977:118).

Yet a study of attitudes toward menopause found that the majority of older women saw postmenopausal women as "feeling better, more confident, calmer, [and] freer than before [menopause]," while the majority of younger women disagreed with this view. Middle-aged women seemed to be more likely than younger women to see menopause as creating no major discontinuities in a woman's life and to feel that a woman has some degree of control over her symptoms (Neugarten, et al, 1968: 198–99).

Men do not experience a counterpart to women's menopause. While women are born with their lifetime supply of ova, men continually produce sperm and can father children virtually until their death. Yet men do age, and some writers have noted what they call the male climacteric. All men experience a decline in testosterone levels as they age, and, apparently, about 15 percent of all men experience a sharp and sudden drop in these levels. The symptoms reported for males parallel to some extent the symptoms cited for females, including depression, nervousness, irritability, hot flashes, and dizziness (Sheehy, 1977:458–59 citing Ruebsaat and Hull, 1975). Because men and their significant others do not ordinarily expect such changes to occur, Sheehy suggests that the climacteric may be more disconcerting for men who experience it than for women.

Status and Role Changes

Along with physical changes, there are also role changes at middle age. In fact, as we noted above, women tend to define the departure of children from the home as the start of middle age. This can bring about basic changes in the lives of American women. As Lopata notes, when a woman's children reach preadulthood, the "basic tasks of womanhood, as defined by American society, those of bearing and rearing children, are completed" (Lopata, 1971:41). If women do not find other ways to fill their lives, their self-definitions as a mother or a housewife can have "very narrow boundaries with empty lives" (Lopata, 1971:41). Lopata suggests that the loss of children when they are launched into adulthood involves an "automatic drop of status for women," a situation similar to that of retired men. She found that this situation could be most disturbing to working-class or less well educated women who do not have the opportunity or resources to broaden their activities.

Interestingly enough, this drop in status at middle age does not occur in all cultures. In societies that have extended families, strong mother-child relations that extend into adulthood, strong institutionalization of the mother-in-law and grandmother roles, and a high cultural valuation on age, women's status actually rises as they become older. Notably enough, our own society has few of these characteristics, thus accounting in some part for the drop in status for women at middle age (Bart, 1969).

In contrast to women, men do not experience sharp role changes at middle age. They do not associate middle age with their children's leaving home but rather with the growing approach of old age. The middle-aged men in one large study tended to be actively involved in life, focusing on their work. The men were both more committed to their work and saw it as more central to their lives than did their working wives. It is not surprising that these men were happier than their wives (Lowenthal et al., 1975:18–20).

Role Strains and Developmental Crises in Middle Age

Erik Erikson suggests that the last developmental crisis concerns integrity and despair, the point at which individuals try to come to grips with what they have done in their lives, accept their surroundings, and feel connected with the rest of humanity. From the empirical studies of Roger Gould (1972) it appears that this crisis may be a continuous process. People in their early thirties often began to question their life course. These questions continue with subjects in their late thirties and early forties, who also begin to sense the finiteness of time and their lives. The subjects in their mid and late forties appear to have begun to live with these questions and to have developed more autonomous relations with their own children. Finally, in their fifties they show more self-acceptance and come to rely more on their spouses. (Unfortunately, Gould's studies were cross-sectional rather than longitudinal, and it is impossible to tell to what extent generational changes in experiences or situations can affect these stages.)

While the popular literature tends to emphasize the "crises" associated with these developmental changes, it is important to realize that they do not always reach crisis proportions. Many of the changes people experience at this time are not seen as losses; some are seen as gains. Midlife changes appear to be most stressful when they do not occur as expected, as for instance when adult children remain in the home or when a spouse dies (Neugarten, 1976; Brim, 1976). The different roles of men and women influence the nature of their developmental changes. While women must adjust to their loss of the mother role and their culturally defined physical attractiveness, men usually try to come to terms with what they have accomplished in their work role. They begin to realize that they are mortal, and they compare their achievements with the dreams of their youth (Levinson et al., 1976; also see Vaillant, 1977).

Strains for women Pauline Bart has studied the depression some women experience in middle age and concludes that it occurs because of their role loss at that time. Middle-aged women with severe depression tend overwhelmingly to be devoted to a mother role that includes extensive involvement with the lives of their children. As their children grow older, this involvement lessens. This is understandable in our society, which stresses that adults not depend emotionally on their family of orientation. When their children no longer need them, these women have no other roles to take the place of motherhood. Bart suggests that women whose husbands provide both financial and emotional support during their time of role loss, whose children fulfill her expectations for them, and who continue to maintain contact with her are much less likely to experience depression with these role changes (Bart, 1975).

Relatively few women experience this severe depression at middle age. In fact, while all mothers experience role loss when their children leave home, many also experience a sense of relief as their responsibilities lessen and they may devote more attention to other activities (Rubin, 1979). Many women return to participation in the labor force when they have no children at home. There is some evidence that women who are involved in jobs they enjoy are less likely to experience depression (Radloff, 1975; Campbell et al., 1975; Birnbaum, 1975). In fact, after a period of adjustment, most women are likely to note a sense of increased freedom by preretirement age (Neugarten, 1968b:96; also Lowenthal et al., 1975:74).

Besides experiencing the loss of their mother role, middle-aged women begin to look older. In our society a middle-aged woman is often seen as losing her looks or going downhill, but a middle-aged man is perceived as sexually attractive and available. In fact, younger women often think an experienced older man is a good catch. Thus while older men can compete successfully with younger men for women, older women cannot compete successfully with younger women for men. Since men show signs of aging more than women do and since their sexual capacity declines to some extent while women's does not, it is probably not men's physical attractiveness or sexual prowess that allows them to continue to appeal to women, but, at least within the middle class, their successful careers. The male provider role, especially if played successfully, can keep middle-aged men desirable to women, but middle-aged women have nothing comparable to keep them desirable to men. This situation is further exacerbated by the cultural taboos against liaisons between older women and younger men. These taboos, which have no counterpart for older men and younger women, are clearly related to the male dominance norms that require husbands to be older than their wives. Any woman older than her mate is suspected of dominating him, particularly when the woman is noticeably older than the man.

Strains for men While women try to adjust to the loss of the importance of their status as a parent and of their physical attractiveness, men at middle age appear to take stock of their lives, to judge how well they have met earlier goals. Because men's lives center much more on work than on family, this stocktaking generally focuses on their status as worker. This illustrates a major strain in male sex roles in our society, for a man is not allowed to feel he is really a man unless he achieves in one sense or another. Thus all through their lives most men are engaged in proving themselves. This activity in the middle class mainly centers on the world of work, but, because it is connected with maintaining masculine identity and male dominance, performance anxiety can spill over into all areas of life from sexuality to childrearing. While men are subject to performance anxiety, performance also keeps many men going. When they can no longer perform, they become vulnerable. Thus, most men perceive old age as a threat because it endangers their performance capacities.

OLD AGE

Attempts to find meaning from life continue into old age. However, as the possibility of death comes closer and as the roles of men and women change, the concerns of men and women may become somewhat more similar. While sex roles in middle age and young adulthood involve a fair amount of divergence, in old age the roles men and women play appear to converge through changes both in the work patterns and in the family lives of men and women.

Role Changes

Women are more likely to work as the children leave home, and as both men and women reach retirement age, they leave the workforce and tend to concentrate their energies in other areas. When there are no longer children at home, the energies of the mother need not be directed so much toward her children, and the father's role as breadwinner for his family becomes less important. When grandchildren are born, both grandmother and grandfather may take a nurturant or a playful role toward the grandchild. Some grandmothers may take over maternal functions, but rarely will the grandfather have to play either an authoritative or a breadwinner role (Neugarten and Weinstein, 1968). In other words, the roles of grandfather and grandmother are much less differentiated than the roles of mother and father.

Men and women also appear to come closer together on personality variables in old age. In a study of people from an age range of fifty through eighty Neugarten concludes that as they age "men seem to become more receptive to affiliative and nurturant promptings; women, more responsive toward and less guilty about aggressive and egocentric impulses" (Neugarten, 1968a:140). Lowenthal's cross-sectional study suggests that older women in their study, who were at a preretirement stage, felt most competent and independent. They were more like middle-aged men than preretirement men in the sample. The Lowenthal group suggests that this upsurge in good feelings of the women is not related to age as much as to the women's new freedom (Lowenthal et al., 1975:74–76). Freed from worries about their children and their future, because most children were already settled in their own lives, these women are at last able to indulge themselves.

In line with these changes, the preretirement women in the Lowenthal study tended to become more dominant in their families, especially with their husbands. The preretirement men seemed to need more physical comfort and attention than earlier and, although the preretirement women noted needs for "reciprocity and mutuality," they seemed to sublimate these needs by becoming more assertive in their marriage relations while also caring for their husband's needs (Lowenthal et al., 1975:237–38).

Jeanne McGee and Kathleen Wells (1978) caution that we must not exaggerate the extent of convergence of sex roles in old age. Because aging inevitably involves the loss of a number of highly sex-differentiated roles acquired earlier in adulthood, some kind of convergence in roles of the sexes is inevitable. Yet, women do not give up the role of housewife and remain tied to domesticity. Moreover, their observations of group behavior of older men and women document the persistence of male dominance in conversations and in decision-making patterns.

Both men and women, as long as they are healthy, appear to maintain a wide variety of possible role patterns in old age. In a follow-up study of couples who participated in the Berkeley Growth Study with their children beginning in 1928 and 1929, Maas and Kuypers (1974) interviewed ninety-nine mothers and forty-seven fathers. All of the men were still married to women who had originally been in the study. Some of the women, however, were divorced or widowed. The parents ranged in age from sixty to eighty-two at the time of the study and were generally economically well-off and in good health. Maas and Kuypers note that the mothers with the least problems in their older years had expanded their interests and involvements beyond their family roles. This resembles conclusions found with women in the midlife crisis. Retirement did not seem to affect the men in Maas and Kuyper's sample as much as it affected the women. The authors suggest that the fathers in the sample had a more balanced range of roles than the mothers, and that the mothers with a more expanded role set encountered fewer difficulties (Maas and Kuypers, 1974:205–6). Interestingly enough, the life style of one spouse was generally uncorrelated with the life style of the other. Probably because more of the mothers were divorced or widowed and were more likely to have limited incomes, the life styles the mothers adopted were more influenced by the context or situation in which they lived than were the lives of the fathers, who had more money and thus more choices.

The Death of a Spouse

The final stage of life for men and women often involves the death of a spouse. Although women have always lived longer than men, women are living even longer than men because of the increasing lifespan. By the time a woman is sixty-seven years old there are only 70 men for every 100 women. This means that widowhood may well be part of a married woman's life. Married men are much less likely to be widowed than married women are. According to the 1970 census, 79 percent of all women at age fifty to fifty-four were married, but only 11 percent of women who were eighty-five years or older were married. Ten percent of all women were widowed at age fifty to fifty-four; 77 percent were widowed at age eighty-five or older. Because of the higher death rates for black men, the percentage of widows among black women is higher at each age group (Williams, 1977:373–74).

Widowers are much more likely to remarry than are widows. Similarly, divorced men are much more likely to remarry than divorced women. Only part of this difference may be accounted for by the greater availability of marriageable women than men (Bell, 1975:147).

An increasingly common situation is that of divorced older women. Divorced older women are often left without adequate financial resources, and if they have spent most of their lives as housewives, they often have inadequate job skills. They face many of the same financial hardships and problems of loneliness that widows do. In addition, older divorced women are not entitled to some of the financial benefits that widows can acquire. For instance, they usually cannot collect Social Security payments earned by their ex-husbands.

Women without husbands, especially if they have children, are much more likely to be poor than other people. For instance, in 1977, 50 percent of all families headed by females and with children under eighteen had incomes below the poverty line. Of the families with an adult male in the household, only 8 percent of those with children had poverty level incomes (Statistical Abstracts, 1978:466).

While widowhood may be a tragedy for an individual person, Helena Lopata suggests that it is so common that it should be seen as the final stage in the typical career of a wife. In her study of widows in an American urban area Lopata (1973) indicates that the way in which a woman deals with widowhood corresponds to the way she dealt with the wife role. Largest differences are found between widows of different social class backgrounds. Women who have the educational and social resources to participate in the larger community are the most likely to adjust well to new social relations and the least likely to become isolated.

TRENDS AND CONTINUITIES IN SEX ROLES DURING THE LIFE CYCLE

Part of our discussion of sex roles throughout the life cycle has been based on studies of people at various life stages. Other evidence comes from cross-sectional studies of people at different stages of life, and a small amount of evidence is available from longitudinal studies of people over a number of years. In this final section, we briefly review information on general trends in self-concepts of men and women over the life cycle and then discuss evidence on continuities—that is, how behaviors and capabilities at one point in time influence later sex role behaviors.

Self-Concept over the Life Cycle

The changes in social roles and physiology over the life cycle are often accompanied by changes in self-conception and personality orientation. The Lowenthal group summarizes the changes in the self-concepts of men in their sample at different life stages (1975: 67–68).

> In essence, there is reflected through the successive stages a change from an insecure and discontented self-image [in high school] through a buoyant and sometimes uncontrolled [newlywed] phase to the stage of control and industry [in middle age], to a later point of decreased demands on the self and greater acceptance of others and one's environment [at preretirement].

As the authors note, these changes parallel Erikson's overview of developmental stages throughout life.

Lowenthal and her associates found that women's self-concepts do not change as much as men's from one life stage to another. Generally, they found that high-school and newlywed women are similar to men of that age in being unsure of themselves and feeling powerless over the future. The newlywed women also tend to have less energy than their husbands and to exhibit greater warmth. The middle-aged women are least happy and see themselves as absent-minded. By preretirement, however, this pattern appears to dissipate, with the preretirement women feeling more effective and self-controlled than ever before. The Lowenthal group suggest that this comes from women's greater freedom at this stage as their children are on their own. They suggest that life stage may be more important in explaining psychological differences than chronological age (Lowenthal et al., 1975:72–76). Stage of life is more influential than age because life stages denote different kinds of interactions in different social situations.

Block and Haan's follow-up study of young people involved in the University of California, Berkeley Growth Study in the late 1920s supports at least part of the Lowenthal group's findings. Block and Haan's subjects were in their late thirties when they were contacted. The men were found at that time to have become more self-confident and certain; the women saw themselves as less sure of themselves (Sheehy, 1977:159–60 citing Block and Haan, 1971). When these subjects are contacted again in middle age we would expect that the women, whose responsibilities will have shifted so that they may focus more attention on themselves, will have regained some of their self-confidence.

Longitudinal Studies

Longitudinal studies, such as the Berkeley Growth Study, provide a unique opportunity to see continuities in sex roles as people grow older. While longitudinal studies are very expensive and time-consuming, they are often preferable to cross-sectional studies because we can control for different cultural and historical experiences of the subjects. For instance, a cross-sectional study may compare people who were thirty years old with some who were sixty years old in 1978. Yet these two groups of people had strikingly different experiences when they were in their twenties because of historical circumstances. For example, the thirty-five-year-olds were young during the Vietnam War, while the sixty-year-olds experienced World War II. Because, however, longitudinal studies deal only with a single generation, their results may not totally apply to other generations.

The results of three longitudinal studies can enhance our knowledge of continuities in sex roles over life: the Fels Institute Study of children begun in 1929 (Kagan and Moss, 1962), the Berkeley Growth Study of children and their parents that began about fifty years ago (e.g., Block and Haan, 1971; Maas and Kuypers, 1974), and Terman's studies of highly gifted children begun in the 1920s (e.g., Terman and Oden, 1947; Burks et al., 1930). From these studies it is apparent that as children grow older they tend to mold their behaviors more in accordance with the societal definitions of sex-appropriate behavior. Also, because men do have more power and prestige in the society, it is somewhat more difficult to predict women's future than men's future from their early years. Women may have less objective control over their fate.

Kagan and Moss's follow-up study of the Fels Institute children illustrate how sex role expectations in the society influence the development of personality characteristics and related behaviors. Stereotypically feminine traits that appeared in childhood were related to similar traits in adulthood in women, but not in men. Stereotypically masculine traits were related to adult behaviors for men, but not for women. Kagan and Moss found these results even in families "that did not consciously attempt to mold the child in strict concordance with traditional sex-role standards." They suggest that children in these families "responded to the pressures of the extrafamilial environment. The aggressive girls learned to inhibit direct expression of overt aggressive and sexual behavior; the dependent boys gradually placed inhibition on urges toward dependent overtures to others" (Kagan and Moss 1962:268).

The children did not actually discard their childhood traits. Instead when a child had behavior patterns that were not concordant with sex role expectations, the adult behavior tended to be related to those behavior patterns, but was more in accord with traditional sex role expectations. For instance (Kagan and Moss, 1962:268–69):

> Passivity among boys predicted noncompetitiveness, sexual anxiety, and social apprehension in adult men, but not direct dependent overtures to parents or love objects. A tendency toward rage reactions in young girls predicted intellectual competitiveness, masculine interests, and dependency conflict in adult women, but not direct expression of aggression. It appears that when a childhood behavior is congruent with traditional sex-role characteristics, it is likely to be predictive of phenotypically similar behaviors in adulthood. When it conflicts with sex-role standards, the relevant motive is more likely to find expression in theoretically consistent substitute behaviors that are socially more acceptable than the original response. In sum, the individual's desire to mold his overt behavior in concordance with the culture's definition of sex-appropriate responses is a major determinant of the patterns of continuity and discontinuity in his development.

Kagan and Moss did find that some characteristics show no continuity from childhood to adulthood. These traits included compulsivity, irrational fears, task persistence, and excessive irritability during the first three years of life. Yet when traits were consistent or stable over time, they tended to be congruent with acceptable sex roles.

Evidence that women are more affected than men by the opportunities they encounter comes both from studies that began with children and studies starting in adulthood. The parents in Maas and Kuyper's study (1974) were first interviewed in the early 1930s when they were generally in their early thirties, and they were contacted again in 1968–69 when they were in their late sixties and early seventies. In general the fathers in this study showed more continuity in life style from their thirties to old age than the mothers did. Maas and Kuypers note that "the continuities in [the] fathers' life styles are associated with few changes in context, aside from retirement, over their adult years" (1974:130–31). In contrast, many mothers had extensive life style changes from their early years of mothering. Changes in the women's situation and especially their age and health, economic conditions, and marital status all influenced whether their old age was more pleasant than their earlier lives. Maas and Kuypers suggest that because the women had to adapt to more changing conditions than the fathers over their lives, they showed less continuity.

While Maas and Kuyper's study of parents shows how women more often experience changes in their life styles in adulthood than men do, Terman's study of gifted young people shows how the future occupational status of young women is much less likely than the status of young men to be related to their actual potential. Terman and his associates identified a large number of highly intelligent students in the 1920s and continued to follow them through their adult lives. Both boys and girls usually did very well in school, and the girls performed somewhat better than the boys in high school. Many of the men had very successful careers and were in the professions eight times as often as would be expected by chance (Terman and Oden, 1947:193). Only about half of the women were employed in adulthood. Almost 35 percent of these employed women were in "business occupations, chiefly secretarial and clerical" (Terman and Oden, 1947:194), 10 percent were college teachers in four-year schools, and 22 percent taught in lower levels (Terman and Oden, 1947:181). While both the men and women generally did quite well in college, over half of the men but only 29 percent of the women graduating from college went on to get graduate degrees. In general, while highly gifted men may be expected to show occupational success, highly gifted women may be more hidden, and "there are highly gifted women working as secretaries, filing clerks, elementary teachers, and telephone operators" (Terman and Oden,

1947:311). Even though Terman's data were gathered a number of years ago, we suspect that the situation has changed only a little. Women and men are still equally represented among the gifted population, yet men overwhelmingly dominate the most prestigious and well-paid occupational areas.

SUMMARY

Men and women grow from childhood—where they have remarkably similar body shapes and abilities—through adolescence—where males become larger and stronger and both sex groups reach sexual maturity—and young adulthood—where women can bear and nurse children—to middle age—where women lose their reproductive capability and both sex groups begin to show signs of aging—and old age—where men tend to weaken and die earlier than women. At the same time males and females enter different social roles and relationships. Young children gradually expand their relationships to involve their peers more, until by adolescence they tend to focus more on peers than on their families. By young adulthood most young people begin to form their own families through marriage and having children. Women tend to assume the primary responsibility for caring for the children, although they also usually remain in or soon return to the roles associated with the status of worker. Men's roles tend to center on their work, and they tend to see their main function in the family as that of provider or breadwinner. By the time parents reach middle age, children have usually left home, and, while some women may find this loss of a mother role difficult, others, especially those with adequate educational and economic resources, adjust by expanding their interests to work and more attention to themselves. By old age men's and women's roles become more similar as both leave the labor force and as they become grandparents, a role that in our culture emphasizes nurturance. Children who display atypical sex-typed behaviors in childhood generally modify these to more sex-appropriate forms by adulthood. More continuities over the lifespan may be found in the lives of adult men than adult women, probably because men have greater economic independence and control over their lives.

We have also seen how the achievement of males and females begins to diverge in anticipation of sex differentiated adult roles. Even though more and more women will combine work with marriage, evidence indicates that their family roles are expected to take precedence over their outside work. Thus men are much more likely to reach their intellectual potential in the occupational world than are women.

Suggested Readings

KONOPKA, GISELA, *Young Girls: A Portrait of Adolescence.* Englewood Cliffs, N.J.: Prentice-Hall, 1976. Report of a study of one thousand adolescent girls in the United States. Includes descriptions of their future plans and their relationships with others.

LOWENTHAL, MARJORIE FISKE, MAJDA THURNHER, AND DAVID CHIRIBOGA, *Four Stages of Life.* San Francisco, Calif.: Jossey-Bass, 1975. Report of an ongoing study of women and men in four different age groups from high school to retirement.

MAAS, HENRY S., AND JOSEPH A. KUYPERS, *From Thirty to Seventy.* San Francisco, Calif.: Jossey-Bass, 1974. Report of a longitudinal study of parents of children in the Berkeley Growth Study, following them through adulthood to old age.

NEUGARTEN, BERNICE L., ed., *Middle Age and Aging.* Chicago, Ill.: University of Chicago Press, 1968. A collection of articles dealing with social roles and psychological changes in middle and old age that takes sex differences into account.

SHEEHY, GAIL, *Passages: Predictable Crises of Adult Life.* New York: Bantam, 1976. A popularized, easy to read discussion of developmental crises in adulthood.

12: The Future

The previous chapters have shown that male dominance exists in our cultural symbol system, in informal everyday interactions, and in social institutions and roles. Even in the same organizations, the activities of males and females tend to be separate, and what males do is more highly valued than what females do. In general, domestic roles in all societies are emphasized for women, and public roles for men. This sex stratification is reproduced in each generation, in social institutions, and in the personalities of individuals as men's motive to deprecate women develops along with their early notions of their gender identity.

While some sex differences such as males' tendency to aggress more than females may have some biological basis, psychological studies show few sex differences in basic capacities. Sex differences that do appear as people grow older can generally be better explained by the different social roles that males and females are expected to play. Children first develop their understandings of these different social roles, and boys first develop the motive underlying male dominance in their interactions in the family. As children grow older and interact more with their peers, their notions of appropriate sex roles are elaborated. The male peer group is especially important in reinforcing the deprecation of women. Throughout life, men and women generally face different role expectations, although the extent of sex differentiation and how this affects individuals' self-concepts may vary from one life stage to another.

Parts of this chapter originally appeared in "The Social Origins of Male Dominance," by Jean Stockard and Miriam M. Johnson, in *Sex Roles,* 5 (1979), pp. 199–218, and are included here with the permission of Plenum Publishing Corporation.

We believe that the world would be a better place for all of its inhabitants—both male and female—if male dominance and sex inequality could be lessened. Both men and women could have more opportunities to explore new fields of work and to enjoy a greater variety of types of relationships with others. What would this world be like? How could our world be changed to approximate it? Could these changes really occur? In this chapter we explore each of these issues.

A WORLD WITHOUT MALE DOMINANCE

People have often approached the question of sex inequality by asking, Why can't women be more like men? Our analysis suggests that a world without male dominance would not be one in which women become more like men, but one in which men become more like women in the sense that a female paradigm or world view would be substituted for the now-dominant male paradigm. This means that cultural symbols would be altered to show an equal valuation of females and males, and cultural values would express complementarity and interdependence rather than priority and social hierarchy (Giele, 1978:x). It would be recognized that nurturance, expressiveness, and concern for other people are more important than the maintenance of hierarchies and dominance over others (cf. Neal, 1979). Aggression would be viewed as a threat to social integration and to human survival itself. In this world, all forms of domination would be seen as undesirable, and stratification by race, class, and sex would lessen.

Such changes in cultural values and symbols imply changes in social institutions and in the personalities of individuals. In a society without male dominance, there would be no unfair legal restrictions on women's activities, women and men would have equal access to educational opportunities, and sex segregation and wage disparities in the labor force would no longer exist. Women and men would have equal access to all roles in the society.

Because a society without male dominance would attach greater value to nurturant and expressive roles, work patterns and regulations would support family roles and the involvement of both women and men with the care of children. Most people would probably continue to marry, and marriage itself could temper tendencies toward male aggression and male bonding. Marriages would, however, be more egalitarian than they are now, with men and women sharing household tasks and important family decisions.

Because men would be more involved with the early care of children, gender identities would be retained but would probably be stronger and less problematic than they now are because masculinity would seem less formidable. Gender itself would be less salient, and men would not feel a need to deprecate women to shore up their masculinity. Some sex differences in personalities and even social roles would probably remain, but there would be no different value attached to those of women and those of men.

Today these changes may seem unrealistic or at least very difficult to promote. The preponderance of evidence amassed in this book shows that male dominance persists in social institutions. Throughout the world, women still do the bulk of the housework, even when they also work many hours outside the home. Sex stratification permeates the economy. From country to country, women hold different jobs than men do, and even when they have similar qualifications and do similar work, women are paid less than men are. In our own country, men and women have the same average amount of education; yet full-time, year-round women workers earn on the average less than two-thirds what full-time men workers earn. Any attempts to alter male dominance must recognize the multiple areas in which it appears.

NEEDED INSTITUTIONAL CHANGES Changes that would lead to a less male dominant society must attempt to deal with inequalities that are perpetuated in social institutions, within individual personalities, and in cultural symbols. We believe that the most fruitful way to approach change is to focus not directly on individual motivation but on how the structure of social institutions and the patterns of interactions within them reinforce sexual inequalities on the institutional, individual, and cultural levels. Because individuals live and mature within social institutions, one way to alter their motivations and self-definitions is to change these institutions. Because cultural symbols ultimately reflect existing social reality, they may eventually alter to reflect institutional changes. It must also be recognized that societies may more easily legislate changes in institutions than in individual attitudes, thus making institutions the easiest area in which to intervene.

Our analysis of sex inequality in social institutions has focused on the economy, the family, education, and the polity. Providing women with education appears to be a basic necessity in starting the trend toward greater equality. With increased education, the birth rate tends to decline, more women become involved in occupations outside the home, and women themselves may begin to demand greater legal equality (cf. Youssef and Hartley, 1979). The extent of inequality in education, and to some extent in the polity, tends to vary from one society to another. For instance, while in many countries women have much less education than men and are much more likely to be illiterate, in this country and in some others such as France, women and men have virtually the same amount of education. While no country has an equal representation of the sexes in its governing bodies, many countries guarantee equal rights for women and men in the political sphere and have legislation that calls for equal treatment in the economy. This is especially true of both Eastern and Western industrialized countries. These legal guarantees, along with increased education, are probably necessary steps to guarantee the end of sex inequality and can help promote changes in other institutions. Yet, changes in the polity and education are probably not sufficient to guarantee the end of male dominance.

Despite legal guarantees and relatively equal educational opportunities, extensive inequalities persist in both the economy and the family. Cross-culturally, women remain the main providers of early child care, both in the home and in other care settings. While some countries with socialist parties in power have been able to lessen the wage gap between men and women by lowering the overall disparity in wages between various levels of workers, in all societies women generally do different work than men and receive less money and less prestige for their work than men. These inequalities in the economy and in the family continue to be seen in all contemporary societies including our own. Changes in both the economy and the family will be necessary to lessen inequality in social institutions and to decrease men's motive to devalue women. These changes should be accompanied by, and reflected in, alterations in our cultural beliefs and values.

Dealing with Sex Stratification through the Economy

Laws requiring that men and women be paid the same amount for the same work and regulations such as affirmative action programs that call for an end to sex segregation of occupations provide the basis for the equal participation of women and men in the economy with equal rewards. Some laws also require the end of discrimination in admission to educational programs leading to certain kinds of jobs. By law in this country, women cannot be denied admission to vocational training programs in the traditionally male craft areas or to traditionally male professional areas in medicine or law solely on the basis of their sex. The various equal employment opportunity laws also give women who have been discriminated against an opportunity to legally claim jobs. Proponents of these laws and regulations hope that as more women are trained in male dominated areas, the sex ratio in the applicant pool for these jobs will change, and eventually employers will be forced to hire either unqualified men or the trained and qualified women. This assumes, of course, that the demand for these workers does not decline and the services of all trained people will be needed.

If these economic changes occurred, they could help promote greater sex equality in the family. When women work outside the home *and* contribute a large proportion of the family income, they may have more input into family decisions. Moreover, at least when a family has young children, the father may contribute more time to child care if his wife works outside the home.

Even though there is the legal basis in the United States for ending sex segregation of occupations as well as sex disparities in income, there has been little progress toward this end. As we have seen, sex differentials continue to appear in all countries. As more women are trained for an occupational area, they may begin to enter the field; but the field then appears to develop greater internal sex segregation, and the areas within the field where men are employed provide higher pay. It appears, then, that economic changes are also necessary, but not sufficient, to produce lasting change in sex inequality. The laws related to job discrimination are not strictly enforced, and the individual motives underlying male dominance appear unchanged. Moreover, the balance of attention women and men give to their roles connected with work and the family has not altered. Simply focusing on women's work role does not appear to directly change the attention men give to the family role, nor does it assure that the various laws will be followed. To deal with these problems, we turn to additional changes that focus on the family.

Dealing with Sex Stratification through the Family

One step that might minimize the psychological motives underlying male dominance is for men to become more involved in the nurturing of young children. While the universal pattern of early child care by women is certainly linked to the biological fact that women bear children and can nurse, this pattern is actually a social one. The introduction of the bottle has long separated women's capacity to breast feed from the necessity of their doing so. Moreover, it would be possible for women to continue to breast feed and still have less than primary responsibility for the care of infants and children.

Based on our earlier analysis, we would hypothesize that as men become more involved in nurturing young children, gender identity will not disappear but will become less problematic and less salient. Studies of matrifocal societies where considerable worth is given by both men and women to the maternal role and of societies where males are more exposed to young children also indicate that male dominance is less in these than in other societies (Johnson, 1977; Tanner, 1974).

Because father-daughter incest is already all too common, it might be argued that if males were encouraged to nurture it would increase their tendency to sexualize the relationship with children even more. This could increase incest and the sex objectification of women even further. Studies of nonhuman primates, however, suggest that an incest taboo may develop between adult nurturers and those they care for. There is ordinarily an incest taboo between mothers and their young among macaques, and male macaques who nurture a young macaque show an incest taboo with that child (Eaton, 1976:102). Among humans, then, one might expect that fathers who were actively involved in child care and who felt genuinely responsible for their children's well-being would be less inclined toward a sexual and seductive relationship with them. In this case, incest might actually decline.

If male children were exposed to warmly supportive fathers in early childhood, their lessened need to dominate and to sex objectify women might also lessen the incidence of rape. As males no longer need to repress their positive expressiveness in denying "femininity," their overall aggressiveness might lessen, especially since nurturing itself requires a repression of aggression. Finally, some evidence indicates that heterosexuality (whatever one may think of its desirability) would be promoted in both sexes by fathers interacting in a warm and caring, but not a seductive, manner with their children.*

Because sex objectification and male dominance are strongly reinforced in the male peer group, it will be important to devise ways to strengthen ties between males and females that are not necessarily sexually oriented and that can compete with the bonds of the male peer group. With such ties males and females could come to see each other more as individual personalities rather than as objects for conquest or use. Although it is probably too early to tell, the recent moves to minimize sex segregation in school activities in the United States required by the Title IX regulations may help to bring this about as boys and girls participate together in classes and extracurricular activities more often than in earlier years. Although the wife role is now subordinate to the husband role in the family, marriages in a relatively egalitarian society may have the effect of tempering the masculine tendency fostered in peer groups to consider women sex objects.

*In speaking of fathers, mothers, and families, we do not mean to imply that the only desirable family situation is that of the isolated nuclear family with both parents present. Children of divorced parents often have an opportunity to interact with more adults of both sexes after the divorce than when their parents were married. Also, many children receive more mothering from fathers after their parents have been separated than when their parents were married.

The Interrelatedness of Institutional Changes

While the United States already legally guarantees educational and economic equality, additional policies must focus on ways to strictly enforce these regulations. Because the changes in family roles that we have advocated can only occur with concurrent changes in the economy, other economic policies must focus on ways to encourage changes in the family.

Altering women's subordinate economic status will be most important in bringing about these changes. If men and women were rewarded equally for their work, it would be possible for either men or women to lessen their workforce participation to care for infants. For this to succeed it would also be necessary to alter the "clockwork of male careers" (Hochschild, 1975b). Many typically male jobs now require continuous participation and heavy dedication in the first years on the job—when people generally have children. For instance, both blue-collar and white-collar workers devote many hours to "working their way up the ladder" by doing extra work, attending evening meetings, and devoting continuous time periods to their occupations. If both males and females were to help with early childcare, employers would have to alter this typical pattern by legitimating and financially supporting parental leaves.

Since the start of the current feminist movement, attitudes toward women's roles have become greatly liberalized, and we can see changes in some behavior. Yet, the gap between men's and women's income remains large, and there has been only minimal token compliance to attempts to place women in positions of more authority. We suspect that this difficulty in developing long-term and effective change comes because there have been no policies aimed at the deeply held motives that underlie male dominance. These are the motives that are fostered in male peer groups and in family structures where only women mother. Consciousness raising efforts of feminist groups, affirmative action programs in employment, and equal opportunity laws that apply to schools are necessary programs. But, specific policies that address the motivational base of male dominance are also needed.

COULD THESE CHANGES OCCUR? In the past century, most countries throughout the world have recognized women as citizens, and many governments have already enacted laws and established commissions to implement greater equality between women and men (Boulding et al., 1976: 248–54). A major impetus for these changes has been the increased education of women, and, in many places, their increased involvement in the public spheres of the economy and polity. Within the United States, there is extensive evidence that attitudes toward women's roles have changed. Polls taken over a period of the last forty years in this country show a consistent trend toward greater acceptance of equality for men and women by members of both sexes (e.g., Mason, et al., 1976; Ferree, 1974; Erskine, 1971).

Changes can also be seen in cultural symbols. Women who are attending seminaries or who are now ordained are challenging and altering the patriarchal symbolism characterizing their religions. Language usage has clearly changed. The names of jobs have been extensively revised, thanks in good part to the policies of the federal government. We now have flight attendants, mail carriers, and postal workers instead of stewardesses, mailmen, and postmen. Signs on construction sites now proclaim "crew working" instead of "men working." Publishing companies require their authors, whenever possible, to avoid the patterns of word usage that reflect male dominance. Images in the media also demonstrate changes. Women newscasters are much more common than just a few years ago. While many prime-time shows maintain the traditional patterns of male dominance, other shows, especially soap operas that are felt to appeal more to women, show many women professionals. They also deal with stories involving males caring for their children and the problems of balancing work and home life.

In fact, it is possible to detect a general cultural trend toward a greater emphasis and value on expressiveness, nurturance, and caring as opposed to competitive striving. The phenomena that indicate this trend surfaced in this country with the counterculture and war resistance movements in the 1960s. Even though hippies themselves may have fallen far short of realizing their ideals, they at least wanted to be gentle, sharing, caring, feeling, and egalitarian. However mysogynist their actual behavior, members of the counterculture did seriously challenge the stereotypical competitive masculine role and did move the rest of society into a position to be critical of its norms (see Johnson, 1977). For instance, in an article entitled "The Waning of Macho America," the sociologist Amitai Etzioni (1978:136) argues that "this country's post-Vietnam war attitude is growing away from the simpleminded dichotomy of fight-or-flight and instead focuses on the middle range of nonviolent involvement." These general cultural trends could be an important precursor to alterations in social institutions and social roles that may help to lessen further the prevalence of male dominance.

Males seem quite capable of learning to care for young children, especially when exposed to them. For instance, cross-cultural evidence clearly shows that in societies where males are constantly exposed to young children, they are as adept at caring for them as are females (Byrne, 1977). Also, young boys who have younger siblings do show more interest in caring for younger children than other boys. While nurturing may not be as "natural" for men as for women (Rossi, 1977), there is no inherent reason why a society could not encourage them to nurture, even if it required compensatory training. This training could teach men nurturing skills they had rejected when they were younger and try to counteract the dangers that male aggressiveness may pose to young children, for it is important to stress that in this care men must assume a maternal role toward children rather than an authoritarian or a sexual role.

There is some evidence that for a number of years in this country fathers have been displaying increasing warmth and affection to their children. There is no longer a "studied coolness" or distance between father and child that was common in the last century. Instead, fathers as well as mothers actively love, fondle, and care for their children (Brenton, 1966). This pattern has been apparent for a number of years and may have contributed to the appearance of the greater cultural stress on expressiveness noted above (Flacks, 1971; Johnson, 1977).

Today, these changes are becoming more and more accepted. Fathers are becoming involved in the actual birth process, attending prenatal classes with their wives, staying with them throughout the birth process, and holding the child almost immediately after delivery. This family-centered birth process appears to enhance the attachment that parents, both mothers and fathers, feel toward their children. Similarly, in countries such as Sweden where fathers are allowed to take paternity leaves to care for newborn children, the number of participating fathers has grown rapidly, so that now over 12 percent of those who are eligible take advantage of this time to be with their offspring.

Before the turn of this century, the common-law rule in cases of divorce provided that since the father was entitled to the services and earnings of his children as compensation for his duty to support and maintain them, he should have preference in obtaining custody of them. By 1925, however, every state had abandoned this rule in favor of the view that what mattered most were the best interests of the child. This led to the practice of awarding children to their mothers because they were their primary caretakers. Now, fathers are obtaining custody again more frequently, not because they "own" their children's services but because mothers and fathers increasingly include child care in their vision of the father role (Eisler, 1977: 55–56). This practice may indicate a growing trend for fathers to include child care skills as part of their self-concept.

Some experiences in other countries also indicate that highly industrialized societies can place a high priority on nurturance and care of children by both mothers and fathers. In addition to allowing fathers to take parental leave when their children are young, Sweden also allows either a mother or father to take paid sick leave when a child is sick (Daniel, 1976). Over 90 percent of the women in China are employed; yet, they are given maternity leaves with full pay for almost two months when their children are born and then may bring their infants to a day care nursery in their workplace, where they can nurse and visit their babies several times a day. Public policies supporting mothering by either males or females are almost nonexistent in this country. In fact, Urie Bronfenbrenner has declared that simply because we ignore the situation, the family policy in this country is an antifamily policy (AP, 1977). Paternity leaves are almost unknown, and day care centers for infants in workplaces are very rare today in the United States.

Besides these general cultural trends and changes in family patterns and values, some changes have also occurred in the economy. As more and more women enter the labor force, pressure continues to mount for the development of anti-sex discrimination laws, and feminists continue to push for their enforcement.

Even though these contemporary changes indicate some promise for the lessening of male dominance, some current movements that superficially appear promising are probably not conducive to greater equality for women and men. While the increase of female-headed households and the rising divorce rate may result in part from women's greater economic independence, female-headed households have less than half the income of male-headed households. Neither is it clear that the various alternative family styles such as communal living have contributed to greater equality between the sexes. While communal groups espouse freedom from traditional roles, men generally have not shared responsibility for nurturing. Women are often totally responsible for the care of infants, and older children may be left with no adult responsible for their well-being (Rossi, 1977).

Women's greater participation in the labor force, the passing of legislation that requires equality in the economy, and the general cultural trend toward expressiveness may have set the stage for men's greater acceptance of a nurturing role with children and men assuming more equal responsibility with women for child care. If our analysis is correct, such changes are necessary if sex inequality is to end. Male dominance has been an integral part of human society for all of recorded time. It will no doubt be hard to change, but we believe that the results will be worth the effort.

Suggested Readings

CHAFE, WILLIAM H., *Women and Equality: Changing Patterns in American Culture.* New York: Oxford University Press, 1977. Essays by an historian concerning women from colonial times to the present, including a comparison of sexism and racism.

FILENE, PETER GABRIEL, *Him/Her Self: Sex Roles in Modern America.* New York: NAL, 1975 An historical look at changing sex roles.

GIELE, JANET, *Women and the Future: Changing Sex Roles in Modern America.* New York: Free Press, 1978. A fact-filled book written by a sociologist; discusses policies that may help produce a society in which female values are given a larger place.

MILLER, JEAN BAKER, *Toward a New Psychology of Women.* Boston, Mass.: Beacon Press, 1976. A psychoanalyst suggests that women have psychological strengths that need to be shared by men.

PIERCY, MARGE, *Woman on the Edge of Time.* New York: Fawcett Crest, 1976. Science fiction dramatizing many of the ideas discussed in this text.

RICH, ADRIENNE, *Of Woman Born: Motherhood as Experience and Institution.* New York: W. W. Norton & Co., Inc., 1976. A view of androgyny by a poet and writer that stresses a female/maternal principle.

References

Acker, Joan

1978 "Issues in the Sociological Study of Women's Work." Pp. 134–61 in Ann H. Stromberg and Shirley Harkess (eds.), *Women Working: Theories and Facts in Perspective.* Palo Alto, Calif.: Mayfield.

Adams, Karen L., and Norma C. Ware

1979 "Sexism and the English Language: The Linguistic Implications of Being a Woman." Pp. 487–504 in Jo Freeman (ed.), *Women: A Feminist Perspective* (2nd ed.). Palo Alto, Calif.: Mayfield.

Alexander, Karl L., and Bruce K. Eckland

1974 "Sex Differences in the Educational Attainment Process." *American Sociological Review* 39:668–82.

Almquist, Elizabeth M.

1975 "Untangling the Effects of Race and Sex: The Disadvantaged Status of Black Women." *Social Science Quarterly* 56:129–42.

Almquist, Elizabeth M., and Juanita Wehrle-Einhorn

1978 "The Doubly Disadvantaged: Minority Women in the Labor Force." Pp. 63–88 in Ann Stromberg and Shirley Harkness (eds.), *Women Working.* Palo Alto, Calif.: Mayfield.

Angrilli, A. F.

1960 "The Psychosexual Identification of Pre-school Boys." *Journal of Genetic Psychology* 97:329–40.

Ariès, Philippe

1962 *Centuries of Childhood: A Social History of Family Life.* (Robert Baldick, trans.) New York: Knopf.

Armstrong, Louise

1978 *Kiss Daddy Goodnight: A Speak-Out on Incest.* New York: Hawthorn.

Associated Press

1977 "Family Serves Prime Function." *Eugene Register Guard,* August 31, p. 12F.

Astin, Helen A., and Alan E. Bayer

1973 "Sex Discrimination in Academe." Pp. 333–56 in Alice Rossi and Ann Calderwood (eds.), *Academic Women on the Move.* New York: Russell Sage.

Atkin, C. K.

1975 "The Effects of Television Advertising on Children: Second Year Experimental Evidence." Report submitted to the Office of Child Development.

Bahr, Stephen J.

1974a "Effects on Power and Division of Labor in the Family." Pp. 167–85 in Lois W. Hoffman and F. Ivan Nye (eds.), *Working Mothers.* San Francisco: Jossey-Bass.

1974b "Adolescent Perceptions of Conjugal Power." *Social Forces* 52:357–67.

Bakan, David

1966 *The Duality of Human Existence.* Chicago: Rand McNally.

Baker, Sally Hillsman

1978 "Women in Blue-Collar and Service Occupations." Pp. 339–76 in Ann Stromberg and Shirley Harkness (eds.), *Women Working.* Palo Alto, Calif: Mayfield.

Balow, Irving H.

1963 "Sex Differences in First Grade Reading." *Elementary English* 40:303–20.

Balswick, Jack, and Charles Peek

1971 "The Inexpressive Male: A Tragedy of American Society." *Family Coordinator* 20:363–68.

Bandura, Albert, and R. H. Walters

1963 *Social Learning and Personality Development.* New York: Holt, Rinehart & Winston.

Bardwick, Judith M.

1974 "The Sex Hormones, the Central Nervous System and Affect Variability in Humans." Pp. 27–50 in Violet Franks and Vsanti Burtle (eds.), *Women in Therapy: New Psychotherapies for a Changing Society.* New York: Brunner/Mazel.

Barfield, Ashton

1976 "Biological Influences on Sex Differences in Behavior." Pp. 62–121 in Michael Teitelbaum (ed.), *Sex Differences: Social and Biological Perspectives.* Garden City, N.Y.: Anchor Books.

Barry, Herbert, Margaret K. Bacon, and Irvin L. Child

1957 "A Cross-cultural Survey of Some Sex Differences in Socialization." *Journal of Abnormal and Social Psychology* 55:327–32.

Bart, Pauline B.

1969 "Why Women's Status Changes in Middle Age: The Turns of the Social Ferris Wheel," *Sociological Symposium* 3:1–18.

1975 "The Loneliness of the Long-Distance Mother." Pp. 156–70 in Jo Freeman (ed.), *Women: A Feminist Perspective.* Palo Alto, Calif.: Mayfield.

1976 "Review of Psychoanalysis and Women." *Contemporary Sociology* 5:9–13.

Baude, Annika

1979 "Public Policy and Changing Family Patterns in Sweden: 1930–1977." Pp. 145–76 in Jean Lipman-Blumen and Jessie Bernard (eds.), *Sex Roles and Social Policy: A Complex Social Science Equation.* Beverly Hills, Calif.: Sage Publications.

Baumrind, Diana, and A. E. Black

1967 "Socialization Practices Associated with Dimensions of Competence in Preschool Boys and Girls." *Child Development* 38:291–327.

Bell, Colin, and Howard Newby

1976 "Husbands and Wives: The Dynamics of the Deferential Dialectic." Pp. 152–68 in Diana L. Barker and Sheila Allen (eds.), *Dependence and Exploitation in Work and Marriage.* New York: Longman.

Bell, Inge Powell
1975 "The Double-Standard: Age." Pp. 145–55 in Jo Freeman (ed.), *Women: A Feminist Perspective.* Palo Alto, Calif.: Mayfield.

Bem, Sandra L.
1974 "The Measurement of Psychological Androgyny." *Journal of Consulting and Clinical Psychology* 42:155–62.
1975 "Sex-Role Adaptability: One Consequence of Psychological Androgyny." *Journal of Personality and Social Psychology* 31:634–43.

Bem, Sandra L., W. Martyna, and C. Watson
1976 "Sex-Typing and Androgyny: Further Explorations of the Expressive Domain." *Journal of Personality and Social Psychology* 34:1016–23.

Bengis, Ingrid
1973 *Combat in the Erogenous Zone.* New York: Knopf.

Bennett, Edward M., and Larry R. Cohen
1959 "Men and Women: Personality Patterns and Contrasts." *Genetic Psychology Monographs* 59:101–55.

Benston, Margaret
1969 "The Political Economy of Women's Liberation." *Monthly Review* 21:13–27. Excerpted in Nona Glazer and Helen Y. Waehrer (eds.), *Woman in a Man-Made World* (2nd ed.). Chicago: Rand McNally, 1977, pp. 216–25.

Berger, Bennett M., Bruce M. Hackett, and R. Mervyn Millar
1974 "Child-rearing Practices in the Communal Family." Pp. 441–63 in Arlene Skolnick and Jerome H. Skolnick (eds.), *Intimacy, Family, and Society.* Boston: Little, Brown.

Bergmann, Barbara R.
1971 "The Effect on White Incomes of Discrimination in Employment." *Journal of Political Economy* 79:294–313.
1973 "The Economics of Women's Liberation." *Challenge* 16:11–17.

Bergmann, Barbara R., and Irma Adelman
1973 "The 1973 Report of the President's Council of Economic Advisors: The Economic Role of Women." *The American Economic Review* 63:509–14.

Bernard, Jessie
1975a *The Future of Motherhood.* New York: Penguin.
1975b *Women, Wives, Mothers: Values and Options.* Chicago: Aldine.

Bers, Trudy Harrison
1978 "Local Political Elites: Men and Women on Boards of Education." *Western Political Quarterly* 31:381–91.

Bettelheim, Bruno
1954 *Symbolic Wounds: Puberty Rites and the Envious Male.* London: Thames and Hudson.

Beyers, Charlotte
1972 "Beauty and Her Beasts." *Saturday Review of Science* 1:34–37.

Bieber, Irving, J. J. Dain, P. R. Dince, M. G. Drellich, H. G. Grand, R. H. Gundlach, M. W. Kremer, A. H. Rifkin, C. B. Wilbur, and Toby Bieber
1962 *Homosexuality: A Psychoanalytic Study.* New York: Basic Books.

Bielli, Carla
1976 "Some Aspects of the Condition of Women in Italy." (Beverly Springer, trans.) Pp. 105–14 in Lynne B. Iglitzin and Ruth Ross (eds.), *Women in the World: A Comparative Study.* Santa Barbara, Calif.: Clio Books.

Birnbaum, J.

1975 "Life Patterns and Self-Esteem in Gifted Family-Oriented and Career-Committed Women." In Martha Mednick, Sandra Tangri, and Lois Hoffman (eds.), *Women and Achievement.* Washington, D.C.: Hemisphere.

Birns, Beverly

1976 "The Emergence and Socialization of Sex Differences in the Earliest Years." *Merrill-Palmer Quarterly* 22:229–54.

Blau, Francine O.

1975 "Women in the Labor Force: An Overview." Pp. 211–25 in Jo Freeman (ed.), *Women: A Feminist Perspective.* Palo Alto, Calif.: Mayfield.

Blau, Francine O., and Carol L. Jusenius

1976 "Economists' Approaches to Sex Segregation in the Labor Market: An Appraisal." *Signs* 1:181–200.

Block, Jack, and Norma Haan

1971 *Lives Through Time.* Berkeley: Bancroft.

Block, Jeanne H.

1973 "Conceptions of Sex Role: Some Cross-cultural and Longitudinal Perspectives." *American Psychologist* 28:512–26.

1974 "The Relationship of Parental Teaching Strategies to Ego-resiliency in Preschool Children." Paper presented at the meeting of the Western Psychological Association, San Francisco.

1975 "Another Look at Sex Differentiation in the Socialization Behaviors of Mothers and Fathers." Paper for Conference on New Directions for Research on Women, Madison, Wisc.

1976 "Issues, Problems, and Pitfalls in Assessing Sex Differences." *Merrill-Palmer Quarterly* 22:283–308.

Blood, Robert O., Jr., and Donald M. Wolfe

1960 *Husbands and Wives.* Glencoe, Ill.: Free Press.

Blumberg, Rae Lesser

1978 *Stratification: Socioeconomic and Sexual Inequality.* Dubuque, Iowa: Wm. C. Brown.

Blumberg, Rae Lesser, and Robert F. Winch

1974 "Societal Complexity and Familial Complexity." Pp. 94–113 in Robert F. Winch and Graham B. Spanier (eds.), *Selected Studies in Marriage and the Family* (4th ed.). New York: Holt, Rinehart & Winston.

Blumstein, Philip W., and Pepper Schwartz

1976 "Bisexuality: Some Social Psychological Issues." Available from P. W. Blumstein, Department of Sociology, University of Washington, Seattle, Washington.

Bose, Christine

1976 "Social Status of the Homemaker." Paper presented at the annual meeting of the American Sociological Association, New York City.

Boskind-Lodahl, Marlene

1976 "Cinderella's Stepsisters: A Feminist Perspective on Anorexia Nervosa and Bulimia." *Signs* 2:342–56.

Boulding, Elise

1976 "Familial Constraints on Women's Work Roles," *Signs* 1:95–117.

1979 "Introduction." Pp. 7–16 in Jean Lipman-Blumen and Jessie Bernard (eds.), *Sex Roles and Social Policy: A Complex Social Science Equation.* Beverly Hills, Calif.: Sage Publications.

Boulding, Elise, Shirley A. Nuss, Dorothy Lee Carson, and Michael A. Greenstein

1976 *Handbook of International Data on Women.* New York: Halsted Press.

Bowerman, C. E., and J. W. Kinch
1959 "Changes in Family and Peer Orientation of Children between the Fourth and Tenth Grades." *Social Forces* 37:206–11. Reprinted in Martin Gold and Elizabeth Douvan (eds.), *Adolescent Development.* Boston: Allyn & Bacon, 1969, pp. 137–41.

Brenton, Myron
1966 *The American Male.* New York: Coward, McCann & Geoghegan.

Brim, Orville
1958 "Family Structure and Sex Role Learning by Children." *Sociometry* 21:1–16.

Brim, Orville
1976 "Theories of the Male Mid-life Crisis." *The Counseling Psychologist* 6:2–9.

Brøgger, Suzanne
1976 "Prohibition." Pp. 215–34 in Brøgger, *Deliver Us from Love.* (Thomas Teal, trans.) New York: Dell.

Bronfenbrenner, Urie
1961 "Some Familial Antecedents of Responsibility and Leadership in Adolescents." Pp. 239–71 in L. Petrullo and B. M. Bass (eds.), *Leadership and Interpersonal Behavior.* New York: Holt, Rinehart & Winston.

Broverman, Inge K., Frank E. Clarkson, Paul S. Rosenkrantz, and Susan R. Vogel
1970 "Sex-Role Stereotypes and Clinical Judgments of Mental Health." *Journal of Consulting Psychology* 34:1–7.

Broverman, Inge K., Susan R. Vogel, Donald M. Broverman, Frank E. Clarkson, and Paul S. Rosenkrantz
1972 "Sex-Role Stereotypes: A Current Appraisal." *Journal of Social Issues* 28:59–78.

Brown, Judith K.
1975 "Iroquois Women: An Ethnohistoric Note." Pp. 235–51 in Rayna R. Reiter (ed.), *Toward an Anthropology of Women.* New York: Monthly Review Press.

Brownmiller, Susan
1975 *Against Our Will: Men, Women and Rape.* New York: Simon & Schuster.

Bullock, Charles S. III and Patricia Lee Findley Harris
1972 "Recruitment of Women for Congress: A Research Note." *Western Political Quarterly* 25:416–23.

Burks, Barbara Stoddard, Dortha Williams Jensen, and Lewis H. Terman
1930 *The Promise of Youth.* Stanford, Calif.: Stanford University Press.

Burton, Roger V., and John W. M. Whiting
1961 "The Absent Father and Cross-sex Identity." *Merrill-Palmer Quarterly* 7: 85–95.

Byrne, Susan
1977 "Nobody Home: The Erosion of the American Family." An interview with Urie Bronfenbrenner in *Psychology Today,* May, 41–47.

Caldwell, Bettye M.
1973 "Infant Day Care—The Outcast Gains Respectability." Pp. 20–36 in Pamela Roby (ed.), *Child Care: Who Cares?* New York: Basic Books.

Campbell, Angus, Philip E. Converse, and Willard L. Rodgers
1975 *The Quality of American Life.* New York: Russell Sage.

Campbell, Jean W.
1973 "Women Drop Back In: Educational Innovation in the Sixties." Pp. 93–124 in Alice S. Rossi and Ann Calderwood (eds.), *Academic Women on the Move.* New York: Russell Sage.

Cantor, Muriel S.
1978 "Where are the women in Public Broadcasting?" Pp. 78–90 in Gaye Tuchman, A. K. Daniels, and J. Benet (eds.), *Hearth and Home: Images of Women in the Mass Media.* New York: Oxford University Press.

Carey, Max L.
1976 "Revised Occupational Projections to 1985." *Monthly Labor Review,* November. pp. 10–22.

Carlson, Rae
1971 "Sex Differences in Ego Functioning: Exploratory Studies of Agency and Communion." *Journal of Consulting and Clinical Psychology* 37:267–77.

Cassell, Frank H., Steven M. Director, and Samuel I. Doctors
1975 "Discrimination within Internal Labor Markets." *Industrial Relations* 14:337–44.

Center for the American Woman and Politics, Rutgers University
1976 *Women in Public Office.* New York: Bonker.

Centers, Richard, Bertram H. Raven, and Aroldo Rodrigues
1971 "Conjugal Power Structure: A Re-examination." *American Sociological Review* 36:264–78.

Chafetz, Janet Saltzman
1974 *Masculine/Feminine or Human? An Overview of the Sociology of Sex Roles.* Itasca, Ill.: F. E. Peacock.

Chafetz, Janet Saltzman, Paula Beck, Patricia Sampson, Joyce West, and Bonnye Jones
1976 *Who's Queer?: A Study of Homo- and Heterosexual Women.* Sarasota, Fla.: Omni Press.

Chamove, A., H. Harlow, and G. D. Mitchell
1967 "Sex Differences in the Infant-Directed Behavior of Preadolescent Rhesus Monkeys." *Child Development* 38:329–35.

Chasseguet-Smirgel, Janine
1970 "Feminine Guilt and the Oedipus Complex." Pp. 94–134 in Chasseguet-Smirgel (ed.), *Female Sexuality.* Ann Arbor: University of Michigan Press.

Chodorow, Nancy
1971 "Being and Doing: A Cross-cultural Examination of the Socialization of Males and Females." Pp. 259–91 in Vivian Gornick and Barbara K. Moran (eds.), *Woman in Sexist Society.* New York: New American Library.
1974 "Family Structure and Feminine Personality." Pp. 43–66 in Michelle Zimbalist Rosaldo and Louise Lamphere (eds.), *Woman, Culture, and Society.* Stanford, Calif.: Stanford University Press.
1978 *The Reproduction of Mothering.* Berkeley, Calif.: University of California Press.

Coleman, James
1961 *The Adolescent Society.* New York: Free Press.

Condry, John, and Sharon Dyer
1976 "Fear of Success: Attribution of Cause to the Victim." *Journal of Social Issues* 32:63–84.

Connor, Jane Marantz, Maxine Schackman, and Lisa A. Serbin
1978 "Sex-Related Differences in Response to Practice on a Visual-Spatial Test and Generalization to a Related Test." *Child Development* 49:24–29.

Constantinople, Anne
1973 "Masculinity-Femininity: An Exception to a Famous Dictum?" *Psychological Bulletin* 80:389–407.

Cosby, Bill

1975 "The Regular Way." Pp. 58–62 in John W. Petras (ed.), *Sex Male Gender Masculine: Selected Readings in Male Sexuality.* Port Washington, N.Y.: Alfred Publishing Co.

Coser, Lewis A.

1974 "Some Aspects of Soviet Family Policy." Pp. 412–29 in Rose Laub Coser (ed.), *The Family: Its Structures and Functions* (2nd ed.). New York: St. Martin's Press.

Coser, Rose L., and Gerald Rokoff

1974 "Women in the Occupational World: Social Disruption and Conflict." Pp. 490–511 in Rose L. Coser (ed.), *The Family: Its Structures and Functions* (2nd ed.). New York: St. Martin's Press.

Current Labor Statistics

1979 "Household Data." *Monthly Labor Review* 102:78.

Dalla Costa, Mariarosa

1972 "Women and the Subversion of Community." *Radical America* 6:67–102.

D'Andrade, Roy G.

1966 "Sex Differences and Cultural Institutions." Pp. 173–203 in Eleanor E. Maccoby (ed.), *The Development of Sex Differences.* Stanford, Calif.: Stanford University Press.

Daniel, Glenda

1976 "Socialists Stress Motherhood As Parenting Loses Appeal in U.S." *The Oregonian,* September 7, p. C2.

Darien, Jean C.

1976 "Factors Influencing the Rising Labor Force Participation Rates of Married Women with Pre-school Children." *Social Science Quarterly* 56:614–30.

Davis, P. G., and R. D. Gandelman

1972 "Pup-killing Produced by the Administration of Testosterone Propionate to Adult Female Mice." *Hormones and Behavior* 3:169–73.

de Beauvoir, Simone

1953 *The Second Sex.* (H. M. Parshley, trans.) New York: Knopf.

Deckard, Barbara, and Howard Sherman

1974 "Monopoly Power and Sex Discrimination." *Politics and Society* 4:475–82.

Denfield, Duane

1974 "Dropouts from Swinging." *The Family Coordinator* 23:45–49.

Deutsch, Helene

1974 "The psychology of women in relation to the functions of reproduction." Reprinted in Jean Strouse (ed.), *Women and Analysis.* New York: Grossman, pp. 147–61. Originally published 1924.

1944–45 *The Psychology of Women: A Psychoanalytic Interpretation.* Vol. 1: *Girlhood.* Vol. 2: *Motherhood.* New York: Bantam.

DeVore, Irven

1963 "Mother-Infant Relations in Free-Ranging Baboons." Pp. 305–35 in H. L. Rheingold (ed.), *Maternal Behavior in Mammals.* New York: John Wiley.

1965 *Primate Behavior: Field Studies of Monkeys and Apes.* New York: Holt, Rinehart & Winston.

Diamond, Irene

1977 *Sex Roles in the State House.* New Haven: Yale University Press.

Dinnerstein, Dorothy
1976 *The Mermaid and the Minotaur: Sexual Arrangements and Human Malaise.* New York: Harper & Row, Pub.

Doering, C. H., H. K. H. Brodie, H. Kraemer, H. Becker, and D. A. Hamburg
1974 "Plasma Testosterone Levels and Psychologic Measures in Men over a 2-Month Period." Pp. 413–31 in R. C. Friedman et al. (eds.), *Sex Differences in Behavior.* New York: John Wiley.

Douvan, Elizabeth, and Joseph Adelson
1966 *The Adolescent Experience.* New York: John Wiley.

Droppleman, L. F., and E. S. Schaefer
1963 "Boys' and Girls' Reports of Maternal and Paternal Behavior." *Journal of Abnormal and Social Psychology* 67:648–54.

Dwyer, Carol Anne
1974 "Influence of Children's Sex Role Standards on Reading and Arithmetic Achievement." *Journal of Educational Psychology* 66:811–16.

Dyrud, Jarl
1976 "Toward a Science of the Passions." *Saturday Review,* Feb. 21, pp. 22–27.

Eaton, G. Gray
1976 "The Social Order of Japanese Macaques." *Scientific American* 235:96–106.

Edgeworth, F. V.
1922 "Equal Pay to Men and Women for Equal Work." *Economic Journal* 32:431–57.

Edwards, D. A.
1969 "Early Androgen Stimulation and Aggressive Behavior in Male and Female Mice." *Physiology and Behavior* 4:333–38.

Ehrenreich, Barbara, and Deirdre English
1976 "The Manufacture of Housework." Pp. 7–42 in Mina Davis Caulfield et al. (eds.), *Capitalism and the Family.* San Francisco: Agenda.

Ehrhardt, Anke A.
1973 "Maternalism in Fetal Hormonal and Related Syndromes." Pp. 99–116 in Joseph Zubin and John Money (eds.), *Contemporary Sexual Behavior: Critical Issues in the 1970's.* Baltimore: Johns Hopkins University Press.

Ehrhardt, Anke A., and Susan W. Baker
1974 "Fetal Androgens, Human Central Nervous System, Differentiation, and Behavior Sex Differences." Pp. 33–52 in R. C. Friedman et al. (eds.), *Sex Differences in Behavior.* New York: John Wiley.

Eisenhart, R. Wayne
1975 "You Can't Hack It, Little Girl: A Discussion of the Covert Psychological Agenda of Modern Combat Training." *Journal of Social Issues* 31:13–23.

Eisler, Riane Tennenhaus
1977 *Dissolution.* New York: McGraw-Hill.

Engels, Frederick
1972 *The Origin of the Family, Private Property and the State.* (Eleanor Leacock, ed.) New York: International Publishers. Originally published 1884.

Epstein, Cynthia F.
1970 "Encountering the Male Establishment: Sex Status Limits on Women's Careers in the Professions." *American Journal of Sociology* 75:965–82.
1974 "Reconciliation of Women's Roles." Pp. 473–89 in Rose L. Coser (ed.), *The Family: Its Structures and Functions* (2nd ed.). New York: St. Martin's Press.

Erikson, Erik H.
1959 "Identity and the Life Cycle." *Psychological Issues* 1:18–171.
1968 *Identity: Youth and Crisis.* New York: W. W. Norton & Co., Inc.

Erskine, Hazel
1971 "The Polls: Women's Role." *The Public Opinion Quarterly* 35:275–90.

Escalona, Sibylle
1949 "The Psychological Situation of Mother and Child Upon Return from the Hospital." In Milton J. E. Senn (ed.), *Problems of Infancy and Childhood: Transactions of the Third Conference.* New York: Josiah Macy, Jr. Foundation.

Etzioni, Amitai
1978 "The Waning of Macho America." *Psychology Today.* June, p. 136.

Fagot, Beverly I.
1974 "Sex Differences in Toddlers' Behavior and Parental Reaction." *Developmental Psychology* 10:554–58.
1978a "The Influence of Sex of Child on Parental Reactions to Toddler Children." *Child Development* 49:459–65.
1978b "The Socialization of Sex Differences in Early Childhood." Paper delivered at the Meetings of the Oregon Psychological Association, May, 1978.

Fairbairn, W. R. O.
1952 *Psychoanalytic Studies of the Personality.* New York: Basic Books.

Falk, Gail
1975 "Sex Discrimination in the Trade Unions: Legal Resources for Change." Pp. 254–76 in Jo Freeman (ed.), *Women: A Feminist Perspective.* Palo Alto, Calif.: Mayfield.

Fawcett, Millicent
1918 "Equal Pay for Equal Work." *Economic Journal* 28:1–6.

Featherman, David L., and Robert M. Hauser
1976 "Sexual Inequalities and Socioeconomic Achievement in the U. S., 1962–1973." *American Sociological Review* 41:462–83.

Ferber, Marianne, and Helen M. Lowry
1976 "Women: The New Reserve Army of the Unemployed." *Signs* 1:213–32.

Ferree, Myra Marx
1974 "A Woman for President? Changing Responses: 1958–1972." *The Public Opinion Quarterly* 38:390–99.

Feshback, N. D.
1969 "Sex Differences in Children's Modes of Aggressive Responses towards Outsiders." *Merrill-Palmer Quarterly* 15:249–58.

Fiedler, Leslie A.
1968 *The Return of the Vanishing American.* New York: Stein and Day.

Firestone, Shulamith
1971 *The Dialectic of Sex.* New York: Bantam.

Fisher, Seymour
1973 *Understanding the Female Orgasm.* New York: Basic Books.

Flacks, Richard
1971 *Youth and Social Change.* Chicago: Markham.

Fliess, Robert
1961 *Ego and Body Ego: Contributions to their Psychoanalytic Psychology.* New York: Schulte.

Fling, S., and M. Manosevitz
1972 "Sex Typing in Nursery School Children's Play Interests." *Developmental Psychology* 7:146–52.

Fogg, Susan
1977 "Women's Wages Fall below Average." *The Oregonian,* December 8, p. B10.

Foreman, Laura
1977 "Congress Facing Proposals to Improve Its Standards As an Employer." *The New York Times,* August 13, p. I.7.

Fosburgh, Lacy
1977 "The Make-Believe World of Teen-age Maternity." *The New York Times Magazine,* August 7, pp. 29–34.

Fox, Greer Litton
1977 "Sex-Role Attitudes As Predictions of Contraceptive Use." *Sex Roles* 3:265–83.

Freeman, Jo
1975 "How to Discriminate against Women without Really Trying." Pp. 194–208 in Jo Freeman (ed.), *Women: A Feminist Perspective.* Palo Alto, Calif.: Mayfield.

Freud, Sigmund
1933 "Femininity." Pp. 112–135 in Freud, *New Introductory Lectures on Psychoanalysis.* New York: W. W. Norton & Co., Inc.
1963a "Female Sexuality." Pp. 194–211 in Philip Reiff (ed.), Sexuality and the Psychology of Love. New York: Collier. Originally published 1931.
1963b "The Most Prevalent Form of Degradation in Erotic Life." Pp. 58–70 in Philip Reiff (ed.), *Sexuality and the Psychology of Love.* New York: Collier. Originally published 1912.
1963c "Some Psychological Consequences of the Anatomical Distinction between the Sexes." Pp. 183–93 in Philip Reiff (ed.), *Sexuality and the Psychology of Love.* New York: Collier. Originally published 1925.
1963d "The Taboo of Virginity." Pp. 70–86 in Philip Reiff (ed.), *Sexuality and the Psychology of Love.* New York: Collier. Originally published 1918.
1969 *An Outline of Psycho-Analysis.* New York: W. W. Norton & Co., Inc. Originally published 1940.

Friedan, Betty
1963 *The Feminine Mystique.* New York: Dell.

Friedl, Ernestine
1975 *Women and Men: An Anthropologist's View.* New York: Holt, Rinehart & Winston.

Frieze, Irene H., Jacquelynne E. Parsons, Paula B. Johnson, Diane N. Ruble, and Gail L. Zellman
1978 *Women and Sex Roles: A Social Psychological Perspective.* New York: W. W. Norton & Co., Inc.

Frisch, R. E., and R. Revelle
1970 "Height and Weight at Menarche and a Hypothesis of Critical Body Weights and Adolescent Events. *Science* 169:397–98.

Frodi, Ann, Jacqueline Macaulay, and Pauline R. Thome
1977 "Are Women Always Less Aggressive Than Men? A Review of the Experimental Literature." *Psychological Bulletin* 84:634–60.

Frueh, T., and P. E. McGhee
1975 "Traditional Sex Role Development and Amount of Time Spent Watching Television." *Developmental Psychology* 11:109.

Fry, William
1972 "Psycho-dynamics of Sexual Humor: Women's View of Sex." *Medical Aspects of Human Sexuality* 6:124–39.

Galenson, Eleanor, and Herman Roiphe
1974 "The Emergence of Genital Awareness during the Second Year of Life." Pp. 223–32 in R. C. Friedman et al. (eds.), *Sex Differences in Behavior.* New York: John Wiley.

Galenson, Marjorie
1973 *Women and Work: An International Comparison.* Ithaca, N.Y.: Publications Division, New York School of Industrial Labor Relations, Cornell University.

Gallup, George
1975 *Gallup Opinion Index.* Princeton: Gallup International.

Garai, J. E., and Aram Scheinfeld
1968 "Sex Differences in Mental and Behavior Traits." *Genetic Psychology Monographs* 77:169–299.

Garnets, Linda, and Joseph H. Pleck
1979 "Sex Role Identity, Androgyny, and Sex Role Transcendence: A Sex Role Strain Analysis." *Psychology of Women Quarterly* 3:270–83.

Gates, Arthur I.
1961 "Sex Differences in Reading Ability." *Elementary School Journal* 61:431–34.

Gates, Margaret J.
1976 "Occupational Segregation and the Law." *Signs* 1:61–74.

Gelles, Richard
1976 "Abused Wives: Why Do They Stay?" *Journal of Marriage and the Family* 38:659–68.

Geng, Veronica
1976 "Requiem for the Women's Movement." *Harper's,* November, pp. 49–68.

Giallombardo, Rose
1966 *Society of Women: A Study of a Women's Prison.* New York: John Wiley.

Giele, Janet Z.
1975 "Changing Sex Roles and the Future of Marriage." Pp. 69–85 in Henry Gruenbaum and Jacob Christ (eds.), *Contemporary Marriage: Structure, Dynamics and Therapy.* Boston: Little, Brown.
1978 *Women and the Future: Changing Sex Roles in Modern America.* New York: Free Press.

Gillespie, Dair L.
1971 "Who Has the Power? The Marital Struggle." *Journal of Marriage and the Family* 33:445–58. Reprinted in H. P. Dreitzel (ed.), *Family, Marriage and the Struggle of the Sexes.* New York: Macmillan, 1972, pp. 121–50.

Goldberg, Steven
1974 *The Inevitability of Patriarchy.* New York: Morrow.

Goldberg, Susan, and Michael Lewis
1969 "Play Behavior in the Year-Old Infant: Early Sex Differences." *Child Development* 40:21–31.

Goldman, Roy D., and Barbara Newlin Hewitt
1976 "The Scholastic Aptitude Test Explains Why College Men Major in Science More Often Than College Women." *Journal of Counseling Psychology* 23:50–54.

Goldsmith, Barbara

1970 "Grass, Women and Sex: An Interview with Mike Nichols." *Harper's Bazaar,* November, p. 142.

Goleman, Daniel

1978 "Special Abilities of the Sexes: Do They Begin in the Brain?" *Psychology Today,* November, pp. 48–59.

Goodenough, Evelyn W.

1957 "Interest in Persons As an Aspect of Sex Difference in the Early Years." *Genetic Psychology Monographs* 55:287–323.

Gough, Harrison G.

1952 "Identifying Psychological Femininity." *Educational and Psychological Measurement* 12:427–39.

Gough, Kathleen

1971 "The Origin of the Family." *Journal of Marriage and the Family* 33:760–70.

Gould, Roger L.

1972 "The Phases of Adult Life: A Study in Developmental Psychology." *The American Journal of Psychiatry* 129:521–31.

Gove, Walter R.

1972 "The Relationship between Sex Roles, Marital Status, and Mental Illness." *Social Forces* 51:34–44. Also reprinted with an introduction and postscript by Jerold Heiss in Heiss (ed.), *Family Roles and Interaction* (2nd ed.). Chicago: Rand McNally, pp. 156–76.

Gove, Walter R., and Michael R. Geerken

1977 "The Effect of Children and Employment on the Mental Health of Married Men and Women." *Social Forces* 56:66–76.

Gove, Walter R. and Michael Hughes

1979 "Possible Causes of the Apparent Sex Differences in Physical Health." *American Sociological Review* 44:126–46.

Granrut, Claude du

1979 "Women as Policy Makers: The Case of France." Pp. 269–78 in Jean Lipman-Blumen and Jessie Bernard (eds.), *Sex Roles and Social Policy: A Complex Social Science Equation.* Beverly Hills, Calif.: Sage Publications.

Grant, W. Vance, and C. George Lind

1977 *1976 Digest of Education Statistics.* Washington, D.C.: National Center for Education Statistics, United States Department of Health, Education, and Welfare.

1978 *1977–1978 Digest of Education Statistics.* Washington, D. C.: National Center for Education Statistics, United States Department of Health, Education, and Welfare.

Grass, Günter

1964 *Cat and Mouse.* (Ralph Manheim, trans.) New York: New American Library.

Green, Richard

1974 *Sexual Identity Conflict in Children and Adults.* New York: Basic Books.

Griffin, Susan

1975 "Rape: The All-American Crime." Pp. 24–39 in Jo Freeman (ed.), *Women: A Feminist Perspective.* Palo Alto, Calif.: Mayfield.

Grimm, James W.

1978 "Women in Female-Dominated Professions." Pp. 293–315 in Ann Stromberg and Shirley Harkess (eds.), *Women Working.* Palo Alto, Calif.: Mayfield.

Gross, Edward
1968 "Plus ça change . . .? The Sexual Structure of Occupations over Time." *Social Problems* 16:198–208.

Guntrip, Harry
1961 *Personality Structure and Human Interaction: The Developing Synthesis of Psychodynamic Theory.* New York: International University Press.

Gutmann, David
1965 "Women and the Conception of Ego Strength." *Merrill-Palmer Quarterly* 11:229–40.
1970 "Female Ego Styles and Generational Conflict." Pp. 77–96 in Judith M. Bardwick, Elizabeth Douvan, Martina S. Horner, and David Gutmann, *Feminine Personality and Conflict.* Monterey, Calif.: Brooks/Cole.

Haavio-Mannila, Elisa
1971 "Convergences between East and West: Tradition and Modernity in Sex Roles in Sweden, Finland and the Soviet Union." *Acta Sociologica* 14:114–25. Reprinted in Martha Mednick et al., *Women and Achievement.* New York: John Wiley, 1975, pp. 71–84.

Hagen, Randi, and Arnold Kahn
1975 "Discrimination against Competent Women." *Journal of Applied Social Psychology* 5:362–76.

Hamburg, O. A.
1971. "Aggressive Behavior of Chimpanzees and Baboons in Natural Habitats," *Journal of Psychiatric Research* 8:385–98.

Hareven, Tamara K.
1976a "The Family and Gender Roles in Historical Perspective." Pp. 93–118 in Libby A. Carter, Anne Firor Scott, and Wendy Martyna (eds.), *Women and Men: Changing Roles, Relationships and Perceptions.* New York: Aspen Institute for Humanistic Studies.
1976b "Modernization and Family History: Perspectives on Social Change." *Signs* 2:190–206.
1977 "Family Time and Historical Time." *Daedalus* 106:57–70.

Harris, Marvin
1977 "Why Men Dominate Women." *The New York Times Magazine.* November 13, p. 46.

Harrison, James
1978 "Warning: The Male Sex Role May Be Dangerous to Your Health." *The Journal of Social Issues* 34:65–86.

Hartley, Ruth E.
1976 "Sex-role Pressures and the Socialization of the Male Child." Pp. 235–52 in Deborah S. David and Robert Brannon (eds.), *The Forty-Nine Percent Majority: The Male Sex Role.* Reading Mass.: Addison-Wesley. Originally published 1959.

Hartup, W. W., and S. G. Moore
1963 "Avoidance of Inappropriate Sex-Typing by Young Children." *Journal of Consulting Psychology* 27:467–73.

Hays, H. R.
1972 *The Dangerous Sex.* New York: Pocket Books.

Hedges, Janice Neipert, and Stephen E'. Bennis
1974 "Sex Stereotyping: Its Decline in Skilled Trades." *Monthly Labor Review,* May pp. 14–22.

Heilbrun, Alfred B., Jr.
1968 "Sex Role, Instrumental-Expressive Behavior and Psychopathology." *Psychological Bulletin* 80:389–407.

Heller, D. O.
1959 "The Relationship between Sex-Appropriate Behavior in Young Children and the Clarity of the Sex-Role of the Like-Sexed Parent as Measured by Tests." *Dissertation Abstracts* 19:3365–66.

Henley, Nancy M.
1977 *Body Politics: Power, Sex, and Non-Verbal Communication.* Englewood Cliffs, N.J.: Prentice-Hall.

Herman, Judith, and Lisa Hirschman
1977 "Father-Daughter Incest." *Signs* 2:735–56

Hetherington, E. Mavis
1965 "A Developmental Study of the Effects of Sex of the Dominant Parent on Sex-Role Preference, Identification, and Imitation in Children." *Journal of Personality and Social Psychology* 2:188–94.

Heuser, Linda
1977 "Sex Typing in Daycare: A Preliminary View." Paper presented at the annual meetings of the Pacific Sociological Association, April.

Hill, John P.
1967 "Similarity and Accordance Between Parents and Sons in Attitudes Toward Mathematics." *Child Development* 38:777–91.

Hilton, Thomas L., and Gosta W. Berglund
1974 "Sex Differences in Mathematics Achievement—A Longitudinal Study." *Journal of Educational Research* 67:231–37.

Hinde, Robert A.
1972 *Social Behavior and Its Development in Subhuman Primates.* Eugene, Oreg: Oregon State System of Higher Education.

Hochschild, Arlie R.
1975a "Attending to, Codifying and Managing Feelings: Sex Differences in Love." Paper presented at the American Sociological Association meetings, August.
1975b "Inside the Clockwork of Male Careers." Pp. 47–80 in Florence House (ed.), *Women and the Power to Change.* New York: McGraw-Hill.

Hoffman, Lois Wladis
1972 "Early Childhood Experiences and Women's Achievement Motives." *Journal of Social Issues* 28:129–55.
1974 "Fear of Success in Males and Females: 1965 and 1971." *Journal of Consulting and Clinical Psychology* 42:353–58. Reprinted in Martha Mednick et al. (eds.), *Women and Achievement.* Washington, D.C.: Hemisphere, 1975, pp. 221–30.
1977 "Changes in Family Roles, Socialization and Sex Differences." *American Psychologist* 32:644–57.

Hogan, Dennis P.
1978 "Order of Events in the Life Course." *American Sociological Review* 43:573–86.

Holly, Aleen, and Christine Towne Bransfield
1976 "The Marriage Law: Basis of Change for China's Women." Pp. 363–74 in Lynne B. Iglitzin and Ruth Ross (eds.), *Women in the World: A Comparative Study.* Santa Barbara, Calif.: Clio Books.

Holter, Harriet, and Hildur Ve Henriksen
1979 "Social Policy and the Family in Norway." Pp. 199–224 in Jean Lipman-Blumen

and Jessie Bernard (eds.), *Sex Roles and Social Policy: A Complex Social Science Equation.* Beverly Hills, Calif.: Sage Publications.

Horner, Matina S.

1968 "Sex Differences in Achievement Motivation and Preference in Competitive and Non-competitive Situations." Unpublished Ph.D. dissertation, University of Michigan.

1970 "Femininity and Successful Achievement: A Basic Inconsistancy." In Judith M. Bardwick, Elizabeth Douvan, Matina S. Horner, and David Gutmann, *Feminine Personality and Conflict.* Monterey, Calif.: Brooks/Cole.

1972 "Toward an Understanding of Achievement-Related Conflicts in Women." *Journal of Social Issues* 28:157–75.

Horney, Karen

1967a "The Dread of Woman: Observations on a Specific Difference in the Dread Felt by Men and by Women Respectively for the Opposite Sex." Pp. 133–46 in Harold Kelman (ed.), *Feminine Psychology.* New York: W. W. Norton & Co., Inc. Originally published 1932.

1967b "The Flight from Womanhood: The Masculinity Complex in Women As Viewed by Men and by Women." Pp. 54–70 in Harold Kelman (ed.), *Feminine Psychology.* New York: W. W. Norton & Co., Inc. Originally published 1926.

Hoyenga, Katherine Blick, and Kermit T. Hoyenga

1979 *The Question of Sex Differences: Psychological, Cultural, and Biological Issues.* Boston: Little, Brown.

Hunt, Morton

1974 *Sexual Behavior in the 1970s.* New York: Dell.

Husen, Torsten

1967 *International Study of Achievement in Mathematics: A Comparison of Twelve Countries.* New York: John Wiley.

Hymowitz, Carol, and Michaele Weissman

1978 *A History of Women in America.* New York: Bantam.

Israel, Joachim, and Rosmari Eliasson

1971 "Consumption Society, Sex Roles and Sexual Behavior." *Acta Sociologica* 14:68–82.

Jacklin, Carol N., Eleanor E. Maccoby, and A. E. Dick

1973 "Barrier Behavior and Toy Preference: Sex Differences (and Their Absence) in the Year-Old Child." *Child Development* 44:196–200.

Jaquette, Jane S.

1976 "Female Political Participation in Latin America." Pp. 55–76 in Lynne B. Iglitzin and Ruth Ross (eds.), *Women in the World: A Comparative Study.* Santa Barbara, Calif.: Clio Books.

Jay, P.

1963 "Mother-Infant Relations in Langurs." In H. L. Rheingold (ed.), *Maternal Behavior in Mammals.* New York: John Wiley.

Jeffrey, Kirk

1972 "The Family as Utopian Retreat from the City: The Nineteenth Century Contribution." Pp. 21–41 in Sallie Teselle (ed.), *The Family, Communes and Utopian Communities.* New York: Harper & Row, Pub.

Jencks, Christopher, Marshall Smith, Henry Arland, Mary Jo Bane, David Cohen, Herbert Gintis, Barbara Heyns, and Stephen Mickelson

1972 *Inequality: A Reassessment of the Effect of Family and Schooling in America.* New York: Harper & Row, Pub.

Joffe, Carole

1971 "Sex Role Socialization and the Nursery School, or As the Twig Is Bent." *Journal of Marriage and the Family* 33:467–76.

Johnson, Miriam M.

1963 "Sex Role Learning in the Nuclear Family." *Child Development* 34:319–33.

1975 "Fathers, Mothers and Sex Typing." *Sociological Inquiry* 45:15–26.

1976 "Misogyny and the Superego: Chauvinism in the Moral Sphere." *Indian Journal of Social Research* 16:372–83.

1977 "Androgyny and the Maternal Principle." *School Review* 86:50–69.

1979 "Heterosexuality, the Father and Male Dominance." Available from the Center for the Sociological Study of Women, University of Oregon, Eugene, Oregon.

Johnson, Miriam M., Jean Stockard, Joan Acker, and Claudeen Naffziger

1975 "Expressiveness Reevaluated." *School Review* 83:617–44.

Johnson, Miriam M., Jean Stockard, Mary K. Rothbart, and Lisa Friedman

in press "Sexual Preference, Feminism, and Women's Perceptions of Their Parents." *Sex Roles.*

Johnson, Paula

1976 "Women and Power: Toward a Theory of Effectiveness." *The Journal of Social Issues* 32:99–110.

Jones, Ernest

1933 "The Phallic Phase." *The International Journal of Psychoanalysis* 14:1–33.

1935 "Early Female Sexuality." *The International Journal of Psychoanalysis* 16:263–73.

Jourard, Sidney M.

1971 *The Transparent Self.* New York: D. Van Nostrand.

Juillard, Joelle Rutherford

1976 "Women in France." Pp. 115–28 in Lynne B. Iglitzin and Ruth Ross (eds.), *Women in the World: A Comparative Study.* Santa Barbara, Calif.: Clio Books.

Kaats, Gilbert R., and Keith E. Davis

1970 "The Dynamics of Sexual Behavior of College Students." *Journal of Marriage and Family* 32:390–99.

Kagan, Jerome

1964 "The Child's Sex Role Classification of School Objects." *Child Development* 35:1051–56.

1972 "The Emergence of Sex Differences." *School Review* 80:217–27.

Kagan, Jerome, and Howard A. Moss

1962 *Birth to Maturity: A Study in Psychological Development.* New York: John Wiley.

Kanter, Rosabeth Moss

1975 "Women and the Structure of Organizations: Explorations in Theory and Behavior." Pp. 34–74 in Marcia Millman and R. M. Kanter (eds.), *Another Voice.* Garden City, N.Y.: Doubleday.

Kanter, Rosabeth M., and Marilyn Halter

1976 "De-housewifing Women, Domesticating Men: Changing Sex Roles in Urban Communes." Pp. 197–216 in Jerold Heiss (ed.), *Family Roles and Interaction* (2nd ed). Chicago: Rand McNally.

Katchadourian, Herant A., and Donald T. Lunde

1975 *Fundamentals of Human Sexuality* (2nd ed.) New York: Holt, Rinehart & Winston.

Kaye, Harvey E., Soll Berl, Jack Clare, Mary R. Eleston, Benjamin S. Gershwin, Patricia Gershwin, Leonard S. Kogan, Clara Torda, and Cornelia B. Wilbur

1967 "Homosexuality in Women." *Archives of General Psychiatry* 17:626–34.

Kempner, Kenneth, Rita Pougiales, and Jean Stockard

1979 "Ideological Development in Planned Social Change Projects." Unpublished paper, Center for Educational Policy and Management, University of Oregon.

Kephart, William M.

1967 "Some Correlates of Romantic Love." *Journal of Marriage and the Family* 29:470–74.

Key, Mary Ritchie

1975 *Male/Female Language.* Metuchen, N.J.: The Scarecrow Press.

Keyserling, Mary Dublin

1976 "The Economic Status of Women in the United States." *American Economic Review* 66:205–12.

Kincaid, Diane D.

1978 "Over His Dead Body: A Positive Perspective on Widows in the U.S. Congress." *Western Political Quarterly* 31:96–104.

Kinsey, Alfred C., Wardell B. Pomeroy, and Clyde E. Martin

1948 *Sexual Behavior in the Human Male.* Philadelphia: Saunders.

Kinsey, Alfred C., Wardell B. Pomeroy, Clyde E. Martin, and Paul H. Gehbard

1953 *Sexual Behavior in the Human Female.* Philadelphia: Saunders.

Klaus, Marshall H., and John H. Kennel

1976 *Maternal-Infant Bonding.* St. Louis: C. V. Mosby.

Klein, Melanie

1960 *The Psychoanalysis of Children.* New York: Grove Press. Originally published 1932.

Kline, Crysee

1975 "The Socialization Process of Women," *Gerontologist* 13:91–99.

Kling, A.

1968 "Effects of Amygdalectomy and Testosterone on Sexual Behavior of Male Juvenile Macaques," *Journal of Comparative and Physiological Psychology* 65:466–71.

Koedt, Anne

1973 "The Myth of the Vaginal Orgasm." Pp. 198–207 in Anne Koedt, Ellen Levine, and Anita Rapone (eds.), *Radical Feminism.* New York: Quadrangle/The New York Times Book Co.

Kohlberg, Lawrence

1966 "A Cognitive-Developmental Analysis of Children's Sex Role Concepts and Attitudes." Pp. 82–172 in Eleanor Maccoby (ed.), *The Development of Sex Differences.* Stanford, Calif.: Stanford University Press.

Kohlberg, Lawrence, and Edward Zigler

1967 "The Impact of Cognitive Maturity on the Development of Sex-Role Attitudes in the Years 4 to 8." *Genetic Psychology Monographs* 75:89–165.

Komarovsky, Mirra

1953 *Women in the Modern World.* Boston: Little, Brown.

1974 "Thirty Years Later: The Masculine Case." Pp. 520–31 in Rose L. Coser (ed.), *The Family: Its Structures and Functions* (2nd ed.). New York: St. Martin's Press.

1976 *Dilemmas of Masculinity: A Study of College Youth.* New York: W . W. Norton & Co., Inc.

Konopka, Gisela

1976 *Young Girls.* Englewood Cliffs, N.J.: Prentice-Hall.

Korda, Michael

1973 *Male Chauvinism! How It Works.* New York: Random House.

Koyama, N.

1970 "Changes in Dominance Rank and Division of a Wild Japanese Monkey Troop in Arashiyama." *Primates* 11:335–91.

Koyama, Takashi, Hachiro Nakamura, and Masako Hiramatsu

1967 "Japan." Pp. 290–314 in Raphael Patai (ed.), *Women in the Modern World.* New York: Free Press.

Kreps, Juanita

1971 *Sex in the Marketplace: American Women at Work.* Baltimore: Johns Hopkins University Press.

Kreps, Juanita, and Robert Clark

1975 *Sex, Age and Work: The Changing Composition of the Labor Force.* Baltimore: Johns Hopkins University Press.

Kronick, Jane C., and Jane Lieberthal

1976 "Predictors of Cross-cultural Variation in the Percentage of Women Employed in Europe." *International Journal of Comparative Sociology* 27:92–96.

Kummer, H.

1971 *Primate Societies: Group Techniques of Ecological Adaptation.* Chicago: Aldine.

Lakoff, Robin

1975 *Language and Woman's Place.* New York: Harper & Row, Pub.

Lamb, Michael E., and Jamie E. Lamb

1976 "The Nature and Importance of the Father-Infant Relationship." *The Family Coordinator* 25:379–85.

Lambert, Helen H.

1978 "Biology and Equality: A Perspective on Sex Differences." *Signs* 4:97–117.

Lambert, W. E., A. Yackley, and R. N. Hein

1971 "Child Training Values of English Canadian and French Canadian Parents." *Canadian Journal of Behavioral Science* 3:217–36.

Lamphere, Louise

1977 "Review Essay: Anthropology." *Signs* 2:612–27.

Lancaster, Jane Beckman

1976 "Sex Roles in Primate Societies." Pp. 22–81 in Michael Teitelbaum (ed.), *Sex Differences: Social and Biological Perspectives.* Garden City, N.Y.: Anchor Books.

Lang, Sylvia Wanner

1977 "Affirmative Action as Employment Policy: Its Impact on Women's Role and Position." Unpublished master's thesis, California State University, Sacramento.

Lansky, L. M.

1967 "The Family Structure Also Affects the Model: Sex Role Attitudes in Parents of Preschool Children." *Merrill-Palmer Quarterly* 13:139–50.

Lapidus, Gail Warshofsky

1976a "Changing Women's Roles in the USSR." Pp. 303–18 in Lynne B. Iglitzin and Ruth Ross (eds.) *Women in the World: A Comparative Study.* Santa Barbara, Calif.: Clio Books.

1976b "Occupational Segregation and Public Policy: A Comparative Analysis of American and Soviet Patterns." *Signs* 1:119–36.

Lasch, Christopher

1977 *Haven in a Heartless World.* New York: Basic Books.

Laschet, Ursula
1973 "Antiandrogen in the Treatment of Sex Offenders: Mode of Action and Therapeutic Outcome." Pp. 311–20 in Joseph Zubin and John Money (eds.), *Contemporary Sexual Behavior: Critical Issues in the 1970's.* Baltimore: Johns Hopkins University Press.

Leakey, Richard E., and Roger Lewin
1977 *Origins.* New York: Dutton.

Lederer, Wolfgang
1968 *The Fear of Women.* New York: Grune & Stratton.

Lehne, Gregory K.
1976 "Homophobia among Men." Pp. 66–88 in Deborah S. David and Robert Brannon (eds.), *The Forty-Nine Percent Majority: The Male Sex Role.* Reading, Mass.: Addison-Wesley.

Leibowitz, Lila
1975 "Perspectives on the Evolution of Sex Differences." Pp. 20–35 in Rayna R. Reiter (ed.), *Toward an Anthropology of Women.* New York: Monthly Review Press.

Leifer, A. D.
1970 "Effects of Early, Temporary Mother-Infant Separation on Later Maternal Behavior in Humans." Unpublished Ph.D. dissertation, Stanford University.

Leifer, A. D., P. H. Leiderman, C. R. Barnett, and J. A. Williams
1972 "Effects of Mother-Infant Separation on Maternal Attachment Behavior." *Child Development* 43:1203–18.

Lemon, Judith
1978 "Dominant or Dominated? Women on Prime-Time Television." Pp. 51–68 in G. Tuchman, A. K. Daniels, and J. Benet (eds.), *Hearth and Home: Images of Women in the Mass Media.* New York: Oxford University Press.

Leonard, Marjorie
1966 "Fathers and Daughters: The Significance of Fathering in the Psychosexual Development of the Girl." *International Journal of Psychoanalysis* 47:325–34.

Lerner, Gerda
1969 "The Lady and the Mill Girl: Changes in the Status of Women in the Age of Jackson." *American Studies Journal* 10:5–15.

Levinson, Daniel J., Charlotte M. Darrow, Edward B. Klein, Maria H. Levinson, and Braxton McKee
1976 "Periods in the Adult Development of Men: Ages 18 to 45." *The Counseling Psychologist* 6:21–25.

Levi-Strauss, Claude
1969 *The Elementary Structures of Kinship.* Boston: Beacon.

Lewis, Diane K.
1975 "The Black Family: Socialization and Sex Roles." *Phylon* 36:221–37.

Lewis, Edwin C.
1968 *Developing Woman's Potential.* Ames, Iowa: Iowa State University Press.

Lewis, Michael
1972 "There's No Unisex in the Nursery." *Psychology Today,* May, pp. 54–57.

Lidz, Ruth W., and Theodore Lidz
1977 "Male Menstruation: A Ritual Alternative to the Oedipal Transition." *International Journal of Psychoanalysis* 58:17–31.

Lindzey, Gardner

1967 "Some Remarks Concerning Incest, the Incest Taboo, and Psychoanalytic Theory." *American Psychologist* 22:1051–59.

Lipman-Blumen, Jean

1976 "Toward a Homosocial Theory of Sex Roles: An Explanation of the Sex Segregation of Social Institutions." *Signs* 1:15–31.

Litewka, Jack

1977 "The Socialized Penis." Pp. 222–45 in Eleanor S. Morrison and Vera Borosage (eds.), *Human Sexuality* (2nd ed.). Palo Alto, Calif.: Mayfield.

Lloyd, Peter C.

1965 "The Yoruba of Nigeria." Pp. 547–82 in James L. Gibbs (ed.), *Peoples of Africa.* New York: Holt, Rinehart & Winston.

Lopata, Helena Znaniecki

1971 *Occupation: Housewife.* New York: Oxford University Press.

1973 *Widowhood in an American City.* Cambridge, Mass.: Schenkman.

Lowenthal, Marjorie Fiske, Majda Thurnher, and David Chiriboga

1975 *Four Stages of Life.* San Francisco: Jossey-Bass.

Luce, G. G.

1970 *Biological Rhythms in Psychiatry and Medicine.* USPHS Pub. No. 2088. Washington, D.C.: U.S. Department of Health, Education, and Welfare.

Lynn, David B.

1969 *Parental and Sex-Role Identification.* Berkeley, Calif.: McCutchan.

1976 "Father and Sex-role Development." *Family Coordinator* 25:403–28.

Lynn, Naomi B.

1979 "American Women and the Political Process." Pp. 404–29 in Jo Freeman (ed.), *Women: A Feminist Perspective* (2nd ed.). Palo Alto, Calif.: Mayfield.

Maas, Henry S., and Joseph A. Kuypers

1974 *From Thirty to Seventy.* San Francisco: Jossey-Bass.

McCall, George J., and J. L. Simmons

1978 *Identities and Interactions.* New York: Free Press.

McClelland, D. C., J. W. Atkinson, R. A. Clark, and E. L. Lowell

1953 *The Achievement Motive.* New York: Appleton-Century-Crofts.

Maccoby, Eleanor Emmons (ed.)

1966 *The Development of Sex Differences.* Stanford, Calif.: Stanford University Press.

Maccoby, Eleanor Emmons, and Carol Nagy Jacklin

1974 *The Psychology of Sex Differences.* Stanford, Calif.: Stanford University Press.

McGee, Jeanne and Kathleen Wells

1978 "Life-span Model of Gender Role Identity." Paper presented at the Annual Meetings of the Gerontological Society, Dallas, Texas.

Mackie, Marlene

1977 "On Congenial Truths: A Perspective on Women's Studies." *Canadian Review of Sociology and Anthropology* 14:117–28.

McNeil, Jean C.

1975 "Feminism, Femininity, and the Television Series: A Content Analysis." *Journal of Broadcasting* 19:259–69.

Madden, Janice Fanning

1973 *The Economics of Sex Discrimination.* Lexington, Mass.: Lexington Books.

1975 "Discrimination—A Manifestation of Male Market Power?" Pp. 146–74 in Cynthia B. Lloyd (ed.), *Sex, Discrimination and the Division of Labor.* New York: Columbia University Press.

1976 "Comment III," *Signs* 1:245–50.

Madigan, F. C.

1957 "Are Sex Mortality Differentials Biologically Caused?" *Milbank Memorial Fund Quarterly* 35:202–23.

Malinowski, Bronislaw

1974 "Parenthood, the Basis of Social Structure." Pp. 51–63 in Rose L. Coser (ed.), *The Family: Its Structures and Functions* (2nd ed.). New York: St. Martin's Press. Originally published 1930.

Margolin, Gayla, and Gerald R. Patterson

1975 "Differential Consequences Provided by Mothers and Fathers for Their Sons and Daughters." *Developmental Psychology* 11:537–38.

Martin, M. Kay, and Barbara Voorhies

1975 *Female of the Species.* New York: Columbia University Press.

Maslow, Abraham H.

1942 "Self-esteem (Dominance-Feeling) and Sexuality in Women." *Journal of Social Psychology* 16:259–94.

Mason, Karen Oppenheim, and Larry L. Bumpass

1975 "U.S. Women's Sex-Role Ideology, 1970." *American Journal of Sociology* 80:1212–19.

Mason, Karen Oppenheim, John L. Czajka, and Sara Arber

1976 "Change in U.S. Women's Sex-Role Attitudes, 1964–1974." *American Sociological Review* 41:573–96.

Masters, William H., and Virginia E. Johnson

1966 *Human Sexual Response.* Boston: Little, Brown.

Mead, Margaret

1949 *Male and Female: A Study of the Sexes in a Changing World.* New York: Dell.

1963 *Sex and Temperament in Three Primitive Societies.* New York: Morrow. Originally published 1935.

1974 "On Freud's View of Female Psychology." Pp. 95–106 in Jean Strause (ed.), *Women and Analysis.* New York: Grossman.

Meiselman, Karin C.

1978 *Incest.* San Francisco: Jossey-Bass.

Merkl, Peter H.

1976 "The Politics of Sex: West Germany." Pp. 129–48 in Lynne B. Iglitzin and Ruth Ross (eds.), *Women in the World: A Comparative Study.* Santa Barbara, Calif.: Clio Books.

Meyer, Jon K., and Donna J. Reter

1979 "Sex Reassignment Follow-up." *Archives of General Psychiatry* 36:1010–15.

Michelson, Stephan

1972 "Rational Income Decisions of Blacks and Everybody Else." Pp. 100–119 in Martin Carnoy (ed.), *Schooling in a Corporate Society: The Political Economy of Education in America.* New York: David McKay, Co.

Middleton, Russell, and Snell Putney

1960 "Dominance in Decisions in the Family: Race and Class Differences." *American Journal of Sociology* 65:605–9.

Miller, Jon, Sanford Labovitz, and Lincoln Fry
1975 "Inequities in the Organizational Experiences of Women and Men." *Social Forces* 54:365–81.

Minton, C., Jerome Kagan, and J. A. Levine
1971 "Maternal Control and Obedience in the Two-Year Old." *Child Development* 42:1873–94.

Mirsky, A. F.
1955 "The Influence of Sex Hormones on Social Behavior in Monkeys." *Journal of Comparative and Physiological Psychology* 48:327–35.

Mischel, Walter
1970 "Sex typing and Socialization." Pp. 3–72 in Paul H. Mussen (ed.), *Carmichael's Manual of Child Psychology* (3rd ed., Vol. 2). New York: Wiley.

Mitchell, Gary, William Redican, and Judy Gomber
1974 "Lesson from a Primate—Males Can Raise Babies." *Psychology Today,* April, pp. 88–89.

Mitchell, Juliet
1974 *Psychoanalysis and Feminism.* New York: Vintage.

Moltz, H., M. Lubin, M. Loon, and M. Numan
1970 "Hormonal Indication of Maternal Behavior in the Ovarisectionized Rat." *Physiology and Behavior* 5:1373–77.

Monahan, L., D. Kuhn, and P. Shaver
1974 "Intrapsychic versus Cultural Explanations of the 'Fear of Success' Motive." *Journal of Personality and Social Psychology* 29:60–64.

Money, John, and Anke A. Ehrhardt
1972 *Man and Woman, Boy and Girl.* Baltimore: Johns Hopkins University Press.

Money, John, and Patricia Tucker
1975 *Sexual Signatures: On Being a Man or a Woman.* Boston: Little, Brown.

Money, J., A. A. Ehrhardt, and D. N. Masica
1968 "Fetal Feminizing Syndrome: Effect on Marriage and Maternalism." *Johns Hopkins Medical Journal* 123:105–14.

Morgan, Marabel
1975 *The Total Woman.* New York: Pocket Books.

Morgan, Robin
1977 "The Politics of Sado-Masochistic Fantasies." Pp. 227–40 in R. Morgan, *Going Too Far.* New York: Random House.

Morgenthaler, Eric
1979 "Dads on Duty." *Wall Street Journal,* January 29, pp. 1, 22.

Morris, Desmond
1970 *The Human Zoo.* New York: McGraw-Hill.

Moyer, Kenneth E.
1974 "Sex Differences in Aggression." Pp. 335–72 in R. C. Friedman et al. (eds.), *Sex Differences in Behavior.* New York: John Wiley.
1976 *The Psychobiology of Aggression.* New York: Harper & Row, Pub.

Mumpower, D. L.
1970 "Sex Ratios Found in Various Types of Referred Exceptional Children." *Exceptional Children* 36:621–24.

Mussen, Paul, and E. Rutherford
1963 "Parent-Child Relations and Parental Personality in Relation to Young Children's Sex-Role Preferences." *Child Development* 34:589–607.

Narain, Vatsala
1967 "India." Pp. 21–41 in Raphael Patai (ed.), *Women in the Modern World.* New York: Free Press.

National School Boards Association
1974 *Women on School Boards.* Evanston, Ill.: National School Boards Association.

National Science Foundation
1977 NASULCG. Circulation Letter, no. 9, pp. 9–10.

Neal, Marie Augusta
1979 "Women in Religious Symbolism and Organization." *Sociological Inquiry* 49:218–50.

Nelson, Cynthia, and Virginia Olesen
1977 "Veil of Illusion: A Critique of the Concept of Equality in Western Thought." *Catalyst* 10–11:8–36.

Neugarten, Bernice L.
1968a "Adult Personality: Toward a Psychology of the Life Cycle." Pp. 137–47 in Neugarten (ed.), *Middle Age and Aging.* Chicago: University of Chicago Press.
1968b "The Awareness of Middle Age." Pp. 93–98 in Neugarten (ed.), *Middle Age and Aging.* Chicago: University of Chicago Press.
1976 "Adaptation and Life Cycle." *The Counseling Psychologist* 6:16–20.

Neugarten, Bernice, and Joan W. Moore
1968 "The Changing Age-Status System." Pp. 5–21 in Neugarten (ed.), *Middle Age and Aging.* Chicago: University of Chicago Press.

Neugarten, Bernice L., Joan W. Moore, and John C. Lowe
1968 "Age Norms, Age Constraints, and Adult Associalization." Pp. 22–28 in Neugarten (ed.), *Middle Age and Aging.* Chicago: University of Chicago Press.

Neugarten, Bernice L., and Karol K. Weinstein
1968 "The Changing American Grandparent." Pp. 280–85 in Neugarten (ed.), *Middle Age and Aging.* Chicago: University of Chicago Press.

Neugarten, Bernice L., Vivian Wood, Ruth L. Kraines and Barbara Loomis
1968 "Women's Attitudes toward the Menopause." Pp. 195–200 in Neugarten (ed.), *Middle Age and Aging.* Chicago: University of Chicago Press.

Newson, John, and Elizabeth Newson
1968 *Four Years Old in an Urban Community.* Harmondworth, England: Pelican.

Nichols, R. C.
1962 "Subtle, Obvious, and Stereotype Measures of Masculinity-Femininity." *Educational and Psychological Measurement* 22:449–61.

Oakley, Ann
1975 *Woman's Work.* New York: Pantheon Books.

O'Brien, Denise
1977 "Female Husbands in Southern Bantu Societies." Pp. 109–26 in Alice Schlegel (ed.), *Sexual Stratification: A Cross-cultural View.* New York: Columbia University Press.

O'Connor, J.
1977 "Changes in the Sex Composition of High Status Female Occupations: An Analysis of Teaching: 1950–1970." Unpublished paper, University of Illinois at Urbana-Champaign.

Offer, Daniel
1969 *The Psychological World of the Teenager.* New York: Basic Books.

Oleson, Virginia L., and Frances Katsuranis
1978 "Urban Nomads: Women in Temporary Clerical Services." Pp. 316–38 in Ann Stromberg and Shirley Harkness (eds.), *Women Working.* Palo Alto, Calif.: Mayfield.

Omark, D. R., M. Omark, and M. Edelman
1973 "Dominance Hierarchies in Young Children." Paper presented at the International Congress of Anthropological and Ethnological Sciences, Chicago.

O'Neill, Gena, and George O'Neill
1972 *Open Marriage.* New York: M. Evans.

Oppenheimer, Valerie Kincade
1968 "The Sex-Labeling of Jobs." *Industrial Relations* 7:219–34. Reprinted in Martha Mednick et al. (eds.), *Women and Achievement: Social and Motivational Analyses.* Washington, D.C.: Hemisphere, 1975, pp. 307–25.
1970 "The Female Labor Force in the United States: Demographic and Economic Factors Governing Its Growth and Changing Composition." Population Monograph, Series No. 5, University of California. Berkeley: Institute of International Studies.
1974 "The Life-Cycle Squeeze: The Interaction of Men's Occupational and Family Life Cycles." *Demography* 11:227–45.

Pagels, Elaine H.
1976 "What Became of God the Mother? Conflicting Images of God in Early Christianity." *Signs* 2:293–303.

Parlee, Mary Brown
1975 "Review Essay: Psychology." *Signs* 1:119–38.
1976 "The Premenstrual Syndrome." Pp. 124–36 in Alexandra G. Kaplan and Joan P. Bean (eds.), *Beyond Sex-Role Stereotypes: Readings Toward a Psychology of Androgyny.* Boston: Little, Brown.

Parsons, Talcott
1954a "Age and Sex in the Social Structure of the United States." Pp. 89–103 in Parsons, *Essays in Sociological Theory* (rev. ed.). Glencoe, Ill.: Free Press.
1954b "Certain Primary Sources and Patterns of Aggression in the Social Structure of the Western World." Pp. 298–335 in Parsons, *Essays in Sociological Theory* (rev. ed.). Glencoe, Ill.: Free Press.
1955 "Family Structure and the Socialization of the Child." Pp. 35–131 in Parsons and R. F. Bales, *Family Socialization and Interaction Process.* Glencoe, Ill.: Free Press.
1966 *Societies: Evolutionary and Comparative Perspectives.* Englewood Cliffs, N.J.: Prentice-Hall.
1970 *Social Structure and Personality.* New York: Free Press.

Parsons, Talcott, and Robert F. Bales
1955 *Family, Socialization and Interaction Process.* Glencoe, Ill.: Free Press.

Patterson, Michelle
1973 "Sex and Specialization in Academe and the Professions." Pp. 313–32 in Alice Rossi and Ann Calderwood (eds.), *Academic Women on the Move.* New York: Russel Sage.

Patterson, Michelle, and Laurie Engelberg
1978 "Women in Male-Dominated Professions." Pp. 266–92 in Stromberg and Hockners (eds.), *Women Working.* Palo Alto, Calif. Mayfield.

Patterson, Michelle, and Lucy Sells
1973 "Women Dropouts from Higher Education." Pp. 70–92 in Alice S. Rossi and Ann Calderwood (eds.), *Academic Women on the Move.* New York: Russell Sage.

People
1976 "Renee Richards." Sept. 6, p. 18.

Person, Ethel S., and Lionel Ovesey
1974 "The Psychodynamics of Male Transsexualism." Pp. 315–26 in R. C. Friedman et al. (eds.), *Sex Differences in Behavior.* New York: John Wiley.

Peterson, Gail Beaton, and Larry R. Peterson
1973 "Sexism in the Treatment of Sexual Dysfunction." *The Family Coordinator* 22:397–404.

Pettman, Barrie O. (ed.)
1975 *Equal Pay for Women: Progress and Problems in Seven Countries.* Bradford, West Yorkshire, England: McB Books.

Pleck, Joseph H.
1975 "Masculinity, Femininity: Current and Alternative Paradigms." *Sex Roles* 1:161–78.
1977 "The Work-Family Role System." *Social Problems* 24:417–27.

Porter, Mary Cornelia, and Corey Venning
1976 "Catholicism and Women's Role in Italy and Ireland." Pp. 81–104 in Lynn B. Iglitzin and Ruth Ross (eds.), *Women in the World: A Comparative Study.* Santa Barbara, Calif.: Clio Books.

Potts, D. M.
1970 "Which is the weaker sex?" *Journal of Biosociological Science Supplement* 2:147–57.

Quadragno, Jill
1976 "Occupational Sex-Typing and Internal Labor Market Distributions: An Assessment of Medical Specialties." *Social Problems* 23:442–53.

Quattelbaum, Cynthia
1977 "Perceived Television Model Attributes and Consequent Modeling Behavior As Described by the Viewer." Unpublished paper, Department of Speech, University of Oregon.

Radloff, Lenore
1975 "Sex Differences in Depression: The Effect of Occupation and Marital Status." *Sex Roles* 1:249–65.

Ramey, Estelle
1976 "Men's Cycles (They Have Them, Too, You Know)." Pp. 138–42 in Alexandra G. Kaplan and Joan P. Bean (eds.), *Beyond Sex-Role Stereotypes: Reading Toward a Psychology of Androgyny.* Boston: Little, Brown.

Raymond, Janice
1977 "Transsexualism: The Ultimate Homage to Sex-Role Power." *Chrysalis* 3: 11–23.

Rebecca, Meda, Robert Hefner, and Barbara Oleshansky
1976 "A Model of Sex-Role Transcendence." Pp. 90–97 in Alexandra G. Kaplan and Joan P. Bean (eds.), *Beyond Sex Role Stereotypes.* Boston: Little, Brown.

Reich, Michael, David M. Gordon, and Richard C. Edwards
1975 "A Theory of Labor Market Segmentation." Pp. 69–79 in Martin Carnoy (ed.), *Schooling in a Corporate Society.* New York: David McKay.

Reid, Elizabeth
1977 "The Forgotten Fifty Percent." *Populi Special* 4:19–35.

Rich, Robert
1974 "Ellie Brown Loves the Kentucky Colonels." *The Saturday Evening Post,* 246:56–57.

Robinson, Donald Allen
1979 "Two Movements in Pursuit of Equal Employment Opportunity." *Signs* 4:413–33.

Roby, Pamela A.
1976 "Toward Full Equality: More Job Education for Women." *School Review* 84:181–211.

Roby, Pamela A. (ed.)
1973 *Child Care—Who Cares? Foreign and Domestic Infant and Early Childhood Development Policies.* New York: Basic Books.

Rosaldo, Michelle Z.
1974 "Woman, Culture and Society: A Theoretical Overview." Pp. 17–42 in Michelle Z. Rosaldo and Louise Lamphere (eds.), *Woman, Culture and Society.* Stanford, Calif.: Stanford University Press.

Rose, R. M., T. P. Gordon, and J. S. Bernstein
1972 "Plasma Testosterone Levels in the Male Rhesus: Influences of Sexual and Social Stimuli." *Science* 178:643–45.

Rose, R. M., J. W. Holaday and I. S. Bernstein
1971 "Plasma Testosterone, Dominance Rank, and Aggressive Behavior in Male Rhesus Monkeys." *Nature* 231:386–88.

Rosenberg, Bernard G., and Brian Sutton-Smith
1960 "A Revised Conception of Masculine-Feminine Differences in Play Activities." *Journal of Genetic Psychology* 96:165–70.

Rosenberg, K. M., Denenberg, V. H. Zarrow, M. Z. and L. F. Bonnie
1971 "Effects of Neonatal Castration and Testosterone on the Rat's Pup-Killing Behavior and Activity." *Physiology and Behavior* 7:363–68.

Rosenblatt, J. S.
1969 "The Development of Maternal Responsiveness in the Rat." *American Journal of Orthopsychiatry* 39:38–56.

Ross, Heather L., and Isabel V. Sawhill
1975 *Time of Transition: The Growth of Families Headed by Women.* Washington, D.C.: The Urban Institute.

Rossi, Alice
1977 "A Biosocial Perspective on Parenting." *Daedulus* 106:1–31.

Rothbart, Mary K., and Eleanor E. Maccoby
1966 "Parents' Differential Reactions to Sons and Daughters." *Journal of Personality and Social Psychology* 4:237–43.

Rothbart, Mary K., and Myron Rothbart
1976 "Birth Order, Sex of Child, and Maternal Help-Giving." *Sex Roles* 2:39–46.

Rubin, Gayle
1975 "The Traffic in Women: Notes on the Political Economy of Sex." Pp. 157–210 in Rayna Reiter (ed.), *Toward an Anthropology of Women.* New York: Monthly Review Press.

Rubin, Jeffrey Z., Frank J. Provenzano, and Zella Luria
1976 "The Eye of the Beholder: Parents' Views on Sex of Newborns." Pp. 179–86 in Alexandra G. Kaplan and Joan P. Bean (eds.), *Beyond Sex-Role Stereotypes: Readings Toward a Psychology of Androgyny.* Boston: Little, Brown.

Rubin, Lillian
1976 *Worlds of Pain: Life in the Working Class Family.* New York: Basic Books.

1979 *Women of a Certain Age: The Midlife Search for Self.* New York: Harper & Row, Pub.

Rubin, Zick

1977 "The Love Research." *Human Behavior* 6:56–59.

Ruebsaat, Helmut J., and Raymond Hull

1975 *The Male Climacteric.* New York: Hawthorne.

Saario, Terry N., Carol Nagy Jacklin, and Carol Kehr Tittle

1973 "Sex Role Stereotyping in the Public Schools." *Harvard Educational Review* 43:386–416.

Sade, D. S.

1965 "Some Aspects of Parent-Offspring and Sibling Relations in a Group of Rhesus Monkeys, with a Discussion of Grooming." *American Journal of Physical Anthropology* 23:1–18.

Safilios-Rothschild, Constantina

1967 "A Comparison of Power Structure and Marital Satisfaction in Urban Greek and French Families." *Journal of Marriage and the Family* 29:345–52.

1969 "Family Sociology or Wives' Family Sociology? A Cross-cultural Examination of Decision-Making." *Journal of Marriage and the Family* 31:290–301.

1977 *Love, Sex, and Sex Roles.* Englewood Cliffs, N.J.: Prentice-Hall.

Sattel, Jack W.

1976 "The Inexpressive Male: Tragedy or Sexual Politics?" *Social Problems* 23:469–77.

Sawhill, Isabel V.

1976 "Discrimination and Poverty among Women Who Head Families." *Signs* 1:201–12.

Schnitzer, Phoebe Kazdin

1977 "The Motive to Avoid Success: Explaining the Nature of the Fear." *Psychology of Women Quarterly* 1:273–82.

Schuetz, Stephen, and Joyce N. Sprafkin

1978 "Spot Messages Appearing within Saturday Morning Television Programs." Pp. 69–77 in Gaye Tuchman, A. K. Daniels, and J. Benet (eds.), *Hearth and Home: Images of Women in the Mass Media.* New York: Oxford University Press.

Schulz, Muriel R.

1975 "The Semantic Derogation of Women." Pp. 64–75 in Barrie Thorne and Nancy Henley (eds.), *Language and Sex: Difference and Dominance.* Rowley, Mass.: Newbury House Publishers.

Scott, Hilda

1979 "Women in Eastern Europe." Pp. 177–98 in Jean Lipman-Blumen and Jessie Bernard (eds.), *Sex Roles and Social Policy: A Complex Social Science Equation.* Beverly Hills, Calif.: Sage Publications.

Scott, John Finley

1971 *Internalization of Norms: A Sociological Theory of Moral Commitment.* Englewood Cliffs, N.J.: Prentice-Hall.

Sears, Robert R., Eleanor E. Maccoby, and H. Levin

1957 *Patterns of Child Rearing.* Evanston, Ill.: Row, Peterson.

Sears, Robert R., Lucy Rau, and Richard Alpert

1965 *Identification and Child Rearing.* Stanford, Calif.: Stanford University Press.

Secombe, Wally

1974 "The Housewife and Her Labour under Capitalism." *New Left Review* 83:3–24.

Serbin, Lisa A., K. Daniel O'Leary, Ronald N. Kent, and Illene J. Tonick
1973 "A Comparison of Teacher Response to the Preacademic and Problem Behavior of Boys and Girls." *Child Development* 44:796–804.

Sewell, William H., and Vimal P. Shah
1967 "Socioeconomic Status, Intelligence, and the Attainment of Higher Education." *Sociology of Education* 40:1–23.

Sheehy, Gail
1976 *Passages: Predictable Crises of Adult Life.* New York: Bantam.

Sherman, Julia
1967 *On the Psychology of Women.* Springfield, Ill.: Chas. Thomas.

Shulman, Alix Kates
1973 *Memoirs of an Ex-Prom Queen.* New York: Bantam.

Sidel, Ruth
1973 *Women and Child Care in China.* New York: Penguin.

Smith-Rosenberg, Carroll
1975 "The Female World of Love and Ritual: Relations between Women in Nineteenth-Century America." *Signs* 1:1–29.

Spaulding, Robert L.
1963 *Achievement, Creativity, and Self-Concept Correlates of Teacher-Pupil Transactions in Elementary Schools.* Cooperative Research Project No. 1352. Washington, D.C.: U.S. Department of Health, Education, and Welfare, Office of Education.

Sprafkin, Joyce N., and Robert M. Liebert
1978 "Sex-Typing and Children's Television Preferences." Pp. 228–39 in Gayle Tuchman et al. (eds.), *Hearth and Home: Images of Women in the Mass Media.* New York: Oxford University Press.

Stannard, Una
1977 Mrs. Man. San Francisco: Germain Books.

Statistical Abstract of the United States
1978 *Statistical Abstract of the United States,* 99th Annual Edition. Washington, D.C.: U.S. Department of Commerce.

Stayton, Donelda J., Robert Hogan, and Mary D. S. Ainsworth
1971 "Infant Obedience and Maternal Behavior: The Origins of Socialization Reconsidered." *Child Development* 42:1057–69.

Stein, Aletha H., and Margaret M. Bailey
1975 "The Socialization of Achievement Motivation in Females." Pp. 151–57 in Martha Mednick et al. (eds.), *Women and Achievement.* Washington, D.C.: Hemisphere.

Stein, Aletha H., and Janis Smithells
1969 "Age and Sex Differences in Children's Sex-Role Standards about Achievement." *Developmental Psychology* 1:252–59.

Sternglanz, S. H., and Lisa A. Serbin
1974 "Sex-Role Stereotyping in Children's Television Programs." *Developmental Psychology* 10:710–15.

Stevenson, Mary
1973 "Women's Wages and Job Segregation." *Politics and Society* 4:83–96.
1975 "Relative Wages and Sex Segregation by Occupation." Pp. 175–200 in Cynthia B. Lloyd (ed.), *Sex Discrimination and the Division of Labor.* New York: Columbia University Press.

Stiehm, Judith
1976 "Algerian Women: Honor, Survival, and Islamic Socialism." Pp. 229–42 in Lynne B. Iglitzin and Ruth Ross (eds.), *Women in the World: A Comparative Study.* Santa Barbara, Calif.: Clio Books.

Stockard, Jean, and Miriam M. Johnson
1979 "The Social Origins of Male Dominance." *Sex Roles* 5:199–218.

Stoller, Robert J.
1968 *Sex and Gender: On the Development of Masculinity and Femininity.* New York: Science House.
1974 "Facts and Fancies: An Examination of Freud's Concept of Bisexuality." Pp. 343–64 in Jean Strouse (ed.), *Women and Analysis: Dialogues on Psychoanalytic Views of Femininity.* New York: Grossman.

Stouffer, Samuel A., et al.
1976 "Masculinity and the Role of the Combat Soldier." Pp. 179–83 in Deborah David and Robert Brannon, *The Forty-Nine Percent Majority: The Male Sex Role.* Excerpted from *The American Soldier: Combat and Its Aftermath.* Princeton: Princeton University Press, 1949.

Suter, Larry E., and Herman P. Miller
1973 "Income Differences between Men and Career Women." *American Journal of Sociology* 78:962–74.

Swafford, Michael
1978 "Sex Differences in Soviet Earnings," *American Sociological Review* 43:657–73.

Szalai, Alexander
1972 *The Use of Time.* The Hague: Mouton and Co.

Talkington, Tracy Faulconer
1976 "An Analysis of Sex Role Stereotypes in Popular Songs, 1955 to 1974." Unpublished master's thesis, University of Oregon.

Tanner, Nancy
1974 "Matrifocality in Indonesia and among Black Americans." Pp. 129–56 in Michelle Z. Rosaldo and Louise Lamphere (eds.), *Women Culture, and Society.* Stanford, Calif.: Stanford University Press.

Tanner, Nancy, and Adrienne Zihlman
1976 "Women in Evolution. Part I: Innovation and Selection in Human Origins." *Signs* 1:585–608.

Tasch, R. J.
1952 "The Role of the Father in the Family." *Journal of Experimental Education* 20:319–61.

Tavris, Carol, and Carole Offir
1977 *The Longest War: Sex Differences in Perspective.* New York: Harcourt Brace Jovanovich.

Task Force on Sex Bias and Sex-Role Stereotyping in Psycho-Therapeutic Practice
1975 "Report." *American Psychologist* 30:1169–75.

Taylor, S. P., and S. Epstein
1967 "Aggression As a Function of the Interaction of the Sex of the Aggressor and the Sex of the Victim." *Journal of Personality* 35:474–96.

Terman, Lewis M., and Melita H. Oden
1947 *The Gifted Child Grows Up.* Stanford, Calif.: Stanford University Press.

Terman, Lewis M., and Leona E. Tyler
1954 "Psychology Sex Differences." Pp. 1064–1114 in L. Carmichael (ed.), *Manual of Child Psychology* (2nd ed.). New York: John Wiley.

Tiger, Lionel
1969 *Men in Groups.* New York: Random House.

Trause, Mary Anne, Marshall H. Klaus, and John H. Kennel
1976 "Maternal behavior in mammals." Pp. 16–37 in M. H. Klaus and J. H. Kennell (eds.), *Maternal-Infant Bonding.* St. Louis: C. V. Mosby.

Treiman, Donald J., and Kermit Terrell
1975 "Sex and the Process of Status Attainment: A Comparison of Working Women and Men." *American Sociological Review* 40:174–200.

Tresemer, David W.
1977 *Fear of Success.* New York: Plenum.

Tuchman, Gaye
1978 "Introduction: The Symbolic Annihilation of Women by the Mass Media." Pp. 3–38 in Tuchman, A. K. Daniels, and J. Benet (eds.), *Hearth and Home: Images of Women in the Mass Media.* New York: Oxford University Press.

Tuchman, Gaye, Arlene Kaplan Daniels, and James Benet
1978 *Hearth and Home: Images of Women in the Mass Media.* New York: Oxford University Press.

Tyler, Leona E.
1965 *The Psychology of Human Differences* (3rd ed.). New York: Appleton-Century-Crofts.

Udry, J. Richard
1974 *The Social Context of Marriage* (3rd ed.). Philadelphia: J. B. Lippincott.

Ullian, Dorothy Z.
1976 "The Development of Conceptions of Masculinity and Femininity." Pp. 25–48 in Barbara Lloyd and John Archer (eds.), *Exploring Sex Differences.* New York: Academic Press.

United States Commission on Civil Rights
1979 *Window Dressing on the Set: An Update.* Washington, D.C.: U.S. Government Printing Office.

United States Department of Commerce
1976 *A Statistical Portrait of Women in the U.S.* Bureau of the Census, Current Population Reports, Special Studies Series P-23, No. 58.
1977 *Consumer Income.* Bureau of the Census, Current Population Reports, Series P-60, Number 105, June.
1978 *Current Population Reports.* Bureau of the Census, Series P-60, No. 114, July.

Vaillant, George E.
1977 *Adaptation to Life.* Boston: Little, Brown.

Van Allen, Judith
1976 "African Women, 'Modernization,' and National Liberation." Pp. 25–54 in Lynne B. Iglitzin and Ruth Ross (eds.), *Women in the World: A Comparative Study.* Santa Barbara, Calif.: Clio Books.

Verbrugge, Lois M.
1976 "Sex Differentials in Morbidity and Mortality in the United States." *Social Biology* 23:275–96.

Veroff, Joseph
1977 "Process vs. Impact in Men's and Women's Achievement Motivation." *Psychology of Women Quarterly* 1:283–93.

Veroff, Joseph, Lou McClelland, and David Ruhlard
1975 "Varieties of Achievement Motivation." Pp. 172–205 in Martha Mednick et al. (eds.), *Women and Achievement.* Washington, D.C.: Hemisphere.

Waller, Willard
1951 *The Family, a Dynamic Interpretation.* (Revised by Reuben Hill.) New York: Holt, Rinehart & Winston.

Warren, James
1979 "Path to Top of City Hall Differs for 5 Women." *The Oregonian,* April 13, p. C2.

Weinbaum, Batya, and Amy Bridges
1976 "The Other Side of the Paycheck: Monopoly Capital and the Structure of Consumption." *Monthly Review* 28:88–103.

Weitz, Shirley
1977 *Sex Roles: Biological, Psychological, and Social Foundations.* New York: Oxford University Press.

Weller, R. H.
1969 "The Employment of Wives, Dominance, and Fertility." *Journal of Marriage and the Family* 30:437–42.

Werner, Emmy E.
1968 "Women in the State Legislatures." *Western Political Quarterly* 21:42–46.

Whitebook, Joel
1974 "Wish I Could Give All I Wanted to Give. Wish I Could Live All I Wanted to Live." Pp. 464–74 in Arlene Skolnick and Jerome H. Skolnick (eds.), *Intimacy Family and Society.* Boston: Little, Brown.

White House Conference on Child Health and Protection, (sect. 3)
1936 *The Young Child in the Home: A Survey of 3000 American Families.* New York: Appleton-Century.

Whiting, Beatrice, and Carolyn Edwards
1973 "A Cross-cultural Study of Sex Differences in the Behavior of Children Aged Three through Eleven." *Journal of Social Psychology* 91:171–88.

Whiting, Beatrice B., and John W. M. Whiting.
1975 *Children of Six Cultures: A Psychocultural Analysis.* Cambridge, Mass.: Harvard University Press.

Wilensky, Harold L.
1968 "Women's Work: Economic Growth, Ideology, Structure." *Industrial Relations* 7:235–48.

Williams, Juanita
1977 *Psychology of Women: Behavior in a Biosocial Context.* New York: W. W. Norton & Co., Inc.

Wilson, Edward O.
1975 *Sociobiology: The New Synthesis.* Cambridge, Mass.: Harvard University Press.
1978 *On Human Nature.* Cambridge, Mass.: Harvard University Press.

Wolff, Charlotte
1971 *Love between Women.* New York: Harper Colophon.

Wright, James D.
1978 "Are Working Women Really More Satisfied? Evidence from Several National Surveys." *Journal of Marriage and the Family* 40:301–13.

Yarrow, Marian R., John D. Campbell, and Roger V. Burton
1968 *Child Rearing: An Inquiry into Research and Methods.* San Francisco: Jossey-Bass.

Young, Michael, and Peter Willmott
1973 *The Symmetrical Family.* New York: Pantheon.

Young, W. C., R. W. Goy, and C. H. Phoenix
1964 "Hormones and Sexual Behavior." *Science* 143:212–13.

Youssef, Nadia Haggag
1974 *Women and Work in Developing Societies.* Population Monograph, Series No. 15, University of California. Berkeley: Institute of International Studies.
1976 "Women in the Muslim World." Pp. 203–18 in Lynn B. Iglitzin and Ruth Ross (eds.), *Women in the World: A Comparative Study.* Santa Barbara, Calif.: Clio Books.

Youssef, Nadia H., and Shirley Foster Hartley
1979 "Demographic Indicators of the Status of Women in Various Societies." Pp. 83–112 in Jean Lipman-Blumen and Jessie Bernard (eds.), *Sex Roles and Social Policy: A Complex Social Science Equation.* Beverly Hills, Calif.: Sage Publications.

Zaretsky, Eli
1976 "Socialist Politics and the Family." Pp. 43–58 in Mina Davis Caulfield, Barbara Ehrenreich, Deirdre English, David Fernback, and Eli Zaretsky, *Capitalism and the Family.* San Francisco: Agenda.

Zihlman, Adrienne L.
1978 "Women in Evolution, Part II: Subsistence and Social Organization among Early Hominids." *Signs* 4:4–20.

Zimmerman, D. H., and C. West
1975 "Sex Roles, Interruptions, and Silences in Conversation." Pp. 105–29 in Barrie Thorne and Nancy Henley (eds.), *Language and Sex: Difference and Dominance.* Rowley, Mass.: Newbury House.

Index

Name Index

Subject Index